SCAR...

Paul Routledge, political corres... *Independent on Sunday*, has covered the mining industry and its troubles since the late Sixties, first for *The Times*, then for the *Observer*, and most recently for the *Independent on Sunday*. Raised in a Yorkshire mining town, he knows Arthur Scargill personally and has got closer to this complex figure than any other national newspaper journalist.

SCARGILL

The Unauthorized Biography

Paul Routledge

HarperCollins*Publishers*

HarperCollins*Publishers*
77–85 Fulham Palace Road
Hammersmith, London W6 8JB

This paperback edition 1994
1 3 5 7 9 8 6 4 2

First published in Great Britain by
HarperCollins*Publishers* 1993

ISBN 0 00 638077 8

Set in Linotron Janson

Printed in Great Britain by
HarperCollinsManufacturing Glasgow

Contents

List of Illustrations

Arthur Scargill arrested at Orgreave coking plant in May 1984 (*Syndication International*).

Scargill at the 1984 TUC, with Peter Heathfield, Mick McGahey, Roger Windsor, and George Rees (*Observer*).

Scargill sharing a platform with Labour leader Neil Kinnock, Stoke-on-Trent, 30 November 1984 (*Observer*).

Scargill with Kevan Hunt and Ian MacGregor, September 1984 (*Syndication International*).

Scargill addressing the TUC at Brighton in September 1984 (*Observer*).

John Walsh, who challenged Scargill for the NUM Presidency in January 1988 (*Press Association/Topham*).

Scargill's mansion, Treelands, Worsbrough, near Barnsley (*Syndication International*).

Interior of Treelands (*John Marshall*).

Yews Lane, Worsbrough, the Scargill family home for many years before the controversial move to Treelands.

Maurice Jones, Scargill's editor, first of the *Yorkshire Miner*, then of the *Miner* (*Martin Jenkinson*).

Terry Pattison, industrial editor of the *Daily Mirror* (*Martin Jenkinson*).

Gavin Lightman QC who conducted the inquiry in allegations into Russian and Libyan financial donations to the Mine Workers' Union during the 1984 strike (*Syndication International*).

Scargill leaving his headquarters in Sheffield, March 1990 (*David Mansell*).

Roger Windsor, former Executive Officer of the NUM (*Observer*).

Jim Parker, Scargill's chauffeur and long-standing friend (*Press Association*).

Altaf Abbasi, a Pakistani businessman (*Syndication International*).

Scargill with Jean McCrindle.

Introduction

Arthur Scargill is an important figure in any reckoning of the post-war history of the labour movement and British politics generally. He deserves serious critical analysis, even if he does not always welcome it. This book is an attempt to provide such an assessment. To essay that task, I have gone back to his trade union and political associates of the past forty years, and to those in the British Coal Corporation who have relevant experience. I have also relived the last twenty-five years of my own life as an industrial correspondent responsible for reporting the affairs of the mining industry, first for *The Times* and latterly for *The Observer*.

In some ways, it has been a voyage of disillusion. It is easy to believe you know a man, before you begin to write the story of his life – especially a man as superficially well-known as Scargill. He has always set himself the highest industrial and political goals. He has challenged those who would be with him to commit themselves as single-mindedly as himself to the achievement of those aims. Very few have stayed the course. His long march has left a small army of disillusioned, and sometimes embittered, supporters by the wayside.

He is still out there in front, fighting what he sees as the good fight. No surrender! Not a single pit shall close! But the ranks of his myrmidons are heavily depleted, ragged and unsure. For Scargill, the Marxist in a hurry, doubt is unthinkable. Say not that the struggle availeth nought: the struggle *is* the victory. Where others have tired of the doctrine of perpetual fight, he shows no sign of slackening. For the rest of us, the question must be: what has it all been for?

The origins of this book are very simple. The idea came up during a meal with my wife Lynne in a Thai restaurant in Mortlake in July 1992. Like me, she was raised in a mining town, and she shares my interest in miners, their communities and their union. We were both involved in (quite separate) support groups during the

great strike of 1984–5, and maintained our interest in the problems
facing the miners. We visited, and were made welcome in, the
mining community of South Elmsall, near Doncaster, still dominated by Frickley colliery. Members of that community visited our
home in Yorkshire, and still do. The pit's proud motto was 'Second
to None', because so few strikers crossed the picket line before the
dispute ended. Their struggle *was* our struggle. The miners' experience and example was there before us when the same choice was
thrust upon the journalists of Times Newspapers at the time of the
Wapping dispute.

So it was not very surprising that the desultory talk over dinner
that night turned to the latest crisis in the mining industry: the prospect, yet again, of massive pit closures. What would the miners do?
What would *Arthur* do? No prizes for guessing what his reaction
would be. The miners would have to take industrial action to force a
change in government policy. Would the men follow him? Probably.
Would they succeed in keeping the pits open? Almost certainly not.
Then why drag the miners back to the barricades again? Because
that's what Arthur's like. Somebody should write the story of his life,
I said, shaking my head. You should do it, she urged.

So, *Scargill* was born: just like its subject, in a hurry and with no
certain idea of where it would all end.

There is one piece of unfinished business. On 28 February 1985,
the Queen visited *The Times* on the occasion of the paper's bicenten-
ary. I had intended to be in Sheffield that day, covering a vital meeting
of the NUM national executive. The strike was about to be called
off, though it ran for another week. The day before the royal visit,
Charles Wilson, then deputy editor of *The Times*, called me into his
office and said I should remain in Gray's Inn Road. I demurred,
wanting to be in at the kill of a story that had dominated my life for
a year. He prevailed, and I stayed in the office.

Because I had not been included in the original reception party, I
had not been given any advice on protocol, and found myself asking
colleagues as she arrived: 'How do we address her?' I was stationed
in the newsroom with Julian Haviland, the paper's political editor
and a gentleman, to await the royal party. The Queen arrived with
Rupert Murdoch, the proprietor of *The Times*, an equerry of some
sort and Charles Douglas-Home, the editor, who was in the last
stages of the cancer that was to kill him later that year and got about
on crutches. After some badinage with Julian Haviland about the

Commons, I was introduced to the Queen as the paper's labour editor, the man covering the miners' strike. Her Majesty thought it must be very interesting. Yes, I replied, though also rather distressing at times.

The Queen volunteered that she had been down a coal mine in Scotland, which had closed not long after. Innocently, I asked what her feelings about the strike were. She thought it 'very sad', and after a pause added: 'It's all about one man, isn't it?' – or words to very similar effect. I wasn't taking notes, nor was anyone else. Evidently, it is not done. I offered the view that perhaps it wasn't about one man: knowing the miners, having been brought up among them, I thought that one man couldn't bring out 100,000 men for a whole year. There was a pregnant pause, and the royal party moved on. The exchange had taken thirty seconds at most.

As instructed, I stayed where I was with Julian Haviland for a moment, and then a BBC radio reporter, Graeme McLagan, appeared from behind a pillar, where it seems he had heard the gist of the conversation. He stuck a microphone under my nose. I repeated what the Queen and I had said and he went off with a beam on his face and a story in his tape recorder. In the heat of the moment, I may have slightly hardened up what the Queen actually said. In response to a question from McLagan, I said: 'I think she felt that the dispute was essentially promoted by Mr Scargill.' This was so close to what I perceived to be the Queen's view, from the words she expressed, as to make no very great difference. However, the interview created the most terrible brouhaha. Douglas-Home carpeted me, and made me sign a ludicrous 'apology' that bore a great deal less approximation to the truth than my interview. The tabloid press excoriated me. The persecution went on for weeks. I got to understand just what it can be like to be on the vicious end of Fleet Street's attention. No bad thing, it might be said.

However, with the benefit of hindsight and the knowledge that has come from writing this book, I now feel that I do owe the Queen an apology. By that stage, at any rate, the strike *was* all about one man. Scargill may not have started the strike, but one word, one signal from him could have called it off before the struggle plumbed the depths of misery, violence and failure to which it sank. If I misrepresented the Queen, I am sorry. If, as I honestly believe, I represented her view correctly, I am even sorrier. The Queen was right.

I have no great desire to reopen this controversy, except to put the record straight and also to put in context the myth that I was exiled to Singapore, as *The Times*'s South-East Asia correspondent, as punishment for lesè-majesté.

Another matter should go on public record. When this book was first mooted, in November 1992 I asked Arthur Scargill if he would grant an interview. He declined, verbally, but when I urged him to reconsider, he promised to do so. He replied by letter, an Arthur classic, which warrants a wider audience. 'Dear Paul,' he wrote on 1 December 1992, 'I was not surprised to read that you were writing a biography of Arthur Scargill – I had already been told by three different sources. I explained that I was not prepared to assist or give approval in any way to a project of this kind, and that on previous occasions I have refused to give approval or assist other journalists in writing a biography of Arthur Scargill. The fact that we haven't exchanged a word between 1985 and the Labour Party conference in Blackpool in 1992, together with the vitriolic and inaccurate articles you wrote at the time of the smear campaign by the *Daily Mirror* and the Cook Report, does not help. I have thought over your request for a general interview but feel in the circumstances it would be unwise. It would undoubtedly be used as an occasion for gleaning information towards the production of your book. Yours sincerely, Arthur Scargill.'

Writing about himself in the third person is so characteristic, as is his accusation of smears and inaccuracies. Nor can he resist the instant put-down: 'I know what you are doing.' I replied in reasonably robust fashion, pointing out that he had begun the boycott, and received the following gem on 17 December: 'The NUM's press officer has confirmed to me that she made clear to you that I would not speak to you, but, with respect, that does not mean the NUM.' There was much more in similar, and more unflattering, vein. As I had feared, this had become the unauthorized biography.

Thankfully, not everyone has been so hostile. I have been reporting the coal industry for most of the last twenty-five years, so have drawn on my own stock of documents and articles. Serving and former members of the NUM leadership and staff have been very helpful, as have MPs and peers, friends in the trade union and labour movement, academics, members of the former Communist Party of Great Britain, serving and retired board members and managers in the coal industry, and a number of miners and retired miners.

During the three months I had to research this book, I spoke to more than seventy interested parties, some two or three times and for many hours at a stretch. It would be unwise to name them all, and invidious to single out a few for particular mention. However, I would like to thank Jim Parker, Scargill's 'minder' and political confrère for so many years, for his unstinting help. I wish I could have used everything that everyone said. Each had his or her own insight into Scargill the man. But even a biography of Arthur Scargill must stop somewhere. The information is all theirs; any faults are all mine.

Thanks, also, to my agent at Curtis Brown, Jane Bradish-Ellames, for her constant encouragement and for keeping my nose in front of the screen until the project was completed, and Michael Fishwick of HarperCollins for making a book out of a manuscript. I am grateful to colleagues at *The Observer* for their forbearance and support, particularly my former editor Donald Trelford for allowing me time to finish the writing.

Finally, I must thank my wife Lynne for sending me down the road of 'desperately seeking Arthur', and the British miners (particularly John Stones, delegate at Frickley colliery) for being such good comrades and exemplars of how to live life with some dignity. To them both this book is dedicated.

CHAPTER I

MINERS

WHEN MICHAEL HESELTINE got to his feet in the House of Commons on 13 October 1992 to announce the virtual demise of the British coal industry, he cannot have had any inkling of the furore that would follow. Politicians make calculations based on power and influence: this group must be placated, that group can safely be ignored. The conventional wisdom of the time was that the miners were finished. They were no longer the shock troops of the trade union movement. The National Union of Mineworkers, once the 750,000-strong power brokers of the TUC and Labour Party, now had fewer members than the actors' union Equity. They had been broken by the great strike of 1984–5, and had been unable to mount any effective industrial action since. Above all, their charismatic and militant leader Arthur Scargill, once the darling of the Left, was now a virtual outcast from political society, a humbled man, irrelevant in the present-day scheme of things. Since the strike, he had been unable to prevent the closure of almost 140 pits and the enforced redundancy of 100,000 men. The rhetoric was still there, but he was speaking to an empty hall.

So John Major's new Conservative government could proceed with the final dismemberment of the industry ahead of privatization, secure in the knowledge that Scargill and his NUM could do nothing. Heseltine announced that thirty-one collieries would close, some of them within a few days, and 30,000 miners and white-collar staff would lose their jobs by 31 March 1993. Only nineteen mines would remain. Less than forty years ago, there were more than 800. In a narrow, blinkered sort of way, the president of the Board of Trade was right. Judged solely on the balance of power, the mineworkers were wanting. By themselves, they were not capable of mounting an industrial or political challenge strong enough to force the government to change course. But this time they were not alone.

Heseltine had forgotten, or chosen to ignore, the deep, emotional – sentimental, even – regard in which 'the colliers' are held by Britons of all classes and every political persuasion. Their industry, for which they sacrificed so much through generation after generation, had fuelled the Industrial Revolution and the nation's prosperity. The coal they dug warmed our houses, powered our industry, bunkered our Navy and won colossal export earnings. At one time, a million men toiled underground. Their hard way of life in tough, proud communities was legendary, celebrated in countless thousand paintings, poems, songs, novels, plays and then films. Unlike the coal seams, they were an inexhaustible subject for creative artists.

This was not just an industry, it was a way of life, and a self-made millionaire politician was going to close it down. Heseltine had the grace, or the political nous, to admit that he was shocked by the reaction of Middle England: the middle-aged, middle-class housewife in leafy Hertfordshire crying into the sink while washing the dishes; the waxed jacket and pearl earring demonstrators in Cheltenham; the Congregational minister saying: 'It's the turning point where people realize money isn't everything.' He heard these voices, and hesitated. In his eleventh-floor eyrie at the Department of Trade and Industry, Victoria Street, he begged people to understand his personal anguish. 'I am dismayed by this decision. I had to take it, and I have lived with it for months. I understand the outrage,' he fumbled. 'It is very human to be outraged.'

But did he *really* understand? Did he understand in the same way as 'natural' Tory voter Paula Radford of Horsforth, Leeds, who wrote to her local paper asking: 'What can I do to fight this? I will write, picket, anything. Please help me and other little people to stop this happening.' With support slipping away on the back benches behind him, and an avalanche of mail reaching MPs from the 'little people', Heseltine's position began to erode. Sir Marcus Fox, chairman of the influential Tory 1922 committee of MPs, warned that the cuts were 'unacceptable' and that a review was 'imperative'. Winston Churchill, MP, whose grandfather sent in troops to quell the rebellious miners of the Rhondda, appealed to the miners at Silverhill colliery in Nottinghamshire: 'Put your faith in the democratic process. I believe we can get this decision changed.'

The democratic process brought 100,000 protesters on to the streets of London, headed by Arthur Scargill, his faced wreathed in smiles as shoppers, tourists and toffs greeted a miners' support march through the capital's West End. Three days later, despite pouring autumn rain, the numbers doubled. It was the biggest demonstration since the poll tax riots, but impassioned rather than violent. Faced with a parliamentary revolt big enough to overwhelm the government's reduced Commons majority of only twenty-one, Heseltine backed down and announced a review of the coal industry. Of the thirty-one pits scheduled for closure, only ten would be provisionally shut and the other twenty-one would go into a comprehensive review. Parliament accepted his decision, but set up its own investigation of coal's future to be carried out by the all-party Commons Trade and Industry Select Committee. The Cabinet breathed a huge sigh of relief and returned to its troubles over the Treaty of Maastricht and preparations for the forthcoming Edinburgh summit of the European Community.

Once the euphoria of the initial climbdown had evaporated, the miners began to have doubts. Scepticism was justified. Had they not always been let down? Had the whole history of the coal industry not been one betrayal after another? The cynical abandonment of the miners by the TUC General Council after the botched general strike of 1926, when they were left to soldier on alone to defeat. The false dawn of nationalization of the mines in 1947, which only seemed to accelerate pit closures and force them down the industrial wages league. The failure of 'our' Labour governments to construct a coherent energy policy in which British coal had a guaranteed place. The incentive pay schemes of the 1970s, which made a man work so hard he put his fellow miner out of a job. The failure of the labour movement to take action alongside pitmen in the year-long Strike for Jobs. The Tory privatization of the electricity generating industry, deliberately fixed to encourage rival fuels. And now the promise of a Conservative grandee to 'do something' about a crisis of his own making. The outraged public might be taken in. But what faith could miners have in the silken pledges of the class enemy?

None. As they sat in their clubs and pubs, they dismissed Heseltine's apparent change of heart as a cynical political ploy. Wayne Lingard, branch president of the NUM at Houghton Main colliery, one of the ten given only a ninety-day reprieve to allow 'consultations' with British Coal, said: 'It's like waiting to be hanged. The government are not bothered about us. They want to save their necks.' At nearby Grimethorpe, home of the famous colliery band that regularly won the national brass championships, there was a similar sentiment.

Johnny Wood, a thirty-four-year-old miner, said: 'Some of our relations died in that colliery. There's blood, sweat and toil gone into that pit, not just for us but for our country. Soldiers get a medal when they retire. We get nothing.' As he left his pit, miners' wives outside were singing an old strike song: 'They talk about statistics, about the price of coal. The cost is the communities, dying on the dole.'

Only one leader talked the language they believed: Arthur Scargill. The more reviled he was by politicians, of whatever party, the closer now they clung to him as their only salvation. They knew his faults: the bombast, the penchant for big cars and the hypnotic self-belief. The old joke ran that he was 'the first man ever to have brainwashed himself'. He aroused the strongest passions, for and against. The landlord of a pub in Bentley, a mining village north of Doncaster was compelled to put up a sign in the bar saying 'No Discussion of Arthur Scargill' to avoid heated arguments getting out of hand. A few miles down the road, at the Empire Club, South Elmsall, the branch NUM president 'Chick' Picken would fold his arms and declaim so all could hear: 'Arthur Scargill is the greatest thing that has ever 'appened to this union and to Yorkshire.' Scargill was the man who said he would *never* betray them, or prostitute his principles. He would never agree to pit closures, unless there was no more coal to be mined. He would never apologize for his members, even when there was violence on the picket line. He would never give *them* anything. He had broken, forever, with the NUM tradition of shabby compromise. There could be no deals with people who had conned and exploited the miners.

In the threatened communities where the promises of politicians had proved worthless so many times, this certitude was the only lifeline they trusted. Had Scargill not done precisely what he promised when he was 'nobbut a lad', breathing defiance towards the National Coal Board and his own area leaders for their complaisant relationship with management? This was a language they could understand, particularly in Yorkshire, which was now the heartland of resistance to the run-down of the industry. It may be a classic case of the stubborn streak that makes a Yorkshireman take a strong idea beyond its logical conclusion. But after a century of shifts, accommodations, and hole-in-the-corner deals that got the miners nowhere except the dole queue, what had they got to lose? The history of the industry was clear evidence of the dictum of Lawrence Daly, the brilliant self-taught intellectual who became general secretary of the NUM, that 'we only get what we are strong enough to take'.

Britain needed her coal miners, but never offered them respect or a halfway decent place in society. They were 'a people apart, and an inferior race'. In the first half of the last century, they were regarded as reckless, degraded and semi-barbarous, living more like savages than civilized human beings. Considering the conditions in which they worked, this is scarcely surprising. A witness to the Children's Employment Commission of 1842 volunteered: 'I have often been shocked in contemplating the hideous and anything but human appearance of these men who are generally found in a state of bestial nakedness, lying their whole length on the uneven floor . . . Black and filthy as they are in their low, dark, heated and dismal chambers, they look like a race fallen from the common stock.'

Lest it be thought that such sights disappeared in Victorian times, this is Jack Collins, a forty-two-year-old ripper at Snowdown colliery in Kent, giving evidence to the Wilberforce Court of Inquiry in 1972, more than a hundred years later: 'I am working in a pit which is much hotter than the previous one. Indeed, the men at the pit where I now work wear no clothes at all when working. Eight out of ten men in the headings work with absolutely no clothes on because of the heat and, because of the amount of sweating they do, they have to drink a lot of water. Many, many men at Snowdown drink eight pints of water a day and the Coal Board has provided them with salt tablets to stop them getting whatever they are supposed to get by drinking a lot of water. This is a way of encouraging the men to work in hot conditions rather than of improving the conditions in the pits. What I have said is no exaggeration. It is there for everybody to see at any time.' For this work, Collins took home 'a couple of coppers over' £23 week. He died of leukaemia in his fifties, an angry and worn-out man.

The common thread running through the intervening century is the exploitation of the miners by the coal owners, including the nationalized industry, and the false prospectuses of politicians feigning to be their friends. To defend themselves, they had only their union and their sense of community. In a time of rampant individualism, their collective view of the world can seem old-fashioned, even quaint, to outsiders. For the miners, it has always seemed natural. As far back as 1792, colliers employed in Sheffield by the Duke of Norfolk combined to strike until their wages were raised. Despite being made illegal by the Combination Acts of 1799 and 1800, trade unions continued to be formed. When miners struck, or were locked out, coal owners would usually bar re-employment to those who would not sign the hated 'paper' abjuring trade unionism.

Strikers and union officials were often evicted from their homes, a practice that survived well into the twentieth century. In the famous Kinsley evictions of 1905, twenty-five families were evicted by police in one day, 15 August, because the man of the house was on strike at Hemsworth colliery. Knowing many more would follow, they put up a tent village, which became a local tourist attraction. The *Barnsley Chronicle* described a typical eviction: 'The few sticks in many of the houses were soon placed outside on the King's Highway. By the side of them was usually the sad-eyed lonely-looking housewife, a pathetic figure, with a baby in arms.' Some miners tried to make light of the grim business. A miner-musician, Bob Battye, played 'The Dead March' on his concertina when the police arrived to evict him and his family. A dozen constables entered as he played, tore down the pictures, removed the tables and chairs and pots and pans and dumped them in the street. A crowd of onlookers pleaded with him to play an Irish jig. He began to play, and then broke down in tears. The crowd fell silent, one bystander scolding the others for expecting him to play a jig after being evicted from the home where he had paid rent for eighteen years. Rubbing his eyes, Bob Battye tried to play 'Home Sweet Home', but this was too much. He turned to 'Bill Bailey', 'The Lost Chord' and 'Jolly Good Company'. Between laughter and tears, the family was turned out. Pennies were showered on the miner and his son as police left them amid their furniture. That strike went on for three and a half years. The colliery closed in 1969.

Miners and their families were reared on folk memories of this sort. The tradition of mutual support that enabled the pitmen of the affluent eighties to get through a year of struggle was rooted deeply in the lives of generations of miners who had gone before them. It was not unknown for three generations to be working the same pit, and, living in this close-knit world, miners and their wives were more inclined to believe one of their own, like Arthur Scargill, than any number of 'outsiders'.

There is a downside to this intense loyalty. A leader who was stupid enough, or unscrupulous enough, could lead the miners into struggles that they could not win, but which nonetheless involved great – and needless – sacrifices. There are those who argue that Scargill was just such a leader: clever enough to win the presidency of the National Union of Mineworkers, but not smart enough to walk away from a battle he must have known he could not win. His critics say he knew he could count on the loyalty of the men and their families, but by going on with the great strike of 1984–5 long after any responsible leader would have called it off, he abused that precious loyalty. And, by putting it to the test yet again in the spring of 1993, he was putting the miners under tremendous strain. Yet they voted for the policy of strike action, in a secret pithead ballot, in the teeth of criticism from the very Conservative back-benchers whose support disappeared just when they needed it.

Trade unionism in the mining industry has long been a thing apart. The miners formed unions in the various coalfields throughout the nineteenth century. Some collapsed under the pressure of lockouts, some lay dormant for years and then revived. The instinct for collectivism was always there. It is not hard to see why. Mutual dependence comes naturally to men working closely together underground in conditions of great danger, sharing the risks and coming to each other's aid in times of trouble. That inter-dependence transfers easily to the homogeneous communities where they live, and the social organizations they have fashioned for themselves.

The first proper national union – the Miners' Federation of Great Britain – was formed in 1889 in Newport, Monmouthshire. It was born from an initiative by Ben Pickard, the Yorkshire miners' leader, who brought together ten coalfields for a successful pay strike in 1888. Within four years, the MFGB was put to the test when the coal owners locked out the miners in pursuit of a twenty-five per cent pay cut. During the bitter dispute that followed, two colliers were shot dead in the Yorkshire pit village of Featherstone by soldiers acting on the orders of magistrates. Sixteen others were injured, and the 'Featherstone Incident' passed into mining folklore. The men fought on for three months, and won after the prime minister W. E. Gladstone instructed his foreign secretary, Lord Robesberry, to arbitrate. They resumed work at the old rates. This was very near the zenith of the mining industry. Coal was fetching nineteen shillings a ton on the London market, an increase of thirty per cent on four years earlier. Despite the strike, Britain produced 164 million tons of coal that year. Output climbed in 1894, and went on rising to a pre-Great War peak of 287 million tons in 1913. Of this, no less than ninety-four million tons went to export and ship bunkering.

The MFGB went from strength to strength after this signal victory, and in 1912 felt powerful enough to call an all-out strike for a national minimum wage. With the nation so dependent on coal for its life-blood, the government intervened to prevent a dispute and rushed through an Act of Parliament compelling coal owners and the union to set up joint boards in each coalfield to establish area minimum rates. The miners wisely accepted half a loaf.

Their mettle was tested again in the strike of 1921, over wage cuts. They were defeated, and within weeks employers right across the industry slashed the wages of more than six million workers. The MFGB felt betrayed by the failure of their fellow trade unions, the railwaymen and the transport workers, with whom they had formed the Triple Alliance, to come to their aid. This pact, signed in 1913, was the forerunner of similar alliances over the years. None of them came to very much. The last, formed in 1981, with the rail and steel workers, came to be known derisively among militant miners as 'the Cripple Alliance'.

The miners may have been naïve to believe that other groups of workers would share their fixity of purpose and toughness of spirit, and put their own jobs at risk by coming to their aid. But their sense of betrayal was nonetheless real for that. They retreated to their communities to lick their wounds, only to have to fight again in 1926, the year of the general strike. The issue was the same: the imposition of lower wages. The TUC came to their aid with a general but half-hearted mobilization of the entire trade union movement. The general strike began on May Day, and lasted nine historic days. Then the TUC General Council, fearing that some or all of their number might be prosecuted, took fright and called off the strike. The miners were left to fight on alone, and went down to defeat in December. The MFGB had to concede wage cuts and the loss of the seven-hour day.

There are parallels between the 1926 strike and the great strike of 1984–5. Both began to peter out in a return to work before they were called off. Both resulted in catastrophic defeat of the declared objective: in 1926, it was to sustain rates of pay and the seven-hour day; in 1984, it was to prevent the closure of 'uneconomic' coal mines. And both will be remembered for the enormously charismatic performances of the NUM leaders of the day. In 1926, it was Arthur James Cook, general secretary of the MFGB, an eloquent agitator but regarded by fellow left-wingers as a poor negotiator. His slogan

'Not a penny off the pay, not an hour off the day' rallied the strikers in their hundreds of thousands. But after the long months of struggle, wages went down, and the men had to work an extra hour every day. In 1984, it was Arthur Scargill, who hero-worshipped Cook as the sea-green incorruptible, and modelled himself on the great 'AJ'. Scargill, too, went down to defeat on his key objective of no pit closures, and tens of thousands of miners were made redundant.

Cook, described by Will Paynter, his Communist successor as general secretary of the NUM, as a master of his craft on the platform with terrific support throughout the coalfields, often said: 'When you hear that A.J. has been dining with royalty, he will have deserted you.' When he dined with the Prince of Wales towards the end of his life, the miners at Porth colliery accused him of betraying them. More distressingly, Cook was accused of holding secret negotiations with associates of the coal owners and the government during his lock-out. He did not tell his fellow MFGB leaders of these talks, but a committee of inquiry upheld the charge. There is an oblique parallel with Scargill here, too: Scargill opened bank accounts and conducted policy initiatives such as the ill-fated mission to Libya during the great strike without telling his executive, and was subjected to an official inquiry by the executive. The parallels are not as flattering as he might wish them to be.

But the fact that he could still invoke Cook's name and the treachery of the TUC in his speeches points to the powerful nature of the myths in mining trade unionism. Lord Murray, former general secretary of the TUC, makes the rueful point that 'Arthur's whole attitude towards the TUC seemed to be shaped by the events of 1926, the year in which the TUC "sold the miners down the river" and refused to acknowledge the capacity of the Miners' Federation to solve the economic problems by failing to get behind them in their industrial action. I don't think he ever forgot that. He always bore a grudge. He always regarded the TUC as unable to deliver the support that was necessary and desirable.' That analysis chimed with Scargill's view of the NUM as 'the spearhead of the labour movement', meriting the unquestioning support of other trade unions. 'He saw members of unions, and unions, in that order as being more reliable supporters and reliable allies for the NUM than the TUC,' said Murray.

The MFGB survived the Hungry Thirties heavily reduced in numbers, but with unity intact. Men in the despised and hated 'Spencer union' were brought back into the fold. This was a

breakaway 'industrial' union formed in the Nottinghamshire coalfield by area president George Spencer, who had been expelled from
the MFGB after the 1926 dispute for agreeing to talk with one of
the coalfield branches about a return to work. In 1926, as in 1984,
Nottinghamshire split over the dispute. Like the Union of Democratic Mineworkers today, the moderate Spencer union, which did
not believe in strikes, enjoyed sole recognition rights in the county's
pits. After a particularly vicious dispute at Harworth colliery, the
Spencer union and the Nottinghamshire Miners Association amalga-
mated under the umbrella of the MFGB.

  There had been calls down the decades for a truly national union,
rather than a loose federation of coalfield fiefdoms. These demands
became more strident during the thirties, and the advent of war
brought the various areas into a much closer working relationship.
The MFGB succeeded in winning an across-the-board pay rise for
all miners, the first national agreement for many years. It was not
universally popular with the union barons in the big coalfields of
Yorkshire, Scotland and South Wales, who felt their independence
and authority being eroded. But the conditions of wartime were pushing the union towards a truly national entity. Ernest Bevin introduced
an essential work order to keep men in the pits, and when Hugh
Dalton became president of the Board of Trade in 1942, he introduced government control of the coal industry. Advisory boards, with
miners on them, were set up at national and regional level. Machinery
for regulating wages was established, giving the men a guaranteed
weekly wage for the first time in the history of British coalmining.
That same year, the MFGB set up a working party to draw up a
blueprint for a national union. The die was cast at a conference held
in Nottingham in August 1944, when delegates accepted a new rule
book for the National Union of Mineworkers. Late amendments
committed the NUM to seek nationalization of the industry and 'the
complete abolition of capitalism' – a political dimension that gave
comfort to the Left in years to come. The old coalfield areas were
not dissolved, merely made subject to the 'overriding authority' of
the national union. By failing to break up these fiefdoms, the NUM
sowed the seeds of dissent for the rest of its natural term. The areas
became legally registered unions in their own right, some, like Yorkshire, with funds larger than those of the NUM. However, that
compromise was the price of unity, and the National Union of Mineworkers came into being on 1 January 1945.

For generations, the miners had wanted their industry to be taken into public ownership. The landslide victory of Clement Attlee's Labour government in 1945, coming after three years of national control of coal by the wartime coalition, provided the conditions for their wish to be fulfilled. On New Year's Day, 1947, notices went up at more than 700 pits all over the country stating: 'This colliery is now owned and managed by the National Coal Board on behalf of the people.' It was the new dawn, but it proved a chilly one. Faced with a crisis of supply, the government demanded greater output and harder work while ignoring the fact that coalmining was failing to attract the workers because pay and hours were better in other industries. The supply crisis combined with the bitter winter of 1947 to produce widespread power cuts. Two million people were thrown out of work, a foretaste of what was to happen when the new NUM staged its first national strike in 1972. But at least the miners had got what they wanted, and their new union was courted by the Attlee administration. The NUM assumed its mantle of power with some satisfaction.

A different flag might now be flying from the pithead gear, but life underground had not changed very much with nationalization. The same managers were in charge, the same pressure for production continued, and the same insistence on wage restraint came from the employer. Only now it also came from the union as well. The natural result was desertion among the ranks. More and more miners quit for better paid and more congenial jobs. By late 1950, the number of men in the industry was the lowest since the turn of the century. Early in 1951, with the entire NUM executive in 10 Downing Street, the government was forced to make big pay concessions and agree to set up a pension scheme. In return, the miners agreed to cut down on strikes and absenteeism – and accept foreign workmen in the pits. The first train load of Italian workers was seen off from Milan railway station on 21 May by Alf Robens, Minister of Power and a future NCB chairman.

But Labour was losing its grip on government, and the miners were fearful that their traditional enemy Winston Churchill would reverse the advances they had won under Attlee. Not long before the 1951 general election, Arthur Horner, Communist general secretary of the NUM, warned of 'industrial resistance by the miners' if the Tories carried out their threat to break the industry into smaller units. With the Conservatives in office, the tone changed. The threat to end Saturday working was quietly forgotten and Sir William Lawther, the union president knighted by Attlee, rejected the use of the miners' industrial power for political objectives as 'a great evil', and outraged his members by attending Sir Winston Churchill's birthday celebrations.

Despite the arrival of the new-fangled curse of inflation, the early fifties were on the whole a conciliatory period. But the pressures were building up. The government's 'cheap coal' policy gave industry a hidden subsidy, allowing Britain to compete more easily in international markets. The other side of that coin was an undeclared policy of pay restraint. The miners saw the hand of government in the Coal Board's refusal to maintain wages in line with inflation. The ministerial veto of an arbitration award in October 1952 confirmed their fears. After the relentless pressure for coal, demand was now beginning to slide and the industry was moving towards a period of massive contraction. Yet the NUM pinned its faith on the return of a Labour government, rather than the industrial muscle of its members.

Into this cauldron stepped a nervous teenager, fresh from secondary modern school, a bit of a mother's boy, who was so shocked by his first day at the pit he nearly ran away. Arthur Scargill went into the coal industry at the age of fifteen in the summer of 1953. He hated virtually everything he saw: the dirt, the noise, the sheer crudity of life on the pit top, where men crippled by work underground jostled with young boys on the freezing coal screens. Not much had changed since 'the people' took over the collieries. He was determined that it would. His extraordinary career has become one of the great myths of the labour movement, greater even than that of his hero A. J. Cook and infinitely more tantalizing because he fashioned his own myth – and still lives by it.

CHAPTER II

ORIGINS

ARTHUR SCARGILL WAS born on 11 January 1938, in a 'very old' one-up, one-down collier's house on Pantry Hill, a steep back street in Worsbrough Dale, two miles south of Barnsley. His father Harold was a quiet-spoken man by all accounts, a miner and a devout Communist, though not particularly prominent in the small local party. It was a close-knit household. His mother Alice, who worked in the local bobbin mill, was deeply religious. She was 'strictly non-political' and may have been unhappy about her husband's politics, for she certainly disapproved of her son getting mixed up with the Young Communist League. But he was an only son, and he worshipped his parents, particularly his mother, who was the mainstay of his early life and who died while he was still a teenager, long before fame came his way. In later years, he confessed to Joan Bakewell: 'My mother had lost a child many years before I was born and been told she couldn't have any more. She was thirty-two when I was born – it was quite a shock. I was an only child.'[1]

It could scarcely have been 'many years before' that his mother had lost a child. His parents' marriage certificate records that Harold Scargill, aged twenty-five, a coal miner (hewer) of 6, Wellington Crescent, Bank End, Worsbrough Dale, married Alice Pickering, aged twenty-five, a spinster, and a 'borer' (the handwriting is virtually unintelligible) at the bobbin mill, of 37, James Street, also Worsbrough Dale, at Barnsley Registry Office on 30 January 1932. That is little more than six years before baby Arthur emerged into the world, and she must have been carrying him from the spring of 1937, only five years after entering the marriage. The mother–son relationship was very close. 'We had a warm, lovely relationship,' he told the *Daily Mirror* in 1980. 'She was a very religious woman. She had a brother crippled for life and a father who died at forty-four from working in the pit. All she wanted was for me to have a safe job.'

There is another mystery on the Scargill family wedding certificate. His mother Alice is listed as the daughter of Joseph William Pickering, coal miner, deceased. But in the space provided for Harold's father's name and profession, a discreet black line is drawn. The mystery is compounded in his father's birth certificate, which records that he was born on 23 July 1906 at 379, High Street, Worsbrough Dale, to Clara Scargill, a velvet cutter, living at that address. The mother registered Harold's birth herself just over a month later. Again the columns giving details of the father's name and occupation bear only a thin black line. Who was Harold's father and Arthur's grandfather?

Scargill has talked of being partly brought up by grandparents because his father was away at the war and his mother working in a munitions factory. He told the *Yorkshire Evening Post* in 1973 that 'my father was a miner, and his father before him'. Both worked at Wombwell Main colliery, he said a year later. Scargill has occasionally unburdened himself of the story in private, but rarely in public. He told an interviewer in 1979 that his name would have been McQuillan 'if an Irish male forbear had married before fathering his first child, but as it was, the child was born out of wedlock and took his mother's name, Scargill, and Arthur Scargill, several generations later, is proud of it'.[2]

In April 1993, he was a good deal more forthcoming in an interview with Hunter Davies in *The Independent*. His grandfather, Joe McQuillan, was a miner from Drogheda who had fathered Harold before marrying the boy's mother three months after the birth. The McQuillans went on to have three girls and two more boys, all taking the family name.

For the young Harold, however, there followed a lifetime of discreet shame. Scargill told Davies: 'My father went through life in this small mining village, the same one I was brought up in, with a different surname from his brothers and sisters – so everyone knew what happened. It was a stigma he took through life. He was an active Communist, but I think this stigma was the reason he never stood for any public office. When I became president of the Yorkshire miners in 1973, he said to me it was the first time in his life he hadn't been ashamed of his name.'

Scargill is a Yorkshire name to be proud of. It means 'the place at the foot of the cliff', and by extension the people who live there. Indeed, Scargill does live at the foot of a dale, scarcely a mile from where he was born, in his luxury stone villa, Treelands, bought shortly after the great strike of 1984–5 and the subject of so much controversy. He has come full circle from the grinding poverty of his childhood, though the revolution has not been the one he has so passionately preached all his life. He started his crusade from a small home as a humble activist in a big union. He is ending it in a big house, as the leader of a small union facing extinction.

His later success would have been unthinkable in those pre-war days of privation. 27, Pantry Hill, long since demolished in the slum clearances that were the pride of municipal socialism in the 1950s, had no gas, no electric light, no hot water and an outside lavatory. Cold water was piped to the kitchen sink, and lighting was by a storm lamp. Scargill recalled: 'There were three toilets across the yard. Seven families shared them. They had a flat roof on top, and every kid in the neighbourhood used to play on top, clattering around.'[3] Worsbrough Urban District Council's Medical Officer of Health targeted 'this whole unhealthy area', condemning entire streets such as Pantry Hill and Jarrotts Buildings nearby. He complained of 'unpaved yards, inadequate sanitary accommodation and general dilapidation aggravated by mining subsidence'. Young Arthur's home was condemned as unfit for human habitation. Only a stone wall, with infills where doors and windows once were, now marks the spot. The site is now in a private garden. 'We lived there till I was four, and then we got a council house. It had both a kitchen and a living room. I thought it was huge. I thought we had moved into paradise,'[4] he recalled later.

This is classic Yorkshire mining country. In the Domesday Book, it was Wirc's burg – the defensive place of Wirc – and coal has been dug here since the Middle Ages. A Victorian history states: 'It is to the coal trade that Worsbrough owes mainly its present commercial prosperity. It has gone on growing rapidly in wealth and importance; its hidden mineral treasures have been sought for, and brought to the surface – in late years in an abundance that would astonish our forefathers. It is now sent to the surface in this township alone by thousands of tons daily, and despatched to all parts of the kingdom, the canal and railway communication affording every facility for transit.'

Upwards of a thousand men, women and boys were employed in eight pits in the dale. Initially, coal was got by 'day holes', primitive pits dug directly into the seams outcropping on both sides of the valley of the River Dove. Fire-damp was a constant danger, and the parish register records the first known explosion in 1755, when three men were 'slain by the damp' in Mr Boden's coal pit in Genne-Lane. As the pits went deeper, the dangers increased correspondingly. Outside the parish church of St Thomas stands to this day a small, elegant monument to the 145 men and boys killed in an explosion down Swaithe Main colliery on 6 December 1875.

This was the way of life – hard, but warm – to which the young Arthur became accustomed. 'Worsbrough was a very close-knit mining community. It seemed to me everybody in the world lived there. I've seen men boxing, Sunday afternoons, bare-knuckled, for a side-stake of two and sixpence. I've seen whippet-racing, pigeon racing. It was a complete community. Nowhere was there such a growth of brass bands and marvellous choirs as Yorkshire. The Welsh haven't got a monopoly. And when we had a disaster – twelve or fifteen men killed in a pit – the sense of grief and shock was something I've not witnessed anywhere else. As a child I had that sense of a mining community setting themselves apart – not because they wanted to, but because they were compelled to.'[5]

Worsbrough Dale, easily visible from the southbound lanes of the M1, wears a kindlier aspect now than it did in the heyday of King Coal. The pits have all gone. The last, Barrow, from which many Scargillite policies emerged into the councils of the National Union of Mineworkers, was abandoned in 1985, and few traces remain. The River Dove meanders quietly through open farmland that once echoed to the noise of collieries, chemicals and munitions works, and the coal trains of the London North-Eastern Railway blasting their way up Worsbrough Bank. In Arthur's childhood it must have seemed like a self-contained universe. Lads did not stray far. Ian Linford, a school contemporary, recalls that a walk across the valley to the old Dove Cliffe station of the LMS railway was regarded as something of an adventure. The township was big enough. 'And it was always a friendly place,' he remembered.[6]

Scargill's earliest recollection of his surroundings is of going as a very young child with the family dog to meet his father coming home from work. He could hear the sound of his clogs on the cobblestones long before he could see him, and the dog 'went mad barking'.[7] He recalled that his father was 'always suffering from some sort of infirmity, so he didn't work much as a miner'.[8] In fact, he retired incapacitated in 1965, aged fifty-nine, though he lived on into his eighties. Despite being in a reserved occupation, and approaching middle age, Harold Scargill was called up in 1940 and went into the RAF, serving in West Africa for much of the war. Alice Scargill went to work full-time in the munitions factory, and in later years Scargill blamed the war for damaging his family life. 'My mother was having to work, and I was an only child left with my grandparents,' he told a TV-am interviewer in 1983. Young Arthur was only twenty months old when his father went off to the war, and the separation naturally tightened the bond with his mother. 'I grew very, very close to my mother,' he told David Dimbleby on BBC1's 'Person to Person' in August 1979. 'She was always there when I wanted her.'

He later revealed to Sue Lawley on the BBC Radio programme 'Desert Island Discs': 'I remember my mother with probably more vivid recollection than anything else in my life. She died when I was eighteen. It was the most devastating period of the whole of my life when she died, and for three months it literally rendered me unable to function properly. I was very, very close to my mother because my father was in the Royal Air Force and so my mother and I became inseparable. She was a Christian, a very lovely women, and obviously I loved her very much indeed. I often think back and regret deeply that she never saw any of the things that I was able to achieve in later life because the only thing that she ever saw me do was go down a pit and join the Young Communist League, and both of those things she disapproved of because she didn't want me to get hurt going down the pit and she didn't want me to get hurt by joining the Young Communist League.'

He was sure that 'my mother would have been as proud of me as I was of her'. He chose 'a beautiful hymn', 'Oh Love That Will Not Let Me Go', sung by the London Emmanuel Choir, to take with him to the mythical island, because it epitomized his feelings about his mother. 'She was a Christian,' he said, adding: 'Incidentally, so am I.' And, asked which record he would keep if a wave snatched away the other seven, he came back swiftly: 'Without question, the one that would remind me of my mother.'

His father, he said on the same programme in April 1988, was 'in many ways the opposite of my mother'. She was strictly non-political, he was very political indeed, 'and I was brought up in a household filled with love but also filled with this marvellous contradiction – my mother, who used to go to church, and my father, who used to go to the Communist Party meetings and meetings of the National Union of Mineworkers'. Didn't that make for an argumentative household, asked Ms Lawley. No, insisted Scargill. 'There were no arguments in the house, funnily enough. My mother totally supported my father – absolutely loved him and of course it was reciprocated.'

This idyll was interrupted by the war, and Arthur was sent to the village junior mixed and infants primary school in Worsbrough Dale, a two-storey Victorian stone building with high, south-facing windows looking across the valley. The school was on two sites divided by a narrow road. One building has been demolished, and the site is occupied by smart semis – Worsbrough is a respectable address these days. The other building still stands on a sharply rising hill. The headmaster during the war years, recalls Ian Linford (now a bookseller in Harrogate), was Harold Hemingway, something of a tyro even for those days. 'The regime was very strict. Nobody got away with anything with that headmaster. Nobody stepped out of line.'[9]

Little is recorded of his time at that school, although pert little Arthur clearly impressed one of his teachers, Mrs Dorothy Bamford, who remembered: 'He was always saying: "I've done, Miss – what shall I do next?" When I was on yard duty, he'd pop up in front of me, asking questions. He liked puzzling, and arguing for the sake of arguing – but he kept you on your toes.'[10] There is anecdotal evidence that Scargill was badly bullied at school. His conduct in the school yard sounds more like that of a young boy who craves attention, and the warmth of a caring mother substitute.[11]

Even at this tender age, he began to show the first, critical signs of an inner fear of wider horizons that has dogged him all his life, prompting accusations of insularity and insecurity that are hard to dispel completely. 'I went to the board school and refused to take the eleven-plus,' he told Joan Bakewell. 'If I'd got a scholarship I'd have had to go to the grammar school in Barnsley, and I didn't want to go out of my village. In retrospect, I can see that I was wrong.'[12] Much later, he produced a class-based argument for not going to the grammar school. In 1993, he told Hunter Davies: 'I thought the grammar school was a place for snobs and I didn't want to go.' It was also a place of open academic competition, and he has never shone in such surroundings. This is the first manifestation of the intellectual agoraphobia that characterized, and vitiated, his mature years.

His refusal to take the eleven-plus is all the more remarkable because Harold Hemingway put his top year, the examination class, through a work-intensive curriculum that was the envy of the neighbourhood. 'You didn't play games in the last year. You didn't play football. There was no time for that. Not even for painting and that kind of thing. It was entirely devoted to getting you through the eleven-plus, and he had a tremendous success rate,' recalled Ian Linford,[13] who was a class above young Arthur and did pass his eleven-plus. He remembers little of the boy who would become king. 'There were quite a few characters there who stood out as personalities, but he certainly didn't. I can recall nothing ever being said about him or indeed his family.'

So Arthur eschewed the bright lights of Barnsley, and settled for White Cross secondary modern (now Worsbrough High), a gaunt redbrick school built by the education authority on what were once cornfields crossed by the collier's path to Swaithe pit. There, he was put in the B-stream 'because I refused to try'.[14] He readily confessed later: 'While I was at school, I was never a brilliant or enthusiastic scholar – the real studies came later.'[15] But if school was not the most satisfactory educational experience, he was learning at home.

He told John Mortimer in January 1982 in an interview for *The Sunday Times* that his father was the greatest influence on him. 'Not directly – he never told me anything directly – but he read about eight books a week. The house was full of books, the Bible, Shakespeare, we had everything. My father still reads the dictionary every day. He says your life depends on your power to master words. I read Jack London and *The Ragged Trousered Philanthropists*. Those were the books that formed my political opinions.'[16] Rather more conventionally for a boy in his early teens, he was also reading Huckleberry Finn, a present from his mother. This was 'the book that brings back memories, that was bought for me by my mother' that he would take as his only book on to the BBC's Desert Island. 'It's given me enormous pleasure as I've read it and re-read it over the years,' he told Sue Lawley. How much, one wonders, from the intrinsic interest of Mark Twain's classic of a Mississippi boyhood, and how much from the emotional connection with his mother?

His political interests were beginning to take shape in this unusual domestic forcing house. 'My dad was a very strong unionist and active member of the labour movement and he taught me all I knew,' he told the Communist writer Len Doherty.[17] 'I was about twelve when he started taking me to meetings.' This was a unique interview involving father and son, and Harold Scargill cut in to say: 'It was always up to him whether he came with me or not, but from the first meeting he was always with me, and we heard many a famous speaker and took part in many a debate.' Just what these meetings were is, alas, not recorded. It is inconceivable that he took a schoolboy to CP branch meetings, but he may refer to parliamentary hustings and town council gatherings. Scargill *père* insisted: 'From being a boy, Arthur was always a great reader. He went through Marx and Lenin and others while he was still at school, and he was a lad who always seemed to know what he wanted – and if he wanted something, went all out to get it.'

At this distance, Harold's engaging picture of a determined boy is easily recognizable. The lad in shorts poring over *Das Kapital* and *Left-wing Communism, An Infantile Disorder* is rather less convincing. In later life, his comrades on the Left found Scargill's Marxism hesitant and superficial. Nor did he speak naturally in the approved 'party manner', as did those well schooled in the Marxist classics. Mercifully – and to his advantage – his style has always been more demotic.

He left White Cross school in the summer of 1953, and initially sought work in a local engineering factory in deference to his mother's wishes. 'I thought I was the greatest gift to engineering since the wheel,' he remembered with characteristic modesty. 'Somehow, no one seemed to agree,'[18] he added, with equally characteristic self-deprecation, of the sort that is designed to get you on his side. So, despite Alice's forebodings, it was the pit. But he didn't go down 'the one in the village', or Wombwell Main, where his father worked. He chose instead to go to Woolley colliery, some eight miles north of Barnsley and ten miles from home – two bus journeys at four a.m. or a long bike ride on summer mornings. He later rationalized this choice by arguing that the shift at Woolley was half an hour shorter than elsewhere. Colliery managers in the Barnsley area at the time contest this, insisting that shift times were common across the coalfield, and a young trainee like Arthur Scargill is unlikely to have had that kind of working grasp of the industry in any event.

Whatever the truth of the matter, the light this incident sheds on Scargill's character is interesting. He feels obliged in later life to portray himself as a precocious fifteen-year-old school leaver who could already put one over on the bosses by finding the least punishing place to work. In fact, it comes out as more smart-aleck than smart: the long journey time to Woolley from Worsbrough would have been greater than any time he could have saved through a shorter shift – which could only have been made short by cutting back on 'snap' (meal) times. No pit manager would have been able to operate a working week two and a half hours shorter than the rest of the industry.

However long his shift was, Scargill found the work quite literally terrifying. He has given a number of descriptions of his first day working on the coal screens on the surface at Woolley. He was taken into the screening plant, where coal on a conveyor belt is separated from stones and other debris, with the other raw new recruits and old miners no longer fit to work anywhere else. 'You couldn't see more than two yards for dust, and the noise was so intense you had to speak with your hands. I had to scrape the caked dust from my lips before I could eat my sandwiches. I couldn't understand how such awful conditions could exist in 1953. It probably sounds corny, but on that first day I promised myself I would try one day to get things changed.'[19] In a more colourful version eight years later, he vouchsafed to John Mortimer: 'I got up at four to walk a mile to the bus. We were in the engineer's office at six in the morning and he came in, a big man in a brown suit with oil stains on it, a brown pork-pie hat and thick glasses. His name was Lomas. "I want no bloody trouble from any of you." He glared round at us fifteen-year-old lads. "You do a six-hour shift and your snap time is twenty minutes. If I get any bloody trouble, you're on your way. All right, take them away."'

The foreman was a one-eyed man, Alf Melson, another villain of the piece. 'Melson used to stalk up and down a sort of raised gantry in the screening plant. He was just like Captain Bligh glaring at his crew. We were picking bits of stone and rock out of the coal as it passed us on conveyor belts. The place was so full of dust you could barely see your hands, and so noisy you had to use sign language. When it came to snap time, your lips were coated in black dust. You had to wash them before you could eat your snap.'

In a third version, he remembered that his snap consisted of a bottle of water and bread and jam sandwiches, and that on the engineer's office was 'the biggest clock outside Big Ben'. He also added some serious socio-political observations: 'There were two sorts of people in the section: us, and disabled rejects of society. I saw men with one arm and one leg, men crippled and mentally retarded. I nearly turned and ran. I thought: "I can't work in this lot." But I did for a year, and I suppose it had a direct effect on my life. I saw people who should never have been working, having to work to live. They were a danger to themselves and everyone else.'[20] This strikes the ear as genuine. Young Scargill was no longer cosseted at home. He was in the cruel environment of the pre-mechanization mining industry. Today, coal is washed by machines. There is no hand picking, and disabled miners are no longer found eking out a living alongside boys straight from school.

The impact that such conditions made on Scargill has plainly stayed with him all his life. At the time, the shock was seismic. He quickly became involved in the NUM, attending his first branch meeting at the age of sixteen. He also veered into politics. According to the version he published in *New Left Review* in 1975, 'at the age of 15 I decided that the world was wrong and I wanted to put it right, virtually overnight if possible'. He did two things. 'First of all I wrote to the Labour Party and asked them if there was any youth organization I could belong to, or if there was any association at all where I could play a part. Additionally, I wrote to the British-Soviet Friendship Society. I was reading the *Daily Worker* at this time, and asked them if I could join because I wanted to further friendship between peoples. I got a reply from them, but I didn't get a reply from the Labour Party, in spite of two more letters. I thought here I am, I want to contribute to a world where I know everything's wrong and I want to try and put it right, or at least play my part. I read Jack London's novel *The Iron Heel* and many other of his works. I was shocked that we can have a world of plenty and still starvation. And so I wrote to the *Daily Worker* and asked if there was a young Communist Party I could join. Within twenty-four hours they were at my house and I joined the Young Communist League.'[21]

In another version 'the Young Communists were at our house the same night'. He also told John Mortimer he was fifteen when he began his political odyssey. In fact, he was seventeen years and two months, according to the Barnsley Young Communist League minute book that he used to produce for the entertainment of visitors. The entry for 31 March 1955 reads: 'Today the comrades visited Billy Smart's circus. Arthur Scargill and Derek Stubbings joined the party. The membership is now 11.'

The party activist who visited the Scargills was David Larder, a young former Second Lieutenant who had witnessed British atrocities against prisoners in Kenya and quit the army in disgust. He was a hero of the YCL at the time, regularly lionized in *Challenge*, the Young Communist paper started in 1938 ('written by young people and controlled by young people', presumably as long as they toed the party line). Miners were certainly the flavour of the month, for two weeks after he signed up, *Challenge* published a photograph of Scargill and Stubbings, with a caption saying they were old school-mates 'and do everything together'. Scargill admitted that he encoun-tered 'some hostility from families, but not from friends. And some of my friends were sympathetic: so much so that I was able to build the organization from six members when I joined into about 168 or 170 when I finally left the organization when I was twenty-three, which is not a bad achievement in an area like this.'[22]

Quite apart from the fact that he understated the membership when he joined by about half, his estimate of the membership when he left is a gross overstatement. He would have had to be the Pied Piper of Barnsley to have recruited so many young people. The figures he refers to must be for the whole Yorkshire region, which in the mid-1950s ran at about 120.

It was, on the whole, a congenial political home. Scargill's picture was in *Challenge* once again later that year, on 5 November, when he was shown taking part in a National Peace Lobby the previous month. A loud check scarf round his neck, he beams for the camera, in company with Violet Gill, an engineering worker and another YCLer. *Challenge* also reported in July 1955 that Barnsley, which was not a particularly long-established branch, was celebrating its first birthday, and that 'starting from scratch a year ago they now have sixteen members, five of whom are miners'.

Monty Meth, who later became industrial editor of the *Daily Mail*, was then a young freelance reporter living in Leeds, earning part of his living as Yorkshire correspondent for the *Daily Worker*. This post would not have made him much of a living. The party paper was a notoriously poor payer. Some of its London staffers would joke that there was no 'Moscow gold', adding ruefully: 'Wish there were.' Meth was also secretary of the Yorkshire YCL, and he still remembers the fresh-faced Scargill joining the Communist youth organization. 'He was very bright, always articulate. He did stand out from the crowd, there's no doubt about that.'[23]

The YCL was a serious business, but it had its social side too. Branch meetings would usually start off with a talk, often on labour history. Then the members would fall to discussing 'activity': winning support for petitions against rearmament, or cutting national service from two years to one – a radical measure that young men found attractive, for obvious reasons. They would also plan sales of *Challenge* in the streets of Barnsley. It wasn't all preparation for the revolution that never came. On Saturday nights, they staged a social, and on fine Sundays, a ramble in the countryside. In the summer, there was invariably a YCL camp, often at Hardcastle Crags, the Yorkshire beauty spot. It sounds unbelievably virtuous by today's standards, and Meth confirms that. 'You couldn't have a youth organization like that today,' he muses.[24]

Perhaps it wasn't always so demure. Fellow Young Communists still tell the story that on one hike Scargill was boasting about his popularity with 'the lasses'. Four of the girls tired of his bragging, and stripped him to his boots, according to his comrade of the time Jim Parker, later his driver and bodyguard. 'He wasn't so manly then. He didn't like it.'[25] If he was gauche with girls, it is all the more surprising that his first serious relationship was with a young French woman, named Hélène, from the city of Lyons. 'I was engaged for three years,' he told Hunter Davies in 1993. 'We met at a Young Communist meeting in Prague. We used to meet five or six times a year. I don't speak French, but her English was good. We grew apart in the end. Then I met my wife.' Quite apart from the uncharacteristically bourgeois and old-fashioned concept of 'being engaged' for three years, this episode offers another interesting sidelight on his tastes. 'Londoner's Diary' in the *Evening Standard* reported in March 1987 that Scargill had told an audience in Cork that his relationship with Hélène gave him a passion – for bread and red wine. In private, that is his favourite tipple.

Scargill evidently threw himself into the YCL with some vigour. He organized seaside outings, jazz concerts and political lectures. Jean Miller, an active member at the time, recalled: 'He was never shy of voicing his opinions even then. Every Sunday afternoon we had meetings, Marxist classes, poetry readings, rambles. He was very fond of Burns, I remember. In the Marxist classes, he was always very dynamic, always asking questions and wanting to get people to talk to us who knew more about the subject than we did.'[26]

He came to the notice of the YCL leadership quite quickly, but perhaps not as quickly as his first biographer, television journalist Michael Crick, seems to believe. He states that Scargill was on the

YCL national executive committee within eighteen months, in 1956, the year of the Hungarian counter-revolution.[27] Jimmy Reid, the young hero of the Clydeside shipbuilding apprentices' dispute, believes it was a good deal later, in 1958 or 1959. Reid was national secretary of the YCL from 1958 to 1964, and he insists: 'He came on in 1959, and purely on the basis that he was a young miner from a big coalfield, and that was it.'[28]

The national executive was around twenty-five to thirty strong, composed of young miners, engineers, students – male and female – drawn from as wide a geographical area as possible. 'I have got no recollections of thinking: "This is a great potential, politically",' recalls Reid. 'He wasn't on very long. I cannot remember any significant contribution.' The one thing he could remember is Scargill's passion for cars. 'He has always been fascinated with big cars. He had bought a second-hand Jaguar and couldn't afford to run it.'

But his fascination did not evidently run to orthodox Communist theory. Reid again: 'I have never heard Arthur Scargill, while he was in the YCL, or subsequently, revealing any evidence of having studied Marx.' Some of Reid's strictures may be put down to the spectacular fall-out between the two comrades during the great strike of 1984–5, but he was in a position to know at the time, and his analysis is shared by others. 'There is not a great deal of evidence of a coherently thought-out position,' he argues. Pressed to pin him down philosophically, he remarks: 'It would be a crude form of syndicalism. There was always this implication that militant trade unionism on its own could become a dynamo to change society. Syndicalism has been tried and abandoned because it doesn't work. That is not to say that trade unions do not have a political role. But Scargill was saying more than that.' He was openly cynical of the role of MPs and the political process 'in favour of the things you could do through trade unions'.

Partly for the obvious reason that the Communist Party conducted its affairs in a semi-clandestine manner, very little survives of Scargill's contribution to British Communism. The party itself is now defunct, having been transmogrified into the Democratic Left after the victory of the 'Eurocommunist' reformers in the late eighties – a political shift triggered in no small part by the miners' strike and the lessons learned from it. But in a warehouse in Hackney, the old party still keeps some records. Among these, George Matthews, former editor of the *Morning Star*, turned up a speech by 'Arthur Skargile' (sic) made at a party conference in Easter 1957. By CP standards, it was a brief contribution, and it deserves to see the light of day in full. The party paper *World News* reported his speech, noting simply that he was a delegate from Yorkshire.

Scargill told the conference: 'At the last National Congress an analysis was made regarding young people, which showed that they were the most prone as victims of the Tory attack. They are still exploited, still called up for conscription and to fight in colonial wars. But they are prepared to fight with us and have a go whenever the opportunity presents itself. During the recent strike, we got the apprentices to come out on strike with the engineers at Metro-Vicks in Manchester, they stormed the gates to get in to work and then came out on strike with the other engineers.

'I would like to bring some experiences from my own pit in Yorkshire, which show how the young workers will fight. On the afternoon of the shift when they finish at seven, the management said they must stop down a further two hours. They approached me on the question and approached me to get in touch with the management to get out early. I put it to the young workers, and we held a meeting and discussed the matter. We held the meeting at the pit bottom and we had forty-five young people in the cabin at the pit bottom, which has never been used before. We took six of the lads to see the management the next day.

'These are the same young people who are irresponsible – everyone at the present moment says so. Even in the eyes of the Communist Party they are irresponsible.

'The management refused to let us come out early. We came out and won a victory. The question of winning young people to our cause is very important. We can see this quite clearly. Look at the Tory Party – they know how to win them. They have 150,000 Young Conservatives. I think it shows a criminal neglect by the Communist Party when you look at the state of the Young Communist League since the Twenty-Fourth Congress. I am calling for action now.

'I want to call for volunteers to come into the YCL from this Congress. This will help strengthen the Communist movement right where it needs to be strengthened – among the young people of Britain, who alone can determine the future of socialism in this country.'

Scargill spoke those words when he was just nineteen, but already a veteran of his first strike. It could be argued that his speech is a little crude, and that Reid's complaint of naïve syndicalism is upheld.

But there is a freshness and zest to his appeal, a passion that illustrates like a clear shaft of light. He tells the story of his strike simply, unlike the previous speaker, George Bridges, who has disappeared into obscurity. He drowned in a welter of 'only a party of Marxists is able to lead the workers out of their despair and betrayal . . . only a party with the aim of class political power is able to fulfil the correct role in Britain'. Some of Scargill's rhetorical tricks are already becoming evident: the party's neglect is 'criminal'. Fights and victories abound. His demand is for action 'now'. It is a practical but stirring speech: a celebration of a strike and a call to arms. The formula was to become very familiar, and very polished.

These were critical days for the Communist Party in Yorkshire. In World War Two, when membership rose sharply across the country, the party in Yorkshire made considerable inroads in the steel and engineering industries of Sheffield, the clothing industry in Leeds and the great textile centres of Bradford, Halifax and Calderdale. In 1950, the party elders appointed a young Canadian lawyer, Bert Ramelson, a veteran of the Spanish civil war, to be district secretary of the party in Yorkshire, based in Leeds. Ramelson swiftly grasped that the CP had a secure power base in the big conurbations. But in the vast Yorkshire coalfield employing more than 150,000 men in 130 pits, dispersed for the most part in semi-rural locations, it was not yet a force to be reckoned with. Loyalty to Labour, the party that had nationalized the industry was taken for granted. In the words of an NUM branch secretary, bemused by talk of a 'political strike' that was bringing down the Heath government: 'We're not political here, we always vote Labour.'

Ramelson remembers: 'We didn't have so many members. But those we had were respected by the miners: Jock Kane, Sammy Taylor, Tommy Degnan, Percy Riley. The problem we had was that the entire NUM leadership in the coalfield was right-wing. If I was going to do anything that was useful, of importance, it would be to change the character of the Yorkshire coalfield. When I got the job, I discussed it with Harry Pollitt (general secretary of the CPGB). I put this idea to him and said we should concentrate on this. The Yorkshire miners could change the character of the NUM, which in turn could change the composition of the labour movement as a whole. The miners at that time had a big vote. If they could be changed, it could change the role of the TUC General Council.'[29]

The party had full-time workers in Leeds and Sheffield, but nobody in the coalfield. So, in 1952, Ramelson proposed bringing a party apparatchik into the mining country from outside. He wrote to the Scottish Party, which was very strong in coalmining, and they sent Frank Watters, a thirty-one-year-old ex-collier from West Lothian where he was party secretary. He had only been out of the pit six months. He came down to Yorkshire in 1953, and came into contact with young Scargill soon after. They became firm comrades and their careers have been continuously intertwined for the ensuing four decades. In a fulsome tribute to Watters' acerbic autobiography, *Being Frank*, published in late 1992, Scargill wrote: 'Frank has been my friend for nearly forty years, ever since the days when as an eager youngster to help change the world I joined the Young Communist League.'

Watters estimated that in 1953 the party had fewer than a hundred members in less than twelve pits, out of a total CP membership of approximately 300 covering Rotherham, Doncaster, Barnsley and Worksop. On the vital area council of the National Union of Mineworkers, the party had only three members out of 136. By 1960, when Scargill was treading the path of disillusion with the CP, there were 440 Communists in the South Yorkshire coalfield. The party had made 'big advances in our contacts' and could regularly win nominations in thirty pits – around a third of those still remaining open. Communists felt they were 'at the centre of things in the Yorkshire coalfield'.[30]

Watters insists that 'there can never be any doubt that it was the Communist Party that mainly made the challenge to the right-wing machine in Yorkshire and nationally'.[31] The man chosen as the party's standard bearer in the county was Sammy Taylor, into whose shoes Scargill would eventually step. Taylor, a fluent speaker and well-liked pit official from Barnsley, was chairman of the Yorkshire area of the Communist Party. With Watters as his election agent, Taylor 'made the first major breakthrough for the party' by winning a seat on the national executive of the NUM in 1959, and went on to capture the Yorkshire Compensation Agent position in 1964, the same road later trodden by his protégé, Scargill.

At pit level, the CP was making headway, but it was not always plain sailing. Despite the party's condescending remarks about right-wing leadership, Yorkshire was the most strike-prone coalfield in the nation's most strike-ridden industry. In the fifties, coalmining accounted for three strikes out of four in Britain, and a Ministry of

Labour report in 1965 disclosed that Yorkshire accounted for forty-six per cent of all days lost through disputes in the mining industry, yet the coalfield had only twenty per cent of the industry's manpower.[32] They punched their weight, twice over. But most of these strikes were unofficial 'rag-ups' over local or even single-pit issues, and formed no part of a cohesive political direction. Watters complains bitterly that Bob Wilkinson, a lifelong friend of Scargill and Communist delegate at Woodlesford colliery, 'jumped the gun' on a dispute in 1954 over tonnage bonuses and sent out pickets into South Yorkshire before any groundwork had been done. The outcome was disastrous. In a head-shaking condemnation of what would now be called mindless militancy, Watters reports: 'Woodlesford opted for the easy pickings, but in the process undid the years of work devoted to getting clarity along with the necessary preparation for an all-out coalfield strike.'[33] That was clearly the party's objective: not just the capturing of key positions, but an all-out strike of the coalfield. It was to come, but not for another decade.

Meanwhile, Scargill was busy in the YCL and making a name for himself in the Woolley NUM branch. At first, surprisingly, he failed to make the connection between the pit and the party. Considering that he was supposed to be immersed in Marxism, and to be the product of a home deeply imbued with Communism and the labour movement, this is inexplicable. Yet he confessed later: 'Looking back, I regarded my life at the pit as a job to be done. Full stop. And I regarded my political activities as another job to be done . . . but as something separate. It was only later that I began to realize the need for a trade union.'[34]

He went to work underground at seventeen and a half, not at the face but 'out-bye', in the roadways at the bottom of the shaft. There he looked after a pit pony named 'King', a story he likes to tell with a wry face, knowing that his present-day audience will be familiar with the soubriquet 'King Arthur' he was given in the seventies – coined incidentally, by Bob Houston, pop music journalist and scion of a Lanarkshire mining family who edited the NUM national journal, *The Miner*, until Scargill became national president.

The only thing royal about Scargill in the mid-fifties was his own sense of destiny. He told David Dimbleby in August 1979: 'I began to recognize that in order to advance the interests of the people at the pit, I needed to become involved in the trade union movement. The older miners viewed me with great suspicion because it was

unknown for a young miner to be involved in the trade union movement. The young miners around me were very great supporters of
mine, and the miners who were in between those two categories first
of all questioned what my motives were and then later supported
me full-heartedly, and this was to lead on to many other measures,
including, of course, subsequently election to office.'[35]

It may have been unusual for young men to be active at Woolley
– a big pit, employing some 2,700 men, and run by an old-fashioned
NUM right-wing 'baron', Elijah Benn – but it was by no means
'unknown' in the union. The pages of *Challenge* often featured young
Communist miners in South Wales, Scotland and even Lancashire
at this time. Scargill may have been 'for'ard' for his age but he was
by no means unique. Because of his youthful high profile, he had to
live with some hostility down the pit. 'Every time something appeared
in the newspapers about the Communist Party of Great Britain, I
was immediately attacked, in the verbal sense, down the pit by older
miners and I had running debates day in and day out.' However, he
was stoic about such attacks. 'It didn't worry me because I knew it
was essential to argue my case both as a politician and also as a trade
unionist.'[36]

As time went by, by his own account, he became more interested
in the trade union than in the YCL. He told *New Left Review* in 1975:
'I went on very actively in the Young Communist League until I was
about eighteen years of age. And then I gradually began to be interested in the union itself because it appeared to me that irrespective
of what I did politically in the Young Communist League or the
Labour League of Youth as it then was, the Labour or Communist
Party or any other political organization, the *real power* – and I say
that in the best possible sense – the real power lay either with the
working classes or the ruling classes.

'Now the working classes were obviously identified with the trade
union movement and not directly identified with the Labour Party,
which in my opinion had, and indeed still has, lost complete contact
with the basic problems of the movement and the rank and file.

'And so I started to attend union meetings. I'll never forget the
first one. I stood on my feet and started to speak and I thought I was
making a very good contribution, but the leadership of the pit, which
is a very large one of 2,700 men, stood up, walked out and left me
speaking to myself.

'What a fantastic state of affairs. This was just a forerunner of what was to happen to me over the years at the pit. I suffered terribly as a result of the right-wing domination. My pit was even more of a right-wing centre than you can imagine. It made some of the antics in the ETU look like Sunday school.'[37]

It is easy to believe that Scargill was given a hard time by the aldermen of his branch. But it was not necessarily, and certainly not wholly, based on his politics. In common with others, the Yorkshire area of the NUM attached great importance to hierarchy and long service. In some ways it was a deeply conservative movement. Sagacity went hand in hand with experience, it was assumed. Scargill does not tell us what his speech was about on that fateful day, but one can almost hear the older men saying they were not going to be told how they should run the pit by a young whippersnapper scarcely out of short trousers who ran jazz evenings in a Barnsley cellar. 'And a Commie to boot.' It is possible to have some sympathy with such a point of view.

Such was his self-belief, even at that age, that Scargill refused to give up. Worse was to come, however. 'The leadership were responsible for some of the worst things that could be done to any workman, let alone a trade unionist. I was compelled to work for three years on a shift that started at six o'clock at night and finished at two o'clock in the morning. Because of the right-wing trade union branch, there was no transport to take me home and I didn't get home until half past four or five in the morning. Now, you've got to imagine that I'd got to set off at four o'clock in the afternoon, so that my day was destroyed and my night had gone. I was getting home early the next morning, and I was shattered.'[38]

There are glimpses here of a conviction that others were out to do him down, which later developed into full-blown paranoia at times. 'The idea was a very simple one – to get rid of me, to force me into a position where I would no longer tolerate the intolerable shifts and get out of the industry. Well, I was equally determined that they wouldn't get rid of me.' Indeed, his sufferings were to be rewarded. 'While I was on the shift, the men elected me to be their leader. This was the first step in breaking the right-wing domination in the pit. This happened in 1960–1. That was when the breakthrough came.

'I had started working there in 1953 at the age of fifteen. From '53 to '59 I led a whole series of battles as a young miners' leader. Once we had 2,000 miners demonstrating for the right to attend the branch meetings of our union. We were at that time unable even to attend our branch meetings because of the policies of the right wing – supported, of course, by the mass media.'

He insisted: 'We had to demonstrate and even come out on strike in order to establish the right to attend our own trade union branch meeting. The branch arranged the meetings on a Friday, when we couldn't attend because we were on awkward shifts.'[39] The casual observer might be forgiven for thinking that Scargill was always on awkward shifts, but he unquestionably had a point. The self-perpetuating oligarchies who ran union branches in those days, would deliberately organize meetings so that members could not attend and 'get in the way'. 'We were young, we were militant, and putting forward a line which they didn't like, and so the only way they could think of stopping us was preventing us attending the meetings.'

Scargill and his young Turks staged a walkout over the issue, pointing out that attendance on Friday would, for many, mean a day's lost pay and the loss of a week's bonus. One irate Woolley branch official condemned the strike as 'Communist inspired' (which, strictly speaking, it was, being led by an inspired Young Communist) and demanded the expulsion of Communists from the union. This was a familiar theme. An earlier coalfield leader, George Rhodes, had promised to 'cut out communist influence like a surgeon cuts out cancer'.[40] In the end, after Scargill had led a march of a thousand men through the streets of Barnsley, the area leadership authorized a change to Sunday evening meetings. 'The net effect was a transformation from an attendance of forty to an attendance of about 200 per time, and this had a profound effect on our branch and, of course, increased my scope and standing and influence in the pit as a whole.'[41]

It was, he says, a very broad militant and progressive group of miners. 'In fact, many of them had no political convictions at all, apart from the fact that they could see injustice. They didn't accept that this should be the order of the day and they were determined to put it right. This went on for several years. Finally I led a strike at the pit over the question of training and I was expelled from the union at local level. It took the intervention of the Area President of the NUM to get me reinstated.'[42]

The dispute he most likes to talk about we have already heard described at the Communist Party conference. In later years, the story began to acquire a characteristic Scargill gloss. In 1979, he told

Joan Bakewell: 'There was an agreement that just before the holidays all the people on the coal face could go home as they finished work. But a group of us, young lads, were at the pit bottom, and we had to stay until the end of the shift – it made two hours' difference. So I represented the lads and went to see the manager, who said he couldn't give us permission to go home. When I came out, I suddenly realized he hadn't said "no", so I took the decision we'd go home and no one stopped any money, so we'd won. My popularity rocketed. It was the first recognition of some sort of leadership role at the pit.'[43]

This was a clearer account of the dispute, and brings his own role into much sharper relief. Three years later, he retold the story to John Mortimer in a much tighter, more entertaining fashion, which pitted him in a battle of wits with the manager – won, of course, by the young Scargill. He also indicates that the dispute took place 'as soon as I started working', when it was probably at least a year later. 'They were letting the faceworkers go earlier than us at the pit bottom, so I put our case to the manager. He was a huge, pipe-smoking man named Fred Steele. When I'd finished talking, he said: "I can't agree", and walked away. Then I realized he hadn't said: "No." "I can't agree" doesn't mean "No", does it? So I reported back to the lads and we left early and no one ever said anything about it.'[44]

The direction of Scargill's career was becoming clear by the spring of 1960, when he led the walkout over branch meeting times. He was going to become a leader of men, his own men, not a disparate collection of students and workers in other industries grouped under the revolutionary banner of the Young Communist League. Barnsley was home, and it was his power base. Having recovered – as much as he was ever to – from the loss of his mother when he was eighteen, he was launching himself into the mainstream of the labour movement, seeking office at the pit and then in the coalfield. The branch meeting dispute had brought him forcibly to the attention of the area NUM leadership, and he was becoming known to the media. Indeed, he was already complaining about press attention, while making sure he was noticed. But he was uncomfortably conscious that he had encumbered himself with an unsuitable liaison. The YCL was rather like a girlfriend from one's youth who suddenly becomes embarrassing when success beckons. She simply had to go.

CHAPTER III

AMBITION

O F THE MANY contradictions at the heart of Arthur Scargill, his long romance with Communism and revolutionary change has been the most critical. At various times he has declared himself a Marxist, a class warrior of the most indefatigable kind, and a disillusioned ex-Communist. He has sometimes expressed grudging admiration of the Tories, seeing in the Conservative Party a political force more class-conscious and cohesive than the Labour Party, of which he has been such a scathingly dismissive member for thirty years. If his myth-making is to be believed, he joined the Young Communist League out of pique at Labour's slowness in replying to a letter from a seventeen-year-old boy, and because a dishonourably discharged British army officer was prompt on his doorstep. This is scarcely the stuff of revolution. Nor does it quite measure up to the high seriousness with which joining the Communist Party was treated in the traditionally militant coalfields of Scotland and South Wales, where Communism was elevated to the status of a lifelong political vocation.

By contrast, Scargill's own relationship with the party was more of a flirtation, a teenage passion that cooled as he grew to manhood and found something more worthy of his ardour: his own destiny as the revolutionary class warrior. But even after the estrangement, he would still ask favours of his first love, and she, fool that she was, would oblige in the cause of 'Left unity'.

The whole issue has been cloaked in secrecy for decades. Not only because Scargill is such a secretive man, and not even for obscure reasons of Left 'security'. The truth is more mundane. Scargill was a man in a hurry, and the Communist Party got in the way. He quit because he was ambitious for himself and for the men he represented.

It is a long story, and difficult to piece together, not least because many of the key players are now dead. By his own admission, Scargill wrote to the *Daily Worker* (or the Communist Party: the story varies) and asked to join the party's youth organization. The most colourful version was the one he gave to John Mortimer: 'I couldn't understand why they were burning wheat in the steam engines in Canada while half the world was starving. I decided to join the Labour Party, so I wrote to them. No reply. So I wrote to the Communist Party. They sent round a wonderful man called David Larder, who'd been dishonourably discharged from the Army in Kenya because he refused to shoot coloured workers who were accused of belonging to the Mau Mau. He had a great influence on me. So I discussed it all with my friend Derek Stubbings, and we signed up with the Communists.'[1]

Just like that. As if it was of no more significance than signing up for the village football team. Others took longer, found it harder, and stayed the course rather longer. Will Paynter, the Welsh miners' leader who rose to be general secretary of the NUM throughout the turbulent sixties, has left his own account. First, he read, and read, and read. In the workmen's library attached to Cymmer pit, in the Rhondda valley, he read with the aid of an oil lamp and a dictionary, 'meandering indiscriminately through a wide range of subjects before anchoring to political philosophy'. He worked his way through the available literature and found most satisfaction with Marxism.

In his autobiography, *My Generation*, Paynter cheerfully confessed: 'I still find it difficult to give a positive reason for my gravitation to Marxism and revolutionary politics. Was it the hammering we had taken from the employers and the government that produced this reaction? If so, why had it not similarly affected thousands of others who had endured the same hammering? It was a period of naked class war with the working class suffering defeats, but I was not consciously aware of this at the time. Perhaps the bitter experiences had planted a seed that needed a few years of gestation before the revolutionary was born. I prefer to think that I was conceived from the marriage of experience with study, to become an active communist for more than forty years.'[2]

Paynter joined the Communist Party at the age of twenty-five in 1929, 'although I was a communist in outlook long before this'. He attended CP public meetings intending to join, but found it difficult to make the approach. Then a general election was called and his friend Arthur Horner, who was to become general secretary of the NUM before him was given the menial task of leaflet distributor. But, having broken the ice, he joined the CP after the election, and

remained a party member until 1968, leaving quietly and without
fuss when he retired from the miners' leadership. This, too, was not
a sudden decision, 'but in accordance with a family understanding
decided on many years before'.[3]

The contrast with Scargill could hardly be greater. The young
Arthur threw himself into the YCL with characteristic energy and
not a little flash. 'I introduced jazz sessions in cellars, coach trips to
Blackpool illuminations – with a fish and chip supper before we
came back at night,' he told Joan Bakewell.[4] 'Within six months
membership grew from ten to 190. We were one of the biggest
political youth organizations in the north of England. Another six
months and I was on the national executive of the YCL.' His recollection is a little gilded, but it is not just the exaggeration that leaps out
of this brief description. He talks almost entirely of himself, and the
size of the YCL. The League, it seems, was a place for young Arthur
to strut his stuff and become known. And, as in trade unions, the
numbers game is important: size produces clout. The numbers never
grew to anything like the figures he has bandied about – sometimes
180, sometimes 200, on one occasion 600 was mentioned – but they
always had to be bigger than anyone else's. This was a serious ego
trip. Even his first strike victory was measured on this scale: 'My
popularity rocketed. It was my first recognition of some sort of
leadership . . .'

Yet alongside this rampant careerism, he espoused the most hardline Stalinist approach of them all. The Hungarian uprising of 1956,
when Russian tanks crushed a 'people power' revolt for democracy,
took place the year after he joined the YCL, triggering mass deser-
tions from the Communist Party. It left him unmoved: 'I'm always
amazed Hungary affected any Communist. I thought the Russians
were absolutely right and still do. The CIA were responsible for
organizing that lot. I suspect the argument that it was a genuine
uprising on the part of the people. The people who were strung up
– hanged on lamp posts – were trade union leaders, Communist Party
leaders. The hundreds who came in and fought with American arms
were emigrants who'd once fought with the Fascists. They took a
genuine revolt against high prices and used it for something wider.'[5]

Quite apart from the blinkered hero-worship of the then Soviet
Union, his opening remarks in this interview in 1979 are particularly
interesting. Scargill has always denied being a full member of the
Communist Party. He does not quite belong to the 'I am not and

never have been...' school of non-Communist. Given his track record in the YCL that would be difficult, but he has gone to very considerable lengths to play down his involvement with the CP.

That came much later. In 1957, soon after he had appeared as 'Arthur Skargile' at the Easter CPGB conference and barely months after the brutal Soviet suppression of the Hungarian uprising, he was only too happy to go as a delegate to the World Youth Festival in Moscow. He has since dined out on the story that he had supped in the Kremlin with Khrushchev. So he did, it seems, though he sometimes forgets to add that there were 1,650 other Young Communists there. He told the *Yorkshire Evening Post*: 'Khrushchev was a dynamic man. An amazing strength of personality and magnetism. And an ex-miner as well...;'[6] Another version of this trip downgrades the dinner to a reception, but adds the fantastic detail that Scargill gave Bulganin and Khrushchev a dressing-down (or their cohorts, at any rate) for disgracing Stalin. 'I told them: "You can't get rid of him by removing his body from the mausoleum, you know. You can't rewrite history – and he did play a valuable part during World War Two."'[7] He was also quoted in 1982 as saying: 'I also objected to the moving of Stalin's body outside the mausoleum and changing the name of Stalingrad.'[8] Two years later, he told reporters, he visited Hungary and met the Communist president, János Kádár.

The revolution may have been going well in the homeland of socialism, but there were hiccups back home. Scargill decided that the time had come to offer the voters of Worsbrough an opportunity to embrace Communism. On 14 May 1960, the travelled veteran of Moscow and Budapest and champion of the oppressed at Woolley stood as Communist Party candidate for the North Ward of Worsbrough Urban District Council. The folded A4-sheet election address has his photograph on the front. He has thick hair combed back in a quiff, a prominent, sharp nose, ears quite tight to the head, a full mouth, and chiselled chin. He is dressed in collar and tie, and a suit or jacket. His eyes appear to be looking just to the right of the camera. Beneath his picture is the legend 'Arthur Scargill, Your COMMUNIST Candidate'. A thumbnail profile says: 'Arthur Scargill is 22 years of age * Miner, well known for his Trade Union activities in his local branch * Constant fighter for a square deal for young miners * Active among young people for better social activities * He will fight for the needs of the people both young and old, to make Worsbrough a model mining village with all the social amenities for all the people.' He called for 'a Socialist system of society in which the Communist Party will play a major role'.[9]

Unlike the voters of Thorne Rural District, who had elected a Communist miner as councillor two years previously, the burghers of Worsbrough were plainly not ready for the revolution. Scargill got 138 votes, and his Labour opponent Alderman Charles Boland sailed home with 945. Frank Watters, his election agent, recalls that 'Arthur won on the first count by a majority of one in the postal ballot returns. We tried to get that accepted by the Returning Officer as the final vote, but consistent with his usual lack of humour we got the reply "no".'[10] Watters thought it was 'not a bad result for a first time contest', and he was probably right. Scargill was fighting a well-entrenched Labour veteran, and his achievements to date were confined to Woolley miners who are unlikely to have been living in the ward. Nonetheless, it must have been something of a blow. As he once admitted, 'I don't like losing.'[11] He rarely spoke of his candidature, and he has never stood for publicly elected office since that day.

Scargill's battle to persuade the Woolley miners that they needed a Communist leader had not been blessed with much success either. He stood for office several times, but failed to get elected. Then, after he had lead the walkout and demonstration over branch democratization, came the breakthrough. In the summer of 1960, at the age of twenty-two, he was elected to the branch committee for the first time. This was the turning point in his life. Henceforth, he looked to the union rather than to politics to work out his sense of mission.

It was an unlikely spot to begin a crusade to change the world. Woolley mine was a 'big hitter', capable of producing a million tonnes of coal a year. Today, its gaunt remains sit on a hillside east of the M1 motorway, just beyond Woolley Edge service station. The pit closed in 1987 and the colliery buildings were dynamited in February 1993, as Scargill waited for president of the Board of Trade Michael Heseltine to deliver his verdict on the coal industry.

One of Scargill's first jobs when he got on the committee was running the pit's home coal delivery scheme. This job freed him from the endless drudgery of working underground. Fellow miners say that once 'on the committee', union men got the pick of the work. Scargill, they insist, never again had a regular job at the coal face. In the context of a large colliery supplying house coal to three thousand miners, retired members and their families, the home coal man was important. Moreover, it was a job that brought him into close contact with the colliery electorate, putting him in good stead when he ran for more important office. Most pits had endless trouble with home coal delivery. Not so Woolley. The pit ran its own delivery waggon. Scargill drove an impressive Wolseley.

Woolley, known in those days as 'the Mafia pit', certainly has its place in history. In Victorian times it was evidently a hotbed of militancy. The coal owner's agent John Marsden sent his men a printed address in 1859, exhorting them: 'The proprietors of the colliery recommend you, by your sober and steady conduct, to cement the union between themselves and you, and to bear in mind that good servants make good masters: and instead of listening to the advice of those who would keep you always in an unsettled state, and who live a life of idleness out of the subscriptions arising from your earnings, and instead of going to the Public-house to spend your money, to remain at home and spend your time out of working hours in cultivating your gardens, or in innocent recreation, and to invest any money you can spare in the Savings bank to accumulate at interest; by which you may hope to have sufficient to keep you in comfort and independent of the parish, in sickness or old age. If you do your duty, and are steady and industrious, you may rely on your masters doing all they consistently can to promote the comfort and happiness of yourselves and your families.'

Like the managerial warnings to the young Scargill almost exactly a century later, this patronizing circular had little effect. Taking up their pen in the Old White Bear Inn, Barnsley, the Miners' Association union chairman and secretary raged defiance. Complaining that the agent was 'victimizing the best Men among us', they declared: 'The right to combine for a proper Object is no longer considered to be the peculiar privilege of a Few . . . The Counter Combinations are a tangible fact. They are permanent institutions – A part of our natures, and cannot be destroyed. We believe it to be wrong, if not coercive Tyranny, for employers to deprive the Men of their Natural Liberties, by holding over their heads the Ban of instant dismissal.' The men of Woolley were not coerced easily. They struck in 1861 over the coal owner's demand for a twenty per cent pay cut, and when 'black sheep' were imported from Bilston, Staffs, the miners met them at the railway station 'shouting, waving their arms, hats, and making other signs of disapprobation'.[12] When the situation was explained, the 'black sheep' refused to break the strike, and the union gave them railway tickets home. Six men were later jailed for two months at York Assizes on charges of intimidation.

That was the tradition of struggle inherited by Scargill, but in the years following nationalization the NUM was motivated by a powerful desire to support the Labour government that had nationalized the mines. Redeeming this debt of gratitude, points out academic Andrew Taylor, son of Scargill's successor as Yorkshire NUM president Jack Taylor,[13] involved a cost: securing the maximum output of cheap coal meant the union actively co-operating with management in production and insisting that the conciliation machinery be used to the full. 'Naturally, this gave the impression to many miners that their union had "sold out" and the result was unofficial industrial action and internal conflict.' After 1945, coal production became 'an index of political loyalty'.

In Yorkshire, the Coal Board management and NUM officials had a comfortable working relationship, strikes notwithstanding. It was not uncommon for branch officials to join the NCB's area industrial relations team as managers. The country needed all the coal it could get, and the emphasis was on production. 'We were going through a "coal at any price" situation,' recalls Michael Eaton, former director of the North Yorkshire NCB area. 'The biggest cause of managers getting pushed out in those days when it was coal at any price was that they were continually having strikes. It would be called "incapable of handling the men". You were definitely schooled into the fact that we just had to get the volume of production. A week's strike could be ruinous to the results of a pit for the whole year, and be a terribly serious set-back for the manager because he was judged on the value of the coal.'[14]

This 'coal at any price' situation greatly helped young Scargill, argues Eaton, and probably made him think he was a better leader than he actually was. Woolley was going through a difficult period, working thin seams. Its 'glory days' came later when the men got into the Parkgate seam. So when young Scargill led the 'pit bottom lads' out, the manager would have to listen to their grievances. 'It would be highly flattering for a teenager to be met on the surface by the manager, almost on bended knees, asking him to go back to bloody work. That will have influenced him for the whole of his life, and made him infinitely the worse as a trade union official. That would particularly apply to anyone as egotistical as he is. It would enable him to say to the men "Don't worry, I can get the manager out of his office."[15]

The policy of the area leadership in the late fifties and early sixties was in tune with the NUM nationally: to seek to persuade the Tory government to adopt an integrated fuel policy in which coal had a secure future, and to work long-term for the return of a Labour government. Both were forlorn hopes, and the NUM was consequently impotent. 'Perhaps if an assault had been made on miners' wages the NUM might have reacted more militantly, but it was the productive capacity of the industry, not wages that was attacked,' observed Taylor.[16] 'Capacity was very difficult to defend by strike action, particularly when the overall market for coal was contracting.' This was precisely the scenario inherited by Scargill when he became national president twenty years later.

For once, Arthur had more homely matters on his plate at this time. Not long after he made it to the branch committee, he was asked to deliver a message to a fellow committee member, Elliott Harper, in the Barnsley suburb of Barugh Green. He drove over, and was met at the door by Harper's eighteen-year-old daughter Anne. Scargill told Sue Lawley: 'I never suspected for one moment that he'd have a daughter. I discovered that she was learning to drive, so I promptly offered my services as an expert driver to teach her how to drive. We went for a drive, and I invited her to a jazz concert to hear Chris Barber, and within a few months' time we had played together and got married.'[17] Other versions have it that their first date was a Young Communist League debate.

'We knew in a week that we wanted to get married,' he told the *Daily Mirror*.[18] The wedding took place at Gawber Parish Church on 16 September 1961, and the marriage endures to this day. The Scargills had a daughter, Margaret, a year after they got married. She is now a doctor, practising in Yorkshire. Anne Scargill, like his mother, is 'basically non-political. In the main she shares my views, but not in an active sense. She's strongly anti-Fascism, and a member of the Anti-Fascist League.'[19] For many years, Anne Scargill worked as a comptometer operator at Barnsley Co-operative Society. She emerged from the suffocating privacy of the family home in the campaign of 1992-3 to save the thirty-one pits earmarked for closure by Michael Heseltine. For most of their married life she was at her husband's side but out of the limelight. There was only room for one Scargill there.

With domesticity came another new direction. In 1962, Scargill the committee man was chosen by the union to take part in a day-release education scheme at Leeds University. One day a week during the university term, he drove to Leeds to study industrial relations and social history. These were the days of close collaboration between the union and the employer, and the scheme was jointly financed by the NUM and the Coal Board. In the same class of about a dozen men was John Walsh, a face worker at Glasshoughton colliery in Castleford, who was to be his rival for the presidency a quarter of a century later. He was from an utterly different, though more influential, tradition: the North Yorkshire moderates, sometimes known derisively as 'the Castleford Mafia'. From that one, big, staunchly anti-Communist pit came a steady stream of area leaders and miners' MPs who were sponsored by the union. Such backing gave the local party extra cash, and the NUM a voice in Parliament.

Walsh recalls: 'As I remember, what concerned Arthur primarily was speaking. The tutors used to put us on tape as if we were speaking in public. When he made a speech, he used to ask the others: "Did I do it right?" The tutors were shoving you, so that eventually you could think on your feet.'[20] 'Arthur was well in front of me in knowledge of trade unions. Putting it bluntly, I knew bugger all. I went to see how the system worked. Arthur seemed to know a lot about history, particularly Marx and Communism. He seemed to be spouting about that endlessly. I was interested in how agreements were made, and the contents of agreements, how we were bound by them and how to negotiate. He was always political from the start.'

Scargill recalled it rather differently to Sue Lawley: 'The National Union of Mineworkers had a scheme for sending what it called its talented young people to university on a day-release course for three years. We could go along and take economics, industrial relations and social history. And I went to the University of Leeds for three years. I actually got offered a place at Oxford as a result of that, but I couldn't afford to go.'[21]

This is the first occasion he mentions the possibility of his going to Oxford. Originally, it was assumed that the offer was of a place at Ruskin College, which specializes in educating adult working men to degree level. Then, in April 1993, he told Hunter Davies he had been offered a place at University College, Oxford. How come, his interviewer asked, without an entrance exam or interview. 'I'm just telling you what I was told. I was told it could be fixed. But I didn't want it.' A classic Arthur story, hinting obliquely at greatness, but absolutely uncheckable. It is fascinating, but idle, to speculate what he might have done as an Oxford graduate, with academia and politics beckoning. Finance aside, however, he does not strike one as having the temperament or the application to bury his head in books for three years: not just once a week, but every day.

Leeds was congenial, politically. Walsh remembers the tuition as 'slanted towards the left-wing. They wanted you to ask questions, not to accept anything but to question everything. They would say things like: "Who is asking you the question? Who is he? What methods has he got? Has he got a vested interest?" Walsh actually led a strike on the issue of fall-back pay during the time he was at university with Scargill. 'I wasn't political to that extent. All we used to argue about was the money for the job. Once I had got into my head how the system works, I was happy with that. I had to deal with the present. Arthur was always on about what happened in nineteen-ought-blob.'[22] Scargill confirmed the tutors' interrogatory style. 'It taught me to think and to question. I began to dissect everything that came my way in minute detail, so that I could argue.'[23]

The question uppermost in his mind during the early sixties was 'What am I doing in the Young Communist League?' He was clearly heading for a break with the Communists. The only questions that his fellow comrades had were when, and what over? There were those who had doubted his suitability for the party almost from the beginning. Jim Parker, the chairman of the Barnsley YCL branch who welcomed him in with a handshake, stood by him through thick and thin for thirty-five years – latterly, during the great strike, as his driver, confidant and bodyguard. Parker had doubts from the outset. The Communist way was to reach a collective decision, and then stand by it. Scargill could not accept that. 'If a decision was taken collectively, and he disagreed with it, he wanted and did go his own way. Arthur Scargill was more interested in creating Scargillism rather than Marxism or Socialism – for the glory of Scargill. It is nonsense to say that Scargill was a deep Marxist thinker.'[24]

Parker's assessment is critical, because he was closer than any other man to Scargill, and for longer. And he remained a devout Communist until the party imploded in the late eighties. He broke with Scargill at the time of the 'Gaddafi-Russian money' scandal in 1990, when he gave evidence to the *Daily Mirror*/Roger Cook Central TV investigation. The total membership of the Barnsley YCL, he says, was never more than forty-two, 'and not all of those were totally active'. Within that group, 'and not due to Scargill, by the way', the young comrades had trips to Blackpool and joint canal trips with Leeds YCL. Each Whitsuntide, they would go camping at Hardcastle Crags, 'To my knowledge, he only went to one camp. It was not his bent at all, the outdoor life. Everything's a myth with Scargill, everything.' Scargill was willing, insists Parker, 'to trample on anybody to get where he was going, regardless of comradeship and friendship. I think I know him better than anybody. I spent more time with him than his wife. I know how he thinks. He has no friends, only associates.'

Woolley had its own pit branch of the Communist Party, he remembers, and Scargill was associated with this. 'One has to take part by selling the *Daily Worker*. He didn't want to be seen selling the *Daily Worker* because it prevented him making progress in the union and put him in the opposite corner to Elijah Benn.'

Scargill's leave-taking of the Communist Party has spun more myths than any other aspect of his life. It is a standing joke in the labour movement that Britain's biggest political party is the ex-Communist Party. Many trade union leaders of the front rank passed through the CP, gaining valuable education and a sense of discipline that enabled them to see when to advance and when to retreat. Most former Communists were quite happy to acknowledge their debt, and to admit they once carried a card. In those days 'the party' only meant one party. Of those who came to public prominence in that era, only Scargill seems compelled to expunge this part of his life, as if cauterizing a wound.

Previous versions of the break have tended to flatter Scargill. His first biographer Michael Crick writes that in late 1962 or 1963, there being extant no record or exactly when, Scargill left the YCL. He concedes that 'the circumstances of the departure are still not certain', and that Scargill has given varying accounts of them to different journalists. 'This is not to suggest that Scargill is trying to hide anything – he may not remember the exact details and there were probably several different reasons for his decision.'[25] But by this time in his career, Scargill never did anything without a very good reason. He knows precisely when the break took place, and why he made it.

He has at times been flamboyant with the truth, and at others economical. He told Anthony Bailey in 1979 he fell out with the Communists not because of Soviet policies, the domination of

Eastern Europe, or even British CP policy. 'Basically it was because the CP insisted I should work in a certain way when I became a trade union official. They wanted me to sell the *Daily Worker* and promote CP ideals through the pit branch of the NUM. I resented this. It meant I wouldn't be exercising all my efforts for the men as miners.'[26] Heaven forfend that a good Marxist should be asked to sell the *Daily Worker* or promote CP ideals. Wasn't that what his father had stood for all his life?

Six weeks later, he was telling David Dimbleby a very similar story, but with some fascinating hardening of terminology. Asked 'Why did you leave the Communist Party?' he did not jib at the question, which suggests that he must have been a member, but replied: 'I think the main reason was because of the Communist Party's (author's note – not the YCL's) insistence that I conform to what they thought I should do as a trade union leader because I'd been elected as a Communist to a trade union position. I said that I wasn't prepared to do that. I wasn't prepared to do that because my first responsibility was to the members of the NUM branch where I had been elected to serve.'[27]

In 1977, Scargill told Chapman Pincher of the *Daily Express* that he had been 'expelled' 'because I wouldn't stick to any rigid party line'. This 'expulsion' story was also told to Ann Leslie of the *Daily Mail*, in December of that year. However, on other occasions, Scargill has insisted that he simply resigned.

In keeping with the tone of the rest of the interview, he gave his most exotic explanation to John Mortimer in 1982. Mortimer asked: 'You left the Communist Party in 1961. That wasn't because of Hungary?' Scargill riposted: 'Oh no. I supported the Soviet Union over Hungary. The Hungarian revolution was supported by known Fascists. Quite different from the situation in Czechoslovakia. No. I disagreed with the Russians not allowing dissidents to leave the country.

'I also objected to the moving of Stalin's body outside the mausoleum and changing the name of Stalingrad. It would be like us trying to pretend Churchill had never existed. And I didn't like the personal discipline of the party. They wanted me to sell the *Daily Worker* on Friday, but I had union business to look after on a Friday, so I joined the Co-operative Party.'[28] This confession that he did not like the personal discipline, which was the hallmark of the party, rings true and squares with Parker's version of events.

Crick plainly found this to be a minefield. He points out that in recent years Scargill has frequently said that he was never a member of the Communist Party, claiming that he was only a member of the YCL. This fine political distinction might not mean very much to the public at large, who might think: 'Young Commie or old Commie, you're still a Commie.' But it is evidently important to Scargill, who even told Crick during an interview in August 1984 that one could not be a member of both the YCL and the party. This is not true.

Three leading Communist officials who knew him at the time all expressed surprise when told that Scargill was never actually a party member, Crick added. According to Jimmy Reid, all members of the YCL National Committee were expected to join the party. Frank Watters remembered that Scargill regularly attended party meetings. Furthermore, he had even stood as a Communist in a local election, and it should be noted that he was asked to sell the party paper, rather than simply the YCL paper, *Challenge*. This latter point may not be of much significance. Scargill would undoubtedly have been roped in to sell *Challenge* on the streets of Barnsley, particularly when he graced its pages. But there would have been precious little point trying to flog a youth paper to older miners coming off shift. They would have told him where to stuff it.

However, considerable weight does attach to his other arguments. They back up the evidence of Parker, and of another witness who cannot be identified, but who was a top-level official of the Communist Party intimately connected with the labour movement at this period. This witness insists: 'Of course Arthur was a member of the Party.'[29] But 'under Elijah Benn, no Communist would be allowed to hold a position at Woolley'. Indeed, such was the virulence of anti-Communism in the branch that Woolley wrote to the NUM area council in March 1961 demanding that all Communists be expelled from NUM membership. If implemented, this would also have entailed sacking the men, because the mineworkers' union had a de facto closed shop in the industry.

Scargill was in a quandary. If he did not quit the Communist Party, the right-wing old guard would block his path towards higher office – and power, and fame. If he did quit the party, or if he was expelled, he would risk alienating the only election machine he could trust. And one that was becoming increasingly important in the coalfield. He would have to bid goodbye to his pals in the YCL for the greater good.

The precise mechanics of the mystery may never be known. It was the practice of the Communist Party to shed itself of embarrassing or truculent members by the simple device of not renewing their card when annual subscriptions became due. Sometimes this developed into a more elaborate gavotte. A member wanting to quit would not pay his subscription on time, and the party would not strive too strenuously to chase up the arrears. He would then automatically drop out of the membership.

In Scargill's case, sources say he made several telephone calls to King Street, the party's headquarters in Covent Garden, London (and now, ironically, a bank), asking that his card 'not be taken away'. These communications would suggest that the CP took the active step of withdrawing his card, rather than the less painful route of allowing his membership to wither on the vine. This explanation is supported by his admission in the seventies to the two Fleet Street writers Pincher and Leslie that he had been 'expelled'. His expulsion could perfectly well be justified on the grounds that he would not accept the collective discipline of the party, which by his own admission he found irksome.

Despite the rift, which passed unnoticed among the mass of Yorkshire miners, Scargill was able to rely on the party's organizational support in the coalfield when he ran for election at branch and area level subsequently. This uniquely comfortable arrangement owed something to Frank Watters' friendship, but also to the CP's pragmatic assessment that their protégé was going places and it was better to have him more or less on side than in outright opposition. In any event, the comrades often sustained a lingering attachment to those they could not quite hold on to, but who nevertheless shared common values and took cognizance of the Left whip. As Mick McGahey, the stern Communist leader of the Scots miners, used to say in later years of the wayward ex-CPer Lawrence Daly, the NUM general secretary, 'He may be a bastard, but he's *oour* bastard.'

So it was that Scargill was able to win the key role of NUM delegate at Woolley in 1964, beating the incumbent moderate, Gough Sunderland. Ambitious Arthur had initially been attracted to the more prestigious post of branch secretary, where the administrative talents he later displayed as compensation agent would have shone. But he was persuaded round to the party's view that the delegate's role was more important. Frank Watters said: 'I told Arthur there wasn't much point in being king of your own men. "You will only get known throughout the coalfield by your contributions as a delegate to area council." '30

He ran for the post several times before winning, once even sitting up all night in the pit NUM office to guard against ballot-rigging, which was not unknown at Woolley. Later, he rationalized his ambitions in terms acceptable to the Left. 'My background really was one of continuous struggle, of expulsion from the union, reinstatement, physically being barred from branch meetings until finally it built up and I was elected branch delegate,' he told *New Left Review*.

Scargill was anxious to assure his interviewer he had identified the correct route to power. 'Don't be misled by the word "delegate",' he said. 'It's the position that carries the political authority in the union. The delegate is the man who attends all meetings of the branch, he is the man who comes to the area council meetings, which is the *government* of the union, and he is the man who takes the policy decisions of the branch back to the area council. So it is a very powerful position.

'A lot of people don't understand how the miners' union is constituted and it is important that you should. It is not like any other union and this is why the area officials – area presidents and general secretaries – have so much power as compared say to the AUEW or the TGWU. We have a separate, registered trade union here in Yorkshire. No other union has this, of course, but we really are a federation. We come together on a national basis but we still maintain autonomy in many, many areas in the coalfields.

'We have more money in Yorkshire than the union does nationally. This is an indication of the influence of the old union and this is why the area officials of the union are able to speak with so much authority, in spite of what the national officials of the union may do, say or think at any particular time. Many historians, unless they are historians of the mining industry, do not understand the reasons why the area officials of the NUM carry so much weight on the national political stage as compared to any other union.'31 He spoke truly then, in 1975, when he had just captured the Yorkshire presidency and was revelling in the power it gave him. But he was to rue the devolution of power in the NUM when it came to the great strike, and his writ did not always run in the coalfields.

Freed of the constraints of Communist Party direction and responsibility, Scargill wisely reached an accommodation with his right-wing branch committee on his conduct in the council chamber in Barnsley, where he was to claim Woolley's seat on the front row.

'I went along with the majority decisions at the pit, and they were content to let me speak for them on the area council.'[32] This arrangement appears to err on the side of generosity. He accepts that he is outvoted by the moderate majority at the pit, but says what he likes at the area council, where he is their sole representative. A characteristic Scargill deal, reminiscent of the old Soviet formula 'What's ours is ours; what's yours is negotiable.'

He turned up for his first council meeting dressed rather like a dandy, in grey flannels and a fancy blazer with a badge, 'looking as if he was taking the field at Lords', prompting subdued guffaws from some of the older men who made up the bulk of the council. 'I can remember thinking, we've a darling here! Seeing this young fellow come in dressed like that, it wasn't very impressive from a rough collier's point of view. They were always respectably dressed, but in a sober fashion,' recalled veteran left-winger Don Baines.[33] But Scargill swiftly made his mark. At that period, Yorkshire still had more than one hundred branches, each entitled to send a delegate to the ornate council chamber.

This magnificent hall is the holy of holies, its atmosphere deliberately solemn. The hall was built in 1912, almost forty years after the splendid neo-Gothic union headquarters in Huddersfield Road, to which it is attached. The windows are stained glass; plaster reliefs of underground scenes decorate the high back wall facing the platform, and stone busts of bygone leaders stare down on the delegates, mentors from another age.

They sat – and the few remaining still sit – in rows of high-backed, hard wooden chairs facing the platform. Each man (and they were all men) occupied the seat allocated to his branch. In a small drawer underneath the chair in front was his card vote. On the platform were the full-time elected officials: area president Sam Bullough, the traditional Yorkshire moderate who chaired the meetings, and general secretary Sid Schofield, a devout anti-Communist from the 'Castleford Mafia'. To their left and right sat the treasurer and compensation agent. Behind them sat the four agents, responsible for day-to-day dealings with management for the pits in their area, which coincided with the NCB production area. At the back of the hall, behind the delegates, sat the sponsored MPs, often a dozen in number, indicating the grip the miners had on the political scene in Yorkshire. But, unlike Westminster, here they could not speak or vote.

Debates in this chamber could be fierce and uncompromising,

sometimes lasting all day. John Stones, delegate from Frickley, a big, militant pit in the Doncaster area, who was also a newcomer to the council, remembers Scargill's contributions as 'very forcible'. 'He was definitely against the leadership of Bullough and Schofield. He wanted change within the union, in favour of more left-wing attitudes. He wanted change in the area council, and that change occurred over the next two or three years.'[34] Don Baines recalls that debate was usually dominated by about fifteen speakers, and Scargill was one of them: 'He always had something to say about everything, not always significant. The miners were then very right-wing; even speakers in the chamber were very right-wing. What he and others had to say didn't necessarily find a lot of favour. But he commanded respect for the fact that he had something to say, and was quite capable of saying it.'

Other delegates took a less charitable view, seeing him as a cheeky young upstart, a careerist, a vain boy too fond of the sound of his own voice. What particularly irked some of the old right-wing machine politicians in the coalfield was Scargill's discovery of the media, particularly television. 'That's what made him stick out from the others,' observed John Stones. 'It was still a new thing, even in the sixties, using TV to explain your point of view. But here he was, appearing on BBC TV's "Calendar" regularly on Sundays, with Austin Mitchell and Richard Whiteley.'[35]

Jim Parker takes a customarily robust view of this august body: 'The delegate was the position where you went to the council chamber. You got up and spouted in front of all the other delegates, and your name got known for when it comes to running for area position. Even if you have nothing to say, you get up and say something just to be seen.' He also offered an insight into Scargill's public speaking and media skills: 'A lot thought he was born with an ability to speak. He wasn't. I can remember Scargill going to the studios, and I was with him, he wouldn't have a drink of tea or anything. He was frightened of going in front of the cameras, but the more he has done it, the better he has got.'

Notwithstanding his break with the CP, Scargill had his own political agenda. 'We had to struggle on two fronts. First of all, struggle within the industry against the Coal Board, and, far more importantly, we had to struggle in the union for democracy, bearing in mind that we had an ultra-right leadership, holding back not only Yorkshire and the miners, but holding back the whole of the trade union movement in Britain.'[36]

Here is a startling admission: the fight against the right-wing leadership of the NUM was 'far more important' than the struggle against the Coal Board on bread-and-butter issues. Scargill would, of course, argue that capturing the high command of the NUM was the only way in which Left policies needed by the miners could be pursued effectively. Indeed, he did. He scorned the traditional Left coalfields of Scotland and South Wales as 'pockets of resistance' less than half the size of Yorkshire even when combined. What mattered was Yorkshire. At one time, he conceded, there were nine left-wingers or Communists on the area council, 'and yet the role that they played, brilliant though it was (and I would be one of the first to admit that some of them were outstanding leaders), was in fact insignificant. They were never able to exert sufficient pressure, they were never able to push through those resolutions which were necessary to change the union.'[37]

It wasn't until the early sixties, he argued, that the Left in the Yorkshire coalfield 'began to see the necessity for some kind of organization, to put forward co-ordinated policies.' This strategy had worked for a while because it got two Communists elected to the area leadership: Sammy Taylor as compensation agent in 1961, and Jock Kane as financial secretary in 1966. But these two men, 'while they were tremendous leaders and made a marvellous impact on the area, in many respects changing the whole concept of the union, were still never able to affect the fundamental right-wing apparatus as it stood because the right held the presidency and the general secretaryship of the union in Yorkshire'. This analysis, correct in its own way, nonetheless feeds the notion that the coalfield was waiting for a saviour: someone who could smash the supremacy of the right-wing NUM leadership in Yorkshire, driving the union to the Left and taking the rest of the labour movement with it. Not even ambitious Arthur could do that. He needed a political coalition to get him there, and fortunately for him just such an organization was already meeting secretly, plotting the downfall of the Right.

CHAPTER IV

UNION MILITANT

THE LONG-AWAITED return of a Labour government in 1964 should have boosted the moderate leadership of the National Union of Mineworkers, particularly in Yorkshire, where so much hope had been invested in sympathetic political change. The reverse turned out to be true. Coalfield leaders who had asked the men to be patient over pay and understanding about pit closures, in the sure expectation that Harold Wilson would deliver a 200-million-tonne industry, found themselves trying to explain the unexplainable. The Wilson Cabinet ratted on what the NUM thought was a deal entered into by the Labour Party in Opposition to treat the coal industry as a 'special case', built on an agreed fuel policy that would maintain employment. Instead, the new Minister of Power, Fred Lee, gave miners' leaders only vague promises that the government was 'pro-coal' without committing himself to the 200-million-tonne target.

Lee went to the NUM annual conference in 1965, and told them the bad news. Coal would remain, but as a smaller industry: uneconomic pits, not just exhausted pits, would be closed and the remainder would be modernized and then employ fewer miners. 'The Labour government was to continue the strategy of the previous Conservative government.'[1] George Brown's much-vaunted National Plan published in September confirmed that production would fall to between 170 and 180 million tonnes by 1970. High-cost pits would close, whatever their coal reserves, and many thousands of jobs would go.

A subsequent White Paper on Fuel Policy went further, warning that 'the size of the industry ... will depend significantly on its success in reducing costs'.[2] In plain English, in an industry where labour was the largest single cost, higher pay would mean a faster rate of closures.

This must have been music to the ears of Scargill. By now he had joined the Labour Party via the circuitous route of the Co-operative

Party, but he had few illusions that Harold Wilson would usher in the socialist millennium. Now he could point out that a Labour government had backtracked on an agreed fuel policy – aided and abetted by the TUC, whose general council had scolded the miners for expecting too much from a government that had 'gone as far as could be reasonably expected in existing circumstances'.[3]

There was uproar in the coalfield. Branches bombarded Barnsley with protests, to little avail. The leadership did nothing, but the council put down a marker, voting 103 to two to defy any moves towards statutory incomes policy. In Yorkshire, the Coal Board determined that seventy-five pits had a long life, ten were in some danger of closure and eighteen had a maximum life of three years. The area council promised 'strenuous opposition' on closures on solely economic grounds.

Opposition to wage restraint, seen by the official leadership as the only way to slow down the rate of contraction, and to the whole idea of 'economic' closures, now provided the fertile ground needed by the Left to win support among the men for a challenge to the supine leadership in Barnsley. A nascent organization already existed – the Left Caucus. This, according to one of its founder members, Don Baines, was 'a very tight organization'.[4] 'Your credentials had to be fairly correct, in terms of left-wing attitudes.' It had begun to develop in the late fifties, when Arthur was still a boy militant at Woolley. In those days, any unofficial organization of the NUM was regarded as subversive (in this case, quite rightly) and ruthlessly suppressed by invoking the rule book. But men will meet in pubs and clubs whatever the rule book says. And, by their inactivity, the moderate Yorkshire leaders were inviting the grass-roots revolt that eventually destroyed their hegemony.

Scargill became involved with the caucus, but he was 'only one of very many able members' who made up the Yorkshire Left: men like Sammy Taylor and Jock Kane, who became full-time officials and won seats on the NUM national executive; John Weaver, a quiet but tough operator from the Thorne branch; Mick Welsh, who later became an MP; Owen Briscoe, an ex-Guardsman from the notoriously hardline Armthorpe colliery; Peter Tait, a wiry Scots electrician with a ready sense of humour from Wharncliffe Woodmoor; Ron Rigby, Percy Riley and Baines himself. 'He was among class in that,' said Don Baines. The Left Caucus was not just a talking shop. It was designed to shift entrenched right-wing policies, such as the annual pay claim.

'We never stipulated a figure, or gave any indication that we would do anything except sit round a table and accept what they were giving us,' said Baines. 'The idea was to change all that, and be ready to fight for what we wanted.'[5]

Partly under pressure from the official leadership, which was complaining of 'secret meetings', but mainly in an attempt to win broader support for their policies, the Left Caucus agreed to go public. 'We decided to have open meetings, calling them the Barnsley Miners' Forum, where anybody could go. It was a very respectable title. We invited prominent speakers. They were always left-wing, of course,' added Baines.

Professor Vic Allen, professor of the Sociology of Industrial Society, who emerged as the *éminence grise* of the NUM Left in the sixties, described the opposition to the area leadership as 'a mixture of Communists, ex-Communists, and left-wing members of the Labour Party'.[6] The demands of a campaign to capture the two top jobs in Yorkshire, due to fall vacant through retirement in a few years, 'tapped the leadership qualities of this group and fairly quickly a number of miners emerged as potential union officials'.

The most important organization innovation in Yorkshire, says Allen, 'was the formation of the Barnsley Miners' Forum by Arthur Scargill, a face worker and delegate from Woolley colliery. Scargill had been active as a militant rank and file miner since the late 1950s.' Scargill would argue that his militant career began a good deal earlier. His comrades in the caucus would dispute his role in starting up the forum. Yet others would quarrel with the term 'face worker'. Michael Eaton, NCB North Yorkshire area director, dismisses him derisively as 'a canteen ripper'. Jim Parker insists: 'He talked as if he was a miner for twenty years. But if you actually analyse that, and put him from the age when he started to when he became a trade union official, there is no way he could have been a miner for twenty years. As you get to be pit delegate, you have no job down the pit. Even as boss of the coal scheme, he would have no regular job down the pit. I once remember when he was a delegate, he came down the pit for an inspection. We were supposed to be best mates, and he didn't even recognize me in my pit muck.'[7]

If he wasn't digging much coal, Scargill was digging his leaders' political grave. Allen reports that 'hundreds of miners' attended the Barnsley Forum meetings in the town's Co-operative Hall on Friday evenings, though local journalists who turned up usually found only a few dozen and soon gave up covering the event. Those who attended heard speeches by Lawrence Daly, the ex-Communist Scots miner who was to win the NUM general secretaryship; Michael McGahey, the Communist who ran for the presidency, lost to Joe Gormley, but became vice-president in a political troika with Scargill; Emlyn Williams, the Left-Labour president of the Welsh miners, who was to serve on Labour's national executive; Jack Dunn, the gravel-voiced Communist hardliner who was secretary of the Kent coalfield and others.

'For the first time, many young miners heard arguments against pit closures, in favour of high wages and a shorter working week,' gushes Prof Allen. 'Through this medium, Scargill acted as a catalyst in the Barnsley district and beyond. He worked closely with a small group of Barnsley miners, including Peter Tait, George Wilkinson, Ron Rigby and Don Baines. They met in a room of a Barnsley hotel [the Queens] where Roy Mason, who became Minister for Power in July 1968, often drank in an adjoining bar.' Events moved apace in the coalfield. Daly was chosen as Yorkshire's nominee for the general secretaryship. The area leadership's position became vulnerable. 'The combination of aggressive determination of miners such as Arthur Scargill and circumstances propitious for campaigning ensured that left-wing influence would continue to grow. That is what happened.'

Prof Allen, himself a Communist, was the Left's fixer, first in Yorkshire and then nationally. He booked the rooms and acted as convenor. He was in a position to observe the key players at close quarters, and he offers this fascinating pen-portrait of Scargill: 'This period proved to be a learning experience for Scargill. He always acted competently with confidence but he was rarely at this stage given more than a grudging respect by the others.

'He was, and still is, essentially a shy person who projects himself as a compensation for his shyness. Those miners who worked alongside Scargill in the newly formed left-wing grouping in Yorkshire, however, did not engage in personality analysis and treated him as they found him. There was a tendency, therefore, for them to react to his brashness by trying to argue him down before looking at the merits of his case.

'He perpetually had to defend his stance from criticism by miners such as Ian Ferguson, branch secretary at Yorkshire Main, Jimmy Miller [Communist branch secretary from 'the big K' Kellingley colliery], and Ron Rigby, who could always detect the wider political consequences of action in the Yorkshire coalfield. Arthur Scargill selects himself for attention because of his later achievements, but in the early days of the campaign it would have been difficult to identify the future leadership pattern in Yorkshire because the field was so rich with talent.'[8]

As a brief essay in hagiography, this would take some beating. It is certainly true that Scargill can be a very shy man, uncomfortable in company and given to a nervous tic of the shoulders. He is most at home one-to-one, or one to a thousand in an audience. This may be traceable to an inner insecurity, or, strange as it may seem in such a public figure, a lack of confidence. Behind the bluster and the mask of self-belief, one feels, lies the little boy who was bullied in the school playground, the sensitive lad who doted on his mother, and was smothered with affection in return. It is not difficult to imagine that his painful efforts at self-assertion irritated the older comrades, or that his ideas sometimes came out the wrong way. They would not 'engage in personality analysis' in Allen's sense, giving him the benefit of the doubt over his display of nervous energy. More likely, they would wonder what he was scheming.

The plotting in Yorkshire was mirrored at national level, in the formation of a national Left organization. On 5 August 1967, the group met for the first time in the County Hotel, Sheffield, to discuss the campaign to win the NUM general secretaryship for 'progressive' forces when Will Paynter retired at the end of 1968. This conference brought together left-wingers who had been delegates to the NUM annual conference the month before, 'friends with similar political commitments', reports Allen: that is to say, Communist and Left-Labour. Jock Kane, the Yorkshire Communist, took the chair. About thirty activists attended, from Yorkshire, Scotland, South Wales, Kent and Derbyshire. Scargill, who had emerged on to the national scene with a speech to the annual conference, was among them. Supporting an emergency motion from the executive that demanded a guaranteed size for the industry, Scargill berated Fred Lee and accused the Labour government of 'a betrayal of the mining industry'.

The comrades agreed that 'someone of the same calibre, cast in the same broad political image – though not necessarily Communist – should take over from Paynter'. The selection fell on Lawrence Daly, general secretary of the Scottish miners and a brilliant intellectual given to singing Robert Burns' love songs in his cups. Daly, a former face worker from Glencraig colliery, Fife, had been in the

Communist Party, but quit in 1956. He formed his own political party, the Fife Socialist League, and stood for parliament before joining the Labour Party. A short, thickset man in the classic miner's mould, he possessed great charm and natural oratorical skills. Scargill, one always felt on the industrial circuit in those years, quietly feared him, because he was so much more intelligent and easy-going, without the brittle self-esteem of the Yorkshireman. But it was Scargill who survived, whereas Daly destroyed himself with drink.

In 1967, however, Daly was at the height of his powers. Once the succession had been determined, 'it was necessary to project him throughout the major coalfields in much the same way as a new packet of soap flakes was introduced to consumers,' said Allen. But the Sheffield conference took another key decision that summer Saturday: it decided that the election should be waged around policies and not the personalities of candidates. This would involve the formulation and publication of policies that 'challenged the logic of the consensus' in the NUM. Here was a role for Prof Allen, the Left's faithful amanuensis, who had done research for some of the areas and prided himself on being able to articulate the aims and objectives of the miners. The general secretaryship election had provided a finite and specific purpose for the national Left to get together, 'but the aim was to alter the consciousness of miners with implications well beyond that election. It intended, moreover, to convert right-wing areas to left-wing policies and to start right there in Yorkshire.'[9]

Scargill took the fight back to the area council, with a strong personal attack on Roy Mason, then the NUM-sponsored MP for Barnsley and Labour's new Minister of Fuel and Power. Mason, a former pit electrician at Wharncliffe Woodmoor and a right-winger of the old school, was still held in high regard by the unreconstructed council. Woolley branch complained about a sponsored MP being in charge of pit closures and demanded withdrawal of financial support. 'It was a motion of condemnation, really,' said Lord Mason.[10] 'I was summoned by the Yorkshire miners' council to appear before them to answer the charge. Scargill made a speech, and I responded. Halfway through my speech, I remember a voice shouting out from the floor: "Throw in the towel, Scargill!" When it came to the vote, he got terrifically beaten. I think he got eight votes out of a council chamber of more than a hundred votes. I don't think he ever forgave me for that.' The voting was actually ninety-six to eight, revealing Scargill's weakness at this stage. The Left could only count on eight or ten votes.

Events were moving his way, however. As the toll of pit closures grew, so did the simmering resentment in the coalfield over the government's 'betrayal'. In 1968, a Houghton Main motion to call a strike in Yorkshire 'in protest at the government's policy of pit closures' fell by sixty-one votes to thirty, but it marked an increase in the votes supporting the Left. A special national conference on the issue found Yorkshire divided, left-winger Tommy Mullany insisting: 'After talk, talk, talk, the policy that you have to come to is some kind of industrial action', while right-winger Tommy Burke argued that: 'Today our lads have set on things like £800 cars and £3,000 bungalows . . . it is a different system of life and I do not think they will jeopardize all those things for the sake of a strike which could have no impact whatsoever.' Taylor notes 'a distinct groundswell in Yorkshire for a change of policy by the NUM. For the moment, fuel policy was not enough to mobilize the mass of miners'.[11]

But an issue was waiting in the wings, one that would ignite Yorkshire and the other militant areas, changing utterly the nature of the biggest coalfield and the NUM at large – and creating the conditions for Scargill to ride to power. As so often in industrial relations, it was not the obvious issue. Not pit closures. Not wages for face workers, which since 1966 had been equalized throughout the industry through a universal day-wage system – the national power loading agreement. The issue was hours of work for surface workers. Choosing this highly emotive issue was a brilliant tactical stroke by the Left. Surface workers, as Scargill had found on his first frightening day at Woolley, were often men bowed and broken by years of work underground. Their wages were low, and they worked up to an hour longer than men underground.

The NUM annual conference had demanded that their hours be lowered to seven and three quarters as long ago as July 1968, but the national executive had done nothing to progress the claim. More than a year later, on 11 October 1969, when the coalfield leaders reported back to the area council that the national executive was still vacillating, Scargill seized his chance. The president, Sam Bullough, unwell and losing his grip, ruled him out of order. Delegates voted him out of the chair and approved the strike call by eighty-five votes to three. Within forty-eight hours, 70,000 men were out, the coalfield was stopped and strike action had spread to the Midlands, Scotland

and South Wales. The strike, which was unofficial, drew the condemnation not just of the NCB's chairman Lord Robens, but of Lawrence Daly, who had only just been installed as general secretary with the votes of Yorkshire miners.

Robens, a crafty ex-Labour politician with an inside working knowledge of the labour movement, sought to defuse the crisis by conceding the union's current wage claim in full: the princely sum of 27s 6d a week (£1.37). The Board's apparent generosity was put in perspective by a new agreement giving women bus conductors in Yorkshire a minimum wage of £18 a week – considerably more than the wages of a surface worker in coalmining. Instead of calling off their action once the NUM claim had been conceded, the strike leaders demanded the resignation of Daly and the union's weak president, Sidney Ford. 'In my opinion,' intoned Robens loftily, 'the militant leaders could not be affected by our reasoned arguments. It was the most senseless strike of any size ever to affect the mining industry.'[12]

Scargill was playing for higher stakes, of course. The strike was not just about surface hours. Just as importantly, it was about who was going to run the union, and with what policies. He later admitted: 'It was obvious to us in Yorkshire that if we had left it to the official leadership, in Yorkshire nothing could have been done.'[13] Having elbowed aside the leadership in the council chamber, the Left organized an unofficial strike committee based on the four NUM 'panels' (pit groupings) in North Yorkshire, Barnsley, Doncaster and South Yorkshire. Then they sent emissaries to friendly coalfields, and pickets into Nottinghamshire and Derbyshire. 'We decided to have rapid mobile pickets. We'd used this before in the Yorkshire coalfield, but on a very limited scale and never in an organized way. We launched from the coalfield here squads of cars, minibuses and buses, all directed on to pre-determined targets, with five, six hundred miners at a time. Of course, the police were going to come, but they couldn't cover forty points at a time, without bringing the British armed forces in.

'I believe in a class war you have to fight with the tools at your disposal. 1969 was a foretaste.'

The strike lasted a fortnight and coal losses amounted to more than 2.5 million tonnes. Robens was obliged to ask the government to put up coal prices to cover the £15 million cost. At its height, the strike shut down 140 of the 307 collieries then operating. Robens conceded: 'The capture of the Yorkshire coalfield by the militant Left had been complete. Their victory had been met with success. Not a pit in Yorkshire turned a wheel at the peak of the dispute.'[14]

In terms of its stated objective, the strike was an abysmal failure. The men began to drift back in the second week. Vic Feather, TUC general secretary, saved the Left's public face by producing a formula for a return to work. The issue of surface hours was put off for further negotiations. Robens observed shrewdly: 'Always, militant leaders of unofficial strikes dread that the stoppage will end in such a way that their authority is affected and their future influence reduced.'[15] And this is what happened. Despite a ballot in which the men approved the 27s 6d deal by 194,000 votes to 41,300, Scargill and his co-conspirators in what one commentator called 'the October Revolution' retained the political initiative.

Scargill admitted that the outcome 'wasn't a victory in the sense that you can say: "We've got it."' But since the ostensible aim was not the overriding one, he could claim a victory. 'We took a decision to go back to work victoriously, and we led them back. I don't care who the historian is, but if he regards 69 as anything other than a complete victory, it's time that he went and did some more thinking,' he told New Left Review. 'Because 69 was responsible for producing all the victories to come.

'After the 69 and 70 disputes it was clear that the union was never, ever going to be the same again.

'The pressure on the right wing was so intense that they saw that if they did not do something about the rules of the union for calling a strike, the left and the rank and file would sweep them aside and there would be an alternative leadership. So they changed the rules of the union to allow strike action to be called with a fifty-five per cent majority vote instead of a sixty-six and two thirds per cent majority. This was to be the most decisive change of rule ever in the history of the union.'[16]

Scargill conflates events here. But he correctly divines the importance of the Left's next step. A strike ballot over the Coal Board's annual pay offer in October 1970 yielded a fifty-five per cent majority for action, on a turnout of eighty-three per cent. This was too low under existing union rules, which required a two-thirds majority to authorize a national stoppage. Only the Communist-dominated coalfields of Scotland and South Wales achieved the required figure; Yorkshire managed only sixty per cent – indicating that, despite the

1969 strike, the area has not turned overnight into a Left monolith. It never did.

Perhaps Scargill is less keen to emphasize the events of 1970 because they did not fall his way. This time out, he was officially making the running. The Left had agreed that Yorkshire would move the annual wage resolution at the NUM conference. The Left in Yorkshire gave it to their new champion. In conformity with the Left's prescription, the motion specified ambitious figures: a weekly wage of £30 a week for face workers; £22 for those elsewhere underground, and £20 for surface workers. The area council had decreed that rank-and-file delegates should move their resolutions, so Scargill strode to the rostrum and warned that failure to secure this demand 'will release an anger that will make last October look like a Sunday school picnic. No longer will our membership accept that a small increase is better than none. They are fed up with being asked not to rock the boat. We have remained passive since 1956 and what has it got us? Half the coalmining industry has been obliterated in Great Britain. If this is what passiveness brings us, then we want none of it.'

Unhappily for Scargill, a clear majority of the men were ready to accept that a small increase was better than none. Unofficial strikes did break out, starting at Brodsworth, near Doncaster, sometimes called the Queen's pit because its high-quality coal once warmed Buckingham Palace. The walkouts lasted three weeks, but did not bring Yorkshire to a complete standstill this time. Some 2.8 million tonnes of coal production was lost, costing the industry £21 million. The overall impact of the two bouts of industrial action was however as much psychological and political as industrial. Scargill had got the miners, especially the Yorkshire miners, back into the habit of thinking that strikes could be a strategic weapon in pursuit of their objectives. The action had also had the desired political effect. As Taylor argues, 'The outburst of unofficial militancy in Yorkshire in 1969–70 was the product of the mineworkers' experiences in the post-war period and particularly under the 1964–70 Labour government. The effect of this was to push the NUM as a *whole* further to the Left.'[17]

The right-wing leaders of the Yorkshire coalfields were old enough hands at the game to know what was going on. But they still talked in the stilted code of the Cold War, afraid to come out and name people like Scargill for fear of triggering yet more trouble. Hence Sid Schofield, acting president at the 1970 conference, warned darkly in his presidential address of 'minorities in our union who are arranging unofficial meetings, printing and issuing pamphlets, ignoring the policies agreed upon at annual conference'. Their purpose was 'to undermine the status of area and national officials of our union and incite our members into taking unconstitutional action'.

Well, of course it was. What is revealing about Schofield's contribution is the flabby, hesitant nature of the right-wing's counter-attack. He was appealing to delegates not to allow these minorities to make union policy: they were sitting right in front of him doing just that. Enervated by years of undisputed control, the moderates could not work out how to prevent their power ebbing away. They were being outflanked and outmanoeuvred by younger, smarter, more politically committed miners and their advisers, who were able to argue plausibly that decades of co-operation first with Conservative and now Labour governments had got the miners nowhere. Except a situation where Lord Robens could shut seventy pits in one year, and a clippie could earn more than a collier.

The qualified industrial success of resurgent militancy in Yorkshire prompted a rethink among rank-and-file activists. They published a pamphlet, 'A Future for the British Miners?', which argued that the NUM should abandon its reliance on a 'friendly' Labour government and rely instead on its own industrial strength. The main author was Jim Oldham, branch secretary at Hickleton pit, who was later to emerge as a rival to Scargill. The Left was pushing on an open door in the coalfield, because the post-war generation of Yorkshire miners' leaders, conditioned by their bitter experiences of the twenties and thirties, had abandoned industrial action but had been 'betrayed' by the Wilson administration. 'As the authority of the official leaders declined, that of the unofficial increased,' notes Taylor.[18]

Ted Heath's victory in the June 1970 election, giving the Tories a forty-three-seat majority over Labour in the Commons, finally resolved the argument between political persuasion and industrial action. Freed of the constraints to support 'their' government, the miners could choose their own destiny. Signs of change came from the most unexpected places. Joe Gormley, the canny moderate secretary of the Lancashire miners, who cultivated the image of a 'rough diamond', told his area conference that the union would have to fight for higher wages even if some pits would have to close. 'I am not going to be a miners' leader if I cannot claim a bigger minimum wage for the lads who go underground than the lads carting the dustbins around the streets of London,' he expostulated. 'I can tell you, I'm getting off my knees. I have been on them too long.'

He was to have the opportunity earlier than he expected. Early in 1971, the ailing NUM president, Sir Sidney Ford, who had Parkinson's disease, announced that he was to retire early at the age of sixty-one. The move caught both political camps by surprise, but the right wing was quicker off the mark. This time, it was a straight fight between Gormley, a dyed-in-the-wool Labour man and the Communist Mick McGahey, a leading light in the national Left. McGahey started off with several handicaps. He was a Scot, and another Scot, Lawrence Daly, had just become general secretary. He was a left-winger, and if there was such a thing as a tacit political settlement in the NUM, it was that no tendency had both top jobs. Since the war, the Left had held the general secretaryship, and the Right took the presidency, which carried the key role of chief negotiator.

Lancashire miners, keenly aware that the Left's superior organization had deprived Gormley of the general secretaryship, made it a no-holds-barred contest. Area funds poured into the campaign. Sid Vincent, the area agent who wanted Gormley's Lancashire post, took a 'task force' over to Yorkshire and set up headquarters in a hotel. From there, campaigners fanned out to the pits with leaflets extolling Gormley's record as a bargainer, countering McGahey's 'Miners' Charter.'

Vincent, a bear of a man with dyed black hair and piggy, quizzical eyes, was deliberately taunting Scargill. In 1980, he told labour historian Hywel Francis: 'There was an incident at the time. Arthur Scargill then worked at Woolley, and I got a message that some of our lads distributing leaflets had been turfed off the premises. They had refused to go, and the police had been rung. One of the chaps doing all the bawling and shouting was Scargill.

'I told the lads to come back to headquarters. We got back there at ten at night, me wearing my old neb cap and a dirty old mac (and under the mac there would be about 500 'Vote for Joe Gormley' leaflets). We went into the baths – we weren't trespassing – we had a quick word with the chap in charge of the baths that night shift and asked him, was he interested in the national ballot? He said he hadn't heard anything about it. He wasn't interested in Gormley or McGahey. So I said, were he interested in earning a fiver? (At that time, this would represent a day's pay for a face worker.) What for? he asked. I said, give us a hand putting these leaflets in these lockers.

The chap put the £5 in his pocket, and every man at Woolley had a leaflet in his locker.'[19]

With operators like that in the field, Gormley trounced McGahey, winning by a majority of almost 25,000, the biggest margin for decades. The Left had suffered a reverse, one which would later impact on Scargill's future, straightening his path to the top.

For the moment, he was busily re-establishing his credibility on his home patch. Woolley colliery had rejected strike action in the unofficial strikes of 1970, and even heavy picketing failed to close the pit for any length of time. Nonetheless, Scargill was able once again to take the initiative on wages. Woolley branch submitted the motion demanding minimum rates of £35 for face workers, £28 elsewhere underground and £26 for men on the surface – increases ranging from thirty-five to forty-seven per cent for 280,000 pitmen. Failure to concede the demand would mean consultation 'on various forms of industrial action'. Yorkshire area took up the motion, and it was unanimously approved by the NUM annual conference in Aberdeen on 6 July 1971. Apprehensive Coal Board officials described it as 'a militant claim, aggressively presented and certainly addressed to the government'.[20] Taylor describes the resolution as 'the casus belli of the 1972 strike'.[21] Scargill wasn't in Aberdeen to relish his victory. It was not his turn on the rota to be a delegate to conference that year. That same day, in a decision of even greater importance, delegates voted to lower the threshold for calling a national strike under rule from two thirds to fifty-five per cent.

As negotiations on the pay claim faltered, NUM leaders called an overtime ban in the industry, and mounted a pithead ballot with a recommendation for strike action. In an eighty-five per cent turnout, the men voted by 58.8 per cent to strike. Not without trepidation, the NUM executive called an all-out strike from 9 January 1972. Gormley had been unwilling to commit his troops, fearing that the ballot margin was too narrow. Under the old rules, a strike could not have been called. But, meeting the president just before the fateful executive meeting on the 'bridge of sighs' connecting their two offices in 222 Euston Road, Daly told him: 'It's enough for me, Joe.' Daly's passionate speech, regarded as the finest in his career by those present, carried the day.

The 1972 strike was a watershed in the history of the union and the industry. It began at midnight on 8 January and ended on 27

February. When it started, nobody outside Yorkshire and the Left of the labour movement had heard of Arthur Scargill. When it finished, he had become a household name for militancy, credited with the invention of flying pickets and the technique of mass picketing. Ted Heath's Tory government played it wrong from the beginning, believing the assurances of Fleet Street editors that it was 'a suicide strike'. *The Economist* said the miners could not stop the country as once they could. *The Times* foolishly predicted 'only marginal disruption to industry and commerce as a whole'. But the Left had spent years preparing for this hour. Even Vic Feather, general secretary of the TUC, warned that if the government thought they could break the miners 'they have got an insuperable task'. Although the vote for industrial action was only just over the required figure, the strike was solid from day one. All 280,000 miners at 289 pits struck as one man. The pits did not need picketing. The men were released to spread disruption elsewhere. The age of secondary picketing had dawned.

From the outset, the NUM appreciated that picketing would be critical, to tie up coal stocks at the pithead, prevent coal imports coming into the country and halt the movement of coal, lighting-up oil and vital chemicals into the power stations. Joe Gormley, having originally opposed the strike, was now determined to win it. He promised: 'We shall organize picket lines where they have most effect.' Details of all power stations were sent to the areas by the NUM National Strike Committee, with instructions where to place pickets. Each coalfield was given a non-mining area to picket – Yorkshire was assigned to East Anglia. Transport unions like Jack Jones's TGWU pledged not to cross miners' picket lines, wherever they were. This led to some almost comic scenes. Train drivers belonging to the footplate union ASLEF reported that a rail line into a power station had no pickets. So a handful of miners hung a banner from an overhead bridge, and the coal trains ceased. On the Thames, Kent miners chartered boats and ran a water-borne picket to halt supplies to riverside generating stations such as Battersea.

When the Commons debated the strike during its second week, the government appeared nervous and rattled. Not only Labour but most Tory MPs were at pains to stress the loyalty and moderation of the miners, and the forbearance they had shown during years of painful contraction of their industry. Industry Secretary John Davies – the former director-general of the CBI – was out of his political depth. He defended the NCB's 7.9 per cent pay offer (just inside the government's 'guideline' of eight per cent), but this offer had already been withdrawn by the Coal Board. Employment Secretary Robert Carr, widely regarded as a decent man despite his piloting of the hated 1971 Industrial Relations Act through the House, insisted that the government was not seeking a showdown with the miners, or trying to drive them into submission and humiliation. Vic Feather tried to get the two sides together, and almost teased Carr into breaking the deadlock. But he stood back from the conflict, keeping up the pretence that the government was not involved. On 26 January, the TUC general council called on ministers to look at the miners' case on its merits, without reference to 'doctrinaire considerations'. The next day, Lawrence Daly was given an ovation in South Wales when he told a rally: 'Ours will be a victory not only for the miners, but for the whole working class of Britain.'

That weekend, General Winter came to the aid of the miners. A cold spell exposed the weakness of the Central Electricity Generating Board. Voltage was reduced right across the national grid. Three power stations shut down completely. The CEGB blamed 'sudden severe weather' but admitted that picketing, amounting to an 'unrelenting blockade', of the power stations was the main cause. The popular press, having predicted that the strike would collapse in failure, now began to have second thoughts. The *Sun* gave space for an article by Daly. The *Daily Express*, whose industrial correspondent Barrie Devney was a personal friend of Gormley, turned against the government, demanding that Robert Carr, the NUM and the Coal Board should get negotiations started and get the miners back to work.

The mood turned more ugly on 3 February, when Yorkshire miner Fred Matthews from Hatfield colliery died while picketing outside Keadby power station in Lincolnshire. An articulated lorry driven at high speed by a 'scab' non-union driver had mounted the pavement. The back of the lorry hit Matthews, a thirty-seven-year-old married man, killing him. Peace evaporated on the picket lines. The next day, eighteen men were arrested when 400 miners massed at Markham Main colliery, not far from Hatfield, to stop deputies going in to carry out safety work. At Kilnhurst, near Rotherham, another seven were arrested after scuffles with police. In the Commons, Tom Swain, MP for a Derbyshire mining constituency, warned: 'This could be the start of another Ulster in the Yorkshire coalfield.' He demanded

an immediate statement, failing which he would go home 'and advocate violence'. Home Secretary Reginald Maudling went to the House
and promised a police investigation, adding his sympathy to
Matthews' relatives. The day after Fred Matthews' death, the saga
of what became known as the Battle of Saltley Gate began.

It took place in Birmingham, but the myth it weaved round Scargill
began in Yorkshire, where seventy-five per cent of the men had voted
for industrial action. When hostilities started, the militants moved
in. The men who had experience of the unofficial strikes now had
an official dispute to run, and virtually a free hand from the area
leaders, who left them to get on with it. The four Yorkshire panels
set up strike committees, Barnsley's in a room in the White Hart
pub in the centre of town. Don Baines and Peter Tait took charge
of the direction of the dispute, and Scargill was made the front man –
the spokesman for the strikers. He was the plausible face of militancy.
Austin Mitchell, the Labour MP, then a reporter for Yorkshire Television, had swiftly appreciated his value after the stoppages of 1969
and 1970. 'Yorkshire Television created Arthur Scargill,' he said later.
'He was just the voice of the articulate left-wing Yorkshire miner
that we wanted. It was our Barnsley stringer who put us on to him,
but if he hadn't I think we should have had to invent him.'

Scargill remembers his role rather differently. 'I was appointed
spokesman of the Barnsley Area Strike Committee and also put in
charge of picketing.'[22] Hundreds of pickets had been despatched to
halt coal movements through the ports and to prevent supplies getting
into the region's power stations. There were 'a number of battles' in
the Barnsley strike committee. Some wanted small numbers at all the
power stations and ports. Scargill argued that this tactic would not
work. He wanted mass pickets roaming East Anglia, closing down
any target they chose. He says he won. 'We had a weekend strike
committee meeting and changed the policy. I picked the phone up
and called East Anglia HQ and said: "Move everything in on to
Ipswich dock, move everything we can." We produced a thousand
pickets in an hour and a half on Ipswich dock, and stopped the dock
in an hour. We left a token picket at the docks, moved on, and closed
down the power stations one by one. Within two days, we'd shut the
whole of East Anglia.'[23]

This version has now entered the official myth. Scargill also went
on a speaking and fundraising tour of East Anglia. He was exhilarated
by the revolutionary fervour that the strike sparked on university

campuses. 'We showed to the university students a degree of discipline and organization which they had probably read about in their Marxist books, but had not seen for themselves.' He called together the various factions on the ultra-Left – the International Marxist Group, the International Socialists, the Workers' Revolutionary Party and all the other rag-bag of would-be revolutionaries – into a 'broad left alliance, a united front' to fight the common enemy. 'We had no time to discuss whether Trotsky said X, Y or Z in 1873.'

The picketing miners found campus life much to their liking. The NUM had problems persuading them to go home when the strike was over. Scargill felt their conversion was at hand. 'This was an absolutely tremendous experience. Our people were becoming politically educated and were becoming aware of what the class structure and what the class war was. In a matter of days, they were changing. Never mind about a thousand lectures, this was it! We had men who would never have gone to a political meeting in their life, not only going to the University of Essex and listening to speeches, but actually getting on their feet and speaking themselves. It was amazing.'[24] He might have added that they were also having a bloody good time. Scargill enthuses about audiences packed with students *and* miners. 'The barriers were down,' he proclaimed. And so they were, in more ways than one. The tabloid press finally cottoned on to the fine time the comrades were having. Daly rang the campus pickets, and was assured: 'It's OK, Lawrence, we're doing the work – and we're getting our leg over every night.' Daly, no critic of pulchritude, replied: 'I know, and I'm a miner too – but just get your arse out of that university.'

Back in Barnsley, the strike committee turned its attention to picketing the huge Coalite plant at Grimethorpe. 'Waggons were going in and out of there like nobody's business,' recalled Don Baines.[25] So they decided to stop the plant by what is now called secondary picketing, but was then no more than a natural extension of what they were already doing. 'It got a substantial amount of publicity. We got TV. Some of our rough lads were involved in incidents. There was a half brick through a driver's window.'

When local TV showed the footage, Scargill was quickly on the phone to Baines. 'His words to me were "If I come down, do you think it will do me some good?" That meant, in relation to the compensation agent's position. I said: "Bring yoursen down." He came down, but didn't stop long. The word came through that the same thing was happening at Monckton coke ovens.'

A revealing anecdote. Four months before the strike, Sammy Taylor, the compensation agent in Yorkshire, had died. The Left Caucus had a meeting in the Albert Club, Cudworth, to decide who should be the candidate to succeed Taylor. The contest was between Jim Oldham, branch secretary at Hickleton, a 'reliable' left-winger in his late fifties, and Scargill, who was then only thirty-three years old. The outcome was not a foregone conclusion. 'Jim was a fairly solid chap. Arthur was rather flamboyant,' said Baines. 'Whilst recognizing his abilities, I wasn't convinced that Arthur wasn't seeking glory.'[26]

There were about twenty men at the meeting in a side room at the Albert. A small serving hatch led into the bar, but there was no drinking. 'In these meetings, it was straight talking. There was no question of offending anybody,' said Baines. 'You spoke your mind, and sometimes it wasn't too complimentary. You said what you had to say. The vote came down to Scargill and Oldham. I felt that Jim was the more honest character in that sense, and said so. I didn't think Arthur had developed that kind of responsibility, and was probably glory-seeking. Anyway, the vote went for Scargill. It was not substantial – a clear majority, but not overwhelming.'

That caucus meeting secured his future. Scargill had already made clear the previous autumn to Bert Ramelson, the Communist Party's national industrial organizer, that he thought he was the man for the job. In keeping with party tradition, Ramelson gave the oration at Taylor's funeral, and immediately afterwards over a drink Scargill had indicated his intention to run. He thought he could win, and he wanted the party's backing. Ramelson left him in no doubt that the CP would support him. This was in keeping with the party's view that if a Communist could win, he should run. If not, go for the next best thing. As Watters put it, 'Admittedly, if a member of the party was the most likely to defeat the right wing, then we fought for our corner, as we did with Jock [Kane – elected financial secretary] and Sammy [Taylor]. When Sammy died in 1971 he was replaced by Arthur Scargill, a former member of the Young Communist League, but again the argument was about who was the best placed to succeed. For me, it was never about narrow party advantage.'[27]

All this wheeling and dealing was going on behind the scenes, both before and during the strike. One of the reasons Scargill was made spokesman by the strike committee was to get his name and face into every pit living room in the county. He had already got his name in the papers in the early days for being arrested at Cawthorne colliery. He was later fined £5 for obstructing the police.

Scargill boasted to the *Observer Colour Magazine* that in Barnsley he ran a strike operations room, like a military HQ with a map showing ports, power stations, steel works and coal mines. From this 'ops room', he despatched pickets 'like shock troops'. For someone ostensibly revolted by war and modern weaponry, he seems irresistibly drawn to military analogy, particularly when it merges with the class war. He rhapsodized to *New Left Review*: 'You see, we took the view that we were in a class war. We were not playing cricket on the village green, like they did in '26. We were out to defeat Heath and Heath's policies because we were fighting a government. Anyone who thinks otherwise is living in cloud-cuckoo-land.

'We had to declare *war* on them, and the only way you could declare war was to attack the vulnerable points. They were the points of *energy*: the power stations, the coke depots, the coal depots, the points of supply.'[28]

Tactical picketing, particularly of the power stations, was the key to the success of the 1972 strike. But the key to the final success of Arthur's Private War – as the dispute was, on a different level – was undoubtedly the Battle of Saltley Gate. On 7 February, roughly a month after the strike began, a report was received in Barnsley that police were allowing between 600 and 700 lorries a day to take coke from a depot in Saltley, Birmingham. This large-scale movement of fuel was going on in defiance of the NUM's permit system that was supposed to govern the supply of coal and coke to 'priority customers' such as hospitals, schools and old folks' homes during the strike. As Scargill tells the story, he took the call from the NUM national office, which was asking for pickets to be sent to Birmingham to halt movements from the coke depot. Within five hours, he had despatched 400 men. By then it was nearly nine o'clock at night.

Destiny called. 'I'll never know as long as I live what made me take a decision to go to Birmingham,' he recalled. 'But I thought, it's queer, a depot in Birmingham and they need so many pickets. There's something unusual.' He drove through the night to Birmingham, and went straight to the Communist Party HQ, where 'our lads' had been put up for the night by Frank Watters – now a CP district secretary in the city. Next day, Sunday, he inspected the depot. 'I have never seen anything like it. It was like the most gigantic stack of any colliery that I'd ever seen. It was estimated that there were a million tons. This was no coke depot in the accepted sense. It was an Eldorado of coke, and you can guess the reactions of our boys, fresh from the successes of East Anglia and Yorkshire. Battles raged outside that coke depot, and at ten o'clock they closed it.'

It was reopened the next day, and battles raged for two days. In front of the TV cameras, Scargill yelled instructions through a megaphone. Police threatened him with arrest for incitement, and he replied: 'Go ahead, arrest me.' Scargill complained to *New Left Review* that 'the right-wing leadership in Yorkshire refused to send us reinforcements, I think mainly because I was down there.'[29] But wasn't the strike committee in charge of picketing the same strike committee committed to giving him the maximum exposure ahead of a critical election?

After three days, with a hundred pickets in jail, and fifty in hospital, the lorries were still rolling. Local Labour MPs tried to put pressure on Home Secretary Reginald Maudling, but he warned that troops would be used if necessary to keep the coke moving. It was his last piece of bravura. The government was now severely shaken by the power cuts affecting industry and commerce. People were learning to live with three-hours-on, three-hours-off electricity supplies. But, with stocks at the power stations down to only three weeks, the Cabinet caved in and declared a State of Emergency 'to protect central services and supplies for the community'.

The nation was in a hitherto unimagined crisis, but Scargill was still obsessed with his coke heap. Heavy picketing, involving miners lying down in the road and at other times shuffling in military formation across zebra crossings, had failed to close the gates. It was obvious that something different would have to happen. The picket line had not closed Saltley, so the working class must. Scargill plotted behind the scenes with local engineering, transport and vehicle building unions, and the Labour and Communist Parties, to call a one-day strike in Birmingham factories, with a 'people power' march on Saltley to close the gates.

The plot succeeded beyond his wildest dreams, and the greatest fears of the authorities. Scargill simply says: 'It was the greatest day of my life.' His graphic description has become a minor classic of its kind, still capable of moving the reader twenty years later. On the morning of Thursday 10 February, about ten o'clock, the lorries stopped arriving. No one knew why. 'There was a hush over the Saltley. 3,000 miners altogether, Welsh miners singing, Yorkshire miners, Nottinghamshire miners, Midlands miners. And yet nothing happened.

'Here we had a situation where miners were tired, physically and mentally desperately weary. They had gone through nearly six weeks' strike action, they had gone through a three months' overtime ban, they had gone through the worst battling encountered on strike action at any time in recent years. Their comrades had been arrested, one of them had been kicked to bits, and yet they were still battling on. I readily concede that some of the lads were feeling the effects and were a bit dispirited that no reinforcements were coming.

'Then over this hill came a banner and I've never seen in my life as many people following a banner. As far as the eye could see it was just a mass of people marching towards Saltley. There was a huge roar from the other side of the hill, they were coming the other way. They were coming from five approaches to Saltley. It was in a hollow, they were arriving from every direction. And our lads were jumping up in the air with emotion – a fantastic situation.

'I heard the police talking – Sir Derek Capper was one, Donaldson, his deputy – the tactic was simple: get the pickets coming from the east to go through to the west and get the pickets from the west – the striking engineers – to go through to the east. East to west, west to east, past each other.

'I got this megaphone, and I'm yelling like hell: "When you get to the picket line, Stop! Stop!" They were trying to shut me up and I said: "You try today, no bloody shutting up today. These boys are coming to our picket line." And they were piling up like sandwich cake, as far as the eye could see they were just pouring in. Saltley, the area of Saltley, was now just a mass of human beings, arriving from all over, with banners. The only time this crowd opened was when a delegation of girls from a women's factory came along all dressed in bright white dresses. They plunged through, and one of the lads shouts: "Go on, officer, tell them they can't come. Try and hold them." And no police officer moved, you know. Who'd have dared to try and stop those girls coming into that square? Nobody.

'The crowd was absolutely dense by this time. We were in the centre of it and everybody was chanting something different: some were chanting: "Heath Out", "Tories Out", "Support the Miners", "General Strike", a hundred slogans being chanted. I got hold of the megaphone and started to chant through it: "Close the Gates! Close the Gates!" and it was taken up, just like a football crowd. It was booming through Saltley: "Close the Gates!" It reverberated right across this hollow, and each time they shouted this slogan they moved and the police, who were four deep, couldn't help it, they were getting moved in.

'And Capper, the Chief Constable of Birmingham, took a swift decision. He said: "Close the Gates", and they swung them to. Hats were in the air, you've never see anything like it in your life. Absolute delirium on the part of the people who were there. Because the Birmingham working class had become involved, not as observers but as participants. The whole of the East District of the Birmingham AUEW were out on strike, 100,000 were out on strike, you know. It was tremendous. And they were still marching in from Coventry and other places, still advancing into Saltley. It was estimated that there were 20,000 in this area.

'Maudling, who said the gates wouldn't close, suddenly found that they were bloody closed and locked. The Chief Constable said: "That's it, I'm not risking any more here, those gates stay closed." He then turned to me – this is absolutely factual – and said: "Will you please do us a favour? Will you please disperse the crowd?" And I said on two conditions: firstly that I can make a speech to the crowd. He said: "Agreed." And secondly can I use your equipment, because mine's knackered?" He said: 'Agreed."

'Then I spoke from the urinal in Birmingham, with this police equipment. I gave a political speech to that mass of people and told them it was the greatest victory of the working class, certainly in my lifetime. The lads who were there were overcome with emotion, emotion in the best possible way. Here had been displayed all that's good in the working-class movement. Here had been displayed what for years had been on a banner but had never been transferred from the banner into reality. You know the words: "Unity is Strength", "Workers of the World Unite", "Man to Man Brother Be". They're big words. Sometimes they've been ridiculed. Through all that ridicule, all that sneering, they survived.

'Here was the living proof that the working class only had to flex its muscles and it could bring governments, employers, society to a total standstill. I know the fear of Birmingham on the part of the ruling class. The fear was that what happened in Birmingham could happen in every city in Britain.'[30]

On his day of days, the government appointed a Court of Inquiry headed by Lord Wilberforce to investigate the miners' case. This move signalled capitulation to the miners. It would have come, whatever happened at Saltley, because the power stations were running out of coal. The next day, the government told industry it could operate on three days a week only. Increasingly harsh power cuts began as the CEGB conserved what little stocks it had. Heating and lighting went in offices up and down the country. Secretaries struggled gallantly with candles stuck on their typewriters. The floodlights went off at football matches. Neon signs were shut down. Britons began to realize just how much they relied upon the miners they had forgotten down their black holes. Within a week, 1.6 million workers had been laid off by the power cuts, and Industry Secretary John Davies confessed that the country was just two weeks away from total blackout.

The Wilberforce Inquiry worked quickly, taking evidence in public in Church House, Westminster. Daly was magnificent. He appealed to the conscience of the nation, and voiced his pride in the pickets. 'Our pickets have done something more than hasten the course of this dispute. They have acted as ambassadors of the mining community in every city and port of this country.' Miners had enjoyed, in practical form, and with steadily growing effectiveness, the solidarity and support of the organized workers of Britain. 'Instead of remaining isolated and alone beside our pits we have built the unity of action and understanding that has been the immense positive feature of this strike.' That, and that alone, had forced the government from its 'dictatorship' imposed on all workers. The picket lines had been the one way of shortening the dispute, moving the government from dictation to a just settlement. 'When the industrial workers of Birmingham marched in their thousands to join our picket line, they showed that we do not stand alone, and that the purpose of our picket lines is understood by the working people of this country.'[31]

It was not until more than thirteen years had elapsed that the British Gas Corporation commissioned its own internal investigation into what is described primly as 'The Saltley Incident'. This management report,[32] disclosed here for the first time, was drawn up by Frank Ffoulkes, former personnel director of the East Midlands Gas Board, shortly after Scargill's ill-fated attempt to repeat the success of Saltley at Orgreave during the great strike. It dispels some of Scargill's more exotic claims.

First, there were 138,000 tons of coke at the depot when the strike began, not one million tons. It was the biggest pile of coke in the country, a legacy of the conversion to natural gas. Local newspapers carried stories about coke being freely on sale, without permits, to coal traders the day the strike started. But the media thereafter lost interest until early February, when shortages elsewhere meant that lorries were arriving from all over the country at the rate of over 250 a day.

The coke 'Eldorado' was now reduced to 100,000 tons, and would have disappeared altogether within a fortnight at the current rate of depletion. There were no pickets at the site. Only when the *Birmingham Mail* carried headlines about 'The Long Lorry Queue' on 3 February did the NUM wake up to what was going on. About a hundred pickets were redirected from an opencast mine at Brierley Hill, Staffs, to Saltley, with instructions to impose the NUM's 'special needs' permit system. The TGWU joined in, threatening drivers that their firms would be 'blacklisted' and their union cards withdrawn if they crossed the picket line.

Scargill claimed to have shut down the depot on Sunday, but Ffoulkes points out that it was closed for business that day. It was reported that 'Arthur Scargill, supported by some 200 or more flying pickets, would be arriving in the early hours of Monday morning'. This flatly contradicts Scargill's version. Ffoulkes agrees that violence erupted on the Monday, when 'the pickets from Barnsley in South Yorkshire duly arrived'. Two policemen were injured that day, and fourteen pickets arrested. The depot was closed part of that day.

Ffoulkes insists that 'notwithstanding the evidence of violence depicted in the media, however, relations between police and pickets on the whole remained friendly and low key. Only when lorries and/ or TV crews arrived did the atmosphere change, with the police forming a barrier and the pickets raising their voices and pressing to break the cordon. Once the lorries and TV cameras had left the scene, the atmosphere relaxed, and often cigarettes were exchanged between pickets and police.'

On Tuesday, the violence increased. Drivers who 'felt threatened' lined up nose to tail, forming convoys of up to ten lorries, to approach the depot without attempting to stop. One driver had a large Alsatian dog in his cab, 'while a number were observed to have armed themselves with staves'. That afternoon, an unnamed senior government minister sent a message to the chairman of the West Midlands Gas

Board – owners of the depot – saying: 'Whatever happens, don't close the gates – but don't say I told you, as I shall deny having said that.' A Gas Board spokesman deplored the incidents on the picket line, and said: 'If we were requested by the police or the government to close the depot in the interest of law and order we should do so. Otherwise we consider it our duty to continue to be available for business.'

By Wednesday, the pickets had grown to between 600 and 1,000, their number already swollen by students and car workers; the State of Emergency had been declared and ministers were passing the buck for responsibility. Police at the site had made an offer to allow twelve pickets to communicate with the drivers, but it was not taken up.

Thursday was 'crisis day'. The day was cold, bright and clear. The media had predicted a 'massive assault' by 40,000 striking engineering workers. In the event, 'the number of striking demonstrators increased from 5,000 to more than 10,000 to join the 2,000 pickets already there. Every approach road became rapidly jammed . . . the whole Nechells Place and approaches became a huge solid mass of people.'

At ten forty-five Sir Derrick Capper ordered David Beavis, the chairman of the Board, to close the gates. The chairman had not responded to an appeal on similar lines. Sir Derrick said: 'It is beyond the power of the resources at my disposal to maintain law and order on the street any more. I have been in touch with the home secretary and can get no further help. I have no alternative therefore but to tell you regrettably – "Close the gates."'

Scargill spoke, and 'the crowds behaved like football supporters after their team's victory. There were great bursts of triumphant cheering, but the whole mass of demonstrators and pickets rapidly dispersed – in many cases to the pubs, and an eerie silence descended upon Nechells Place. Only a handful of pickets remained.' An agreement was reached with Scargill and the TGWU at six a.m. on Friday, allowing priority customers to buy coke 'in accordance with the minister of industry's guidance of 9 January'. The depot reopened at seven-thirty a.m. that day, and deliveries continued at a much reduced rate thereafter. At the end of the strike, 55,000 tonnes were left. A month later, there were fewer than 10,000 tons. Publicity had sold the coke.

Interviewed on television at the time of his retirement, Sir Derrick was asked if he had regretted anything in the course of his career.

Yes, he said, the day he had to order the closure of Saltley gate. With hindsight, argues Ffoulkes, the crisis could have been avoided if West Midland Gas Board had restricted supplies to 'hardship cases'. But the Board was selling coke for the whole of January without any suggestions of provocation. 'Only when the local press actively publicized the absence of pickets from the coke pile did the situation suddenly alter. From that time the Saltley saga inexorably developed with all the inevitability of a Greek tragedy.' Ffoulkes exonerated management from blame, arguing: 'Saltley was simply a manifestation of social upheaval in which the nation was embroiled at the time, and became the symbol of a major change in political relationships.'

So far from a Greek tragedy, Scargill turned Saltley into a fairy story, or more precisely a modern myth in which he was the hero who delivered the downtrodden masses from the evil baron Edward Heath. His version is more entertaining, and improves on the re-telling. Ffoulkes may be, almost certainly is, more factual. But how many votes would his version win?

Scargill genuinely believed that Saltley was 'the decisive turning point of the strike, because this is where the government sought to make a stand'. It was certainly the decisive turning point in his career. Television pictures of him making the victory speech atop Nechells public urinal were flashed into every home. In future, his name would be indelibly associated with Saltley, and the defeat inflicted on the forces of law and order and the government through 'people power' – though he never uses the expression. All demonstrations of this kind are 'mass pickets', because that is the only way they fit into his world picture. Saltley was unquestionably a morale-booster for the miners, a source of dismay for the Cabinet and a deeper cause for concern for civil servants and senior police officers concerned with contingency planning.

But Scargill's estimate of the incident's industrial importance is not universally shared, not even by his closest comrade, Frank Watters, who writes: 'Victory was in sight in any case, but what Saltley did was put the icing on the cake.'[33] Taylor observes: 'The struggle before the gates has now entered the mythology of the union movement, and its symbolic importance should not be denied.'[34] In reality, the picketing of the power stations, which prompted the declaration of a State of Emergency on 10 February, was the key industrial factor in winning the strike, though the political and psychological impact of Saltley is undeniable.

There was also a legal knock-on effect. The 1971 Industrial Relations Act, designed to curb trade union power, was a dead letter almost before it reached the statute book. The legislation relied on unions 'opting in', by joining a government register, in order to obtain the few concessions it offered to collective bargainers such as the American-style 'agency shop' instead of closed shops. The TUC, appalled by the negative aspects such as compulsory cooling-off periods before strikes and the legal enforceability of collective agreements, organized a highly successful boycott of the register which made the law unworkable. It remained on the statute book, more an embarrassment and an irritant, until the Labour government that succeeded Heath after the next miners' strike repealed the measure. Along with most major unions, the NUM refused to join the government register. Its de facto closed shop remained intact. Nor did Employment Secretary Robert Carr invoke the emergency 'cooling-off period' provisions when faced with the 1972 coal strike.

But Saltley did focus long-term Conservative thinking on the successor legislation to the Industrial Relations Act. The Tories did not make the same mistake again. When Mrs Thatcher regained power for the Conservatives in 1979, on a manifesto of 'striking a fair balance between the rights and duties of the trade union movement', she appointed Jim Prior as Employment Secretary with the express instruction to act against secondary picketing of the kind that had brought the country to its knees in 1972. Prior's 1980 Employment Act repealed most of Labour's pro-union Employment Protection Act, and specifically the right of secondary picketing it had enshrined. In future, picketing could only be carried on in pursuance of a trade dispute, and then only by a person attending at or near his own place of work. Trade union officials could only attend picket lines of their members at or near their place of work. The picket's only purpose must henceforth be peacefully communicating information to or persuading a person to work or not to work.

Prior buttressed his legislation with a Code of Conduct on picketing, which was not written into the law but gradually came to have the force of law. Taking his cue from the NUM's own instructions in the 1974 strike, he limited the number of pickets permitted on any picket line to six. The code specifically excluded mass picketing. Such activity was 'not picketing in its lawful sense of an attempt at peaceful persuasion, but mass demonstration, which may result in a breach of the peace'. Prior came under fire for not being tough enough, and his laws were eventually taken into wholly new territory by his hardline successor, Norman Tebbit, who opened up trade union funds to legal attack.

The trigger for the legislation against secondary picketing was the 1972 strike in general, and the picketing of power stations and the 'mass picket' at Saltley in particular. Scargill may have felt satisfaction that one day in 1972 wiped the slate clean for the defeat of 1926, and made the miners acting in conjunction with fellow workers unbeatable. But the Conservatives bided their time, took note, and made their next legislative attack on trade unions more sophisticated and more effective. Far from destroying the use of the law as the most powerful weapon in the Tories' armoury, Scargill and Saltley merely made their approach more calculating. Not only mass picketing, but all secondary action eventually became unlawful and liable to bring the most crippling legal sanctions in train. That legal juggernaut has proved politically impossible to halt. No Labour leader will now risk going into a general election saddled with a commitment to restore lawful secondary action.

CHAPTER V

THE MAKING OF THE PRESIDENT

'I CRIED THAT DAY,' Scargill said as the miners went back after their momentous strike. He wasn't talking about the victorious return to work, but about Saltley. The Battle of Saltley Gate may only have been a side-show in the biggest industrial upheaval since the general strike of 1926, but his skilful exploitation of the street theatre in Birmingham had made him an instant hero in Yorkshire. The *Sheffield Star* reported: 'Scargill returned, after threats of being sprayed by acid or shot, to what amounts to a hero's welcome in Barnsley. In the streets, pubs and clubs, at further meetings in halls or pit branches, he was told by his taciturn supporters and their wives: "Well done, Arthur." And when the Court of Inquiry reported, a common comment in South Yorkshire was: "If it's fair enough with Arthur, it's fair enough with us . . ."'[1]

The Wilberforce Inquiry completed its work in a record two days, and ministers assumed that the NUM would accept its recommendations and call off the strike. It was a misapprehension. Wilberforce argued that too much had been asked of the miners in the late sixties, when their pay was rationalized under the National Power Loading Agreement. The national interest required the survival of a viable coal industry in competitive conditions, and that in turn demanded a contented and efficient labour force. Lord Wilberforce and his colleagues, Professor L. S. Hunter of Glasgow University and John Garnett, director of the Industrial Society, agreed that the miners had 'a just case for special treatment'.

Accordingly, they proposed lifting miners' basic rates by an average of eighteen and a half per cent – more than double the Board's final offer of 7.9 per cent, which was the ceiling under government guidelines. Surface workers would get a £5 rise to £18 a week; underground workers a £6 rise to £25; and face workers a £4.50 rise to £34.50 a week. The union had been claiming £26, £28 and £35

Scargill's first powerbase, Woolley Colliery, just north of Barnsley, where he worked from 1953 to 1972, much of that time as a lay official of the NUM. The pit, notorious for being right-wing, was sunk during the First World War and had a manpower of 2500 men at nationalization. Once a 'big hitter' producing a million tons a year, Woolley closed just before Christmas 1987

Scargill (*centre facing camera*), aged eighteen in October 1956, celebrating Barnsley Young Communist League winning a trophy for boosting circulation of YCL newspaper *Challenge*. *Left to right*: Derek Stubbings, later Scargill's best man; Scargill; Jean Hyde, YCL activist; Jim Parker, Scargill's minder after he became President of the NUM

Above: With his mini-skirted wife, Anne, July 1975

Left: First among equals: the composite portrait of key figures in the 1972 strike which lionizes Scargill as the hero of the Battle of Saltley Gate, 'Where the working class took control and provided a turning-point in the strike'

The Administrator: Scargill at his desk preparing for the February 1974 strike that led indirectly to the downfall of Edward Heath's Conservative Government

Arthur's army: Scargill at the head of the Yorkshire miners, seeking to repeat his success at Saltley outside the strike-hit Grunwick film-processing laboratory in north London, July 1977. He was later arrested for obstruction but cleared by the evidence of a *Morning Star* photographer

Striking a pose: while
President of the
Yorkshire Mineworkers
in September 1977,
Scargill swaps his usual
pin-stripe businessman's
suit for miners' gear

A chip off the old block? Scargill pictured with his predecessor Joe Gormley at the miners' offices in Euston Road, London, November 1981, not long before he won the NUM Presidency by a landslide

With his closest political ally, Tony Benn, addressing a meeting in Sheffield City Hall, November 1981

The move from London:
Scargill supervises the delivery
of his 'social realism' portrait
to the NUM's new
headquarters in Sheffield,
April 1983

Solidarity in South Wales: Scargill leads a
defiant parade of strikers through the
militant Rhondda Valley, three months
after hostilities opened

respectively. In retrospect, it is the modesty rather than the ambition of their demands that is most striking. With the country moving towards total blackout, the NUM executive gathered in the Employment Department's old offices in St James's Square, off Piccadilly, on the morning of 18 February to consider the recommendations. After a stormy meeting lasting several hours, they broke the bad news to DE officials: they had rejected Wilberforce. The vote had actually been thirteen to twelve against acceptance, but the vice-president Sid Schofield lied to Robert Carr's assistant and told him it was fourteen to eleven. The Cabinet, sunk in gloom, was called into emergency session and decided to fight the NUM's demand for an extra £1 for surface and underground men.

The stalemate did not last long. Joe Gormley, the miners' canny president, took his twenty-six-man executive to Downing Street and negotiated with the prime minister in his own parlour. Heath stood firm on the Wilberforce basic figures, but the NUM forced an extra fifteen concessions out of the government, ranging from adult rate at eighteen years, free transport to the pit, free working clothes and consolidation of bonuses into shift rates which would greatly increase overtime earnings. At one point, the union's industrial relations officer, Trevor Bell, who was later to challenge Scargill for the national presidency, was scratching round in his files for conference demands that had not been rejected by the Coal Board in previous years. When they couldn't think of anything more to demand, the executive sat down and voted on a package now inflated to £95 million. Still, the Left would not budge, but the ruling moderate coalition asserted its power and agreed to recommend the offer in a branch ballot and call off the pickets outside the power stations meanwhile.

This was their finest hour. The men voted by 96.5 per cent to accept the offer and return to work. The Wilberforce-plus package was enough for the men, but despite the confidence of the citizens of Barnsley, it is unlikely to have been 'fair enough' for Scargill. He never voted for a pay settlement on the national executive – not even the 1974 settlement – on the ground that the claim had not been conceded in full. Anything less than the full claim, he always insisted, was a sell-out.

Wisely, he kept his counsel and basked in the glory of the hour. He was still only the rank-and-file pit delegate from Woolley colliery, where he could not always rely on his own members, but he was already being talked about as a potential president. Indeed, he was talking about it himself. Asked if he envisaged himself becoming national president some day, he struck the right diplomatic note: 'Well, of course, I'd love to think some day I could serve the miners in such a post. But let's face it – you're talking to a man who isn't even a member of the national executive at this moment, so it would be a long way ahead.

'But my life does lie with the union and trade unionism in general. I don't want to be an MP as some people have suggested to me I should aim at. There's too much to be done in the field of the unions, and I've made my choice. You can't do both. I believe a new leadership is emerging in our union – young men sent to study on day courses at university, but ready to go out on the picket line and lead from the front. I believe the strike took us into a new era. As for me, all I ever hoped for in unionism and solidarity, all I've dreamed of, came true on February 10 at Saltley in Birmingham. I cried that day . . .'[2]

His presidential ambitions were to be realized within ten years, but his first priority was to win a full-time position in the NUM. Scargill was already a member of the coalfield 'inner cabinet', the area executive, and he seized the opportunity presented by the election for compensation agent in Yorkshire. Superficially, this was an unglamorous job. It was not about leading from the front on picket lines or confronting the police. It was about the painstaking assembly of a case to prove that a miner's incapacity is due to diseases common in the industry such as pneumoconiosis ('black lung' in the more striking American phrase), and is therefore the fault of the Coal Board. The NUM has a proud record for winning compensation for such diseases, and for more common injuries routinely suffered in the mines.

From Scargill's point of view, being compensation agent would take him all over the coalfield attending to cases at more than a hundred collieries, workshops and other sites. Far more than, say, an area agent, he would be in daily contact with his members, moreover in a social welfare function that is seen as non-political. The compensation agent is the man who brings the NCB cheques. This is not to suggest that Scargill saw the job solely in that way, as a route towards greater popularity. He has a genuine concern for the casualties of coal-getting. But it is an aspect to the job that his party backers would not have ignored. It was a path subsequently trodden by the Communist in Nottinghamshire, Joe Whelan, an engaging Dubliner who died suddenly before the CP could realize its objective of radicalizing that coalfield.

Sammy Taylor, the Communist who had held the compensation agent's post in Yorkshire, had died suddenly in September 1971, but the question of a successor had been put to one side for the duration of the strike. After the funeral, as we have seen, Scargill had discussed the possibility of going for the position. Some argued that Scargill could not always be relied on to 'pull' his own branch, and could not therefore be regarded as the front runner. John Walsh, who is admittedly parti-pris, suggests that Scargill was even at risk of losing the delegate's job when he came up for re-election in 1973. 'If it hadn't been for 1972, he wouldn't have been re-elected,' says Walsh.[3] 'Nothing made him different until 1972. Then it all changed. It all changed with Saltley, which gave him a lot of television exposure. He was in the right place at the right time.'

Scargill, says Prof Vic Allen, was quite simply 'the best known miner in Yorkshire'.[4] 'He had a natural flair for attracting publicity and, because of his confident and intelligent commentaries, he appeared regularly on television in Yorkshire. He had achieved national notoriety for his part in the Saltley Gate affair. He had not been the only candidate before the strike, but after it he stood out on his own.'

The right wing made a desperate effort to regroup in the face of the growing influence of the Yorkshire Left Caucus, but it was a feeble shadow of its former self. Not all the moderates were happy about having an organization within the union that bypassed the formal branch and panel structures. And there were too many individuals who believed they were the right man for the job to sustain any political cohesion. The moderates could not match the Left's discipline in putting forward only one agreed candidate. When the ballot for compensation agent was announced no fewer than eighteen hopefuls put their name forward. By a branch vote, the list was reduced to three: Scargill; Jack Smart, full-time area agent for the moderate North Yorkshire coalfield; and Tommy Roebuck, a maverick right-winger who was delegate at Manvers colliery in South Yorkshire. Voting took place in June, shortly before the NUM annual conference, and Scargill romped home, taking 28,050 votes to 9,824 for Smart and 8,336 for Roebuck. It was the start of a pattern. The man who, by his own admission doesn't like losing, prefers to stack up the votes in vast quantities as a buttress against criticism.

Observers noted 'a new self-confidence, indeed truculence' in the coalfield after the strike and Scargill's election victory. It was apparent in the area's support of a thirty per cent pay claim agreed by the national conference in the Dixieland ballroom, Morecambe, in July against the wishes of Joe Gormley. It was evident in the motions coming to area council calling for strike action to defeat Ted Heath's hated Industrial Relations Act and for defiance of the Housing Finance Act, which put up the rents of miners' houses.

By most accounts, Scargill acquitted himself well in his full-time role. Michael Eaton, North Yorkshire area director of the NCB, fell in with him at a social function at the time and can still recall the pride with which Scargill told him he had just been elected compensation agent at the age of thirty-four. 'But he did that job very well. It's not surprising. It was his first job, and he wanted to be a miner's leader and make a reputation. He is a man capable of a lot of work[5]. Scargill reorganized the department, and the number of claims against the NCB increased sharply. He proved a dogged advocate, and the amounts recovered improved accordingly. His friend and political sparring partner in Worsbrough at the time, Ian Linford, concedes: 'He really did make a lot of ill miners happy.'[6]

It was a period of rapid change at the top in the Yorkshire NUM. Sam Bullough, the ineffective moderate president, was ill for long periods, as was the area secretary, Sid Schofield. A power vacuum opened up, but not for long. In their absence, Scargill deputized, making himself the obvious heir-apparent. In September, the veteran Communist Jock Kane retired from his post as financial secretary, and Scargill immediately took his position on the national executive of the NUM.

This twenty-six-man body, which was historically dominated by the right, met on the second Thursday of every month at the NUM headquarters, a three-storey, purpose-built office block at 222 Euston Road, hard by Euston railway station. Under union rules, the executive was the government of the NUM between conferences, whose policy decisions it is charged with implementing. In practice, the executive was a law unto itself. Years of untrammelled power had given the ruling moderates a collective self-confidence that brooked no interference. With their inbuilt majority, they could simply ignore conference decisions at will, safe in the knowledge that the issue would either be forgotten by the next conference, or, *in extremis*, could be voted down by an executive recommendation in a ballot of the men. It was a cosy, powerful club.

The executive met in a wood-panelled, high-ceilinged chamber of the kind beloved of the labour movement the world over, West and East. On solid wooden easy chairs with leather cushions, they gathered round a huge conference table covered in green leather. The debates took place under the steady gaze of a vast street scene of a miners' gala, with bands, banners and marchers etched on to a two-storey window from floor to ceiling at the back of the hall. After the Scargill takeover, when the union decamped to Sheffield, this masterpiece of proletarian art was unceremoniously bulldozed into the back yard: perhaps the greatest piece of cultural vandalism in trade union history. But when he arrived, the union was at the height of its powers in modern times. Debates could last several hours. Their outcome could shake governments and cause a run on the pound. This was definitely A Place To Be Serious.

The Left could usually count on only nine or ten votes, and there was a close working relationship within this group. Mick McGahey, the Communist Scots president who had failed to win the National NUM presidency, was the accepted leader. The group usually stayed at the County Hotel in Upper Woburn Place, a cheerless sort of establishment, where the room keys were attached to long pieces of wood so that residents wouldn't forget to hand them in.

Here, the Left met on the Wednesday night to plan tactics for the executive. Scargill was automatically invited to attend, and initially did so, though his appearances became fewer. After the plotting came the drinking. McGahey, with his 'hauf'n hauf' (half a pint of beer and a whisky), would lead the conversation, usually about current events but freely interspersed with trade union reminiscences and even jokes. It was a relaxed affair, usually attended by Daly (who did not go to the Left meetings) and by Mick Costello, industrial correspondent of the Communist *Morning Star*, and the author. Scargill, who rarely drinks in public (and then only a sherry or half of lager), was almost never seen at these social occasions. Nor did he stay at the County, but at a more modern establishment off Great Russell Square, a few hundred yards down the road, to which he would repair after a fish and chip supper.

He further established his 'differentness' by leaving the executive before anyone else, so that he could get his version in first to the waiting press and TV representatives. He would then smile 'Thank you, gentlemen' and stride off to King's Cross to catch his train back to Yorkshire. This habit swiftly exasperated Gormley, who formally briefed the press after executive meetings, because he often had to rewrite the Scargill version before giving his own gloss on events. After the executive meetings, left-wing coalfield leaders would adjourn for a lunchtime session at the Crown and Anchor pub at the back of the office. The right walked a little further to drink at the Exmouth Arms in Starcross Street, a pub that even London taxi drivers find difficult to locate. The only time the two warring factions drank together was during disputes or similar times of crisis. Scargill, socially uncomfortable in such surroundings, never went to these sessions. He might have been a better leader if he had.

This arm's-length attitude was also noticed at gatherings of the National Left, where Scargill was now a regular attender. Eric Clarke, now Labour MP for Midlothian, was then a left-winger from Scotland who became general secretary of his coalfield and joined the executive soon after Scargill. He recalls: 'I met Arthur at Left meetings. We used to meet periodically in Birmingham. Jock Kane was chairman, and the discussion was of a very, very high calibre. Like myself, Scargill listened more than he spoke. There was genuine comradeship there. No votes were taken. About fifty or seventy people would attend, covering the Left coalfields, with some individuals from the Midlands and latterly some from the North-East. But nobody from Lancashire. We vetted the people who went. There was a complete mixture of Labour and Communist. Yorkshire representation was dominated by the Doncaster panel. Arthur was a breakthrough because he came from the Barnsley panel. He was a bright lad.[7]

'Arthur was quite well liked. He was a wee bit shy. We used to work hard and live hard. We used to drink quite a bit. But he didn't: he kept himself apart from that side of it, socially. I think that was a weakness of his.' It was also an early signal of the graceless diffidence that was to mark his relationships – or lack of them – in the labour movement. 'A lot of people would have liked to meet him, and mix with him socially. People who were really our friends and wanted to be associated with us,' said Clarke. 'And it didn't happen, because he wouldn't do that. The only time he spoke to them was from a platform, or when he canvassed them in some way to do something. He never built up friendships.' This attitude contrasted with McGahey's:

'He was friendly with everyone – even his enemies. He disarmed them with his charm.'

But if he was beginning to sow seeds of doubt in the Left nationally, Scargill's star was rising fast in Yorkshire. In January 1973, Sam Bullough died, and this time there was no debate about who would be the Left candidate. Not that this pleased everyone. Allen recorded 'growing tensions among left-wing miners as opportunities for official positions increased and potential candidates competed with each other. Personality problems also emerged because Scargill's popularity enabled him to pick and choose posts, and others resented this.'[8]

The Right was still in disarray, and allowed two candidates to run: Jack Leigh, the incumbent vice-president, a lacklustre figure too heavily identified with the *ancien régime*, and Jack Layden, South Yorkshire agent and later to become knighted for services to local government. Against such a divided opposition, Scargill walked it, amassing 28,362 votes to 7,981 for Layden and 7,126 for Leigh. In the autumn of the same year, Sid Schofield retired through ill health and in the ensuing election Owen Briscoe, secretary of the Doncaster panel and an arch-loyalist of Scargill, was elected. And before 1973 was out, the Communist Peter Tait, secretary of the big Grimethorpe branch, secured election to the national executive as Yorkshire's lay representative, giving a prile of militants in the highest council of the union. The Left had now captured the commanding heights in the coalfield leadership, and its national representation. 'The transformation of the Yorkshire area which a small number of left-wing miners had aimed for in 1967 was virtually completed in 1973.'[9] Within seven years, the revolution had succeeded, and it now trickled down into the branches, as more and more pit positions fell to the Left. The old guard who remained felt it sensible to emulate the vicar of Bray.

The leadership had changed. What about the members? For all Scargill's hair-raising talk of miners learning about the class war at first hand, there was no evidence, beyond their willingness to elect tough-talking officials, of a sea change in their attitudes. Allen notes that there had been a tendency to view the behaviour of miners in 1972 as a sign of 'a real, profound alteration' in their attitudes rather than as a response to a particular situation. But the ballot of 28 March 1973, taken during a Tory government-imposed pay freeze, caused something of a rethink. Nationally, just over sixty-three per cent of the men voted against strike action in support of their big pay claim, and even Yorkshire managed only a small majority for industrial action, with forty pits voting for action and thirty-eight against. Only Scotland was there with them, all the other coalfields voting against.

'The miners showed through the 1973 ballot that they did not have political motives,' said Allen.[10] 'They simply wanted wage increases. They were entirely pragmatic in their approach. In this respect their attitude was as it always had been.' To win a pay rise they would strike against the government of the day, but 'they did not make any correlation between the manner in which they struggled for subsistence and the capitalist system ... So what was seen during the 1972 strike was not a raised political awareness so much as the imposition of political consequences upon ordinary economic demands.'

The 1973 ballot asking for authority to take strike action against Phase Two of Heath's statutory incomes policy only went ahead after Gormley used his presidential casting vote to break a twelve–twelve deadlock on the national executive. That he had to do so indicated the increasing strength of the Left on the executive. It was also a foretaste of the leadership test that Scargill would one day face: a deadlocked executive on an issue of national importance. Gormley faced it. Scargill would funk it.

The strike ballot took place shortly after a colliery disaster in the coalfield. On Wednesday, 21 March, an inrush of water caused when a coal-cutter broke into old workings inundated Lofthouse colliery, just north of Wakefield. Seven men died in the disaster, the worst in Yorkshire for many years. Scargill took personal charge of the NUM effort. He was at the mine for six days, sometimes joining the rescue brigades in their battles underground to save the entombed men. He comforted the bereaved and received 'the class enemy' Ted Heath when he paid a visit to the stricken scene. But he still found time to address a rally of 2,000 men on 25 March in Barnsley, telling them that Lofthouse was the kind of situation that changed men's minds. It showed that miners' work was tough and hazardous, and that their pay claim was justified, he argued.

Scargill, appearing as acting general secretary of Yorkshire, was at his forensic best in the public inquiry that followed the disaster. In the Institute of Geological Sciences in Leeds, he discovered old notebooks of underground working in the nineteenth century. This information, he argued, was available to the Coal Board, and had they taken account of it, the disaster could have been avoided. The

Yorkshire Evening Post described Scargill as 'an electrifying questioner' determined to establish the facts. 'As the long, sad hours tick away at the public inquiry into the Lofthouse Colliery disaster, one man is emerging as a compulsive forceful personality,' reported the YEP sketch-writer. 'Mr Arthur Scargill, leading the National Union of Mineworkers' examining team, has only to reach for the microphone and the reporters on the crowded Press benches sit up expectantly, pencils poised.'

The inquiry was in no sense a court of law. It was an inquiry under HM Mines Inspectorate. But Scargill wanted the NCB in the dock. 'For the most part the proceedings follow a quiet, ordered pattern – until Arthur Scargill rises to question a witness. Then the courtroom is charged with expectancy. A current has been switched on. Mr Scargill has no legal training. Yet his style is strongly reminiscent of the assize court. He stands, leaning slightly forward, conducting his own perfectly-measured phrases with a yellow pencil.

'He changes pace, feints, pins down a witness on the precise mean- ing of a word, refuses to be fobbed off. "Can you just tell me simply . . ." he begs. His tenacity has a vice-like grip that will not let you go. "I put it to you . . ." he says. "I put the question again . . . in the light of what we know . . ." The forensic phrases slip out with unconscious ease, while the manner remains ever courteous, almost urbane. There is, too, a nice touch of irony, as in: "Thank you. You've given me the answer I've been trying for for the last five minutes."[11] His appearances at the Lofthouse inquiry coincided with voting in the Yorkshire area presidential election, and must have improved his changes in the poll.

At the NUM annual conference in Inverness that followed very shortly afterwards, feelings were once again rising in the union. Gormley, with genuine passion rather than the ersatz anger he some- times displayed, warned that 'never again will we say we shall be more loyal to the rest of the country than to our members. We will provide the coal they need, but they are going to have to pay the right price for it.' Scargill was more political: 'We are dealing with the most immoral, the most corrupt government in living memory. They have been absolutely sincere and dedicated to their class and the people who support them.' Here again is the back-handed compli- ment to the Tories, the envious admiration of a class solidarity that is almost certainly more perceived than real, but no less influential on Scargill's thinking for all that.

Delegates adopted a £138 million pay claim, the biggest in the union's history, that would mean pay rises of £8 to £13 a week, in defiance of the government's statutory wage restraint policy. Lawrence Daly warned of 'a confrontation not of our own making, but of the making of "Benito" Heath', though the NUM general secretary bore a good deal closer physical resemblance to Mussolini than did the prime minister. The coke at Saltley had gone, but the myth reappeared. The aptly-named Mr Pratt of the Midlands area demanded that if there had to be another mass picketing at Saltley, 'let's do it in November rather than midsummer'.

In this state of confused euphoria, the miners squared up for another conflict. Heath tried to avert it by calling Gormley in for 'absolutely secret' talks only days after the Inverness conference. Over drinks in the back garden of 10, Downing Street, Gormley did what he could to help, signposting a possible compromise through extra payment for the 'unsocial hours' that most miners work. Instead of conceding this only to the NUM, Heath foolishly offered it to all workers in Phase Three of his pay policy. Then came the Yom Kippur War, which caused oil prices to rocket. In October 1973, Egypt and Syria attacked Israel on the Jewish holy day, and the Arab states who were not combatants came to their aid by using the price of oil as a political weapon. They announced an overnight increase of seventy per cent, and by 1 January doubled the price again. The Gulf states were punishing the Americans for their support of Israel, but a by-product of this global confrontation was a sudden shift in the bargaining power of the miners. If Middle East oil was going to be expensive and unpredictable, then the run-down of the British coal industry must be reconsidered. The miners felt more relaxed about rejecting the Coal Board's thirteen per cent pay offer. An overtime ban began on 12 November, and the government declared a state of emergency the day after.

Asked later by *New Left Review* how he saw the second confrontation between the miners and the government, Scargill replied: 'Without being big-headed, a little clearer than many of my colleagues on the Left.' Big-headed? *Toi?* He continued: 'Heath had decided right after the '72 strike that he would have to inflict a defeat on the miners. He had made up his mind on this.'[12] When he made these remarks, Scargill clearly did not know about the secret meeting with Heath; when he heard about it, he insisted he would never participate in such secret meetings.

The entire NUM executive trooped in to meet the prime minister in Downing Street on 28 November. Scargill has claimed: 'the meeting took place at my suggestion in the executive'.[13] Gormley's recollection is that Heath took the initiative. McGahey stole the limelight by telling the premier that he wanted to change the government 'but by democratic means, through the ballot box'. This intervention created a political stir.

Scargill later insisted he had shown the prime minister a way out of the impasse. 'I produced statistics to Heath in Downing Street in the Cabinet Room, proving that the calculations that the Coal Board had made and the Government had accepted were wrong. The comparison of average wage rates was not comparing like with like.' Heath passed the figures to Sir William Armstrong, secretary of the Cabinet, 'who must have decided these figures didn't bear looking at or that they were wrong, or, that, in spite of them they should still maintain their position . . . they ignored these arguments'.[14] Gormley does not mention this proposal in his record of the meeting, mentioning only his irritation with McGahey for his outburst about wanting to change the government.[15]

Unabashed, Scargill claimed that he pre-empted the Pay Board inquiry which eventually resolved the ensuing strike. Many people on the NUM side did not agree with his figures, he said, but 'eventually, of course, the Pay Board proved conclusively that the calculations we made were right. Had Heath accepted them, he would still be prime minister today. He would have been seen as someone who accepted new evidence, subsequently proved by the Pay Board. But he totally ignored representations which were logical on the part of the union, because it was quite clear that he wanted a showdown and that he wanted to teach the NUM a lesson.'[16]

Having single-handedly sought to avert a strike and sustain Heath in office, Scargill then tried to bounce the executive into a strike in early January. He regarded some of his fellow left-wingers as complacent, confident that the overtime ban would deliver a result. 'But you don't win things with comfortable struggle – you never can, you never have and you never will.' Scargill moved a resolution for strike action, but got only the support of his loyal Yorkshire secretary Owen Briscoe. The Communists, clearly acting in unison, refused to back him, and the moderates were awaiting the outcome of yet another peace move. This time, it was through the loophole of 'waiting, washing and winding time', another bright idea doomed to failure.

At about this time, *The Times* carried a series of profiles on the NUM leadership. The feature on 4 January 1974, headlined: 'Newcomers who hardened the miners' line', had a mug shot picture of Scargill wearing long sideburns and long hair swept back from the temple. It recorded the usual early details of his life, and said: 'He held a CP card for several years, but describes himself as "never a very active member". After some deep-seated political differences with the Communist Party, he left in 1962 and became involved with the Co-operative movement until 1966 when he joined the Labour Party ... the Labour Party, even today, is "far too liberal" for his liking.' Scargill described himself as 'the hardest of the hardliners', and heaped scorn on the 'waiting time' initiative. 'We are interested in the basic rate. As far as I am concerned, there can be no compromise on that single issue.'[17]

The TUC became involved, promising that if the miners were allowed through Phase Three of the pay policy, no other union would be allowed to follow. But ministers had by now become too mistrustful of organized labour to believe that salvation might lie that way. That was the last peace formula. A strike ballot was called for 1 February, and in Yorkshire Scargill issued 70,000 leaflets saying: 'You either support your union in this fight to obtain better wages and conditions, or you support government policy and as a consequence weaken the union now and in the future. Support Your Union – Vote Yes.' The ballot paper was less hortatory, asking the men if they were prepared to give the executive authority to call a strike.

The day before polling day in the strike ballot, *The Times* visited Woolley colliery with Arthur Scargill to test the temperature in Yorkshire. It was suitably incandescent. Miners going down on the twelve o'clock shift were asked if they intended to vote for industrial action. *The Times* records: 'A certain amount of derision greeted the query and the men did not hide their voting intentions.'[18] Face worker Robert Riley said: 'Definitely for all-out strike. Everybody will vote that way.' Shearer-driver Michael White agreed: 'You've got to. If you've not got confidence in your leaders, you might as well pack up now.' George Nicholls, a trainee on-setter, married with three children, remarked: 'I can't feed them now, that's why I'm for a strike.' And face worker Colin Darlington declared: 'We ought to have had their leadership twenty years ago, and then we wouldn't have been in this position today.'

Scargill was eminently satisfied. 'The determination of the men has got to be seen to be believed. 1971 pales into insignificance alongside the feeling in every single pit in the coalfield today, and I confidently predict an eighty per cent vote for strike action.' He was right. The miners returned their biggest majority for a strike in their history: 80.9 per cent in favour, every single coalfield and section but for the white-collar group COSA. In Yorkshire, the 'Yes' vote was 90.3 per cent.

An all-out strike was duly called from midnight on 9 February. Gormley, keenly aware that Tory back-benchers and some Cabinet ministers were urging Heath to go to the country on a 'who rules' election, warned: 'What would an election change? It doesn't solve the problem.' Nonetheless, two days after the ballot result was declared, Heath called an election for 28 February. He went on television to tell the voters: 'We can't afford the luxury of tearing ourselves apart any more. This time the strife has got to stop. Only you can stop it. It's time for your voice to be heard, the voice of the moderate and reasonable people of Britain, the voice of the majority. It is time for you to say to the extremists, the militants, and the plain and simple misguided: "We've had enough."' In a statement from Downing Street, the prime minister added: 'I know that the miners themselves are democrats. It is therefore especially disappointing that the politically motivated arguments of some of their leaders should have prevailed.'

The extremists had only just started. They rejected Gormley's suggestion to suspend the strike for the duration of the election. In Yorkshire, plans were laid to immobilize industry through sympathetic trade union links. Scargill held talks with engineering and transport union officials in Birmingham, promising disruption in 'the spirit of Saltley'. NUM headquarters, determined to run a low-key dispute, ordered a maximum of six pickets at any site. There was no desire to have a re-run of Saltley. Television pictures of picket line violence might harm Labour's electoral chances, and while the miners' leaders insisted that it was not a political strike – well, now an election had been called, Labour might as well win.

Scargill, naturally, was itching for another set-piece street confrontation. But this time, he was the official leader, installed in his warm office in Huddersfield Road with its big desk and the big oil painting of himself. He was respectable. He couldn't just dust off the baseball picketing hat, put new batteries in the bullhorn and tear off to the front line. He had to be the spider at the centre of the web. Baulked of a convenient coke mountain, his eye alighted on British Steel's giant Anchor complex in Scunthorpe, Lincs, which the Doncaster NUM panel had failed to bring to a halt. More pickets were sent out from Barnsley, and talks with local rail unions brought the supply of materials to Anchor down to a trickle.

The plant was only operating at fifty per cent capacity anyway, because of power cuts and the three-day week imposed under the state of emergency. Concerted action gradually sealed off the complex. Scargill later claimed: 'It was clear that if we could stop the huge Anchor works we could halt British industry ... While they had prepared very well on the power stations (with coal stocks), they hadn't prepared very well at the steel works and we stopped all the steel works on this occasion. Historians, when they look at this, will see that the real crunch came in the '74 strike with the steel works. That's the reason Heath had to take a decision. He had no alternative. He had to have a general election or concede to the miners.'[19]

He was grasping at straws, and his muddled thinking showed it. Desperate to have 'another Saltley', Scargill elevated the Anchor steel works (which he admitted was only 'in danger of coming to a complete standstill') into the instrument by which the whole of British industry would come to a halt. This was self-delusion. Anchor scarcely figured in the national picture, as Saltley did. It certainly had nothing to do with calling the election, which was well under way before 18 February, when the Doncaster panel was complaining that 'It would seem we are weak on steel works.'[20]

The strike was causing some grief for the Labour leadership. At a Shadow Cabinet meeting on 30 January, Harold Wilson said McGahey had done 'a great deal of damage' with his inflammatory remarks that if troops were brought in, he hoped they would think twice before using their weapons against miners. Ted Short, Leader of the House, said it was essential to make clear that Labour was not linked to the Communists. At this point, records Tony Benn in his diaries, 'Roy Mason pointed out that Arthur Scargill, the Yorkshire president, and Mick McGahey, the Scottish president, were competing for the vacancy that would be created when Joe Gormley retired.'[21] His remark, seemingly apropos of nothing, was prescient. It passed without comment.

The strike-that-never-was, as Gormley tried to make it, ran for little more than four weeks. It was called off by the executive on 6 March, two days after Edward Heath gave up attempts to put together a coalition with the Liberals, and Harold Wilson entered Downing Street as the head of a minority Labour administration. On the basis of a Pay Board report acknowledging they had slipped dramatically in the wages league, the Coal Board offered the miners the biggest rise in the industry's history, conceding their full claim for £45 a week at the coal face and substantial increases for other grades. Two members of the executive voted against accepting the £103 million settlement – Scargill, and Jack Collins, Communist secretary of the Kent pitmen.

Gormley said later that it was 'a strike which should never have happened'. Responding to the allegation that 'the miners brought down Ted Heath', he reacted sharply: 'As far as we were concerned it was *not* a political strike, but an industrial one. It was *not* the miners, but Ted Heath who brought himself down. He didn't need to call an election.'[22] Scargill had made a parallel comment to the *Morning Star* as the strike began: 'A general election will not solve anything.'

In the event, it did. The election may have been something of a fraud, in that Heath had promised at the outset to honour whatever the Pay Board awarded to the NUM, and could not therefore argue that he was going to the electorate to sort out the miners. But it did deliver a victory for the NUM. As Allen admits, 'In reality, the strike was lost by the government more than it was won by the miners.'[23]

With Labour in office, if not perhaps in power, this should have been a time for Scargill to put his feet up and relax for a while. Virtually any other man would have. He could look back on a hectic three years spent politicking for position and organizing the most effective strikes in post-war Britain. But Scargill is a workaholic and, besides, there were other mountains to climb. By now, he had given up judo, which was his chief form of physical relaxation other than walking his Yorkshire terriers on the moors. He had achieved yellow belt status, three grades below black belt. Even in his days at Barnsley Judo Club, it was more a contest than sport. 'His aim was to drop his opponent on the mat as fast as possible.'[24]

He was also a 'passionate' Leeds United fan, making the pilgrimage for ten years to Row HH in the West Stand at Elland Road with his wife and father to watch home games. And he shared the customary

tyke enthusiasm for the county cricket team. 'When Yorkshire play
Lancashire at cricket, I get worked up about it. I don't think there's
any point in supporting anyone unless you feel there's a lot at stake.
When I went to a match and Leeds lost, I didn't feel like eating
afterwards.'[25]

He has been known to take holidays, though some of these ended
in grief. The family enjoyed bed and breakfast weeks in Redruth,
Cornwall, before trying Bulgaria. But in their second outing there,
Scargill complained bitterly about overcharging and petty corruption.
When he got back to good old Blighty, he thundered: 'If that's Communism, they can keep it.' The Scargills also had a holiday in what
was the Soviet Union after the 1972 strike, at the invitation of the
Soviet mining union. They were among thirty families who sailed
across on the *MV Baltika*. George Bolton, then an NUM activist in
Scotland, remembers them well: 'He was stand-offish. He sat on the
beach by himself, with his wife. He didn't mix with people.'[26]

Instead of taking it easy, Scargill threw himself into the job with
renewed vigour. The national union, which pays the salaries of area
officials, wanted to economize as the membership was shrinking.
After a show of protest from Yorkshire, Scargill extended the
president's role to take in the compensation agent's job, which
had been vacant since he captured the coalfield leadership. John
Walsh comments: 'He gobbled up the job of compensation agent.
He was cock of the heap with the men, then.'[27] Others – even
managers – attribute less cynical motives. Michael Eaton observed:
'I believe he genuinely thought he could do it well, and better than
anybody else. I don't think he didn't want another official.'[28]
Whoever was right, it was unquestionably convenient for Scargill
not to have an up-and-coming rival at 'Camelot', as he now liked
Huddersfield Road to be called in line with the soubriquet 'King
Arthur'.

He was a busy man now. He appeared on the Michael Parkinson
show, two Barnsley boys together, and countless other television
programmes. In October 1974, he was on the cover of *Harpers &
Queen* magazine, a name of the future along with Jack Straw and
William Waldegrave.[29] He spoke at university debating occasions.
William Rees-Mogg, as he then was, invited him to lunch at *The
Times* offices in Gray's Inn Road, where he astounded editorial
executives by a Stakhanovite performance at table. 'Did you see
that?' asked bemused news editor Rita Marshall. 'Not only does he

monopolize the conversation – he cleans his plate quicker than anyone else.' His ambitions for the future were pretty transparent. Asked if he would stand against McGahey for the NUM presidency, he riposted: 'Perhaps you should ask McGahey if he would stand against me.'[30]

Scargill was also being noticed politically. Tony Benn noted in his diary for 3 September 1974: 'Arthur Scargill was interviewed by that awful woman Anne Scott-James in the *Evening Standard* last night, where he said he would like to see me as Prime Minister and Roy Jenkins and Shirley Williams thrown out of the Labour Party. He said he was a democratic Marxist, which is a new category the British can't really understand. He's a bright guy and I like him. The point is how, if we get a working majority in the Election, we can use that analysis to carry through some changes within the party, particularly in its internal democracy, and the re-selection of MPs, if local parties want it, between elections.'[31]

Within a very short time, this issue was to become the glue of a political relationship between the two men. Scargill was obsessed with the working of representative democracy, not least because the lopsided nature of the NUM national executive gave the right wing, who represented a minority of the membership, an inbuilt majority over the Left, who represented a majority of the membership. In his context, 'represent' actually means 'elected to represent', because members in the areas did not always vote the way their leaders voted.

The return of a Labour government, Scargill knew, would strengthen the hand of the Right, whose confidence had been dented by the success of militant tactics. As early as June 1974, the moderates reasserted their block-vote strength, rejecting a motion from the Scottish miners which would have committed the NUM to outright hostility to the 'social contract' between the TUC and the new Labour government. This executive decision led to the rejection of Scargill's plans for a massive wage claim at the annual conference in Llandudno a month later. Scargill retaliated by boycotting talks with the NCB on a pit productivity pay scheme. At a special conference on the issue soon after, he clashed sharply with Gormley. Scargill raised obstructive procedural points and the NUM president ruled him out of order. The result was predictable. 'When I wouldn't let Arthur have his way, he shouted "There's no point in stopping here" and led the Yorkshire delegation out with him.'[32] And Scargill had the last laugh, mobilizing Yorkshire votes to crush the productivity scheme – though on live television he invited the Coal Board to give it a six-month trial. He was beginning to use live shows, on which his fast-talking style gave him an advantage over his rivals, as an extension of formal negotiations.

With the second general election of 1974 in the offing, NUM moderates were determined not to allow Scargill to rock the boat. He was not permitted to speak when the TUC debated the social contract and its wage restraint provisions in early September. Scargill seethed. Labour was re-elected on 10 October with a precarious working majority of only three over all other parties. This victory ought to have been a matter of rejoicing to a party member in good standing. For Scargill, it merely made things worse. 'The one thing that annoys me at the trade union movement is that we've got one set of standards when we've got a Tory government, and a completely different set of standards when we've got a Labour government, even though our case may be right,' he complained.

A Labour government made *his* struggle harder. 'We have so many people inside the TUC, inside the NUM, both at Executive level and local level, who because it is a Labour government are prepared to accept treatment and decisions that they would never tolerate from a Tory government. This seems to me totally inconsistent with trade union principles.'[33]

Scargill became locked in a propaganda war with moderates and the Coal Board as the men went to a ballot over the productivity scheme. Wilf Miron, director of the East Midlands coalfield and a member of the Board, argued that the real objection to the scheme was that it would reduce the power of the militant Marxist minority within the NUM to wage industrial strife. 'The saboteurs of the social contract' could not overthrow the country's way of life through the ballot box, 'so these latter-day Lenins, small though they are in number, are apparently setting the stage for another confrontation and strike.'[34] This rant, unfortunately delivered at an ample black-tie dinner, did nothing to help the NCB win the ballot. But Scargill would have been even more intrigued to know what Miron, a lawyer by training rather than a mining engineer, was up to in private.

In December 1973, he sent Derek Ezra, chairman of the Coal Board, a secret report on industrial relations in the mining industry. He warned that 'the strategy of the NUM executive will become increasingly politically-orientated and that its Left Wing (Commu-

nists, Marxists and their ilk, however organizationally fragmented)
will maintain a unified strategy towards the ideological end – the
overthrow of the present system.' He named the left-wingers, singling
out Scargill 'a key figure – he aims to succeed Gormley as president'.
To 'emasculate' the national power of the NUM, Miron proposed a
return to locally negotiated pit or district incentive schemes which
would restore the authority of moderate local officials they had lost
after the introduction of national wage rates in the sixties. The operational aims of the Board, he argued, should be 'to limit the future
manning of the industry to restrict, to neutralize, alien or subversive
political influences' and to recruit as many employees outside the
NUM as possible.[35]

Scargill would have been appalled at sections of this document,
which was also destined for the eyes of Industry Secretary Peter
Walker. But he would have been privately pleased that 'the class
enemy' saw him as the heir-apparent to Gormley. The national Left
certainly did not see it that way. It was regarded as 'the natural thing'
that McGahey, more senior and by now vice-president, would take
over the presidency. Scargill's behaviour at Left gatherings was giving
grounds for apprehension. 'He always seemed to want to appear
further Left than anyone else,' recalls Terry Thomas, then a lodge
secretary at Brynlliw colliery, and later president of the South Wales
area. 'It was more or less taken for granted that McGahey would be
the Left candidate. I can recall Arthur Scargill in the Left meeting
saying that he would support that – *provided his area allowed him to
support it* [my italics]. 'But there was a feeling that the Yorkshire area
would demand that he stand as candidate. I think he would have been
put to the test had we as a Left chosen McGahey as candidate to
succeed Gormley.'[36]

Allen, guru of the national Left, records that after 1974 the unity
of the Left areas was 'fractured'. Faced down by Gormley's adroit
use of his presidential authority, the Left was unable to mobilize the
union on any issue at variance with the Labour government's policies.
Moreover, with Gormley offering sympathetic advice, ministers
framed their strategy with containment of the NUM Left in mind.
Thwarted externally, the revolution began to devour its children.
Allen concedes there were personality differences. 'Arthur Scargill
had intruded as an official leader with national importance with the
speed of a projectile, and had disturbed the fairly settled leadership
relations established during the struggles in opposition. The mantle

of unofficial leader which had been borne my Michael McGahey was carried less securely after Scargill became president for the Yorkshire area.

'Rival Scargill and McGahey camps emerged in the union, and the union's recurrent crises were all blamed on personal rivalry between the two.' Relatively minor differences were transformed by the press into mutual hostility and 'unfortunately between 1974 and 1979 the main persons in this scenario tended to act out the imagery which was created by the media'. Scargill and McGahey felt under attack from each other, and virtually lost the ability to talk to each other. 'McGahey began to perceive Scargill's activities as a form of adventurism, while Scargill felt isolated and shunned. The quality of his contributions was overshadowed by a suspicion about his motives. He felt impelled to act independently.'[37]

Naturally, the impish Gormley stirred the pot with a vigour. From time to time he hinted that he might retire early. No annual gathering of the NUM was complete without an eve-of-conference splash story in the *Daily Express* written by his close friend, industrial correspondent Barrie Devney, yelling: 'I Quit! Says Joe.' It wasn't just tweaking the Left prima donnas' ballet pumps: NUM rules now laid down that candidates for full-time office had to be under fifty-five years of age. Ultimately, the fiercely anti-Communist Gormley stayed on until his sixty-fifth birthday, ruling McGahey out of the running in 1980.

Scargill would have run against McGahey. He could have counted on the deeply 'nationalistic' vote in Yorkshire, which was more than a third of the total. And under the NUM's complex transferable vote system, he would have picked up enough second and third preference votes from other coalfields to win. He must have made these calculations, but it was wiser to maintain the polite fiction that he would support McGahey 'if Yorkshire let me' – knowing full well that Yorkshire miners would have taken a flying leap off Flamborough Head at that time if he had so urged them.

Effectively, his campaign for the top job started in January 1977 when he began publishing the *Yorkshire Miner* in Barnsley as a rival to the national paper, *The Miner*, published from London and edited by Bob Houston, who was not a natural fan of Scargill. The *Yorkshire Miner*, a brisk and newsy tabloid, was widely distributed, even to Fleet Street journalists, giving him a unique publicity platform. And though he invariably urged industrial action in the ballots held during this period, he was never called on to lead a strike while he was

Yorkshire president. He even ticked off Joan Bakewell for believing the 'popular misconception' of him as strike-happy. 'We've lost fewer working days during my presidency than at any time before. I'm a super moderate in terms of days lost. I don't believe you have to go on strike to win advances, but you have to have a militant approach.'[38]

In truth, there were few local reasons for striking. In the seven years after Energy Secretary Tony Benn signed the Plan for Coal with the NUM in 1974, 'nothing happened' argues John Walsh. Yorkshire suffered very few pit closures: only six between 1974 and 1981, and four in his last year at 'Camelot'. These were closures on exhaustion grounds, in the older, worked-out sections of the coalfield, to which the union had difficulty in objecting. Not that that prevented Scargill from seeking to keep the pits open, sometimes with more success than was merited. 'Some pits stayed open that should have shut,' says Michael Eaton.[39] 'It was an absolute farce. He used to attempt to negotiate by wearing you down.'

Around this time, Scargill claims to have been offered the chairmanship of the National Coal Board. In his revealing interview with Hunter Davies for *The Independent* in April 1993, he boasted of outliving Mrs Thatcher, press baron Robert Maxwell, Labour leader Neil Kinnock ('not a friend') – and four chairmen of the NCB. 'That was a job I could have had, by the way. In 1977, I was offered it.' In writing? 'Verbally. My wife was present.' By whom? 'By the person who had it in his power. No, I won't give his name.' The only such person is the Energy Secretary of the day. At that time, his friend and burgeoning political ally Tony Benn held that portfolio, and could have privately offered it to Scargill. If it was casual, it was an entertainment. If it was serious, it would have been an act of consummate folly. The Cabinet would have been up in arms, and the government would have been a laughing stock. Benn does not mention the episode in his diaries. It may just be another part of the Scargill myth: tantalizing his critics with intimations of greatness that cannot be disproved.

Local productivity incentive schemes were introduced in 1977, against strong opposition from Scargill. When he failed through legal action to halt the move to pit-based bargaining, he personally negotiated the Yorkshire deal. In the first year, earnings went up by thirty per cent. 'He always said that he had a better incentive scheme than the rest of the country put together. I don't think that was really the case,' said Michael Eaton. 'He wasn't really a negotiator. All he was able to do is threaten. He would say he had never seen the mood

of the men so ugly. And you would check with the people at the pit
and they wouldn't know what he was talking about.'

Scargill also sought to export the 'mass picket' strategy while running Yorkshire. The Grunwick dispute, over the sacking of 137 Asian
workers at a mail-order film company in Willesden, north London,
offered a perfect opportunity for 'another Saltley'. The strike had
begun in August 1976 as a protest against bad working conditions,
but it turned into a union recognition conflict when the strikers joined
the white-collar union, APEX. The conciliation service ACAS found
in favour of the strikers' claim for recognition, but Grunwick refused
to back down. Picketing directed against the bussing in of 'scabs'
intensified, and in mid-June mass picketing began. On 23 June 1977,
Scargill took hundreds of Yorkshire pickets down to Grunwick in
a convoy of buses. The men were paid £15 a day to compensate
for lost earnings, and £8 expenses – almost a week's net pay for some
of them.

For the miners, Grunwick was an eye-opener. Here they were not
dealing with the Birmingham police constrained by a government
anxious about the great coal strike. Here they were battling it out
with the notorious Special Patrol Group, hand-picked hard-men of
the Metropolitan Police. One Yorkshire miner told Capital Radio: 'I
was at Saltley Gates and it was a children's Sunday picnic by the side
of this.' The strike-breakers got through, and that day fifty-three of
the 2,000 pickets were arrested, including Scargill. No one was very
surprised. One of the Yorkshire branch officials predicted to a Welsh
comrade that he would be 'lifted'. Released from Wembley police
station later that day after being charged with obstruction of the
highway and the police, Scargill was 'flushed, angry and eloquent'.[40]
The editor of his *Yorkshire Miner*, Maurice Jones was 'white, trem-
bling and silent'. Later, claiming that the police had made thinly
veiled threats to his daughter, Jones fled with his family to East
Germany and had to be brought back by Owen Briscoe. With the
aid of photographs from the *Morning Star*, Scargill was able to win
an acquittal on both charges. This was not another Saltley. The
hapless Asian strikers, mostly women, never got their jobs back. The
strike was called off a year later. The SPG was later disbanded.

Early in 1980, when it was clear that Gormley would stay to the
bitter end (in his case, bitter-sweet), at a secret location in the Midlands the national Left meeting formally endorsed Scargill as the
presidential candidate. On 4 April, McGahey publicly buried his dif-

ferences, inviting Scargill to Scotland to speak at a weekend school in Perth. McGahey had been out of the race since the previous spring, when Joe Gormley ruled that no candidate over fifty-five could stand for national office. Scargill gave a flavour of his campaign platform on 1 June 1980, appearing at the Derbyshire miners' gala. He claimed that as a result of the new Conservative government's decision gradually to withdraw subsidies from the pits under the Coal Industry Bill, more than fifty pits would close. The industry would be slimmed down to between eighty and a hundred 'super-pits' with the loss of over 100,000 jobs and the closure of 130 collieries. Later that week, he turned up at Ollerton colliery in north Nottinghamshire, ostensibly to be present at the dedication of a new branch banner, but plainly in search of votes. His candidature was endorsed that day by Joe Whelan, Communist secretary of the Nottinghamshire miners.

At their annual conference in July 1980, the miners adopted a thirty-five per cent pay claim and voted unanimously to defy Jim Prior's Employment Act. Scargill warned that 'if this woman in number 10 wants to fight it will be of her own choosing, not the miners'. Mrs Thatcher took it calmly, telling the Commons it was settlements rather than claims that interested her. She noted that face workers were now earning up to £147 a week. The conference also nominated Scargill for election to the TUC general council, a sure sign of his inexorable rise. Under the old system of block voting, he was duly elected at the September Congress in Brighton by 10,478,000 votes, an outstanding showing for the first time out. He was still only forty-two. He promised to pursue the 'deeply militant and socialist' policies he had always embraced. There would be no compromises.

Later that month, the divided moderates still running the NUM executive agreed that the right-wing challenger to Scargill for the NUM presidency should be Trevor Bell, head of the union's Colliery Officials and Staff Area. It was an unwise choice. Bell, aged fifty-three, a graduate of Ruskin College, Oxford, had been the union's industrial relations officer before taking over the union's 20,000-strong white-collar national grouping. He had worked underground, at Royston colliery in Yorkshire, and he had the scars to prove it. But he was a thoughtful, slightly diffident person, out of tune with the pushy, self-confident mood of the men.

Scargill was busy with another leadership election, that of the Labour Party. He had been involved from the beginning in the secret union campaign to draft Michael Foot and stop Denis Healey. In late October, he sought to ensure that Yorkshire-sponsored MPs would vote for Foot. His coalfield area council voted to instruct miners who sat on constituency general management committees of the Labour Party to call special 'elect Foot' meetings. They also warned Yorkshire's five NUM-sponsored MPs that if they failed to toe the line they could not expect union backing when they came up for re-selection by local parties. Foot was duly elected by fellow MPs on 10 November, and the issue was forgotten. However, Scargill and the Left triumphed that same month, shifting the executive away from the existing election process involving only MPs to the new 'electoral college' in which the trade unions had forty per cent of the votes. Gormley's recommendation to maintain the status quo was thrown out by thirteen to twelve, and the union's 244,000-strong block vote was committed in favour of constitutional reform. This move was enough to tilt the balance in favour of change that proved politically disastrous, and is only now being abandoned. Incidentally, the miners were at this stage affiliating on around 20,000 more than there were men in the industry.

Gormley had his way on wages that winter. Despite Scargill's confident predictions of a strike vote over the Coal Board's thirteen per cent pay offer, the men voted by a substantial majority to accept. The miners could see that the industry was heading for big trouble. With the passage of the 1980 Coal Industry Act, the Coal Board was charged with becoming self-financing by 1983–4. Gormley had privately warned Mrs Thatcher's first energy secretary, David Howell, that the NCB could not meet this objective without cutting 'huge chunks' out of the industry. Even the industry's managers were warning of 'an explosion' if the Act's provisions were enforced. Spurred on by incentive bonuses, the miners were breaking all production records. But much of the coal was going into stock.

Scargill held a ballot in Yorkshire in January 1981, on the principle of fighting pit closures, and secured an eighty-six per cent 'Yes' vote. Of course, men were more likely to vote for the possibility of a strike than for action here and now, but it was still an impressive result, a harbinger of what the Cabinet could expect. On 10 February, Derek Ezra, chairman of the cash-strapped Coal Board, finally admitted to the mining unions his intention to meet his financial targets by closing up to fifty pits over the next five years. Gormley thought this was 'probably the most stupid statement he ever made'. It provoked an uproar in the industry, and unofficial strikes broke out in South Wales, where the closures would hit hard. Scargill said: 'Mrs Thatcher has been out to get the miners since 1972 and 1974. If she throws down the gauntlet, I can assure her of one thing. we will pick it up.' Armed with a unanimous vote for a strike ballot from his executive, Gormley demanded talks with the Cabinet. In the Commons, Mrs Thatcher stood firm, but behind the scenes ministers were advising a tactical retreat. The government was not yet ready for the final reckoning with the NUM.

As the Coal Board gave out details in the areas of which pits were to close, the unofficial strikes snowballed. Within three days, the government was indicating a readiness to talk. On 18 February, the Cabinet bowed the knee to the NUM. A shamefaced David Howell, whose rising political career would be brought to a shuddering halt, agreed to withdraw the pit closure programme, slash coal imports and provide £500 million state aid to the industry. The Left was caught on the hop. Some militant coalfields were still coming out. Gormley ordered them back. After a series of secret phone calls the Left went into reverse and called off the strikes. Scargill did not emerge with much credit among fellow hardliners from this débâcle. The truth was that despite his much-vaunted eighty-six per cent for strike action, there was little stomach for a strike in Yorkshire once the government had signalled a compromise. He knew he would not get a strike through his area council. Scargill held talks with Ezra on a loudspeaker telephone audible in other regional NUM offices, and got off his embarrassing hook that way. The incident continued to rankle years later.

There was no formal firing of a starting pistol to signal 'They're off!', but Scargill signalled the start of the NUM presidential race on 1 September 1981. At a press conference at Huddersfield Road, he produced with a flourish 'Miners in the Eighties', a twelve-page pamphlet with a bright red cover 'based on speeches made by Arthur Scargill'. It was his manifesto. Surprisingly, he had secured a highly laudatory foreword from Will Paynter, not a man normally given to hyperbole. But he described him as 'one of the ablest and most articulate trade union leaders in the country ... a recognized powerful advocate of progressive policies in the miners' union, the general council of the TUC and in the national Labour Party.' Urging support, he said: 'Progressive policies are barren without progressive leadership.'

On the back cover were endorsements from McGahey, Emlyn Williams, president of South Wales, Peter Heathfield, the Derbyshire leader, Joe Whelan, general secretary in Nottinghamshire, Jack Collins of Kent, Abe Moffat, leader of the Scottish craftsmen, and Owen Briscoe, Yorkshire secretary, all trying to outdo each other in lavish praise. It would have turned any other head but Arthur's. In a brief biographical note, he said he spent twenty years at the coal face, and 'prosecuted' for the union at public inquiries into the Lofthouse and Houghton Main disasters, where his advocacy 'won universal acclaim and earned him the title "The Miners' QC".' Coalmining was increasingly a young man's industry, and he stressed his commitment to education for miners, and his election to the TUC general council the previous year 'at the age of forty-two, one of the youngest ever representatives from the miners' union'.

Inside, Scargill outlined his version of Britain's industrial crisis, arguing that Tory policies were accelerating decline and destruction. Then it was straight into overdrive: 'Our bankrupt economy, which resembles a lunar landscape, is being steadily taken towards the ultimate holocaust of a nuclear war. There are elements inside the Tory leadership who are hell-bent on preserving private enterprise, even if it entails the sacrifice of the human race.' Clearly, he had written this himself.

He was on surer ground dealing with the industry. 'Unless the NUM take a determined stand now, the future of the industry could be severely jeopardized. Pits will be closed and thousands of jobs lost.' His own revelation that the Coal Board wanted to close fifty pits had been confirmed by Sir Derek Ezra, chairman of the NCB. And in spite of public declarations by the Tory government that the hit list had been withdrawn, there was evidence that the policy was still being pursued. 'These pit closures will only be stopped if there is a determination on the part of our membership to resist any further rape of our industry and insist that no pits should be closed unless on grounds of proven exhaustion.' The NUM should demand a signed agreement from the government and the Coal Board guaranteeing this 'no closure' policy. On pay, coal face workers should be 'at least on a par with management grades', and there should be a four-day week for all, providing 55,000 new jobs. A whole page is given to 'democratization' of the union. The 'undemocratic' national executive must be reformed by the introduction of block voting, as in conference. He did not point it out, but this would deliver an inbuilt Left majority loyal to Scargill on the executive.

Finally, he served notice of confrontation: 'We should warn both the National Coal Board and the Government that the union is prepared to use industrial action, if necessary, to protect our pits and jobs.'[41] Scargill invariably includes the get-out clause 'if necessary'. A precedent has yet to be set when it has not been deemed necessary.

Once again, as in his Yorkshire elections, Scargill benefited hugely from the divisions among his enemies. The Right could not agree on a single candidate. Gormley had tried to set up a tightly knit group of moderately-motivated men at his home in Sunbury-on-Thames some two years before the poll, but news of the plot leaked out and he washed his hands of the problem. Initially, the Right looked to Trevor Bell, the quiet-spoken head of the white-collar COSA group, and formerly the union's industrial relations officer. He was an ex-miner and had once worked underground with Roy Mason. 'But then, as the election approached, the "moderates" woke up to the fact that the lads were unlikely to repeat the experiment of electing a representative of COSA, as Sid Ford had been,' Gormley chortled.[42] A few months before voting, Ray Chadburn, president of the Nottinghamshire miners, an amiable, middle-of-the-road man but with little fire in his belly, decided to stand. Then he changed his mind, and changed it again – too late to get his own area's nomination, which went to Scargill, along with most of the rest of the coalfields. Lancashire stood out, nominating its area president, the unknown Bernard Donaghy, simply to avoid having to back 'that Yorkshireman'.

It was, as some coalfield leaders have acknowledged, 'a dirty campaign', but Scargill emerged with the most overwhelming majority accorded to a national president: 138,803 votes, or 70.3 per cent, in an 80 per cent turnout of the 248,000 members. Bell trailed a poor second, with 34,075 votes. Chadburn, the on-off candidate, was humiliated with only 17,979 votes and Donaghy picked up a mere 6,442. At forty-three, the boy from Pantry Hill had made it to the top. He had everything. The £20,000 salary. The expenses. The union house in London. The hero-worship of the men. The support of a formidable national Left machine that had worked decades to see this day. A big desk in a big office in Euston Road. An expensive car, and a chauffeur. A guaranteed seat on the TUC general council. The inside-track power of a man with a 300,000 block vote at the Labour Party conference, and a loyal nominee on the party's executive. The close political friendship of Tony Benn. And still nobody really knew what to expect.

CHAPTER VI

POWER

LONDON WAITED WITH interest to see what this man would be like. So much had already been written about him, flattering, analytical and damning, that Scargill had a job to live up to the hype. *The Observer*'s anonymous profile, actually written by its respected labour correspondent Robert Taylor, commented: 'There is more than a touch of showbiz about Scargill. In a trade union world where earnest, grey, elderly men thrive, he exudes a sense of excitement and expectancy. With his coiffured hair and neat suits, he walks about with the self-confident air of a man at the top. Like Arnold Bennett's Denry Machin, he often behaves like the "Card", identified with "the great cause of cheering us all up".[1] The photograph accompanying his feature provided another, less encouraging pointer towards the Scargill style. Photographer Jane Bown had persuaded Scargill to stand in front of the oil painting of himself, frozen in an oratorical gesture with right arm half extended and index finger jabbing at an imaginary audience. What kind of man sits for a portrait like that, and then hangs it in his office?

Some people on the NUM Left had already begun asking that question even before the votes were counted. Dr Kim Howells, MP for Pontypridd, was a humble researcher for the South Wales miners in 1981. He was sent up to Sheffield to interview Arthur, and make a video to show in the miners' clubs back home as part of the Left's campaign to secure his election. Howells made the pilgrimage to Camelot and was 'amused and shocked'. He was shown into an office 'full of portraits of himself, including a Stalinist painting of Scargill making a heroic speech from the back of a truck with adoring people all round him in the classic Socialist Realist tradition. I thought that anyone naff enough to put a thing like that on the wall must be absolutely round the bend.

'I came away feeling desperately uneasy. It was also the first time

I had met anyone who spoke to you in the third person. I thought only Royalty did that. That came as a shock.' As they talked, Howells became aware that Scargill idealized himself as 'a lone voice in the Yorkshire coalfield, a superior human being' compared to Will Paynter and Arthur Horner, who came from a traditional left-wing coalfield and were 'therefore not steeled in the struggles that he was steeled in'. Howells could scarcely believe his ears. 'It showed the most appalling ignorance of recent history, and a kind of megalomania. It disturbed me, that the hopes of the Left were pinned on someone who was so ignorant of reality.'[2]

Others had similar misgivings, particularly in South Wales, where the tradition of cultured and thoughtful militancy ran deep. Terry Thomas, now political officer of the general union GMB in Cardiff, then a member of the national Left, discloses: 'There were a lot of reservations about Arthur Scargill, expressed by a lot of people. My answer was that the responsibility of the office he will take on would tend to control him, in the same way it had controlled people like Horner and Paynter.'[3]

This was the conventional wisdom, and Gormley shared it. Scargill had established a clear image of himself, and could be seen as a strong character who knew what he wanted. But the press immediately assumed – and Scargill did nothing to contradict them – that his leadership would usher in a new era of extreme militancy in the pits. Gormley dismissed these fears. 'I believe no such thing, and for two reasons: the first is the basic commonsense of the miners themselves. They will not be led into battle unless they believe their cause is just.' They certainly wouldn't allow Arthur to browbeat them into backing 'some of his wilder flights of political fancy', nor would they forget that there were methods of deposing presidents as well as electing them.

Gormley evidently had something of a soft spot for Scargill. He reminded him of his own early days, when he was an ambitious young man in a hurry. He was a chip off the old block. He liked big cars, salaries commensurate with those paid to managers in the industry, and the good life that comes of being at the top. He did not believe Scargill was at risk of being deposed because 'men tend to mellow a little when they get power'. Scargill might have made a lot of promises about how he would never change his philosophies, 'but he will find out soon enough that you *can't* be fighting battles all your life'.[4]

Conventional wisdom met the unconventional man when Scargill's presidential victory was declared on 9 December 1981, during a break in pay talks between the NUM and the Coal Board. Gormley thought there was 'no mood for a strike' in the coalfields, but president-elect Scargill immediately denounced the Board's nine per cent pay offer as completely unacceptable, pushed for a strike ballot and warned of a repeat of the 1974 confrontation. In an interview with *The Times* the next day, he came out strongly in support of extra-parliamentary action to defeat Norman Tebbit's labour law reforms and excoriated Labour leader Michael Foot for disavowing the party's Bermondsey by-election candidate, Peter Tatchell. He demanded withdrawal from the EC, extended nationalization, unilateral nuclear disarmament and control of the media.

Scargill welcomed the setting up of the SDP as 'the best development in British politics, the best thing that has happened to the Labour Party. It has provided a siphon to take out of the party those elements that were poisoning it, because of their non-belief in socialism.' He said that if Labour right-wingers stopped their 'sabotage of conference policies' and united behind the Left 'we will not only win the next election, but be in power for evermore'. For good measure, he warned that 'all the ingredients' for a confrontation on the scale that triggered Heath's downfall were now present.'

Nobody could say they hadn't been told. Scargill had repeatedly said that he would not 'prostitute my principles' when he became president. He shouted it from a hundred platforms up and down the land during his long campaign. The activists believed him. The majority, who don't go to meetings, didn't take very much notice. They voted for the man who talked loudest and waved the biggest stick, in the sure and certain knowledge that they could rein him in if they had to. At this period, the NUM was run on an unwritten, but invariably observed, constitutional arrangement. The leaders would take union demands as far as they could, and then go to the members with a proposition – accept the offer or strike – in a secret pithead ballot. The area leaders were free to campaign for, or against, the executive recommendation. The president and general secretary normally stayed out of the fray, confining their views to *The Miner*, the official mouthpiece of executive policy.

This well-understood system of checks and balances now came under intense pressure. The shape of things to come was evident when a special national delegate conference was called within days of Scargill's victory. Hundreds of miners, many from Yorkshire, who had been bussed down to 'lobby' the conference, were allowed into

the hall by the acting president, Mick McGahey. Only three Leicestershire delegates voted against recommending a strike against the
Board's £102 million pay offer. They protested against 'pressure from
militants', adding: 'That's not democracy.' Scargill went on the
stump, addressing rallies 500 and 1,000 strong, publicly expressing
confidence that the men would vote 'Yes'.

Privately, however, he was despondent. He was not yet formally
installed as president, but the ballot was widely seen as the first test
of his leadership. He confided his fears to his driver-bodyguard Jim
Parker: 'To be honest, he said he would lose.' But, of course, it was
not his fault. 'He said they had created this situation to push him
into a ballot before he was ready. He said we would lose but you had
to fight for it. He didn't like losing – nobody does. It was the last
thing he wanted. They really didn't want to fight, the Right wing or
part of the Left wing, so it suited them to go for a ballot knowing
that we would lose it. He wanted a result, because that put him back
on his white horse, but it was too soon for him.'[6]

Gormley, who was not nicknamed 'the old fox' by the tabloids for
nothing, delivered the *coup de grâce* to Scargill's strike hopes in a
signed article in the *Daily Express*, advising the men that industrial
action would not produce 'much more than a few quid'. He doubted
whether miners earning more than £100 a week would go on
strike for so little. Later, he said he had been forced to speak his
mind by statements from left-wing coalfield leaders – of whom
Scargill had been the most vociferous – adding: 'Some people are
trying to turn it into a political argument. That creates dangers
that I don't think any trade union ought to be involved in. If we
want to change the government, we should do it through the
ballot box.'[7]

The Left howled in anguish. Scargill accused Gormley of 'an act
of betrayal without parallel in the history of the NUM', and 'collabor-
ationist use of the capitalist press'. When the executive reconvened
on 12 January, the final results had not come through because heavy
snow had impeded the ballot in South Wales. Even by the robust
standards of the NUM executive, this was a heavy session, almost
degenerating into violence. Leicestershire leader Jack Jones bran-
dished a water jug at George Rees, Communist leader of the Welsh
pitmen, who lost his glasses as he rose to respond.

Order was restored, and Gormley saw Scargill push a note across
the table to Owen Briscoe 'telling him, I believe, to move a vote of

censure against me, which he duly did'.[8] Tommy Bartle, the Durham craftsmen's leader, quickly moved an amendment simply 'noting' correspondence on the issue, which carried thirteen to twelve. The next day, the old fox knew he had won his last battle against the Left. The ballot had gone his way by fifty-five per cent to forty-five. 'The Press lads were keen for it to be seen as a personal defeat for Arthur. Some also wondered if it was "a victory for Maggie Thatcher and her policies".' Gormley demurred, arguing that the miners simply took a rational view about an industrial situation. 'But I did also say that no leader comes to office blessed with complete wisdom. I had to learn my lessons as I went along. Arthur will also have to learn his lessons as he goes along.'[9] As he took a pint of black and tan in the Jolly Gardener (neither a Left pub nor a Right pub, but *Joe's* pub) he was still sanguine about Scargill being a national 'politician' susceptible to the responsibilities of office.

But it was a bitter blow, nonetheless. Within the union, the scapegoating of Gormley served to shift some of the blame away from the poor performance of the Left coalfields and the incoming president. Yorkshire had performed better than at the last strike ballot – sixty-six per cent for strike – but the vote was way down in Scotland and South Wales, where pits 'saved' in the dispute-that-never-was in 1981 were now closing rapidly.

Gormley formally bowed out on 12 March, with a 'golden handshake' of £35,000, a £12,000 a year pension, his black Daimler Sovereign limousine and his luxury union home at Sunbury-on-Thames on a peppercorn rent. He was an unrepentant critic of Scargill's politics to the end, telling reporters summoned to a briefing in Workington, Cumbria, at the close of his last executive meeting: 'I have been a fighter. I have been an anti-Communist all my working life and my political life. And I am a damned sight more opposed to those who are more ultra-Left than the Communist Party.'[10] He saw a danger in poor attendance at branch meetings of the NUM, which was allowing the ultra-Left to make inroads. To some extent, this was true, but the fault did not lie entirely with the militants. Ever since the mid-sixties, when wage negotiations shifted to national level, there was less and less for the branch to do, and there were fewer reasons to attend branch meetings. Attendance fell from around 200 to no more than twenty. A strike of the kind led by Scargill in the late fifties to enable men to attend union lodge meetings would have been unthinkable in the eighties.

The day after Gormley's press conference, Scargill bid goodbye to Yorkshire with a valedictory address peppered with threats of industrial action against the industrial relations legislation being pushed through by Norman Tebbit. The Employment Bill would eventually compel all union bosses, including Scargill, to be elected in a secret postal ballot, evening up the odds between him and his rival, John Walsh. Despite the rhetoric, this was a relatively peaceful period for the new president.

Not for long. His arrival at 222 Euston Road was greeted by the NUM's staff, of whom there were about thirty, with a mixture of optimism and anxiety. Most of the staff, who ranged from clerks to research and industrial relations officers and an office manager, were members of the NUM. They had voted overwhelmingly for the militant Yorkshireman in the presidential ballot, which was all the more surprising since his moderate rival, Trevor Bell, had worked among them as industrial relations officer for a number of years. So they were getting the man whose policies they had endorsed. Except one, which had not emerged as an issue in the campaign, but which had been at the back of Scargill's mind for a long time.

Steve Bundred, a young research officer at Euston Road, a thoughtful Scouser with a ready horse-laugh, had backed the new man, but now had misgivings: 'There was a degree of optimism because, although Joe was popular among the staff, Arthur was seen as an exciting, interesting leader who would be good fun to work for.

'But there was anxiety also, because it was always believed that he would want to move the office out of London. Many people thought that they would lose their jobs. It wasn't treated as an inevitability, and Scargill took great pains to ensure it wasn't treated as inevitable because he started looking round for other premises within the London area. But the significant point was that he never moved his family down. He never looked for a family home.'[11] Instead, Scargill fixed himself up with a smart bachelor pad in the Barbican, on the fortieth floor of the Shakespeare Tower, to which outsiders were very rarely invited.

In the office, certain things did change practically overnight, noted Bundred. 'The atmosphere changed very quickly. By his words and deeds Arthur demonstrated from the very beginning a deep distrust of and prejudice against London and all its works, and all who lived in it. It seemed very strange to me that someone like him could hold such strange views.' Petty issues came to the fore. The Christmas bonus of £50 a year was summarily scrapped. 'It was such a tiny sum in terms of the union's finances, but a significant message in intent and practice. The staff were very pissed off. They took it, they accepted it, but they didn't like it.'

Scargill exhibited a 'general distrust' of the staff. 'For instance, it was common practice for the Areas to invite named members of staff from time to time either to events to celebrate their centenary or to speak to their weekend/summer schools. Joe never troubled about that. He welcomed it. Arthur introduced a practice whereby all such invitations had to be referred to him, and could only be accepted on his say-so. It just seemed petty and insecure.

'It hinted at insecurity, which was amazing given the scale of the majority he just had in the election. Sometimes he would say yes and sometimes he would say no. He may well have had his own reasons. Some people he trusted to say the right things when they were mixing with the rank and file and other people he could not trust. In practice, he mostly said yes. It was the degree of control he wanted to exercise.'

In Gormley's day, the NUM headquarters was sometimes like a bazaar. Though there was a general security and handyman at a counter just inside the main double glass doors, those who were known to the union – particularly those known to be supportive – could walk straight in. On the ground floor, behind a vast statue of miners at the coalface, lay the library. On the first floor, the staff had their offices. On the second floor, separated by the 'bridge of sighs' over a reception area, were the spacious suites for the president and general secretary, each with a secretary in an outer room. Lawrence Daly occasionally entertained guests in his office over a bottle of his favourite Antiquary whisky. Gormley preferred brandy in his lair. Their offices overlooked the busy Euston Road, and the blinds were usually half drawn. Especially after a heavy night the night before.

Scargill ended that open society. 'He made it like Fortress Euston,' recalls Bundred. Suddenly, there was 'an attitude of fear' in the building 'and nobody could ever work out what he was afraid of'. The new president 'controlled everything in a way that Joe Gormley didn't find necessary. For example, he used to open all the post, all the mail. The post was all opened and taken up to him, and he would decide where it would go and who would deal with it.'

In May, only four weeks after he moved in, the worst fears of the staff were confirmed. A motion from the left-wing Kent coalfield appeared on the draft agenda for the annual conference, calling for

the head office to be situated in the coalfields. Scargill had privately
floated the idea many months, if not years, before and there was
'general approval' in Yorkshire, his rival John Walsh concedes. The
move was overwhelmingly approved by the conference. One delegate,
George Crawford from the Scottish coalfield, consciously echoed the
Scargill line: 'One of our great fears is that miners who go up to
London get out of touch. They can be seduced by the life there.
London is a prostituting place.'

The existing building, put up in 1960 as a 7,000-square-foot purpose-built headquarters, was said to have structural problems very
costly to put right. It is true that stone panels had an unfortunate
habit of falling off the front on to the pavement below, but that
had been fixed. Boyd Auger, the architect who later redesigned the
building, said it was constructed of reinforced concrete. He went to
inspect 222 Euston Road, and found Scargill had a desk but no chair,
and they went on to meet McGahey, who appeared to have drink
taken. 'He didn't want to leave London at all.'

Scargill didn't meet the office staff about the move until January
1983, though Sheffield had been mentioned in *The Times* in mid-June
as 'the city most favoured by Mr Scargill . . . who still has a home
in Barnsley'.[12] In the interim, relationships within the office got 'more
and more sour', as staff believed that a wholesale clear-out was on
the cards. Scargill denied that, telling the *Sheffield Morning Telegraph*:
'Every member of staff has been approached by me, at least three
times, and asked to keep their jobs and move to Sheffield when the
relocation takes place.'[13]

This was not how the staff saw it. In a press release issued on 10
January 1983, they said: 'With characteristic modesty, Arthur Scargill
has told the Press that he is "the best President the NUM has ever
had and the most compassionate towards his staff". His staff, on the
other hand, believe that like the worst capitalist employers he is trying
to force them to leave their jobs before the union moves its office to
Sheffield in order to avoid having to meet severance and transfer
payments.'

Plainly, the honeymoon was over. The outraged staff, who
later staged a half-day protest strike against Scargill, listed twelve
grievances. An agreement on overtime pay had been torn up. Staff
were being forced to go over to monthly pay. The Christmas bonus
paid since 1956 had been scrapped without consultation, though Scargill told the press his staff were 'happy'. A report on head office

finances commissioned from accountants Peat, Marwick and Mitchell containing 'false allegations against staff' was being kept secret. Scargill failed to have staff liaison meetings.

And under the heading staff procedures: 'Mr Scargill's vendetta against Head Office staff has at times descended to the most puerile and paranoic [sic] levels. The names of all incoming telephone callers are recorded on a central log. A secret record is kept of the time at which all workers arrive and leave each day. Written authorization is required for the purchase of tea and coffee. Staff members suddenly taken ill, or with long-standing medical appointments, require his personal consent to be absent from the office.' Small wonder that when the move came in April the next year, less than a handful of staff opted to move to Sheffield. Redundancy notices went out to staff on 18 January.

While this disgraceful treatment of his staff was going on behind the scenes, Scargill was in triumphal mode at the annual conference in Inverness in July 1982, arguing that the unprecedented vote for him was a demand for a break with the past, a demand for a different kind of leadership. In his first presidential address, he sought to lay down a new contract between the men and himself. 'Members have every right to demand total commitment from me as President, and to insist that I prosecute Resolutions passed at this Conference. Loyalty, however, works both ways. I also have every right to demand total support from the members of this Union,' he insisted.

This novel concept emerged from his own overpowering personality. There was no support for it in the rule book or in the conventions of the union. No such 'right to demand total support' (author's italics) could or should find a home in the rules and practices of a democratic organization. Scargill had a right to lead, and to invite his members to follow. They had a right to elect him, and to follow his leadership if they wished. But they always knew they had the final veto of a ballot, which by custom and practice had become an annual event. This is the critical distinction between Scargill's subjective view of his role and powers, and the objective reality. He imagined he could simply demand blind loyalty. The men knew differently. In the last analysis, they had a veto over Scargill, and the executive *and* conference decisions. It was bound to end in tears, as it did during the great strike.

Scargill paid lip service to the ballot. This paragraph of his keynote presidential address continued: 'Leadership is only as strong as the backing it receives from the rank and file – and if, at the end of the day, the Union's claims cannot be met through negotiation, we have every right to demand your backing in an individual ballot. Given that support all the demands of this Union can become a reality.' In the Scargill lexicon, nobody ever asks. Everything is demanded. Hence his insistence on 'the right to demand your backing'. Again, no such right exists within the NUM constitution. He has a duty to consult the members in a ballot before industrial action can begin. He has no 'right to demand backing'. To grant such a right would be to elevate his personal whim to the status of a dictatorial order.

However, these thoughts did not intrude at Inverness. His speech was given a standing ovation, and the conference went on to adopt a thirty-one per cent pay claim. Scargill also secured endorsement of a move from the Durham coalfield for amalgamating some of the small, craft-based areas of the union. This seemingly innocuous resolution was hotly contested by the moderate rump. It spelled the end of their long hegemony on the national executive. When delegates removed Ray Chadburn from the TUC General Council and put McGahey in his place, it was a clean sweep for Scargill. The union machine was, if not in his pocket, at least responsive to his wishes. Sid Vincent, secretary of the Lancashire miners, who had opposed the lurch to the Left, showed himself a political weathervane. 'I have decided if you can't beat them, join them,' he shamelessly announced from the rostrum.

Scargill's winter strategy emerged at an evening social for Scots and Welsh delegates. *The Times* reported: 'Soundings among the delegates this week suggest that it would be difficult at present to secure in a pithead ballot the 55 per cent majority required under rule to mount an all-out strike over pay. When the issue of wages is linked to closures, a different picture emerges.' Despite the 'success' of the 1981 bout of militancy, 18,000 jobs had gone in eighteen months. With the Selby super-pits coming on stream, the Coal Board had made no secret of its desire to close down twelve per cent of existing high-cost capacity – equivalent to thirty pits employing perhaps 20,000 men.

This was the gauntlet that Scargill could see at his feet, even if it was not immediately visible to everyone else. His strategy, *The Times* added, 'aims to make a critical connection in miners' minds between jobs, investment and pay through an unprecedented campaign of pithead propaganda, building up to a ballot in the autumn that would give NUM leaders the necessary authority to call strike action'.[14]

The NCB had always denied the existence of a 'hit list' of pits facing closure. Scargill always insisted that such a list was secreted away in Hobart House. Baulked of the official list, he fashioned his own. In late August 1982, he went through the NCB's monthly computer abstract of financial performance for each pit. By dint of choosing the financially weakest performers, he came up with a hit list of forty-six 'uneconomic' pits, which then appeared on the front page of The Times. Scargill was quoted as saying: 'We are rapidly approaching crunch time. We have to make up our minds whether we are prepared to stand and fight. If the miners listen to my advice, they will agree to a massive campaign in a pithead ballot. I feel confident that they will give us the votes that we require to save our industry and our jobs.'[15]

The Scargill hit list caused uproar, not least in the coalfield NUM offices, where local leaders felt they were being upstaged. The NCB continued to deny the existence of any national list, saying pit closures were dealt with locally. Phil Weekes, director of the South Wales NCB area, memorably described it as 'more of a miss list than a hit list'. But within two years, practically all the collieries he named had fallen silent.

On 5 October, a special delegate conference rejected the Board's 8.5 per cent pay offer, and imposed an overtime ban beginning a week later as a prelude to a strike ballot on 28 October. It was not a popular move in the pits. Men who now relied on incentive bonus payments for a third of their wages stood to lose £40 a week, and they did not like it. Nor was the sudden imposition of the ban a vote-winner. Six pits in Durham refused to implement it, and Dawdon branch secretary said: 'We will follow common-sense leadership, but not a dictatorship.' It was all happening too quickly.

Scargill had an ecstatic reception when he addressed huge rallies in Cardiff, Birmingham, Sheffield, Newcastle, Edinburgh and Nottinghamshire in the run-up to the ballot, his first since becoming president. But he was speaking only to the activists. At best, the strike road show reached only one in ten of the 220,000 pitmen.

The average miner was now aged thirty-nine and earned £8,000 a year. He had a mortgage and a car in the drive. More than half the men in the industry had no direct experience of the big strikes of a decade earlier, and they were unhappy about pay being linked to closures. The NCB circulated to the coalfields a letter from Industrial Relations Director James Cowan to Lawrence Daly pointing out that redundancies had not been mentioned in the wage claim, and the offer was not conditional on closures. Scargill countered with a lurid claim that the Board was 'looking for the slightest sign of weakness so that the mad dogs of pit butchery can be unleashed'. In a special edition of *The Miner*, now edited by Maurice Jones, he urged the miners: 'Fight like Men.'

They did. They fought him. By a margin bigger than the Right had dared to hope, the miners decisively rejected the Scargill strategy, voting sixty-one per cent to thirty-nine against giving him authority to call a strike. It was a devastating blow, and Scargill found all manner of excuses to explain it away. Producing more 'leaked documents' from the Coal Board, he now said seventy-five pits employing 50,000 men faced closure. If these documents had been available when the men voted, he argued, the result would have been different. Three weeks later, the NCB did confirm plans to close sixty pits by 1991, and Scargill, appearing before the Commons Select Committee on Energy, called on MPs to sack the entire Coal Board for 'duplicity and deliberately lying'.

Defeated in the field, he returned to the domestic fray, turning the tables on his executive critics to secure the move of NUM headquarters to Sheffield. In a presentation that 'bamboozled the lot of us', according to one right-winger, he won overwhelming backing for the sale of 222 Euston Road for £2 million to an American company, the Thurston Corporation. Most of the thirty-six staff accepted pay-offs ranging from £2,000 to £17,000. The move was scheduled for April 1983 – only a year after his takeover of the top job. The NUM leased temporary offices in a tower block before moving into their £3.8 million new site in the city centre, built with the aid of substantial grants from Sheffield City Council.

With Scargill on the rack of a ballot defeat, the government began to think seriously about bringing the coal industry into a tighter financial discipline under a new chairman. The incumbent, Norman Siddall, retired in mid-1983, and Mrs Thatcher signalled her private preference for Ian MacGregor, chairman of the British Steel Corporation, to take on the job. He had brought capacity into line with demand at BSC, shedding tens of thousands of jobs in the process.

Scargill, who had walked out of consultation procedures in the coal industry, promised mayhem if MacGregor was appointed.

A 'stay down' strike over the closure of Ty Mawr/Lewis Merthyr colliery stopped South Wales in early March 1983, threatening walk outs in Scotland and Yorkshire. Events forced Scargill's hand into another ballot, which he lost by the same margin as before, sixty-one to thirty-nine, despite warning the men: 'It's now or never . . . this is the final chance – while we still have the strength – to save the industry.' Scargill was unrepentant, insisting that the men would respond to the call 'that we shall inevitably make' on the run-down of the industry. Meanwhile, he prudently ended his year-long boycott of consultations with the NCB. At the same time, and without fuss, he let proposals go forward to annual conference that would compel union officials to stand for office every five years. Except for those, like him, already in office on 1 August. This held out the prospect of him remaining president until the year 2003, when he became sixty-five.

Scargill finally shook the dust of the capital off his feet on 16 April, saying: 'I have been president for a year and 10 days. That is a year and 10 days in London too long.'[16] 'My only regret is that we did not leave sooner. London is a place where you can very easily get sucked into the system, and I have no intention of allowing that to happen.' The colossal statue of naked miners hewing coal, 'Vigour of Youth, Wisdom of Experience', was lifted out of the Euston Road entrance hall by a crane, while the president posed for the cameras and indulged his contempt for the capital. *The Times* observed: 'The miners will not miss London. The feeling is probably reciprocated.'

With the June general election in the offing, Scargill likened the prospect of a second term for Mrs Thatcher to Germany under the Nazis, promising to oppose it. As he looked forward to a government headed by Michael Foot – whose election as party leader he had supported – Scargill gave the Labour Party £375,000 from the NUM's political fund to fight the Tories. He knew where the traditional sympathies of the miners lay, even if he had for the most part backed losers in the Labour Party over the years.

His political partnership with Tony Benn dates back to 1973, when Scargill originally revealed that his heart's desire was to see Benn in Number Ten. Not surprisingly, Benn warmed to the provincial savant. He first heard him speak publicly on 10 May 1975, at an anti-Common Market rally in Barnsley, and marked his powerful speech. On Friday, 13 June 1975, as Energy Secretary, he attended the Houghton Main disaster, in which five men died, with Scargill, observing in his diary that 'the only time working class people are allowed to become heroes is when they are trapped, dying or dead'.[17] Being at Energy brought him into contact with Scargill regularly and a genuinely close friendship blossomed. Scargill gave him a miners' banner to hang in his office. Benn had a lot of time for McGahey, but Arthur was 'really of a different order . . . a very fluent guy'.[18] The Scargills dined at Benn's home occasionally, and Arthur confided in late 1978 that Gormley was about to retire early, so, Benn noted in his diary, 'he is busy campaigning all over the place for the presidency of the NUM'.[19] This was another of the old fox's false alarms, but it dates Scargill's determination to run nearly two years ahead of McGahey being ruled out of the race.

The politicking increased after Labour's electoral defeat. On 28 November 1979, the Scargills had dinner with the Benns in the House, and the talk fell to serious matters. 'We talked about the leadership. Arthur thought that, if there was an election in July and Denis was elected, there would be an opportunity to dislodge him after an electoral college had been established.'[20] Benn noted: 'That may be the best strategy.'

The following summer, Benn marched between Scargill and McGahey at the Durham miners' gala, publicly cementing the political friendship. And when the battle for the Labour Party deputy leadership began in earnest, Scargill did not hesitate to throw his considerable weight behind Benn. In February 1981, on the day that the Coal Board announced its swathe of pit closures, Scargill found time to lunch with Benn, who found him 'tremendously bouncy and cheerful' that his pit closure predictions had been proved right. Scargill told Benn: 'If you can pick up the same votes in the NUM for the deputy leadership that I am hoping to pick up for the presidency, that will withdraw a quarter of a million NUM votes from Healey and that would do the trick.'[21]

Joe Gormley was fundamentally at odds with Scargill, and fought with characteristic cunning to prevent the NUM's block vote going to Benn, with whom he had signed the Plan for Coal in the halcyon days of 1975. Gormley, who had long experience on the Labour Party national executive committee, backed Denis Healey, arguing: 'I do not see why we should upset the bloody apple cart. As a party, we cannot afford to keep being torn asunder by these personal ambitions.'[22] Gormley ruled out of order a Scargill move to commit the NUM conference into supporting Benn, but he kept coming back. In June, he swung his Yorkshire area behind an emergency motion for a Foot–Benn ticket, which failed by only twelve votes at the national conference the following month in St Helier, Jersey.

Soon after, Gormley announced his decision to retire, and his influence began to wane. Scargill jumped back in and succeeded in getting a coalfield ballot – not an individual vote, but a poll of those attending branch meetings that was then aggregated up so as to 'represent' the views of the entire membership. By this advice, he won a majority of more than two to one for Benn, and he picked up the NUM's 244,000 block vote. It was almost 'enough to do the trick', as Scargill had predicted seven months previously. Healey only just scraped home, taking 50.4 per cent of Labour's electoral college votes on 27 September 1981, with Benn on 49.6 per cent. It was, as Benn said, only 'an absolute whisker of a difference'[23], and he had Scargill to thank for almost getting him there. Even then, Scargill refused to concede defeat, arguing that the party constitution permitted an annual election.

Benn was also the repository of Scargill's innermost thoughts. Over a reflective lunch the week after the deputy leadership election he told Benn he was 'considering the possibility of a merger between the NUM and the TGWU, in which case he would run for General Secretary'.[24] Benn did not comment on this astonishing – preposterous, even – notion. To imagine that he could just walk into the TGWU, with its tightly controlled political machines of Left and Right, and make the running for the top job, was absurdly naïve. It was, however, in keeping with his self-assessment. It was often remarked that Scargill did not like to be vice-president of anything. Benn did note Scargill's further suggestion that both the miners and the transport workers should increase their affiliations to the party in order to strengthen the vote at the 1982 party conference. This was of course possible at the time. Not a few unions were affiliated on a larger membership than they actually had. The NUM was one of them. It still is.

Never one to give up, in June 1982 Scargill told Benn he 'must stand' against Michael Foot as party leader that summer.[25] Benn was non-committal. Walter Greendale, the Hull dockers' leader and Chairman of the TGWU executive, was 'more doubtful', presumably because he knew the union line-up for Benn as deputy leader would be virtually impossible to reassemble.

Benn sympathized with Scargill's industrial dilemma, and thought he would be shown to be right in the end. Interestingly, he characterizes the NUM demand for thirty per cent pay rises as 'Scargill's demand', but he finds the sight of the press rubbing their hands with glee at Arthur's humiliation in the October 1982 ballot both offensive and wrong. 'He won't be humiliated because he knows that, since the miners have voted down industrial action, the Coal Board and the Government will be able to ride over them completely: there will be pit closures, and the whole coal expansion plan will be set back in favour of a massive expansion of nuclear power. Although Arthur may be attacked in the short run, he will be shown to be right in the long run.'[26]

This is the defence consistently mounted in support of Scargill: that 'he was right'. And of course, in terms of assessing the likely run-down of the British coal industry, he *was*. But he was saying no more than most informed industrial commentators had been saying for years. The Coal Board frequently admitted as much. Other energy union leaders made similar predictions. After the 1972 strike, Lord Robens predicted that fifty pits would close. He was proved more than correct. Ten years later, Norman Schofield, president of the British Association of Colliery Management, foresaw a 'free market' in energy supply, with indigenous coal output falling from 120 million tonnes a year to only fifty million tonnes – a prediction already surpassed by events. Successive chairmen of the NCB, and later British Coal, have consistently foreseen a smaller, more efficient industry. Leadership surely lay in coming to terms with that contraction, as Gormley had argued, rather than standing like a latter-day King Canute in the pit yard demanding that technological, economic and political change comes to a halt at the gate.

Benn shared the top table with Scargill at the Durham miners' gala in July 1983, after the election in which he lost his seat. Afterwards, they talked in Benn's hotel room, where Scargill expressed his disappointment that his political mentor had not got a safe seat. Out of parliament, he was not eligible to stand for the party leadership, bringing Scargill's dream of Prime Minister Benn crashing down in ruins.

In any event, the industry's problems were becoming more pressing. Norman Siddall, chairman of the NCB, had warned the union that 'we are producing too much coal, too expensively'. Sources within the Board indicated that fifteen pits would close, with the loss of 15,000 jobs, in the current financial year ending 31 March 1984. More than three billion pounds had been invested to bring on stream forty-two million tonnes of new capacity, and Siddall insisted: 'We must pull out of the hopeless pits which are preventing the industry from adapting itself to the needs of the market.'[27] Within days came news of Ian MacGregor's appointment as chairman-designate of the Coal Board, which sent a shiver down the spine of both sides of the industry. Even the coal managers, adopting Scargill's language, warned that they would not be with him 'should it become obvious that his objective is to butcher the coal industry'.

Thatcher's massive poll victory on 9 June 1983 confirmed that there would eventually be 'the mother of all battles' between her and Scargill, two conviction politicians who were in many ways two sides of the same coin. She could brook no challenge to her authority and publicly at least, would not admit to a U-turn in strategy. He prided himself on refusing to compromise in any way, a character defect that he elevated into a principle which could not be 'prostituted'. The appointment of MacGregor signalled that these two powerful personalities were now on collision course. Scargill showed every sign of relishing the prospect. He clashed with Len Murray, general secretary of the TUC, who said Scargill's threats of extra-parliamentary action and political strikes were 'daft'. He met the new energy secretary, Peter Walker, and dismissed the talks as a waste of time, claiming: 'They want to smash this industry and sack 70,000 miners.' The political historian of the Yorkshire miners, Andrew Taylor, wrote at this time: 'History shows that there will come a point, as their leaders predict, where the miners will take a collective decision to retreat no further and to stand their ground and fight.'[28]

The NUM annual conference took place in Perth a month after polling day. In his presidential address, Scargill was in a more reflective, less demagogic mood. 'Above all, the responsibility for the two ballot results and what they indicate lies with the union itself, and with our failure over the past twenty years to "politicise" our membership, so that we all understand the economic policies of this or any government, and the implementation of those policies by the National Coal Board.'[29] He conceded that 'the lure of redundancy payments' had made a big impact, and men were now willing to 'sell their jobs' – aided by some NUM branch officials. He admitted that he had taken his members too much for granted, 'something which we must never do again'. It was the nearest he ever came to saying he might have been wrong. He dismissed MacGregor in one sentence as 'Mrs Thatcher's hatchet man brought in to close as many pits as possible'. With sixty million tonnes of coal in stock, he warned, 'We are now dealing with forces that intend to ride over us – and only direct action will stop them from doing that.'

The union adopted a claim for 'substantial' pay rises – a complete shift away from the early Left insistence on a set figure which would tie the executive's hands. With an effective pro-Scargill coalition in power, Scargill no longer needed a negotiating straitjacket. Nor did he want one. Delegates had just endorsed the rule change that made him president for life on £27,000 a year. But the mood of the conference was downbeat. Few delegates thought that the men were ready for a strike; yet they unanimously backed a resolution that called for a pithead ballot on all-out strike action 'at the appropriate time' when MacGregor announced his closure plans. Mick McGahey conceded that after two ballot defeats there was a credibility gap between the leaders and the membership, and Yorkshire president Jack Taylor admitted: 'It is not going to be easy.'[30]

Shortly after conference, Scargill cut his last remaining link with the great whore – London – by ending his brief and inglorious career on the TUC General Council. The union's diminishing size meant that it only qualified for one seat, and Scargill gave it to McGahey, saying: 'I don't believe one should hog all the positions to oneself. I have always believed in collective leadership.' This was rather less than half the story. He was livid with the TUC because his fellow union leaders had rejected a crackbrained scheme to split the NUM – for TUC purposes only – into two 'unions', one representing the peripheral coalfields such as Scotland and South Wales and the other representing the central coalfields such as Yorkshire and Nottinghamshire. By this device, he could have kept two seats on the general council.

Why he should actually want to retain two seats was beyond the understanding of his fellow general councillors. Scargill made little effort to conceal his contempt for the TUC's ruling body, which Joe Gormley once described as 'nothing more than a talking shop'. Scargill's real bind, however, was that he wasn't treated in the manner he expected. Elected in September 1980, with 10,478,000 votes under the old patronage system of election, he was required to conform with Congress House traditions. He had to sit in the new boy's chair at the general council table. And under the iron law of 'Buggins's Turn' he had to serve an apprenticeship on the Social Insurance and Industrial Welfare Committee before he could be promoted to the more grandiose Economic Committee or the TUC's 'Inner Cabinet', the Finance and General Purposes Committee. Although the rules were identical for everybody else (save the two biggest unions, the TGWU and the engineering workers), this irked his self-esteem. The Social Insurance Committee handled health and safety at work, trade union involvement in pension funds, and accidents in the mines – issues near to the heart of the NUM.

Lord (then plain Lionel) Murray, general secretary of the TUC at the time, said Scargill expected to go on the top committees. He did not 'partly because of personality but mainly because everybody had to serve a sort of apprenticeship. He regarded it as distasteful to serve on the Industrial Welfare Committee, for which he was eminently qualified. He was a brilliant man in terms of compensation questions, absolutely first class. He was deeply critical of the whole Citrine tradition that developed as a result of the general strike, and saw it as corrupted by that tradition. Therefore he had to keep at arm's distance from the TUC and so only very reluctantly came on for that year. He never made any mark on the general council. I don't recall him speaking very much.' Murray tells the story that his deputy Norman Willis asked him about which committees he would like to join, and Scargill replied: 'I am only interested in serving on one committee of the TUC and that is the lavatories committee.' That, he added, seemed to sum up Arthur's attitude to the TUC. Murray had tried to have informal talks with the miners' leader to sort out the difficulties, but he invariably refused. It was a bad omen for the struggles to come.

Murray concedes that there was a cultural clash with Scargill. 'I am sure that the TUC had got a tendency to look for solutions to problems. It had got a reputation for intervening in industrial disputes to facilitate solutions if we could. To that extent, the view of the TUC as a body which unduly leaned to the idea of conciliation – as distinct from the idea of challenging a Government's policies by the use of industrial action – was an accurate view.'

Alan Sapper, the cine technicians' leader who acted as convenor for the highly unofficial Left grouping on the general council, was disappointed with Scargill. 'He attacked all the disciplines of the general council, all the structures. He thought they had sold the pass. The general council wasn't worth it. He felt by being on the general council it took away from him something that he had outside. I don't think he could work collectively with the general council.

'He was silly, really. He opposed things that he knew should not be opposed. For example, why has it to be Buggins's turn? Why couldn't he be president [of the TUC] after a year. He asked Chapple [right-wing leader of the electricians' union] for an under-taking to abide by general council decisions. He was outrageous against all the extreme right-wingers there, and made his dislike very apparent.'[31]

Scargill was invited to come to the TUC Left informal policy sessions, held in Sapper's office in Soho the day before general council meetings on the last Wednesday of the month. 'He said "OK, yes" and forgot about them. He was reminded, and never came,' mourned Sapper. Why didn't he accept TUC traditions? 'They weren't his customs and practices, that's why. He felt he should have been up among the good and great immediately. He wanted to be on all nine committees straight away, and he had to wait his turn. He didn't like that. That was his weakness. He had an emptiness in him, that might have been a lack of intelligent appreciation of reality and operational rules. Or it may have been an emotional lack, I don't know. I always felt he was lacking something, something essential.'

In any event, Scargill would not have been at home among the 'new realists' who were now taking over at the helm of the labour movement. The general election result, they argued, could not be ignored. The TUC had to talk to Norman Tebbit, whose labour law reforms would utterly change the landscape in which they were operating. The unions had to press their economic case in the last relic of seventies' corporatism, the National Economic Development Council. Scargill was singularly out of place in this new, pragmatic environment. Besides, the pace of activity in the coal industry was hotting up. In a valedictory interview, Siddall appealed to his suc-cessor at the NCB to continue the 'softly, softly' approach to closures that he had employed, and which had reduced manpower by 10,000 in one year. He disclosed that he had privately argued against the Cabi-net picking a fight with the miners just for a show of strength.[32]

But that is precisely what ministers were planning, indeed had been planning since the humiliation of the Heath government in 1974. If ever there was a conspiracy to have a strike, this was it. The generation of Conservative politicians who planned what Scargill would have termed 'the fightback' have now left government, and in their memoirs are perfectly candid about their motives and their actions. Nicholas Ridley says that after Saltley, 'Arthur Scargill drew the lesson that brute militant force would always secure him victory in a struggle against a Tory government. Keith Joseph learnt the lesson that such tactics must never again be allowed to prevail.'[33] While the Conservatives were still in Opposition, Joseph commissioned Ridley to analyse how a future Tory government could defeat the NUM if it were ever to try another frontal assault.

The infamous 'Ridley Plan' that followed laid the groundwork. Ridley recommended that a year's supply of coal should be stocked inside power stations. Many power stations should be converted to dual coal/oil firing, so the generating industry could survive a 'coal famine'. Haulage firms who could not be intimidated should be hired. And the police should be organized on a specially mobile base to meet the challenge of flying pickets.

His blueprint for conflict was leaked to *The Economist* in 1978, and Ridley felt obliged to apologize to Mrs Thatcher. 'She wasn't in the least put out, and proceeded to file the necessary precautions in her mind against a confrontation which she seemed to know must inevitably come one day. She knew, even as far back as 1978, that she would face a pitched battle mounted by Arthur Scargill. She knew that it would be ostensibly an industrial dispute, but in reality, it would be a political assault designed to overthrow her government. She never doubted that these were Scargill's intentions.'[34] When it came, Ridley said: 'It really was closer to a revolution than a strike . . . it was very much in the nature of a peasants' revolt, or a Luddite assault on new textile machinery, as well as a political attempt to humiliate and perhaps destroy the Government outside the Parliamentary process.'[35]

Peter Walker shared the obsession with Scargill. After the 1983 election, he was ready to step down from the Cabinet, fearing Mrs Thatcher would give him a minor post after the 1983 election. She offered him Energy, and before he could blurt out his carefully prepared demurral, she invoked the Arthur Factor. 'She wanted me there because she believed the government was about to be challenged in a major battle with Arthur Scargill, the miners' leader.'[36]

The Prime Minister stroked Walker's ego with practised guile. No one in Cabinet could conduct the forthcoming battle better than he

could. He had the political know-how and the communications skills
to sell the policy to the public, essential in a major conflict of this
kind. Industrial unrest in the coal industry was probably the greatest
threat to her government, and he was the best person to see it did
not happen. What male, middle-aged politician could hold out against
such a charm offensive? Walker capitulated on the spot. 'Put like
this, the overture was difficult to resist,' he harrumphed, reassuring
himself that if he persisted in returning to the back-benches, 'it would
be said privately that I was running scared of a scrap with Arthur
Scargill'. And he couldn't have anybody saying that.

The new energy secretary began by delving into Scargill's background, reading through several decades of press cuttings. He read
his speeches to Labour and other conferences and his leaflets and
pamphlets. It was 'probably the most thorough read-in anyone had
done on the NUM president'. Evidently he needed it. 'I quickly
realized I was dealing with a person with a close and friendly connection with the Marxists. Communist Party literature which had not
had wide circulation brought this out with crystal clarity.'[37] Walker,
mistakenly thinking Scargill still needed a sixty-six per cent majority
in a strike ballot, decided that his enemy was 'not popular enough
without having a good case. He must never be given that case.'

The best way to defeat Scargill would be to throw money at his
members. After huge public investment in the pits, productivity was
rising and future pay settlements should reflect that. But that still
left a large number of uneconomic pits. To avoid a strike, there had
to be no compulsory redundancies. Walker had been down a number
of pits while at DTI, and was horrified by conditions underground.
He felt 'genuine sympathy' with the miners, and thought they should
be offered extremely generous terms to persuade them to go. Older
men should get a capital lump sum and pensions. Younger men should
be found other mining jobs or given 'generous' redundancy.

The package was honed into a six-point programme, secretly circulated (with Mrs Thatcher's approval) round selected ministers to
avoid a leak to Scargill. A select group of ministers chaired by Mrs
Thatcher approved the strategy, leaving Walker confident that he
could win any struggle with Scargill. 'It was total nonsense to suggest,
as some on the Left and the Labour Party did, that the Conservative
government wanted confrontation, but if it was forced upon us I
intended to win. I was convinced the Cabinet had given me all the
resources I needed to guarantee that there would not be a successful

ballot for industrial action in the foreseeable future. I was right on that.'[38] He was, but he had underestimated his adversary.

Nor is he the only minister to claim credit for the successful conspiracy to ambush Scargill. Nigel Lawson, his predecessor at Energy, had while still financial secretary at the Treasury minuted his boss Geoffrey Howe in July 1981, saying the problem of the coal industry was 'essentially a political one, centring around [sic] industrial relations in general, and outmanoeuvring Arthur Scargill'.[39] Once he arrived at Energy, Lawson subordinated everything to the 'overriding need' to win a strike. Like Walker, he wasn't seeking a conflict. 'But it was clear that Arthur Scargill was, and I was determined that he should lose it when it came.'[40]

One of Lawson's initiatives was to push through the new Asfordby mine in the Vale of Belvoir against the original wishes of Environment Secretary Michael Heseltine. He did this to keep Midlands miners 'on our side'. The Duke of Rutland, then Tory leader of Leicestershire County Council, was not best pleased, but Lawson thought the development of the Vale of Belvoir was a strong factor in the Nottinghamshire miners' decision to carry on working. 'The coal they produced extended the Government's capacity to withstand Arthur Scargill's strike from months to years, if not indefinitely.'[41]

These events took place in the closing stages of Gormley's leadership. When Scargill succeeded him, said Lawson, 'a strike became inevitable. Scargill was a self-confessed class war revolutionary, uninterested in discussion about the future of the industry.'[12] He met Scargill, flushed with success in the NUM presidential ballot, in April 1982. His officials had warned him to be careful what he said because Scargill carried a tape recorder in his pocket. 'I need not have worried,' Lawson recalled, 'since he was determined to do almost all the talking himself. He spouted the most amazing nonsense, garnished liberally with spurious statistics "proving" how even the least productive British pits were highly economic by comparison with their heavily subsidised competitors abroad. It was an extraordinary meeting, at which it became quite clear to me that Scargill's concept of the truth was heavily influenced by what he found it convenient to believe. I told my officials that there was no way we would do business with him.'[43]

Lawson had been warned. Joe Gormley paid him a discreet farewell visit, and marked his card. Gormley 'described Scargill to me as an astute technician but a poor strategist, committed to subverting the government. Age and experience, he thought, might mature him. It proved a forlorn hope.'[44] Lawson clearly felt the Tories owed the old fox something. He persuaded Mrs Thatcher to give Gormley a peerage – 'the first, and probably the last time that a Conservative government has ennobled a president of the NUM'.[45] He also maintained close links with the former electricians' union boss Frank Chapple, 'who detested Scargill and was at one with me in longing for a Coal Board management capable of standing up to him'. Chapple advised him to get someone who was not afraid of Scargill. Most businessmen said they weren't, but in their hearts they were, he told Lawson after a dinner *à deux*. 'The Chapple Test was one good reason why I went for MacGregor,' he wrote.

Though he does not acknowledge his debt to Ridley, Lawson implemented his Plan. He increased coal stocks to fifty-eight million tonnes, brought in strategic reserves of vital chemicals and even set up helicopter landing sites inside power stations. He ousted Glyn England from the chairmanship of the Central Electricity Generating Board, by not renewing his five-year contract in April 1982. England had been appointed by Tony Benn in 1977, after his search for a Labour-inclined power industry executive to take over the top CEGB job unearthed England, a one-time Labour member of Hertfordshire County Council, working as chairman of the South-West Electricity Board. Lawson brought in Walter Marshall, head of the UK Atomic Energy Authority, who had once been sacked by Tony Benn in a row over nuclear policy. 'So he had no affection for Scargill's friend and ally, Scargill.'[46] And, contemptuous of the 'Derek and Joe' show that had dominated the Coal Board, he suggested to MacGregor over dinner at the Garrick Club in November 1982 that he move from steel to coal. As former chairman of the Amax Corporation, MacGregor had experience of the coal industry in the USA, where he had the reputation of being a strike-breaker. 'There was no risk of his running from Scargill,' observed Lawson. Mrs Thatcher was cool at first. MacGregor was doing a good job at British Steel, and moving him to the Coal Board 'would be highly provocative: Ian was widely seen as an over-paid, over-aged American whose main achievement at British Steel had been to slash the workforce'.[47]

Lawson wore down the prime minister's objections, and appointed MacGregor in February 1983, less than a year after Scargill's takeover at the NUM. MacGregor took over the reins from Siddall in September, later confessing that his time at BSC had been 'a warm-up'.

Now, at coal, 'if I was to do the job expected of me, I was going to be running on the ragged edge of acceptability. Or even into the area of unacceptability.'[48]

Apart from a certain shyness in some circumstances, MacGregor and Scargill appeared to have nothing in common. The septuagenarian Scots-American, educated at George Watson's College, Edinburgh, winner of a first-class degree in metallurgy at Glasgow University, who graduated from industrial Clydeside to the upper reaches of American capitalism, was the diametrical opposite of the poorly educated, self-made Marxist union activist who could not tear himself away from his provincial roots. But each brought to this great clash of philosophies an unshakeable belief that he was right.

In MacGregor, the Cabinet had found a perfect vehicle for their strategy, whose convictions meshed seamlessly with theirs. He had a straightforward attitude to unions: he would not compromise on the rights of management, and he had no time for union leaders 'whose guiding light is ideology rather than the interests of their members'.[49] Like Scargill, he came early to his convictions. Too young to be involved like his brothers, driving tramcars in Glasgow in the general strike, he broke his first strike at the age of twenty-four as a young metallurgist driving a crane at Beardmore's factory. In 1940, he went to work on tank production for Lord Beaverbrook's Ministry of Supply, first in Canada and then in the USA. Dismayed by the Attlee victory, he stayed in America after the war, working his way up through industry and winning a reputation for toughness. 'If a union leader wanted to challenge the good management of the business and wanted a scrap – then he could have it.'[50] MacGregor was chairman and chief executive of Amax when he retired in 1977, having taken the company 'from nowhere' to among the top hundred in the Fortune 500 list of businesses, with revenues of $1.1 billion. He never quite forgot British politics, and Sir Hector Laing, chairman of United Biscuits and a considerable figure in the Conservative Party, told him over a dinner party in New York one night: 'My God! You may be the person we need to get British Steel into shape.'

MacGregor re-exported his prejudices back home. His archetypal hate-figure is 'a man who needs to perform, who needs a stage, who needs an audience, who needs applause. Not all are actors or pop singers or politicians. Some are union leaders. But political motivation can also be a driving force and there were those who saw it as their role in the union movement to find a way to destroy the present economic system. The whole rag-bag of anarchists could be found in union leadership in the early seventies. And the most dangerous of all were those who combined both these drives – the craving to be a star plus the desire to destroy.'[51] Too many shop stewards, he added, suffered from 'the wrecker syndrome – a few with the theatrical overtones thrown in such as are demonstrated at their most dangerous in Arthur Scargill'.

Such was the man who told Mrs Thatcher: 'I'll help you all I can.' He assumed that by the time he was in post, Scargill 'had already decided to have his strike. All that remained to be settled was the date.'[52] Scargill had other things on his mind that week, having set the cat among the pigeons at the TUC conference in Blackpool with controversial remarks about Solidarność, the Polish labour organization. With his customary penchant for stealing the headlines during other people's conferences, he said in a letter to the Trostkyist paper *Newsline* that Solidarity was 'an anti-socialist organization who desire the overthrow of a socialist state'. He was also rather less than supportive of the TUC's official line condemning the shooting down of a Korean airliner. NUM moderates were furious that their once proud union was becoming the laughing stock of the movement, as TV cameras and reporters trailed Scargill everywhere, looking for fresh controversy. As *The Times* reported, 'The turnaround in Mr Scargill's fortunes could scarcely be greater. Elected with a landslide majority less than two years ago, and applauded before he could even get to the rostrum at previous conferences, he is now openly derided, though he remains a cult figure for a substantial proportion of delegates.'[53]

The two prospective combatants had an opportunity to size each other up at their first face-to-face talks on 14 September. They held 'a civilized meeting', and posed together for the camera. Over a buffet lunch, MacGregor told Scargill privately: 'There are things we have got to do to improve this industry, and it would be far better if we could do them together.' The chairman made a good impression all round: even McGahey paid the gruff compliment that he was 'competent'. It looked like peace was breaking out, but it was a phoney peace. Scargill insisted: 'We are not being soothed, nor are we being talked to in any way that diverts us from our course. We still firmly believe that there should be no pit closures.'

Yet the industry was on track for a £250 million loss for 1983–4, and the Coal Board had come to the conclusion that at least ten per cent of the pits would have to close. Saleable output had fallen by almost four million tonnes, and stockpiles were growing exponentially. Scargill had taken over just as coal's good fortunes ran out. He reacted by submitting a detailed pay claim which the NCB costed at about twenty per cent, and by calling a special conference on 27 October to consider an overtime ban in the industry. MacGregor countered with a 5.2 per cent pay offer, and a warning that 'we are not playing games'. Scargill returned serve with a claim that MacGregor was planning to close forty-four pits where production costs were more than £60 a tonne.

It went on like this day after day: charge and counter-charge, claim and counter-claim. At the time, most seasoned observers put it down to the usual hotting-up of the industrial temperature before a deal is done – the storm before the calm. But this time it *was* different. MacGregor was aware that the Energy Department had geared up for a long fight. His own appointment was part of the preparations. Scargill was working towards a strike in the classic manner: an overtime ban, imposed from early November, to cut into production and harden attitudes in the pits, leading towards an all-out stoppage. Scargill said: 'It is going to be a long, hard haul, but we are prepared for that.' MacGregor warned that the industry had stocks and supplies 'that will last until 1985'.

Another dispute, between the print union the National Graphical Association and local newspaper proprietor Eddy Shah, temporarily eclipsed the miners' overtime ban. The NGA had been fined £675,000 for contempt of orders not to engage in mass picketing at Shah's Messenger Group plant in Warrington, Cheshire. The NGA's £11 million funds were sequestrated under the 'Tebbit Laws' – the 1982 Employment Act. Scargill, who was watching this groundbreaking conflict with more than an academic interest, was apoplectic about the TUC's refusal to aid the print workers for fear of running into trouble with the labour laws itself. He called it 'the greatest sell-out since 1926', and the actions of the general council and Len Murray, TUC general secretary, 'the biggest act of betrayal in the history of our movement'. It was clear from this date – Christmas 1983 – that the TUC would not stand by its Wembley conference decisions to defy the employment laws, and no affiliated union could expect support from that quarter if it landed the wrong side of the law. Scargill would have expected no more, and began discreet contingency planning accordingly.

His policies were about to undergo an oblique test of opinion among the men. Lawrence Daly, the union's general secretary, was persuaded to retire early on health grounds aged only fifty-eight, to make way for Scargill loyalist Peter Heathfield, secretary of the Derbyshire miners. Heathfield was the nominee of the NUM National Left, whose meetings were now less frequent and certainly less important. The old Communists from South Wales and Scotland complained that Scargill was packing the meetings with 'young guys who were militant, but had no politics'.[54] There was probably also 'a bit of racism' in it, one regular attender concedes. 'They were dismissive of Scargill because he had no political background. And they said "how can you have a discussion with these bastards?"'

Heathfield, who at fifty-four only just qualified to stand, agreed to let his name go forward on the understanding that he would not be Scargill's patsy. 'OK, I will accept,' he told the Left gathering. 'But if anyone thinks I am going to Sheffield just to lick stamps for somebody else, they have another think coming because I'm not prepared to do that.' The Left, alarmed at the way Scargill had simply usurped Daly's function (claiming that he couldn't find him, that he was 'down at the club' so much), said: 'Thank God for that. Now we will get someone there who will take some measure of control. But it never worked out that way.'[55]

The right wing ran John Walsh, area agent in North Yorkshire, on a 'negotiation, not confrontation' ticket in the poll, which was widely seen (perhaps wrongly) also as a referendum on Scargill's developing strike strategy. Walsh, forty-six, a former Rugby League international, was a product of the Glasshoughton school of self-confident moderation that had been little heard of since Scargill's famous victory in the presidential poll. He almost pulled it off, the votes being split fifty-one to forty-nine per cent. Heathfield took office the day before he would have been disallowed on age grounds. But the hoped-for check on Scargill's garnering of power did not materialize. 'He sat back and allowed Scargill to do what he did,' said a disenchanted South Wales NUM leader.[56] Some of the votes cast for Walsh must have reflected the unpopularity of the overtime ban in certain areas. Heathfield was closely, and rightly, associated with the policy, which was now leading to 7,000 men being sent home every week because safety checks normally done during weekend overtime shifts had not been carried out. It was chaos in some coalfields. Winding enginemen, the elite of the industry, wanted to work overtime, and when one crossed the NUM picket line at Silverdale colliery, Staffs, the miners walked out on strike. Similar brush fires and 'rag-ups' broke out in other coalfields. From Scargill's point of view, things were going well. Railway union leaders were promising sympathetic action that would tie up twenty-four million tonnes of coal at the pithead. The coal industry was sliding into a strike. The Energy Secretary was confident that he had thrown enough money at the miners to avert a successful strike ballot, but could Scargill turn the tables on Peter Walker, and mount a national strike *without* a ballot?

CHAPTER VII

STRIKE!

THE GREAT STRIKE for Jobs, as it became known in the NUM, was well planned on both sides, but the actual trigger for the biggest social and political upheaval of modern times took Scargill by surprise. Even the Coal Board's industrial relations director, Ned Smith, claims that the timing of the announcement that Cortonwood pit was to close was 'inadvertent'.[1] But it was enough to set the strike ball rolling. On 1 March 1984, George Hayes, South Yorkshire area director of the NCB, told area officials of the NUM that Cortonwood, a traditionally moderate pit in the Dearne Valley employing 839 men, was to close little over a month later, on 6 April, whether the NUM liked it or not. The Coal Board in London had given him his output reduction target: 500,000 tonnes. Shutting this one loss-making pit with its annual output of 280,000 tonnes would get him most of the way there.

The announcement 'came like a thunderclap to unsuspecting Cortonwood miners'.[2] Only eleven months previously, they had been assured that the pit had enough reserves to stay open for another five years. The pithead baths had been improved just before Christmas at a cost of £40,000, and more than £1 million had been spent the previous summer on modernizing the coal washery and installing new generating plant. Miners had recently been transferred from nearby Elsecar colliery when it was closed with guarantees of work for several years. Yet not many weeks later, they were told they would be out of a job.

Hayes argued that even if the pit was allowed to work until 1989, the closure process would have to commence sooner or later; better to shut it now, so the men could look for alternative work either in the industry or outside. The NUM officials present at the talks – Yorkshire president Jack Taylor, general secretary Owen Briscoe, area agent Arnie Young and Ken Sampey, president of the pit deputies' union NACODS – did not believe him. They saw the guiding hand of Hobart House – and possibly even the government – in this precipitate closure, the first imposed shutdown since the climbdown of 1981. Jack Taylor caught his breath. 'This was the first one on uneconomic grounds, and they spelt it out in great detail, in a way a bit like a challenge.'[3] Veteran industrial commentator Geoffrey Goodman later observed: 'They saw it as a try-on in the heartland of the NUM's Yorkshire stronghold. If they were to accept the inevitability of the Cortonwood closure then, in their opinion, the door would be flung open for closures on similar grounds in other areas and in other coalfields where resistance might not be as strong as it was in Yorkshire. They saw the whole affair as a deliberate testing-ground which they dare not evade.'[4]

Ned Smith is categoric that Cortonwood was not a stalking horse. 'We were told by Peter Walker to avoid flashpoints at area level, to avoid conflict, whatever they now say about a great master plan to drive Arthur Scargill,' he insists. 'And the area directors were advised by me about that. Cortonwood was inadvertent. George Hayes and the other men in Yorkshire were supposed to have been advised, and he was not given that advice.' Hayes had argued that the NCB could not sell Cortonwood's coal. It was 'going on the ground'. If the union agreed to 'front end-load' the capacity cutback he was required to make by closing this one colliery, it would lift the burden on the whole area.[5] Hayes later claimed that Yorkshire NUM leaders, who were under pressure from a whole series of 'rag-ups' blamed on the unpopularity of the overtime ban, were looking for 'an excuse to trigger a strike. They were itching for a strike. I did not choose Cortonwood for economic reasons. I chose that pit because I knew I could transfer the men to nearby pits.'[6]

The men themselves had no misgivings. Two days after the shock announcement, 500 miners crowded into the parish hall in the pit village of Brampton. They voted overwhelmingly to fight the closure. NUM Branch Delegate Mick Carter argued: 'We had no options. If we accepted the closure, then the rest of Yorkshire would go as well.'[7] On Monday, 5 March, several hundred Cortonwood men picketed the area offices in Barnsley, where the coalfield NUM council was in emergency session. Jack Taylor, Scargill's successor at Huddersfield Road, announced that an all-out strike of Yorkshire's 56,000 miners would start at the end of that week. The council's decision was based on the authority of the 1981 ballot on action 'in principle' over closures, mounted by Scargill when he was area president and now three years old.

In the tower-block office, St James's House, in Sheffield, Scargill himself appears to have been taken off guard by the speed of events. But whether the flare-up at Cortonwood was a deliberate provocation or inadvertent, he could not resist the opportunity. Indeed, he seized it with both feet. 'The ball was passed to Arthur Scargill, and he made the foolish mistake of not kicking it into touch,' said Ned Smith. 'He decided to run with it. Do you think the Left would organise a strike at the end of winter?'[8]

The answer to that must be that the Left had determined to have a strike when the most opportune moment came. Cortonwood – a weak economic case, a moderate pit, an ambush by the Board – was not the perfect springboard for the all-out conflict that Scargill undoubtedly wanted and which many of the men felt in their hearts was inevitable. But it was here, and now, and unavoidable. And Scargill had prepared his strategy. In 1983, a week before the failed strike ballot of 8 March, he had suggested in a BBC radio interview that a ballot was not required before the union mobilized national support for a strike. Areas could use Rule 41 to call strikes in their own coalfields, through a local ballot or any other means sanctioned by their own rules. 'This could amount to a national strike but called by different, through still constitutional means.'[9] On that occasion, when his second strike call was rejected by a sixty-one per cent majority, he said defiantly: 'The leadership is looking ahead and I believe that in the not too distant future, the impact of the butchering that will take place will be seen by the members for what is it. I am convinced with the advent of the closures programme and the economic crisis, our members will respond to the call that we shall inevitably make when we call for their assistance.'[10]

There had been other pointers, one from a most unusual quarter. In December 1983, Mick McGahey buttonholed his old sparring partner Jimmy Cowan, former director of the Scottish coalfield and now MacGregor's deputy, at a Coal Board Christmas function 'and sought to alert him to both the date and the nature of the impending battle'.[11] Cowan ventured the opinion that a strike was not inevitable – even though he found Scargill almost completely irrational. He thought Scargill's fellow executive members were powerful enough to ensure that the industry was slimmed down without a lengthy and damaging strike.

McGahey suddenly became grave. He reminded Cowan of his ill health and sympathized over a family tragedy, and then warned: 'If I were you, Jimmy, for your sake and the sake of Harriet [his wife], I would get out now, because it's going to be very unpleasant. The die is cast – it's too late. The strike will take place. It will start in March with the Yorkshire area led by Jack Taylor – and Henry Richardson will look after Nottingham and make sure they join in.' An enraged Cowan accused the lifelong Communist of doing nothing to stop Scargill. 'How can you support a leader who so clearly exploits his members?' he demanded. 'I am not going to stand by and let it happen. I will fight you to the end, even if I do leave you with a broken union. That man will not be allowed to destroy the industry I have worked all my life for.'[12] Cowan also said later: 'The whole thing was calculated and planned. There was nothing spontaneous about it.'[13] McGahey has confirmed the drift of the conversation, though insisting that was in the context of a more general warning to Cowan that the appointment of MacGregor would inevitably provoke a strike.

Later investigation by Michael Arnold, the receiver called in to take over the NUM's assets towards the end of the strike, discovered further evidence of Scargill's war planning. With the crippling sequestration of the National Graphical Association over the Eddy Shah dispute still fresh in the NUM leaders' memory, a scheme had been hatched to put the union's funds beyond the reach of the courts. Arnold found that the plan had been laid to take funds out of the country – or, at least, out of apparent control of the union – in February, some weeks before the Cortonwood announcement. He told the High Court in April 1986 that this disinvestment was motivated by a desire to protect NUM assets 'from the likely consequences of defiance of the orders of this court'.[14]

Further inquiries by Gavin Lightman, QC, during the 'Gaddafi Money Scandal' five years after the strike uncovered yet more compelling evidence. On 7 March 1984, two days before Yorkshire was due to strike, but as the pits were being picketed out, Scargill chaired a meeting of the NUM executive's 'inner cabinet', its Finance and General Purposes Committee, attended by only eight other members of the executive, the finance officer Steve Hudson and Roger Windsor, chief executive officer. The minutes of this meeting record that 'following informal discussions with NUM solicitors, Brian Thompson and Partners', four decisions were taken *in camera*. These decisions instructed the union's trustees to consult with lawyers with a view to investing NUM funds in the Isle of Man, Jersey and Ireland and/or any other location deemed appropriate; to invest the funds 'in any bank and its subsidiaries'; to report these moves briefly to a meeting of the national executive the next day, and more fully at a reconvened meeting later that day in the Royal Victoria Hotel, Sheffield, to be attended by all NUM area finance officers; and to advise NUM areas of steps to be taken to locate their funds abroad. In other words, financial evasive action that assumed a major dispute was under way was planned and executed by Scargill before the executive even met to decide whether to back the Yorkshire strike call. And as the minutes of the subsequent 'Royal Vic' conference indicate, those preparations had been going on for some time. The government was not the only one who could play at contingency planning. Scargill's forward thinking was brought to Lightman's attention by the NUM president himself. He told the investigating QC: 'The message to the National Officials [of the NUM] was clear: in the rules of the forthcoming engagement with the Government [which for the union was a battle for survival] no holds [legal or otherwise] were barred.'[15]

This was the developing background to a critical meeting of the Coal Industry National Consultative Council on 6 March, called ostensibly to establish common ground between the Board and the unions for an approach to the government for tripartite talks on the future of the industry. It was doomed to failure. MacGregor had already made up his mind to go ahead with his restructuring plans, arguing: 'I can't wait for the unions. I work for the government.'[16] For his part, Scargill simply wanted to nail MacGregor into admitting that there was a 'hit list' of pits slated for closure. In this, he more or less succeeded. The NCB outlined plans for a reduction of four million tonnes in deep-mined capacity during 1984–5, bringing output into line with demand. According to the confidential CINCC minutes, Scargill pointed out that a four million-tonne reduction in the current financial year had meant the closure of twenty-one collieries and the loss of 21,000 jobs. Did the Board envisage a similar run-down in 1984–5? Jimmy Cowan admitted that the manpower reduction would be 'broadly of the same order'. Scargill pressed the Board to indicate more precisely the job losses and closures. MacGregor butted in to say this was a matter for local management. Scargill pressed on, insisting that when Selby was fully on stream 'future job losses would be on a massive scale'. He refused to back an approach to government involving cutbacks in jobs and capacity, arguing that his own exotic thirteen-point plan should be the basis of the industry's future. MacGregor suggested a joint working party to devise an agreed agenda. It was never set up. Scargill had the last word: on jobs and pit closures, the unions would be making separate representations.[17]

The nature of those representations was already becoming clear. Many pits in Yorkshire had jumped the gun and were out on strike before the official 9 March 'off'. Scargill had done his sums again, and concluded that the Board was actually planning an eight-million-tonne reduction in capacity, twice the official figure, which was based on output already reduced by the overtime ban. He was right. MacGregor had tried to pull a fast one. On that basis, Scargill projected the strike scenario of seventy pit closures and 70,000 job losses.

A clear picture of the tense executive meeting on 8 March that determined the NUM's next step has been painted by Roy Ottey, the dyed-in-the-wool moderate leader of the Midlands-based Power Group. In his book *The Strike*, Ottey recalled that the union leaders met in an 'impersonal room, lacking in atmosphere' at the top of a glass and concrete office block. 'We seemed to sit a long way from each other, and have to shout rather than talk.' Scargill opened the proceedings by introducing Peter Heathfield as the new general secretary, and strolled through a full agenda of issues such as pay and conditions for canteen ladies but also informing members that 23.4 million tonnes of coal were stocked at the pithead, with the same amount at the power stations.

Then the ordinariness of the meeting abruptly changed. It was stated that Scotland and Yorkshire had submitted requests for strike action in their areas to be recognized. Scotland wanted backing for a strike already under way against the closure of Polmaise colliery, and Yorkshire for the dispute over Cortonwood. Both sought sanction under Rule 41 – the rule mentioned by Scargill in his radio interview a year before. This rule gives the national executive power to strike in individual areas. Ottey recalled: 'Straightaway I smelled a rat. I realised the Yorkshire and Scottish calls could represent the start of a national strike without a ballot. It was obvious that Britain's miners were in danger of being brought out through mass picketing and intimidation. The sickening part was that it was all so predictable. The alarm bells had already sounded when I heard Mick McGahey

saying on the news on television that "we will not be constitutional-
ised out of action".[18]

Militant coalfield leaders, who had co-ordinated their line at a Left
meeting the previous night, fell into line one after the other. Scotland's Eric Clarke said his area would be on strike alongside Yorkshire. Sid Vincent of Lancashire, Scargill's one-time adversary, who
had come to terms with the new regime, thought it was 'now or
never'. Behind the Board's figures 'there is a monster'. Jack Taylor of
Yorkshire insisted: 'We are on our way.' Henry Richardson, Scargill
loyalist in Nottinghamshire, complained of being verbally abused by
miners lobbying the building. Prophetically, he warned: 'Calling us
scabs will not help. I have been called that outside. If Notts are scabs
before we start, Notts will become scabs.' The moderates counter-
attacked, proposing through Trevor Bell of the white-collar COSA
section a national ballot with a recommendation for strike action.
Emlyn Williams, the diminutive Welsh warrior, reacted with a formal
motion to back the striking areas. Ottey thought the resolution had
been prepared in advance. He knew it would have been, and the
argument moved behind it – though Wesley Chambers of the ultra-
Left Kent area rather gave the game away by admitting: 'if we have
got to have ballots, we are starting to lose'.

Scargill wound up the debate, 'demonstrating which side he was
on'.[19] 'It was clear he wanted strike action and he was determined
not to be thwarted yet again by the members deciding for themselves.'
He said the 'constitution' was simple: it was a choice between a
national strike ballot and supporting the strikes already under way.
He wanted to make only one or two points, and to point out 'one
simple fact of life': of the NCB's 179 pits, plus workshops and coking
plants, 115 were 'uneconomic'. The debate would be meaningless
unless the union took some decisions. 'It is now the crunch time. We
are all agreed we have to fight. We have an overtime ban. It is only
the tactics which are in question.'[20] Significantly, though it had been
proposed second, he took Emlyn Williams's motion first. The vote
was twenty-two in favour, and three against. Bell, Ottey and Ted
McKay had voted against. 'I was surprised that only three of us had
voted for democracy,' said Ottey, 'considering how many of the
others had spoken up for a ballot.' But there it was. The NUM
executive had, through the escape-hatch of Rule 41, set in motion a
national strike that the union's leaders were not confident of promoting through a national ballot, as had been past practice – certainly

before the successful conflicts of 1972 and 1974. The strikes in York-shire and Scotland were deemed official, and any similar action else-where would be official too. Scargill's dream of a rolling, all-out strike was being realized: a strike that would put all others in the shade, costing some £6 billion, lasting almost one year, leading to 10,000 arrests of miners, 1,000 injuries, three dead, a hundred pits closed and 100,000 jobs lost, the splitting of the once mighty NUM, and deep social unease.

'Arthur subsequently informed the media that the decision was unanimous by virtue of a substantive motion. It even appeared so later in the minutes of the meeting,' noted Ottey. 'Another devious move, I thought to myself.'[21] He hadn't seen anything yet. At three p.m. the same day, the executive was discreetly summoned to the Royal Victoria for war games. The conference, area leaders were told, would clear up 'blind decisions' taken at Scargill's request during the morning when the executive formally accepted the decisions of the 'inner cabinet' reached the previous day. 'Arthur had presented these minutes and asked us to accept them without giving us any information.'[22] This gathering confirmed in Ottey's mind that not only had there been pre-executive collusion on the strike strategy, but steps had been taken by the NUM officials and union trustees 'well before any decision to strike' to prevent possible sequestration of union funds. Some of the decisions minuted were puzzling. Sammy Thompson of Yorkshire and Henry Richardson of Notts had resigned as trustees, and McGahey and Scargill had been appointed 'to fill the casual vacancies'. The trustees and Heathfield had been given auth-ority to invest the funds of the union in any joint stock bank, and £1 million had been settled on an educational trust. Behind closed doors (and curtains), Scargill, 'in a quiet voice obviously intended to convey the seriousness and secrecy with which the discussions had to be treated', spoke alarmingly of the implications of industrial relations legislation. National and area funds could be sequestrated. This should have been common knowledge to any branch activist who had been on an NUM course. But those present took it to mean that there was an intention knowingly to break the law, by secondary picketing or otherwise.

Speaking sotto voce, Roger Windsor warned that while they were not advising breaking the laws of the land, 'even this meeting could be considered conspiratorial'.[23] But funds could be secured by setting up a charitable trust, and over the last year the NUM had already decided to establish such a trust for educational purposes. All the areas could settle their assets, including property, in such a trust. But it should be done within twenty-four hours. The only other way to protect funds was to liquidate assets and take them abroad – though even here there was only one safe place: 'cuckoo clock land', by which his audience understood Switzerland. The names of three helpful solicitors were given out. 'It seemed we were really in the realms of James Bond: a world of spies and phone-tapping.'[24] The 'conspirators' broke up and went home, conscious that the 'blind decision' they had taken at Scargill's request gave the national officials – Scargill, McGahey and Heathfield – authority to do what they liked with the funds without referring back to the executive. It was a piece of blind loyalty they were later to regret.

When they called the strike in Yorkshire, the area leaders derived their authority from a ballot held in 1981 when Scargill was coalfield president. The men had then voted by more than eighty per cent to strike if any of their pits were threatened with closure. Pits had continued to close during his time there – in fact, eight shut down in the three years following the ballot. John Walsh, the surviving right-wing official in the coalfield, argued that the 1981 ballot was 'too remote', and had been superseded by other national ballots that had gone against strike action. The request for authority to call an official strike should have been ruled out of order by Scargill, he argues. 'Yorkshire had no proper mandate. That should have been pointed out by the president.' He considered seeking an injunction against the strike call, but demurred. 'The activists thought all they had to do was threaten a strike, and the government would collapse. I argued that the prospects of having a successful strike were minimal, because we had had two ballots and lost them.' His dissenting voice was drowned in the enthusiasm for 'having a go'.

The strike was solid in Yorkshire, and pickets from the county fanned out into other coalfields, particularly Nottinghamshire, in defiance of the area executive but in keeping with tradition and the personal philosophy of their national leader. By 14 March, 133 pits had either gone on strike or been 'picketed out'. Scargill clearly approved. He certainly refused to rein in Yorkshire's flying pickets, and was incensed when the Coal Board went to the High Court for an injunction under the 1980 Employment Act restraining the Yorkshire area from picketing other coalfields. When Mr Justice Nolan gave the NCB the legal relief it sought, Scargill sought to widen this 'clear attack' to the whole of the NUM. By invoking the employment legislation, he insisted, the Board was 'setting itself in direct conflict with the national union and all its constituent bodies'. Legally, this was a nonsense, but he was determined to wind up the politics of the strike from the very beginning.

Tony Benn had by now returned to Parliament through a by-election in Chesterfield, where the NUM had played a critical role in restoring him to the Commons. As soon as he heard that the sitting MP, Eric Varley, was resigning to become chief executive of Coalite, Benn was on the phone to Scargill. He took little persuading. 'Arthur rang me back and said "You must move quickly. We will put out statements in the constituency to the effect that they would like you, and you must be ready to say you would be pleased to respond." '[25] The by-election took place on 1 March and Benn was returned with a majority of 6,264. His first diary entry after resuming his parliamentary career was to note that the strike had precipitated a crisis in the mining industry 'and a big political crisis in Britain'. In the Parliamentary Labour Party, there were mixed feelings. Neil Kinnock, for whom the strike was to become a millstone round his neck, argued against giving up an Opposition day to hold a debate on the miners, telling fellow MPs: 'We shouldn't lead with our chins. You're asking me to jump out of the window. This would be just a gesture.' As early as 5 May, Benn was saying: 'It looks as though the miners cannot beat the government,' but he predicted a long strike.

Thousands of Yorkshire miners defied the ban on flying pickets, but Ian MacGregor decided against proceeding against the area union for contempt. After a massive police operation enabled 40,000 working miners to cross the picket lines, lawyers for the NCB told the High Court it would 'not be constructive' to pursue the legal action, and Scargill claimed another victory. The climbdown was due to the 'tremendous solidarity' of the miners, three quarters of whom were now on strike. 'The lesson for the miners and all workers is clear. Through solid unity and maximum trade union support, we can save pits and jobs while resisting Tory anti-union legislation.'

Scargill and Heathfield resisted moves to recall the executive to discuss the question of a national ballot, though twelve of the twenty-four-man NEC had written to them asking for such a vote. The two conferred on policy, but Heathfield vetoed a recall and a ballot on the grounds that relatively prosperous areas like Nottinghamshire could not be allowed to veto a strike for jobs in coalfields threatened with large-scale closures. Coalfield polls in moderate areas had all yielded 'No' votes – as had polls in South Wales and Derbyshire. The moderates countered by holding a 'secret' meeting at a public house in Groby, Leicestershire (so secret that the TV cameras were there). There, they demanded that the executive be brought into emergency session to discuss a national ballot. Scargill refused to bow to their demands, playing it long until the scheduled 12 April executive meeting, by which time the strike was more than a month old and was rapidly becoming a way of life for the men and their families. When the meeting finally did take place, Scargill simply ruled the request for a ballot out of order, demonstrating that anything Gormley could do he could do better. His ruling was challenged, but the right-wing coalition had been destabilized to the point where it could muster only eight votes. They were never to win another vote for the rest of the strike.

Scargill addressed the thousands of cheering 'lobbyists' who had attacked the moderates as they left the NUM offices despite the fact that they had lost. To chants of 'Easy! Easy!' he told the men: 'We intend to continue this fight until MacGregor and Thatcher withdraw their pit closures.' Instead of a ballot, on 19 April Scargill deployed his favoured device of a special delegate conference, which confirmed his ruling and voted to spread the strike by other means. Delegates also agreed to reduce the majority required under rule to hold a strike from fifty-five per cent to a simple majority. A policy paper adopted by the conference said the dispute had been provoked by the Coal Board, supported by the government. A special Cabinet sub-committee was meeting twice a week to monitor the strike, but the day-to-day running of the industry was left in the hands of Mac-Gregor. He said it would be a very long time before the NCB had anything new to offer, and appealed for 'realism' on the part of 'our friends in Sheffield'. But two days later he offered to phase the 20,000 job losses over a longer period. Scargill, sensing that he had got them on the run, rejected this olive branch out of hand, insisting that pit closures and job losses were 'not negotiable'. That being the case, there was nothing to negotiate about.

In any event, Coal Board managers argued, Scargill was not a negotiator. Ned Smith, the NCB's director of industrial relations during the strike, said the miners' leader was good at presenting a brief. 'He could put a case across very well indeed. But once his brief was finished, if the answer was "no", Arthur was buggered because he wasn't a negotiator. What he said was right and had to be accepted.'[26] Scargill offered to talk 'anytime, anywhere', but only on his own terms. Instead of contraction, he wanted an expansion of the coal industry and a capital reconstruction of the NCB to ease the burden of debt.

Ministers noted with quiet satisfaction that he was not getting it all his own way. All the pits in Nottinghamshire were working, despite the area leadership declaring an 'official strike'. On 2 May, 6,000 rebel miners, some carrying 'Adolf Scargill' banners, staged a 'right to work' demonstration at the NUM area offices in Berry Hill, Mansfield. Violence erupted, and there were demands for area leaders to resign. Scargill decided to take his strike call into the rebels' heartland, and staged a demonstration in Mansfield on 14 May, when he said the dispute could go on until November or December, and made clear that his ultimate aim was the downfall of the Thatcher administration. Photographs of him at the rally with his right arm raised in salute to the 20,000 strikers were given very wide publicity. Of course, he wasn't giving a Hitler salute, but it looked uncommonly like that. By now, the football-crowd chant of 'Here we go, here we go, here we go' to the tune of 'Colonel Bogie' had become the anthem of the struggle, along with 'There's only one Arthur Scargill', sung to the tune of 'Guantanamera'. It was perhaps his highest point in the strike. Strikers clambered on to the roof tops to cheer the two-mile procession on its way. Not even the sporadic late-evening violence which led to sixty arrests could spoil that sunny, cloudless day. Scargill basked in the adoration of his men – and their womenfolk, who became involved in this strike as never before. Benn rhapsodized: 'The young miners are just so keen. It was a marvellous day.'[27]

The strike was an uncomfortable issue for Labour leaders. Neil Kinnock and his deputy, Roy Hattersley, both said they would be on strike if they were Nottinghamshire miners, though Kinnock added that he would also be agitating for a ballot. In private, Hattersley expressed the opinion that the miners would lose. Kinnock was dismayed that the NUM's ingrained sense of democracy was being trampled on. Members of the Shadow Cabinet were pressing Scargill to talk to Kinnock. Benn suggested to John Prescott that the lack of liaison might be 'because Neil goes on about the ballot and hasn't come out in support of the miners'.[28] Opinion in the parliamentary party was divided. At a PLP meeting on 16 May, there was a row over whether MPs should pay a £5 a week levy to the strikers. The

Shadow Cabinet opposed the move. It was approved, unanimously, but not before Michael McGuire, NUM-sponsored MP for the Lancashire mining constituency of Makerfield, had accused Scargill of intimidation. He insisted: 'Without a ballot, the strike is doomed. The PLP must win back the support of those who fear totalitarianism.' The issue was raised by Benn at an uncomfortable meeting of the TUC-Labour Liaison Committee the following week, when Len Murray made clear that Scargill had not asked for any help. Quite the opposite. He had asked the TUC not to intervene, and that was why the general council had done nothing.

By late May, after three months of strike, MacGregor had got peace talks going as part of a twin-track policy to end the dispute. He was also encouraging a return-to-work movement at the 119 pits still strike-bound, and the initiative was meeting with some success, particularly in the 'barometer' coalfield of Derbyshire, where the men were almost evenly divided about the strike. But the first talks collapsed before they got under way. The Board pulled out when Scargill reiterated that the closure list must be withdrawn before negotiations could commence. 'That is the only thing we want to discuss,' he said. The meeting was rescheduled for 23 May, but talks broke down after only sixty-five minutes, when MacGregor left the room after saying: 'I have no comment' to Scargill's demand for withdrawal of the pit closures. MacGregor's 'American phraseology' infuriated Scargill, but the NCB chairman denied that there was personal animosity between the two men. 'There is no confrontation between Mr Scargill and me. There is a confrontation by Mr Scargill of the National Coal Board in total. He does not discriminate.'[29]

Scargill had his own twin-track approach: to force the Board to back down on the 'hit list' through negotiation, and to win the strike by picketing. He now switched emphasis to the latter. He was going to have another Saltley. The site this time was Orgreave coke works, just south of Sheffield and only three miles from NUM headquarters. The coking plant, owned and operated by British Steel, was supplying badly needed coke to the Anchor steel complex at Scunthorpe – the scene of Scargill's 'mini-Saltley' in 1974. After train drivers refused to take the coke by rail, convoys of lorries began making the run twice a day. At first, the pickets were few in number, but they rapidly grew to more than a thousand. On Sunday, 25 May, Scargill appeared on the picket line, and tried to persuade the lorry drivers not to go into Orgreave. They ignored him.

The next day was Spring Bank Holiday, and though the plant was closed, 1,200 pickets turned up. Scargill was among them, and he was interviewed on prime-time television news exhorting miners and their supporters to attend at Orgreave. In his report, 'Policing the Coal Industry Dispute', Peter Wright, the chief constable of South Yorkshire, said: 'His personal commitment to the picketing of Orgreave gave an added dimension to the incidents which occurred there and caused parallels to be drawn by the media with the closure of Saltley Coke Depot in 1972, and the success of the miners' strike *as a consequence of that closure*' (my italics).[30] That the chief constable of South Yorkshire could believe that Saltley had been responsible for the victory in 1972 is eloquent testimony to the power of the myth that Scargill had created.

Saltley was a picnic compared to Orgreave. There had been little violence, and it was all over in a few days. But after Scargill's appeal for a mass picket, Orgreave became a bloody battleground. Police in riot gear were deployed for the first time on 29 May, when 5,000 miners answered Scargill's appeal. Amid appalling scenes of violence, 82 pickets were arrested, 104 police officers and 28 pickets were injured. A senior police officer, Superintendent Tony Pratt, blamed Scargill for the trouble, saying it had not happened until he turned up. Scargill was unrepentant, laying the blame at the door of the police. He promised they would be back in force the next day, warning: 'We did it at Grunwick, we can do it here.'[31] He wisely omitted to mention that mass picketing at Grunwick had failed.

Trouble began when the thirty-five lorries, heavily protected by wire mesh, arrived at the plant to load up. Pickets surged forward under a hail of missiles and firecrackers, and mounted police and officers with batons and long shields moved in to make arrests. One officer broke his leg falling from his horse. The convoy got through. When the lorries returned for a second load, violence broke out again and police charged the pickets, scattering them across a field. Fighting broke out again as the second convoy left. Scargill was beside himself with rage. 'Quite honestly, there were scenes of brutality which were almost unbelievable. What you have now in South Yorkshire is an actual police state tantamount to something you are used to seeing in Chile or Bolivia.'[32] He urged miners and other trade unionists to 'come here in your thousands'. Police said half-bricks, spikes, ball bearings and pieces of wood with spikes driven through them had been used as missiles. The next day was almost as bad, with 3,000 pickets taking on the police, at one time using a telegraph pole as a crude battering ram in an attempt to breach police lines. Wires were stretched across the road to unhorse mounted police, and a portable building was commandeered and used as a barricade. Pickets later set fire to it.

That day also, Scargill was arrested and charged with obstruction. In the early morning, he was leading a column of about fifty pickets towards the plant when police officers barred his way and said he could go no further. He said: 'No way, no way.' He was trying to get to a spot where the pickets had been standing the previous day. There were more verbal exchanges with the police, and he was led away to a police van, shouting to reporters: '1984 – Great Britain!' He was later released on unconditional bail by Rotherham magistrates, and promised he would go back to Orgreave to lead the pickets. He denied he had intended to get arrested, insisting: 'No, all I wanted to do was to picket peacefully.'

His driver-cum-bodyguard, Jim Parker, recalls it differently. 'He was adamant he was going to get arrested to show the lads that he was suffering like them. He wanted to be arrested.' Parker had been with him until just before the arrest, but Scargill sent him off to find one of the picket leaders. They had earlier discussed what would happen if and when he was arrested. 'I said to him, if they try to take you, will you go easy or do you go hard, meaning, if I'm there, do I fight? And he said he would go hard.' In the event, he went easy, and months later Rotherham magistrates found him guilty and fined him.

Away from the picket line, but not very far away, the first serious peace moves took place at a Yorkshire country house hotel. In response to an invitation from the NCB to discuss the future of the industry 'within the principles of the Plan for Coal', Scargill met Jimmy Cowan for 'tense but cordial' talks on 30 May. Little hard news filtered out of the meeting, though the NUM side gained the impression that a compromise on the original scale of cutbacks might be possible. Scargill told a public meeting that he had not compromised on his position, and Dennis Skinner, NUM-sponsored MP for Bolsover, claimed with more enthusiasm than accuracy that the union was 'on the verge of possibly the greatest industrial success in postwar Britain'. MacGregor privately assured Mrs Thatcher that this was untrue. The talks were adjourned to the following week, amid signs of cracks emerging in the strike. There was a trickle back to work in Derbyshire, and in Yorkshire Barnsley winding engine-men, who operate the pit cages, voted in a postal ballot to break the strike.

Scargill shuttled from peace talks to picket lines. Trouble continued at Orgreave, the chief constable noting that 'missiles of all descriptions had been thrown at police officers, trip wires laid to injure horses and their riders, barricades built, street furniture destroyed and other moveable property commandeered and used by pickets to overcome police efforts to keep the plant open'.[33] Police also had to send reinforcements to Houghton Main colliery outside Barnsley, where two winders crossed the picket line. Scargill returned to Orgreave on 6 June, and so did the violence. Four thousand miners were unable to prevent two convoys of twenty-nine lorries moving coke to Scunthorpe. Twenty-three pickets were arrested, and police experienced a new weapon: ten officers received injuries to their eyes from 'eggs filled with noxious fluid'.

An unaccountable lull ensued, before the final, explosive day when the Battle of Orgreave was lost. Police intelligence indicated that thousands of miners would converge on the coking plant from as far away as Scotland, Kent and South Wales. The day began ominously at three a.m., when fifty demonstrators were seen pulling stones from the perimeter wall and throwing them inside the works. Hundreds of miners left their buses in the city centre and walked, creating traffic chaos in Sheffield. By nine a.m., an estimated 10,000 men had gathered, but the first convoy got through without trouble. Before the next convoy arrived, in the stiff prose of South Yorkshire's chief constable, 'the president of the National Union of Mineworkers was seen to fall down a bank and injure himself. He was conveyed from the scene by ambulance, and was detained at Rotherham District Hospital, alleging that he had been struck by a police shield.'[34] Scargill has always claimed that he was knocked down by a police officer. Others say he missed his footing and fell down the bank.

Whichever version is correct, on the day the incident appeared to inflame feelings to a dangerous new intensity. When the second convoy rolled in, there was mayhem. A barricade was erected, using heavy boulders, a steel girder and angled steel spikes. Scrap vehicles were dragged from a nearby breaker's yard and set on fire in the road. Pickets stole police truncheons and two 'long shields', which they burned. The violence was not confined to one side. Police officers clearly lost control of themselves, and waded into the pickets lashing out indiscriminately. ITN showed pictures of a policeman beating a miner across the shoulders. Mounted police charged the crowd, and police dogs were also deployed. Stan Orme, MP, chairman of the Parliamentary Labour Party, who was acting as a go-between to keep open lines of communication between Scargill and MacGregor, watched an NUM film of the battle, observing: 'Quite frankly, I've never seen anything like it. It reminded me of Henry V with the armies ranged up on different sides of the hill. It was most disturbing to witness this in the United Kingdom of 1984.'[35]

At the end of the day, according to police, there had been ninety-three arrests. Seventy-two policemen and fifty-one pickets (a serious underestimate) had been injured. In total, over the three-week period, some 32,500 pickets had gone to Orgreave, and 273 of them had been arrested. But the drawn-out orgy of violence had been a waste of time. The plant had not been closed. The coke had got through. What had been planned by Scargill as a repeat of Saltley, offering a psychological and tactical breakthrough, had failed utterly. He had been warned that it would, not just in the executive meetings, where he failed to get support for the move, but in meetings of the Left Caucus too. The political cohesion of the Left was now under heavy strain. Tony Benn had heard them quarrelling, noting as early as 1 April that the Left of the executive were meeting in Chesterfield Labour Club. 'I could hear them shouting away at one another, mainly Arthur Scargill's voice coming through the door.'[36] Experienced coalfield leaders complained bitterly that any criticism of Scargill's tactics, or even expressing a different point of view, risked identifying one with 'the enemy'. As brilliant as he could be on a public platform, in the privacy of the committee room he could be petulant and overbearing, demanding his own way like a spoilt child. And if he didn't get it, as he didn't over Orgreave, he would simply go out and announce it anyway.

The question remains, however, why Orgreave? From a tactical point of view, it was a much more difficult site to close down than Saltley had been. Saltley was an inner-city depot hemmed in by streets and approached by a narrow entrance through a small square. It was perfect territory for a mass picket. Orgreave is set in open country, and approached by a minor road bordered with fields. The plant had a large 'apron' where convoys could line up, and across the road was a disused chemical factory which the police used as an operations base. The police could open and close the road at will, and did so.

Their determination not to repeat the humiliation of Sir Derrick Capper was a critical factor in the confrontation that followed. South Yorkshire's chief constable Peter Wright took enough of his own and other forces' men to Orgreave to ensure that every single lorry got through. He was sharply critical of the mass picketing strategy: 'Wherever people seek to impose their will upon others by sheer weight of numbers, there is a strong likelihood that conflict will arise. Mass picketing proved this contention time and time again during the dispute.'[37]

There are those who argue that Orgreave was almost an accident, and those who claim it was a conspiracy, a trap set up for Scargill that he walked straight into. Kevan Hunt, the NCB's deputy director of industrial relations at the time, recalls telephoning the NUM president on a Friday afternoon before the confrontation started. 'I rang him to say "Arthur, we need more tonnage out of Orgreave." The reaction to that was "Very interesting. What do you want me to do about it?" Malcolm Edwards [NCB member for Marketing] had asked me to have a word about it to the NUM. So I had done just that. Could they relieve this pressure point? What it did to him was to [make him] recognise that here he might have a pressure point. His answer was "I will look at it, but I am pretty certain the answer will be No." The word obviously got round that "We could stick them one on here and apply pressure that will help to crack the dam." What it actually did was to divert [NUM] resources from where they were doing a "better job". Orgreave took some pressure off from collieries and there was a flush of people back to work at a number of places because all the pickets had been pulled off. I think it was technically a bad decision on his part.'[38] His boss, Ian MacGregor, reinforces the point: 'It [Orgreave] became a *cause célèbre* for Scargill, a fight he had to win. We were quite encouraged that he thought it so important and did everything we could to help him continue to think so, but the truth was that it hardly mattered a jot to us – beyond the fact that it kept him out of Nottingham.'[39]

However, David Hart, the freelance libertarian who had the ear of Mrs Thatcher and was later to play a key role in the end-game of the strike, claims that Orgreave was 'a set-up by us'. In an extraordinary allegation, he said: 'The coke was of no interest whatsoever. We didn't need it. It was a battle ground of our choosing on grounds of our choosing. I don't think that Scargill believes that even today. The fact is that it was a set-up, and it worked brilliantly. It is another example of his character. I knew he would see it as another Saltley, with him slugging it out on the streets with his troops. That's what it was all about. He even had the same sort of hat on at Orgreave.'[40] Hart offered no convincing evidence of the 'set-up', and his claims are pooh-poohed by Coal Board senior managers (one of whom is said to have threatened to defenestrate him from Hobart House). But his allegation strikes a chord with some of the men who were there. They could not understand why the police, after weeks of telling them they were not allowed to pass, were now actually directing them off the motorway towards the coking plant. 'They knew what they were doing,' one picket told the author. 'The whole thing stank of a set-up.'

Whether or no, Orgreave was a watershed in the strike. After 18 June, the invasion of Nottinghamshire tailed off. Many of the pickets had been 'lifted' and magistrates freely imposed bail conditions requiring that they stay in their own coalfield. The weapon of mass pickets to spread the strike was not used again, though they did re-emerge when the return to work began in earnest in the autumn. In any case, Scargill's nimble mind had taken off at another tangent. 'When it wasn't working like Saltley, he had another interest,' said Jim Parker. 'It developed into a thing that, if the police were seen beating the hell out of us, then the public would come on our side. But television showed us attacking the police, and them retaliating – though they came into us first. No miner is brave enough to charge horses and police with batons, when you are in there in plimsolls. I was there, I took part in it. They came into us, and television turned that round.'[41]

Baulked of his prize at Orgreave, Scargill switched track to negotiations. There was some progress at the reconvened peace talks at the Norton House Hotel in Edinburgh on 8 June. Verbatim notes taken during the meeting, and disclosed here for the first time, indicate that Scargill was now adopting a more conciliatory line. He stressed the areas of agreement, as well as the differences between the two sides. The aim was 'not for a climbdown by either Scargill or Mac-Gregor; the need was to instil confidence in our men'. He called on the Board to recognize that its proposals of 6 March no longer applied. The union was opposed to economic closures, and was not asking the NCB to come to its position 'but to stay with the Plan for Coal'. He asked MacGregor for a list of pits that would exhaust, and promised: 'You will not find us coming to you where the Areas have agreed a closure.' In return, MacGregor said the idea of a four-day week for miners was a goal towards which the two sides could work together.

MacGregor observed of these talks. 'Throughout the entire session, Arthur's attitude was somewhat difficult to plumb. He seemed on edge. He didn't seem to want to settle anything and he seemed uncomfortable when I asked him to agree to things.' Heathfield and McGahey were more inclined to follow the reasoning, but Scargill remained silent for long periods. 'Then suddenly, he would break in to what the rest of us were discussing with some remark that would vitiate all our efforts.'[42] His deputy Jimmy Cowan divined that 'the Communist Party is ready to settle'. MacGregor thought that McGahey had 'moved out from behind Scargill' and might be ready to settle, but not Scargill himself.

Nonetheless, more talks were arranged for 13 June, but in the intervening period MacGregor agreed to do an interview with me. I was then labour editor of The Times, and had been for ten years. The interview emerged as a direct result of a weekly editorial conference on industrial matters conducted by the paper's deputy editor, Charles Wilson. Like any good journalist, he was never quite satisfied with what we were doing, and wanted to do something different. More out of desperation than expectation, I suggested a formal interview with the NCB chairman. He liked the idea, and I approached Geoffrey Kirk, the Coal Board's director of information, who was also a personal friend. Rather to my surprise (and, I believe, his), he came back with two possible dates. I chose the first one, on the grounds that MacGregor would have less time to change his mind. The interview took place on 11 June in MacGregor's spartan office in Hobart House. He was in an unusually expansive mood and talked in a bullish way of the industry's future, and had some harsh things to say about the NUM president. I pointed out that Scargill was still talking about a victory on the hustings, and asked him how flexible he found his adversary. MacGregor replied: 'He has become a Dr Jekyll and Mr Hyde. He talks one way to audiences ... but I will give him credit for focusing on the realities.'

He went on: 'But then he is no different to any other politician. What they say in the privacy of the boudoir and to the public are two different things. He really is in the wrong business. He should be on the stage. He would make a great living as an actor or an entertainer.'[43] He said there would be a new Plan for Coal, 'but we will write the Plan', and the Board would recover the responsibility for managing the industry. MacGregor was dismissive about Scargill's political aims in the dispute. 'The rhetoric in these situations comes up with all sorts of hobgoblins. Arthur has been quite frank about his position.' The government's only aim was to ensure that coal became 'a positive contributor to our economy rather than a drain on it'. I quote parts of this text not solely out of vanity. The article created a terrible stir, and was blamed for the breakdown of talks that had appeared to be going well. Scargill reacted with extraordinary bad temper at publication of the interview all over *The Times*'s back page. He said it was 'the language of one who tells lies and distorts facts. I would not trust Mr MacGregor if he told me the time of day.' He predicted 'more and more conflict'.

The ensuing peace talks at a Rotherham hotel on 13 June lasted little more than fifteen minutes. The miners asked MacGregor if he would withdraw his pit closure programme, and he said 'Nope.' The needle was stuck. MacGregor noted 'open hostility' for the first time. Scargill repeated his demands, and MacGregor countered by suggesting that the Board might now organize its own ballot of the men. He had successfully used this tactic of a management ballot to undermine the authority of the steel unions at BSC, and at British Leyland to bypass the militant shop stewards there. He was attracted to the possibility of repeating the trick, but was finally dissuaded by his managers, who decided to take a leaf out of Peter Walker's book: throw money at the problem. A package of incentives was hastily put together to speed up the return to work – which had got men back at pits in Lancashire, Derbyshire, Warwickshire and Staffordshire, in addition to virtually normal working in Nottinghamshire. The initiative had only qualified success. About a thousand men went back to work, while 180,000 stayed out. The NCB also began discreetly allowing men to take individual redundancy.

Then the Peace Show was back on the road. The Coal Board invited Scargill back for more talks, beginning the most serious bid yet to end the dispute. Many, if not most, industrial commentators believe that the July meetings offered Scargill an opportunity to declare a victory and call the strike off, and that only his obduracy stood in the way of a settlement. Two days before the talks began, MacGregor had been asked to Downing Street to brief the prime minister. She was worried about the related national dock strike that could suddenly come out of the blue, and anxious that the NCB might be ready to 'give away the store'. MacGregor reassured her, but warned that he had come to the conclusion that Scargill was locked into a death or glory struggle, and would settle for nothing less than a total climb-down by the Board. The NCB chairman was exasperated by the politicians and civil servants who wanted to see Scargill beaten, but without any pain or nastiness. He argued that the confrontation would be over quicker if they planned on it going on for ever.

This cycle of talks went on for nearly two weeks, encompassing four meetings, three in London and one in Edinburgh. Benn met Heathfield in Chesterfield Labour Club after the first sessions on 5 and 6 July, and Heathfield said the talks were going well from the NUM point of view. Cowan was playing the hard-man; MacGregor was trying to be friendly. The 'troika' – Scargill, McGahey and Heathfield – were working extremely well together. 'Arthur is totally unyielding and is a field commander.'[44] 'It became absolutely clear – and this is what I wanted to hear – that the NUM are not going to give MacGregor an agreement.'[45]

Hitherto secret verbatim notes of the talks confirm Benn's bleak assessment. The NUM presented a united front. MacGregor asked what was in the union's mind 'other than Arthur Scargill's views'. McGahey jumped in to say that Scargill's views 'are those of the NUM'. MacGregor replied that this made it difficult to make progress. Heathfield agreed, if the Board's strategy was still to close twenty pits and sack 20,000 men. Scargill accepted that there would be 'some exhaustion of capacity', perhaps as much as two million tonnes a year. MacGregor wondered, if the closure programme was adjusted, 'can we redefine exhaustion in a way which gives some comfort to the NCB?' Scargill had understood the Board's position, but he did not accept 'the concept of uneconomic pits'. If the Board made economic an issue, 'We would be miles apart.' In the past, the union had co-operated, but these five threatened pits that had come to encapsulate the dispute – Polmaise, Cortonwood, Herrington, Snowdown and Bullcliffe Wood – were the sticking point. Mac-Gregor was later to call these collieries in Kent, Yorkshire, Durham and Scotland 'a sort of Maginot line in the Scargill mythology'. After an adjournment, Scargill repeated his demand that the 6 March package be withdrawn and the five pits kept open. If that was conceded in principle, the NUM could discuss exhaustion of capacity and a new Plan for Coal. And on it went, this weary game of negotiating battledore and shuttlecock, each side lazily batting back to the other.

Some of the sessions were quite short: that on the afternoon of 5 July lasted only twenty-five minutes.

The next morning, Scargill put forward a new formula. Where a comprehensive and in-depth investigation by the Board and the union's mining engineers showed that a colliery had no mineable reserves that were workable or which could be developed, there would be joint agreement that such a colliery 'shall be deemed exhausted'. MacGregor immediately spotted the trap. The Scargill formula did not mention economics. The NCB team withdrew, and came back an hour later with a proposal to insert the word 'beneficially' before 'developed'. This one word 'beneficially' was to dog the peace process and eventually kill it off. McGahey said the union side was in difficulties. Heathfield accused MacGregor of 'looking for a formula to take out capacity'. They broke for an hour, and Scargill came back with a flat rejection of 'beneficially'. Heathfield said it would be regarded as a sell-out. McGahey appeared hurt that by responding to Cowan's wish for a third category of pit – other than exhausted or geologically unsafe – the union had been drawn into a lobster pot. 'Every time the NCB attempt to close a pit they try and prove that it is beneficial for the industry,' he growled.

The talks resumed on the night of Sunday 8 July in Edinburgh. MacGregor opened with a discussion paper and invited comments. Scargill argued that the NUM's own formula for pit closures – paragraph 3(c) – was 'a demonstration of positive negotiations' from the union. 'Beneficial' was not acceptable, said Heathfield, adding for no very apparent reason: 'You have the Prime Minister's ear, Mr MacGregor.' The chairman's parting shot was that the Board would not 'withdraw' the 6 March programme. 'You will have to think of another word,' he told Scargill. The next morning, they were back at the game of semantics. The atmosphere was sharper, too. MacGregor expressed sadness that the phraseology could not be got right. Cowan criticized the NUM's rash talk of 'complete victory', and his chairman rejoined: 'I'm too old for victories.' Scargill was saying very little, but Heathfield argued: 'There is not much between us – but your words tell us that your policy has not changed. We could not sell that to the lads. Here is a formula that I am unhappy with. Reluctantly I will campaign for it, but if you wish to change it, I will be forced to oppose it.' MacGregor repeated that retention of 'beneficially' was essential, and nobody should claim a victory except for common sense. Scargill retorted that the union side wouldn't have spent so much time negotiating if they didn't think a settlement was possible. 'We have to find a formula that takes us beyond 6 March.' He came more forcibly into the meeting, laying down the NUM's terms yet again and rejecting 'beneficially' on the grounds that 'it means that all the guidelines and safeguards protect you – not us'. McGahey warned: 'We have stopped running and we cannot be chased any further.'

MacGregor later claimed that Scargill never got a better deal than on 9 July, and the two sides had come quite close to settling. It was only Scargill's 'total intransigence and unwillingness to consider any compromise' that got in the way of a settlement. But a close reading of what the combatants actually said suggests that it was more like six of one and half a dozen of the other. MacGregor's underlying aim was to appear conciliatory and push through a form of words that would give him carte blanche to close pits how and when he wanted. Within his own parameters, Scargill was quite right to fasten on 'beneficially' as a cover-all expression designed to give management complete freedom to operate. Even the industry's existing procedures for joint appraisal of threatened pits, which had in truth counted for very little, would have gone by the board. No pit would have been safe. So, in his blinkered way, he was right. But the problems were greater than his vision of them. For twenty years he had hammered away on his one-club policy that 'there is no such thing as an uneconomic pit', and many of his members believed him. By sheer force of personality, he had persuaded a large and dedicated group of working people that he had the answer to their problems, and by extension to those of all working people. He had mesmerized a generation of miners, and a significant tract of public opinion. It was only when his assertiveness and sense of mission came rudely up against a more powerful force – the state, in all its ramifications – that its weakness and sheer wrong-headedness became clear.

Though the government had scarcely been mentioned in the talks, Scargill did not hesitate to lay the blame at Mrs Thatcher's door. 'It seems to us that throughout the negotiations there has been a third party whose hand has been at the negotiating table. At each stage when we appeared to have a settlement, it was clear to us that central government was pulling the strings of the Coal Board negotiators. We found that sad and regrettable,' he said. Judging by what the NCB top brass said, there would have been no need for them to go running to ministers to avoid the pitfalls carefully excavated by the

NUM, or to seek guidance on how to amend the union's draft settlement to their advantage.

The fragile peace process was adjourned so that Scargill could have his truncated annual conference in Sheffield. The chief bone of contention there was a new rule change introducing a disciplinary code within the union. Nottinghamshire moderates, who had just won sweeping gains in the area council, secured a High Court injunction to prevent delegates from adopting the rule change. They had earlier got a ruling that the strike in their coalfield was not official, as Scargill-loyalist officials had claimed in spite of a seventy-two per cent 'No' vote in an area ballot. Scargill's right-wing critics were less anxious about the disciplinary code and talk of a 'Star Chamber' than about the prospect of the strike going on indefinitely. The NUM president said in his address to conference that the union's bargaining position would improve as the dispute moved 'towards autumn and winter'. He conceded what the miners were up against. 'Through the police, the judiciary, the social security system – whichever way seems possible – the full weight of the state is being brought to bear upon us in an attempt to break this strike. On the picket lines, riot police in full battle gear, on horseback and on foot, accompanied by police dogs, have been unleashed in violent attacks upon our members.

'We have seen in our communities and villages a level of police harassment and intimidation which organised British trade unionists have never before experienced. Preventing the right of people to move freely from one part of the country, or even county, to another; the calculated attacks on striking miners in the streets of their villages; the oppressive conditions of bail under which it is hoped to silence, discourage and defeat us – all these tactics constitute outright violation of people's basic rights.' It was vintage Scargill, passionately delivered and rhapsodically received by the men. Concluding on his usual theme of 'no compromise', he declared: 'Ours is a supremely noble aim: to defend pits, jobs, communities and the right to work. The sacrifices and the hardships have forged a unique commitment among our members. They will ensure that the NUM wins this most crucial battle in the history of our industry. Comrades, I salute you for your magnificent achievements and for your support – together, we cannot fail!'

Alas, they could. Before the peace talks restarted, the Coal Board rescinded the industry's NUM closed shop, which had been a de facto agreement since nationalization. This move was designed to reassure miners who had joined the return to work, and were now fearful of being punished under the new union disciplinary code, that their jobs were safe. They would no longer be sacked for not having an NUM card. Scargill retorted: 'We don't work with scabs.' But it was another sentence in the writing on the wall. The NUM's unique status as an industrial union to which all miners must belong was abolished overnight, opening the way to rival unions. In the sweltering heat of the moment, the issue was quickly forgotten. Its true significance was only appreciated later.

The adversaries returned to the comfortable confines of the Rubens Hotel, hard by NCB headquarters in Victoria, for the resumed peace talks. Scargill was in bullish mood. Recalling the Edinburgh discussions, he had the impression that the NCB was willing to withdraw the 6 March programme. 'We were sufficiently convinced on Sunday night that we could reach agreement and settlement,' the verbatim record shows him saying. But the term 'beneficially' still stuck in their gullet. 'We took a battering at the executive and conference on 3(c),' he confided. MacGregor agreed they had been given food for thought, and asked his deputy to bat. Cowan reiterated the Board's line: demand and supply had to be brought into balance. 'I can't see stability if they don't do the right things.' After a fifty-five-minute adjournment, MacGregor came back to say: 'We are dealing with a lot of pieces that hang together, interlock. We are trying to find the trade-offs that help you.' To this encouraging remark, hard-man Cowan added: 'We would like to accommodate the NUM if we can.' But he then insisted: 'We would need "beneficially"', prompting Scargill's riposte 'You have confirmed our worst fears.' Heathfield denounced the proposal as 'a con-trick'. The Board would be back in six months' time to recover its closure programme. A sharp exchange between MacGregor and Scargill followed. Scargill said: 'Beneficially is a killer.' MacGregor countered: 'Arthur, you've made statements. That makes things difficult', to which Scargill replied: 'I'm not on my own.'

They adjourned for lunch, and two hours later MacGregor was 'being frank' again. He clashed with Scargill and after only ten minutes they adjourned for another hour. That session lasted only five minutes, and this pattern continued for several hours. Neither side gave any real ground, despite their protestations, such as MacGregor: 'We took out the word "economic" to make things easier.

"Beneficial" is a broad-gauge word to help both parties. We are so near and yet so far. We think our total package is a reasonable one. Why don't you take it on trial? We have presented a formula which should put us on the road.' He conceded: 'We do not expect all our mines to be profitable, but we should be moving progressively to better performance.' Scargill was worried about the direction of finance, commenting: 'We are convinced that the vast majority of our pits with the appropriate investment could perform a useful life.'

The miners' leader did not sound like the ranter at the rostrum of a week before. More in sorrow than in anger, he went over his ground. 'From our point of view, we have made it clear that we want to protect our industry. We have argued with politicians of all persuasions and we fight the same battle today – not just the overall balance sheet. We are seeking to protect our people, we would have thought that our document was acceptable to all. We have done our best, and there it is.' He offered to show the NCB where its required four million tonnes of exhausting capacity could be found. MacGregor got down to his bottom line: 'You are saying we can deal with that problem. We are saying that there has to be some means of codifying *what the rules of the game are* [my italics]. We have been prepared to go as far as we could to help your overall position. We also have to have something to see.'

Cowan tried a different ploy. Would the 'troika' take the Coal Board paper back to their executive and say: 'This is the best we can do.' Scargill said the executive and conference were on standby, 'if we had a formula'. Sensing an opening, Cowan said that if the union could accept 3(c), 'then we can perhaps move on the other issues' – keeping the five pits open and withdrawing (rather than revising) the 6 March programme. Scargill shot back: 'We have tried to present you with a cosmetic 3(c).' So close to the brink of something big, they adjourned yet again at ten p.m. until ten-fifty. MacGregor returned 'saddened' that they could not accept the Board's formula for future pit closures. Had they done so, 'We could have come up with ideas to accommodate you on the five pits and suspended the 6 March proposals.' But without acceptance of that formula, there was 'no way' he could reach an accommodation otherwise. Cowan thanked the NUM leaders for their 'helpful and constructive' demeanour. Scargill was sorry that they could not find a resolution to the issue. 'We cannot accept beneficial. We are available when you want us.'

With that, at eleven p.m. the talking was over. On that warm July night, they strode out past the waiting media. For once, Scargill did not want a microphone under his nose. He may not have appreciated it at the time, but that was the beginning of the end. MacGregor subsequently wrote: 'I began to realise that he was going to lead those poor men to the gates of hell rather than admit what I thought was now staring him in the face.'[46]

CHAPTER VIII

DEFEAT

AFTER THE BREAKDOWN of what had looked like a very promising round of peace talks, uneasy government ministers heaped venom on Scargill. Some thought he had taken MacGregor to the brink of conceding the issue at the heart of the dispute – who rules the industry – and they lashed out viciously. Margaret Thatcher described him to the Conservative Back-Bench 1922 Committee as 'the enemy within', an indigenous threat comparable to the Argentinian 'enemy without'. Other Tory grandees accused him of trying to stage a political coup. Conservative Party chairman John Selwyn Gummer appealed to NUM rank-and-file members to rise up in revolt against their militant leader. The loudest and most hysterical voice was that of Alex Fletcher, a junior trade and industry minister who charged that there was 'a strong similarity' between Scargill and General Galtieri, the Argentine dictator who sanctioned the Falklands invasion. 'They both believe in intimidating, in substituting the force of persuasion with the persuasion of force. I predict that Mr Scargill will suffer the same fate as General Galtieri. His threats, his lies, will not even save his own job. He will fail and he will be ousted.' Foreigners hearing and reading their alarmist remarks could have been forgiven for believing that armed detachments of striking Yorkshire miners were massing in Parliament Square to storm the Palace of Westminster. Instead, the miners took the insult as a compliment, rushing out to buy T-shirts emblazoned with the slogan 'Enemy Within'.

They certainly needed their sense of humour as the long, hot summer of strike action wore on. Scargill would joke that you could tell the strikers from the scabs by their sun tan. But beneath the joshing lay a powerful new undercurrent against the strike that was to tie the union up in legal knots, leading to its eventual sequestration and receivership, the success of the return-to-work campaign, and the splitting of the miners into two rival unions.

There had been talk for some time of a mysterious figure calling himself 'Silver Birch', a Nottinghamshire miner opposed to the strike, touring the coalfields trying to drum up support for a challenge to Scargill. Initially, the story was dismissed as 'Rocky Ryan' invention the work of somebody trying to trick Fleet Street. It sounded too far-fetched and conspiratorial. But on 25 July, a week after the break-down of negotiations, concrete details of the plot came to light. 'Silver Birch' was real, though his identity was not yet known. His activities had been uncovered by strike loyalists in South Wales, who dismissed him as a crank. NCB officials were more cautious. If it turned out to be an effective move, they would welcome it.

'Silver Birch' was a thirty-four-year-old working miner whose real name was Chris Butcher. He got the nickname from another working miner at Agecroft colliery in Lancashire, who said he should be known as that because of the grey streaks in his hair. The NUM satirically dubbed him 'Dutch Elm', but the intrigue surrounding his back-to-work movement only grew. Butcher convened a meeting in London of anti-Scargill miners from practically every coalfield. This was the forerunner of the National Working Miners' Committee. When I spoke to him, shortly before he revealed his identity to the *Mail on Sunday* (at whose expense he was touring the country), 'Silver Birch' insisted: 'We don't want to break the NUM, but to make it more democratic. The real enemy of the union is the Marxist leader-ship.' A South Wales miner, opposed to the way his coalfield had been 'picketed out' after voting against a strike, concurred: 'The aim is to "bury" Arthur Scargill. The hardship being caused is terrible and pathetic. Hundreds of men in South Wales want to return to work but dare not because of intimidation.'

At this critical juncture, Energy Secretary Peter Walker ruled out the threat of winter power cuts. He said on LTV's 'Weekend World' that with the Nottinghamshire and South Midlands coalfields work-ing fully and others partially, there was enough coal inside power stations to take the country 'way into 1985'. Scargill, who often spoke of 'General Winter' coming to his aid, carried on as if nothing had happened. He ruled out recommending the Coal Board's Rubens Hotel peace deal, arguing that 'there is nothing on the table to accept or reject'. This was not strictly true. MacGregor had privately pleaded with him to put the controversial 'beneficially developed' formula to his executive as 'the best he could get'. The Board now publicly appealed to Scargill to allow his executive to consider the draft agreement 'coolly and quietly'. Ned Smith, NCB director of industrial relations, asked the NUM to put the proposal out to ballot. Many another union leader would have seized the opportunity to declare a famous victory, and asked the men to endorse the achievement in a pithead vote. It could plausibly have been presented that way, and in truth it was an honourable enough compromise that would have left the miners in a position to fight another day. The miners would have cheered their leader to the rafters, praised his far-sighted leadership and gone back to work. But Scargill is not like any other leader. When he says 'no compromise', he means it. And he knew full well that MacGregor would have used the fig-leaf of 'beneficially developed' to close a whole raft of unprofitable pits. 'We are not talking about a word,' explained Scargill. 'We are talking about a philosophy, an ideology. Either we accept a full-scale butchery of this industry or accept that our pits and jobs are retained.'

So it was no surprise that four days later, on 26 July, the miners' leadership said 'No' and recalled their delegate conference to step up the twenty-week struggle. The NUM was getting considerable indus-trial and financial help through a network of backers, particularly the rail, shipping and transport unions. But it was becoming abundantly clear that the miners could not win alone. Scargill abhorred the idea of involving the TUC. He did not trust General Secretary Lionel Murray after the débâcle of the NGA v. Eddy Shah the previous winter, when TUC leaders shamelessly abandoned their Wembley conference policy of defying the Tebbit employment laws and 'sold out' the print workers. His own experience of the general council was that he was playing a different game to the 'collaborators'. But he reluctantly agreed to explore what might be done to inject a new impetus into the strike, which was cracking in too many places. The Board's financial incentives, personal letters to the men, visits to their homes and adver-tisements in the press were having an impact: officials claimed that 60,000 miners were now back at work. The militant heartlands of York-shire, Scotland and South Wales, however, remained solid.

Scargill went on to attend a secret meeting of TUC Left general secretaries at the offices of the National Union of Railwaymen in Euston Road, almost opposite his old headquarters. Benn, who was present, dates the gathering 24 July; *The Times* dated it – or a remark-ably similar conference – 1 August. Ray Buckton, general secretary of the footplatemen's union ASLEF, was there in his capacity as current president of the TUC with a brief to find out what the NUM might want from the Congress due to take place six weeks later. He was the ideal broker for a better relationship with Congress House and the wider labour movement: a veteran left-winger, though cast in a more pragmatic mould, and a fellow Yorkshireman with a sense of humour as well as a feel for the politics of the situation. And his own members were being suspended for refusing to drive 'blacked' coal trains. With Heathfield and McGahey alongside him, Benn discloses, Scargill put forward the most amazing shopping list of demands. 'What we would like the TUC to do, because we still don't want them to intervene in the dispute, is to say: first, no trade-unionist should cross a picket line; secondly, no industry should accept supplies of iron or coal or anything else delivered by scabs; thirdly, give money and food. About £3 million a week would be necessary to provide miners with £10 a week.'[1]

He must have known that Congress could never even contemplate such a revolutionary programme. An instruction to several million trade unionists not to cross NUM picket lines would have convulsed the labour movement, leading to substantial defections. It would have brought affiliated unions who had no legal, primary dispute into direct conflict with the new employment legislation, leading to widespread sequestration of unions and their funds. Trade unions in the power stations and the steel works in particular would have been immediately vulnerable if their members refused to accept supplies from so-called 'scabs', who were not directly involved in the coal dispute and could not honestly be described as such. Scargill's financial demands were also absurdly high, but that was the least of the anxieties triggered by his approach. Heathfield said the NUM could not afford a defeat at the upcoming Brighton Congress. Buckton's reaction is not recorded, but even Ken Gill, veteran Communist leader of the white-collar union MSF and Scargill's most unstinting supporter, warned: 'The TUC will not call for people to respect picket lines.' He was right. This was not 1972, when General Secretary Vic Feather could drop a heavy hint to Gormley to post his pickets in the right place – outside power stations – and the TUC would instruct all workers not to cross their lines. Such 'secondary' picketing was now unlawful, and Norman Tebbit had legislated to open up union funds to attack if the law was flouted. This was a step whose importance cannot be underestimated. For all their rhetoric, most union general secretaries are intensely conservative about funds: it is almost a sacred duty to leave the union better off when you retire than when you were elected. The idea of dissipating funds in pursuit of some other union's revolutionary struggle, however 'noble', would be anathema.

Within days of the Euston Road gathering of the TUC Left, the High Court made clear that the NUM could not defy the law. On 30 July, Mr Justice Park fined the South Wales area £50,000 for disrupting the business of two Forest of Dean road hauliers. Coalfield leaders ignored the hearing and refused to pay the fines in the knowledge that their union would be sequestrated. Scargill immediately called on 'the whole labour movement' to honour the effectively defunct TUC policy on the Employment Acts and 'give total physical support' to the NUM. 'It has not yet penetrated the minds of this government or the judiciary that you cannot sequestrate an idea nor imprison a belief.' His fine words produced no discernible results. Amid scenes of protest outside the area office in Pontypridd, South Wales was duly sequestrated. Scargill tabled a motion for the TUC conference demanding 'total support' for the strike, a doubling of coal output, an end to the massive police operation that was getting 40,000 of his members into work every day, the 'mightiest mobilisation of the power and strength of the movement at all levels' to smash the employment laws and support for all workers in struggle. This insurrectionary prospectus was listed for debate.

Behind the scenes, PLP chairman Stan Orme laboured to keep lines of communication open in readiness for a fresh peace, but Mac-Gregor was losing patience, threatening to withdraw the draft agreement that still lay on the table. An emergency NUM delegate conference on 10 August endorsed their leaders' rejection of the proposal, and voted to continue the strike indefinitely. Afterwards, Scargill made clear where he stood on the picket line violence. There was 'violence by the police who should go back where they came from. I am not prepared to condemn brave men and women of my union whose only crime is fighting for the right to work.'

.While the strikers soldiered on, two working miners from Yorkshire, emboldened by the emergence from the shadows of 'Silver Birch', took the NUM to the High Court. Ken Foulstone, a forty-five-year-old face worker, and fellow miner Robert Taylor, thirty-three, whose bid to start a return to work at Manton colliery, Worksop, had failed, asked Mr Justice Nicholls for a number of 'reliefs'. Apart from the imposition of a ballot (which could have backfired), they were to get everything they asked for, including declarations that the strike called in Yorkshire and the national strike were both unlawful. The two men were smuggled down to London on 9 August by solicitor David Payne, of the Newark solicitors' firm Hodgkinson Tallent, for a press conference. They voiced their deep dislike of Scargill, Foulstone telling reporters: 'The only person that's given anything is the NCB, and the only person who hasn't given anything is the leader of the NUM.' They could hardly know that – as the verbatim notes have shown – Scargill was taking a substantially more conciliatory line in private than on the hustings. But they unquestionably represented a point of view more widely held than spoken.

The pair had not been discovered by accident. They were channelled into the growing revolt and the legal campaign by the Working Miners' Committee, now strongly under the guidance of David Hart, the libertarian adviser to MacGregor, who was working clandestinely for the downfall of Scargill. Hart contributed occasional leader-page pieces to *The Times* (where he described himself as a 'freelance journalist', rather as Mrs Thatcher might call herself a housewife: true, but not the whole truth), and was a close personal friend of the paper's editor, fellow old Etonian Charles Douglas-Home, who was also fanatically anti-Scargill. The network extended round another way: another partner in Hogkinson Tallent was a local Tory party grandee who knew Douglas Hogg, Conservative MP for Newark. His wife Sarah Hogg, now John Major's policy adviser in Downing Street, was then economics editor of *The Times*. She advised Payne to circulate publicity material round Fleet Street, and an article in the *Daily Express* giving a box number for donations to the working miners produced public gifts amounting to £34,000 in a month – not quite on the scale of the cash being given to the strikers, but enough to fund a High Court action to subvert the strike.

While these legal moves were afoot, Scargill placed his faith in creating a Left-centre coalition to back his hardline motion at the TUC, rather than accept a more vague, diversionary statement of support being prepared by the general council, which held its first debate on the dispute on 22 August. Union leaders belonging to the dominant centre-Right group on the general council were in a dilemma. They did not want Scargill to go down to defeat, but they could not stomach the stone-throwing dimension of the strike and they would not defy the labour laws. Alastair Graham, right-wing leader of the civil service union CPSA, warned that the NUM's insistence on the sanctity of picket lines 'could bring British industry' to a stop'. Three top leaders of the TUC met the NUM's troika for talks in a Brighton seafront hotel – the first since the strike began nearly six months previously. The outcome was a more strongly worded general council statement to Congress promising to impose a blockade on coal and coke and the movement of oil as a substitute fuel to power stations. Len Murray told delegates the plan was to make the dispute more effective 'and make mass picketing unnecessary'. Scargill was given a standing ovation when he declared: 'We are involved in a fight for the survival of our industry. We are fighting the threat of unemployment. We are fighting for the survival of our communities, of our culture and of a way of life.' He told delegates that only half an hour previously MacGregor had offered to recommence negotiations, and with Congress support the Coal Board and government could be compelled to sign an agreement on the industry. But before the cheers had died away, union leaders most intimately involved in making the 'solidarity pact' work were busily rubbishing it. Electricians' leader Eric Hammond said it would not work in the power stations. He revealed that he had privately sought to help the miners in May, offering to ballot power workers to strike in support of the NUM if Scargill would disavow his political objectives and unite the miners through a national ballot. The NUM leadership had rejected his overture. Delegates backed Scargill's resolution and the general council statement, but none of the rhetoric or promises ever came to fruition. The TUC did, however, become closely involved in the peace process.

Everybody else wanted to get in on the act. Robert Maxwell, flamboyant publisher of Mirror Group Newspapers, who was later revealed to be a high-flying crook, claimed his personal contacts had brought the two sides together. The indefatigable peacemonger Stan Orme was also active behind the scenes. Even the Archbishop of York was cited as a go-between. Nor could they decide who had invited who. Scargill said MacGregor had restarted the process; he said it was the miners. The preliminary sparring was ominous. Scargill said the NCB had to back down on all the issues – the five threatened collieries, withdrawing the 6 March programme and no economic closures. MacGregor said there would be no point in discussions unless the union was prepared to talk about 'the realities of life'.

The dispute then moved into the theatre of the absurd. The talks were called off. Scargill said his adversary needed a long rest. Mac-

Gregor said in a BBC TV interview: 'Scargill lies through his teeth.' He thought the miners' leader had been working 'too hard for his physical and mental health – the stress must be very great'. Scargill, who had lost weight (deliberately, he said) but none of his jaunty demeanour, suggested that MacGregor seek professional advice. The NCB chairman said he wasn't usually involved in name-calling, 'but one has to respond to repeated initiatives of that type'. After a flurry of hand-delivered letters up and down the Brighton line, the talks were on again, back in Edinburgh on 9 September.

This was the curtain for a week-long drama, of which the final tragic act was already clear. The talks broke down with monotonous regularity as the Coal Board sought to find another phrase with which to replace 'beneficially' but without losing the purpose behind it. MacGregor tried a new formula that gave the NCB a right to 'exercise responsibility for the human and financial resources in the industry'. The talks brought one unexpected agreement between Scargill and MacGregor: that media harassment was getting in the way. Negotiations shifted from Edinburgh to a 'secret venue' – a country house hotel in the North Yorkshire coalfield. After a 200-mile high-speed chase, the press and TV were back on the doorstep, and stayed there when the parties moved to the offices of British Ropes on an industrial estate in Doncaster. Negotiations went on into the small hours.

Overnight, the steam somehow ran out of the initiative. Kevan Hunt believes there were two possible points at which the dispute could have been solved: at the Rubens Hotel on 18 July and that night in Doncaster. 'There was never a prayer at any other time. All the jollying at Acas and elsewhere was forlorn. At the British Ropes meeting, I wasn't anxious to break up and nor was Ned [Smith] either, because it had all the feel of a settlement about it. The mood was right, the atmosphere. All the chemistry was working within people to reach a solution. These chances only come rarely, especially in situations like that, because everybody had a huge investment in that dispute at this stage. The game was called off. I don't think we blamed the NUM for that. McGahey and Cowan weren't youngsters. There was a general weariness around. We fixed up a meeting in the Post Office building [next door to Hobart House, held on 14 September]. We walked across there and the atmosphere was as cold as a mother-in-law's kiss.

'They came down separately. Anything that had been there at Doncaster had withered. It was clearly and truly forlorn, and we adjourned very quickly. It was one of the few days in my career that I cried. I was bloody distraught at the end of that. That was a chance gone, that I felt pretty sure would not return, to have a negotiated settlement. After that, try though we did, I never believed we would get a negotiated settlement. That was the closest we ever got.'[2] MacGregor later confirmed in his autobiography that he feared a settlement on the wrong terms at the British Ropes talks. He blamed the weariness of 'my own crew', who were 'beginning to waver'.[3]

The verbatim notes of the last meeting in this vital round disclose that the parties never fundamentally changed their positions. At one point, Scargill says: 'One or other side has to concede.' Cowan retorts: 'You can have your ideology! We can have our responsibility.' Heathfield points out that they have reached the stage of sitting and staring at each other. After lunch, Scargill says: 'If you can accept our words, we are in business.' MacGregor counters: 'I feel the same about ours.' For all the world like children arguing in a playground. Heathfield insists: 'We've got to overcome the economic connotations.' MacGregor points out that the NCB has 'tried very hard', but every formula is rejected. He later raps out to Scargill: 'What do you suggest now!', but the miners' leader stays calm, merely offering more talks. MacGregor says they will meet any time they have anything constructive to say. The meeting stood down at 3.05 p.m. Both sides went out and blamed the other. Those were the last rites of the peace process.

The TUC and the government conciliation service ACAS refused to accept that it was dead, and made many attempts to revive negotiations. But the dispute took off in another direction. David Hart privately urged an exasperated and receptive MacGregor to give up the chimerical pursuit of a negotiated settlement, and move in for the kill instead. That meant an end to the farce of peace talks, encouragement of the working miners in their legal battle to tie down Gulliver with the ropes of many writs, a hard new public face for the NCB and a big push to get a majority of the men back to work. The first fruit of this initiative was Mr Justice Nicholls's ruling that the national strike was unlawful in Derbyshire, and the restraining of Yorkshire or NUM officials from calling the strike of picket lines in the county 'official'. Rebel pitman Ken Taylor said: 'The law is made to be obeyed in this country and just because you are Arthur Scargill does not mean that you can flout the law. We are going to bloody

well show him that he cannot.' There are few more alarming sights
than one tyke doing down another.

Mr Justice Nicholls delivered his judgement on the Friday before
the Labour Party conference met in Blackpool, prompting Scargill
to go on Channel 4 News (his favoured television outlet: they gave
him longer to speak) and declare that whatever the High Court said
the strike was official and any miner who crossed the picket lines in
defiance of union instructions was at risk of being disciplined according to NUM rules. The Yorkshire dissidents' solicitors videoed the
broadcast, and reported the contempt to the court on Monday morning. Writs demanding the NUM leaders' appearance within forty-
eight hours were issued, and Hart chartered a helicopter to fly the
writ server to Blackpool that day, with a *Daily Express* photographer.
Armed with a false press pass made out to the newspaper, the High
Court official served the motion for contempt on Scargill and four
other NUM leaders as they sat listening to an otherwise unedifying
debate on local party structure.

With just a hint of incredulity, Scargill told reporters: 'Someone
representing the High Court came up to me and handed me a writ.
I was told it is committal proceedings to put me in Pentonville prison
for contempt.' Labour Party leaders were appalled. That morning,
he had taken Winter Gardens by storm with a *coup de théâtre*, winning
full backing for the strike, towards which the Shadow Cabinet was
deeply ambivalent. Now he was guaranteed martyr status, and headlines as well. Martyrdom could not come too quickly for Scargill,
who had often boasted of his readiness to go to jail for his beliefs.
After getting the rubber-stamp authority of his executive, which was
by now putty in his hands, he hurried to a fringe meeting organized
by the hard-Left *Labour Herald* and hollered: 'I want to make it clear
that if the offence I have committed is contempt, I plead guilty.
Because the only crime I have committed is to fight for my class and
my members.' Forced to choose between betraying his class and going
to prison, it was no choice: 'I stand by my class, by my union, and
if that means prison, so be it.'

No trade unionist had been jailed for what might loosely be
described as trade union activities since the so-called Pentonville Five
were committed to the north London prison in July 1972 for contempt of orders made by the ill-fated National Industrial Relations
Court. The TUC threatened a one-day general strike to secure their
release, but the five dockers were released after five days in jail

when the Law Lords conveniently reversed a lower court ruling and made trade unions legally responsible for the actions of their shop stewards. Scargill had joked about going to prison, fearing that he might have to share a cell with the right-wing union leaders Terry Duffy of the engineering workers and Frank Chapple of the electricians. But this was the real thing, though few seasoned observers believed that he would be allowed the status of St Arthur the Principled, martyr of the mineworkers. Sequestration of the union was a more likely route, having proved effective in the NGA *v*. Eddy Shah conflict.

The High Court adjourned the issue to give him time to reflect. He redoubled his contempt, reading out at another fringe meeting the minutes of the NUM executive reaffirming that the strike was 'official'. On 10 October, the court fined the union £200,000 and Scargill personally £1,000. He appeared on the steps of the NUM headquarters and breathed fresh defiance. On 25 October, Mr Justice Nicholls lost patience with the NUM, who appeared to think the law only applied to others. He sequestrated the entire assets of the union, listed at £10.7 million in funds and property before the dispute started, but much less after seven months of strike. Some £2 million had also been spirited abroad shortly after the outbreak of hostilities, and millions more had been spent since. Scargill, in London for a further abortive round of peace talks, still talked of running the union 'from the streets if necessary', and his wife Anne was seen moving files out of the NUM offices.

The talks he was attending were the last gasp of a faint-hearted move by the pit deputies' union NACODS to come to the aid of the miners. Under their new general secretary Peter McNestry, a talkative and sympathetic Geordie well to the left of the average pit overseer, the 16,000 NACODS members had voted by the remarkable margin of eighty-two per cent in favour of striking in support of the NUM campaign against pit closures. This was one of the few occasions that Mrs Thatcher really took fright. NACODS members perform statutory safety duties down the pit, and without them the Coal Board would have been legally obliged to shut down the mines still working and supplying the power industry with a million tonnes of coal a week. MacGregor was summoned to Downing Street 'in very short order'. He started to tell Mrs Thatcher that he now saw a successful outcome to the main dispute, and he did not think a NACODS dispute was critically important. She cut him short, saying:

'Well, I'm very worried about it. You have to realize that the fate of this government is in your hands, Mr MacGregor. You have got to solve this problem.'[4]

He did. He tickled up the colliery closure procedure by inserting an independent review body to whose views 'full weight' would be given – though that was balanced by the requirement to reflect 'both market and production opportunities'. Closure of Scargill's five named pits would be withdrawn. They would go into the new closure procedure, and the 6 March programme would be carefully reconsidered in the light of output losses due to the NUM dispute. This was a creditable negotiating performance by NACODS, especially as the ballot vote was actively being undermined by anti-Scargill forces in the union. But it did not fool Scargill. He thought the deputies had been duped into believing that MacGregor had given way on the kernel of the dispute. His suspicions were well founded. The independent review body never did keep open a single pit that the Board wanted to close. But MacGregor had effectively cleared the decks for the final showdown with the NUM.

Before it could come, Scargill scored a spectacular own goal. An innocuous little news item from the official Libyan news agency Jana was carried down-page in some of the 'heavy' papers on 27 October. It said that Colonel Gaddafi, the Libyan leader, had met a representative of the NUM and had 'expressed sympathy with the striking miners who suffer from abuse and exploitation at the hand of the exploiting ruling class in Britain'. End of statement, but not the end of the story. Behind this disingenuous paragraph lay the scandal that was to break over Scargill's head within hours, only to subside and detonate again with even greater force nearly five years later. The NUM representative pictured on Libyan TV embracing Gaddafi in his tent was Roger Windsor, the chief executive of the Union, who had been personally appointed by Scargill soon after he became the miners' president. And he was not there just to win sympathy with the striking miners, but to solicit cash aid too. This journey was undertaken at Scargill's behest only a matter of months after WPC Yvonne Fletcher had been murdered in cold blood in St James's Square by Libyan 'diplomats'. The whole idea showed appalling judgement. Most people in the labour movement assumed that the Russian miners and other Eastern bloc unions would be giving financial support, and indeed they were. McGahey openly spoke of help from the Soviet Union. This was different. He was livid, and still is.

'We made a mistake sending Windsor to Libya. I blew my top. I was never consulted.'[5]

Nor, it seems, was virtually anybody else, certainly not the executive, who had become inured to policy being made on the hoof and then brought back for their approval when it was too late to do anything about it. Some moderates protested. Trevor Bell, Scargill's rival for the presidency, said the initiative would put the dispute in a new context in the public eye, 'with heavy political overtones that will not go away whatever the explanations for this incident'. Scargill put out a mealy-mouthed statement that since the dispute began the NUM had been invited to more than fifty countries to explain the struggle against pit closures 'and to seek financial support for the families of striking miners suffering severe hardship'. The invitation to Tripoli had been extended on 6 October during a meeting with Paris leaders of the new International Mineworkers' Organization (which reappears devastatingly later) and had been accepted. Scargill concluded primly: 'Our union welcomes any financial contributions from trade unionists anywhere who support our campaign.' That the man who defied the High Court as the leader of a free and independent trade union could imagine that there were free and independent trade unions in Libya is an interesting sidelight on his thinking. It certainly did not wash with the TUC's new general secretary, Norman Willis, who was desperately trying to get new peace negotiations off the ground with Ian MacGregor. He 'advised' Scargill to have nothing to do with the Tripoli regime. Kinnock, whose relations with Scargill had soured to the point where he was 'too busy' to take part in coalfield rallies to win back support for the strike, was more forthright, denouncing the miners' president.

The issue died down, but it left a nasty taste in the mouth. Scargill had more to worry about nearer home. Now in its thirty-fifth week, the strike was showing real signs of failure. The constant raising and dashing of hopes by 'peace talks' that collapsed within hours or got nowhere was demoralizing the men. The Board had upped its financial incentive to break the strike. Men going back could earn up to £1,400 in wages and special Christmas bonuses, enough for many to pay off debts accumulated during eight months of all-out strike. On one day, 5 November, while yet another NUM delegate conference was going on in Sheffield, 802 men gave up the strike and crossed picket lines outside their pit. There were now 'new faces' at mines in South Wales, and 138 men back in Yorkshire. Scargill said the

strike was solid despite the Board's 'bribes, blackmail and browbeat-
ing' and would go on until MacGregor withdrew the pit closure
programme. The argument over the drift back to work began to take
on an air of unreality. Every day, NCB officials would issue figures
of hundreds of 'new faces' turning up for work. Scargill would ritually
deny their figures as 'misleading' and claim that eighty per cent of
the union's 180,000 members were still out. When the returnees
grew to a thousand a day, and then two thousand, he argued that few
of them were face workers and production could not therefore restart.
He told men at Bersham colliery in North Wales who staged a mass
return to work: 'There can be no forgiveness'.

His worst fears were realized in mid-November, when 'leading
TUC moderates', a euphemism for the dominant centre-Right
coalition, began asserting the right to take the strike out of Scargill's
hands. They were appalled at scenes at a rally in Aberavon, where
striking South Wales miners humiliated Norman Willis by dangling
a noose over his head. They had howled him down for daring to
condemn the violence of 'the brick, the bolt or the petrol bomb' on
picket lines, while Scargill stood impassively by. Willis' condemnation
of violence was not a ritual attack on brutality 'from wherever it
came'. He strongly criticized unprovoked police aggression and
excoriated Tory ministers who made maximum propaganda out of
their version of picket line scenes. But he went on: 'I could leave it
there, but I will not; for I have to say that any miner, too, who resorts
to violence wounds the miners' case far more than they damage their
opponents' resolve. Violence creates more violence, and out of that
is built not solidarity but despair and defeat. I have marched proudly
before many miners' banners and I know there will never be one that
praises the brick, the bolt or the petrol bomb. Such acts, if they are
done by miners, are alien to our common tradition, however, not
just because they are counter-productive but because they are wrong.'

Labour leaders had been waiting for just such a robust condemnation of violence by Scargill for many months. They were never to
get it. Yet Willis spoke at the end of a day of frightening scenes in
Yorkshire, where the return to work had begun in earnest. In Scargill's home village of Worsbrough, more than 2,000 homes were
blacked out after strikers brought down power lines while building
barricades to block the road to Barrow pit, and the drivers of vans
taking men back to work were set upon and injured. At Frickley
colliery, police fought running battles with pickets who set up road

blocks, and strikers at Thurcroft piled up timber and stone barricades and pulled a workman's hut across the road. This was just the start of it. The upswelling of hatred and despair in Yorkshire as more men went back under police protection beggared description. Mass pickets ranging from a few hundred to 6,000 gathered to halt the drift-back – which was now more of a surge. More than 850 police officers were injured (though only twelve were detained in hospital) and unknown hundreds of pickets were hurt.

Yet Scargill continued issuing statements from his bunker in Sheffield that three quarters of his members were still on strike, when the true figure was not much more than half. Energy Secretary Peter Walker taunted him that miners who had been deprived of a ballot were now voting with their feet. 'Mr Scargill's support is slipping away as increasing numbers become disgusted with a political strike which relies on Libyan paymasters and Soviet backing.'

Scargill was also losing his grip on his political constituency in the union. He urged limited co-operation with the receiver appointed by the High Court to seize the unpaid £200,000 fine, and had to rely on the hated moderates to get his way on the executive. Then he was rebuffed by a special delegate conference on the issue, outflanked on the Left by revolutionary Communist Jack Collins. There was a noticeable air of weariness and despondency at the top of the NUM, and relations with the TUC's 'seven wise men' chosen to liaise with the Coal Board on peace talks were strained. They found Scargill virtually impossible to deal with. He would not move away from the parrot-cry of his demands at the beginning of the strike, and the Coal Board simply refused to come back to the negotiating table until he did so. MacGregor spoke to his advisers of 'exorcising the Scargill factor'. In January, another 10,000 men went back to work, and the Board made ready to declare the strike 'finished' when more than half the NUM membership had been seduced or driven back to work.

A breakthrough appeared possible in late January, when informal contacts between McGahey and Ned Smith – noticeably in the absence of Scargill – yielded a draft agreement on the 'third category' of pit. Mines had always closed for reasons other than exhaustion or bad geological conditions, the two agreed. The problem now lay in defining this third category, and that ought not to be beyond the wit of experienced negotiators. The NUM was clearly ready to make the historic compromise on 'uneconomic' collieries. Ned Smith believes there could have been a settlement from these talks: 'We were in negotiations, proper negotiations. McGahey wanted a settlement.'[6] Mrs Thatcher evidently did not. She shot down the draft peace deal on Thames Television's 'TV Eye' programme the next day, saying an awful lot of loss-making pits had to be closed 'and you don't need to argue about the definition'. MacGregor must be free to close uneconomic mines. She insisted: 'Let's get it written down. I want it dead straight, honest and no fudging.' Talks about talks did take place, but quickly foundered. The NCB intensified its return-to-work campaign, and on 28 February the number giving up the strike had passed the psychologically important fifty per cent mark. Total collapse was only a matter of time away.

Yet Scargill did not budge. But others had been working for some time on a different strategy to end the conflict. In South Wales, officials dissatisfied with his leadership thought through the crisis, beyond the end of the strike. They reluctantly shared MacGregor's view that Scargill would never compromise. Terry Thomas, vice-president of the Welsh miners, said: 'If we had 99 per cent of what we wanted on the table, it would not have been enough. It was no compromise, no move at all. He would have said "right, we've got them on the run. We're winning. The lights must be just about to go out, or they wouldn't have asked us to settle." That was the philosophy he had.'[7] When the magic fifty per cent barrier had been breached, he would still only contemplate standing by the 'hard core'.

On that basis, there never would be a settlement. So South Wales, with only two per cent of its men back, took on the burden of getting a return *without* an agreement. Kim Howells, MP, says he first heard of the idea in the North East, and it was being openly discussed in the NUM offices – though not on the executive – around Christmas. 'By that time, things had become inconceivably desperate, and many of us in the coalfields had recognised that there seemed to be a serious credibility gap between what Arthur and Peter were saying on public platforms at these huge rallies and what was happening on the ground. There seemed to be no recognition of the appalling problems which miners' families were suffering. Scargill and the rest of the executive had missed every opportunity possible for arriving at some kind of compromise. A compromise didn't seem to be on his agenda. He was going for total victory and the corollary of that is total defeat. Many of us began to think how it might be possible to save the union. There was a feeling that the union was going to be destroyed totally. We knew there were plots of breakaways in Nottinghamshire, and contacts had been made with people keen on going back to work in South Wales. Some people in the coke workers' section appeared to be linking up on a national basis.

'It was also a period of enormous bitterness. A taxi driver had died, and two NUM guys were about to be convicted of murder. At that point, some of us felt it is really time to take a hand and try to bring a halt to all of this.'[8] The press got wind of the story, and it appeared on Ceefax. Howells recalls that Scargill saw it and rang up the South Wales office and was 'bellowing down the telephone'. An altercation between Scargill and Terry Thomas followed. 'After he reacted like that, we had to go back in an organised way before the whole bloody thing fell to pieces.'

On 1 March, with 95,000 miners back at work, the executive signalled an end to hostilities. A national delegate conference convened in Congress House would have before it South Wales's motion for an orderly return to work. Still Scargill would not let go. On the night before the 3 March conference, the Left held a stormy policy session. According to Emlyn Williams, veteran president of the Welsh coalfield, his general secretary George Rees walked out of the meeting. 'He [Scargill] was getting to the stage where he had tantrums. He wasn't getting his way. He did everything possible to stop South Wales putting that motion. We counted heads, and we knew it would be a stalemate. The next step was to get Scargill to use his casting vote, which any president would have done, one way or another.'[9]

But this wasn't just 'any president'. True to form, Scargill refused to use his casting vote in the event of a deadlock on the executive. Sure enough, the next day the executive voted eleven–eleven not to recommend the South Wales return-to-work motion, and by the same margin not to endorse the rival Yorkshire motion not to go back without an amnesty for hundreds of men sacked during the strike. Since the Board had no intention of ever signing such an amnesty, this was effectively a move to keep the strike going indefinitely. Unlike Gormley, Scargill sat on his hands. He refused to use his casting vote, either to keep the strike going or to call it off. This abdication of leadership was greeted with contempt by some coalfield leaders. Emlyn Williams, who called him a coward to his face, is still bitter. 'That is where Scargill fell down on leadership. He wanted everybody to carry the can bar him. He wanted to come out "pure". That destroyed the unity of the Left. They never met afterwards.'

The confidential verbatim report of that memorable conference makes unhappy reading. Scargill tried to duck and weave, but delegates on both sides of the policy divide sought to bring him back to his responsibilities. With the entire executive (apart from himself, as chairman) gagged by the stalemate, the argument was taken up from the floor. Des Dutfield of South Wales accused the executive of abrogating their responsibilities, and asked them to reconsider. 'They should have the guts this morning to make a recommendation.' Sammy Thompson of Yorkshire made the same plea, adding that if they did not come back with a recommendation, 'they will be looking as if they have rattled out on this strike'. They adjourned for half an hour, and came back still deadlocked. The debate went ahead without any leadership from the leaders. Terry Thomas of South Wales, moving the return-to-work resolution, asked delegates to 'search your hearts, comrades, and make your minds up. The men are calling for leadership . . . either give them leadership and repay the loyalty they have given us, or sit back with your blindfold on and you let the strike collapse around you. That is not leadership. We have got to live in the world as it is, and not as we would like it to be. Save the National Union of Mineworkers, for Christ's sake.'

Scargill, presumably sensing the mood of the meeting, was unusually brief but as upbeat as ever. 'Don't anyone in this conference lower their eyes and be ashamed of what they have done. This union has put up the greatest fight in the history of the trade union movement.' To have signed the agreement that the NCB demanded, conceding the principle of closing pits on economic grounds, 'is something that no trade union and no trade unionist can ever come to terms with. To accept this would be to give away your birthright, to prostitute your principles as a union and a movement.' He blamed the rest of the trade union movement, who had to their eternal shame ignored decisions taken by the Trades Union Congress and left the miners isolated.

A lot of people would look at the miners' struggle and what advances had been made, he went on. 'To do that would be to miss the point. *The greatest achievement is the struggle itself* [author's italics] because we have already shown that provided that we are prepared to fight against their policies we can prevent their implementation. We should say at this conference and at every opportunity that we salute our members, all of them, who have participated in this dispute. Their achievements, I submit, have changed the course of history. I submit that their struggle will inspire workers not only in this country but abroad, who have a completely new outlook as far as the fight for jobs is concerned. Comrades, it is upon struggles such as this democracy itself depends!'

The delegates voted ninety-eight to ninety-one for an organized return to work on 5 March. Amid scenes of anger, passion and dismay as the news filtered out to the strikers penned behind steel fences in narrow Great Russell Street outside Congress House, the great Strike for Jobs was over. So, too, was the dream nurtured over generations, that a left-wing coup in the NUM would change for ever the face of the union and the labour movement as a whole. In the words of Emlyn Williams, 'The Left had power, but they didn't know how to use it. And after the strike, they didn't want to use it because they had nothing to use it for.'

The return to work was inevitably an emotional affair, mostly a dignified march through the streets of the strikers' mining community behind the NUM branch banner. Men who had stayed out for a full year held their heads high. Their womenfolk, often pushing baby buggies or gripping the hands of toddlers, because this had been a young men's strike, walked at their side. Local people turned out and cheered them on their way. At some collieries, the return to work ended at the pit gate. Kent miners had sent out pickets to keep the dispute going over the amnesty issue, and after all their sufferings many men refused to cross the picket line. Scargill joined the return to work march to Barrow colliery, Worsbrough, and would not take the miners through the picket line there. He warned that without an· amnesty for the hundreds of sacked strikers 'you will not have peace in the coalfields'.

His old adversary MacGregor had other ideas. The miners would be punished for their 'insurrectionary insubordination'. The union quickly found that its traditional role of joint regulator of terms and conditions at pit level had gone for good. Managers demanded that the men obey orders and work efficiently, on pain of dismissal. Shift times were changed unilaterally, and – horror of horrors – branch officials of the union were sent back down the pit to work. The sacked men fared badly. None were taken back in Scotland, and apart from South Wales, where the union had better relations with the area director Philip Weekes, they had a hard time being taken on else-where. In a national ballot – the first since 1983 – the miners voted down their leaders' proposal to dock 50p a week from pay packets for the 'victimized' men. The voting was fifty-four per cent against, with only five areas agreeing to the levy. Just under 110,000 men voted, an indication of the collapse in membership.

The overtime ban was called off, and Scargill accepted the outstanding pay offers dating back to 1983. He also indicated willingness to operate the modified colliery review procedure negotiated by NACODS, about which he had been so contemptuous during the strike. He sidestepped questions about economic closures, but the agreement he signed laid down that the future of each pit would depend on 'both market and production opportunities'. His acceptance of the new procedure attracted few headlines. After the convulsions of the strike, the media wanted a rest from labour copy. Not so Mrs Thatcher. On tour in the Far East the month after the strike, she boasted to the premiers of Malaysia and Singapore that she had 'seen off' the miners.

Thus began the locust years for Arthur Scargill. Driven from the main field of battle against the Tory government and its Coal Board allies, he seemed to be looking inward for 'proxy' targets against whom he could succeed. In May, the NUM executive voted in his absence by ten to nine to sack Roy Lynk, moderate leader of the dissident Nottinghamshire miners. Lynk had balloted his members and won overwhelming approval to secede from the national union rather than accept the increased authority given to Scargill and the executive he dominated by the new rule book. The stage was set for the birth of the Union of Democratic Mineworkers.

But first the Left that had spawned Scargill was determined to have its own inquest. Pete Carter, a former official of the building union UCATT, and now industrial organizer of the Communist Party, produced a thirty-three-page internal report for the CP's Political Committee – its 'politburo'. It was so critical of Scargill that it was canned and never saw the light of day. Carter now regrets that: 'They felt it was identifying the politics of Scargill too severely.' He believes it would have cleared the air, especially as there had been an unpleasant argument during the strike between the party's general secretary Gordon McLennan and Scargill about 'Who is the best Marxist?' Scargill argued that he had the better understanding of Marxism in British terms. 'Anybody who has to argue at that level must be basically quite insecure,' observes Carter.[10]

CP leaders had a meeting with Scargill in September during the strike, he disclosed. It did not go well. 'We were prepared as a party to concede that there are such things as uneconomic pits.' In fact, the 'elder statesman' of the party, Bert Ramelson, was brought in to put together the CP's views and advice in a paper he delivered personally to Scargill. According to party sources, the man who once looked to King Street for leadership and guidance threw the document to the floor with an oath, declaring that it could have been written by the Coal Board. Not surprisingly, Carter's secret verdict on the strike was deeply pessimistic. The outcome was a major setback, he argued, for the miners and the working class as a whole, and minimizing the extent of that setback did nobody any service.

Without naming Scargill, but with him clearly in mind, Carter argues: 'The "total victory" argument is a cover-up for politics and strategy that did not succeed, nor could they have done. It is a failure to face up to the real world after the strike, as was the case during the strike. It stems from a philosophy that is unable to understand the politics of Thatcher's Britain, its effects on the people, and above all, how to respond.' He conceded that the miners were right to fight when they did. 'Unions cannot always pick the time and place of struggle.' But the tactic of 'no ballot' came unstuck; the union would have gained a more credible position with potential for wider solidarity if it had gone for a ballot, even if Nottinghamshire had voted against and ignored the national result.

Carter also attacked mass picketing, pointing out that it alienated many miners who might otherwise have been persuaded to participate in the strike. There would also have been an early condemnation of violence. 'The failure to speak out appeared to legitimise such violence. Young, inexperienced miners involved in industrial action for the first time were not given clear guidance that to respond by putting in the boot would not help them advance the cause and would only polarise opinion against them.' And denying the very notion of economics in policy for the coal industry made the NUM seem 'at best evasive and at worst not credible'. Nor did cold-shouldering the TUC help. Overall, Carter's verdict is damning. It helped confirm the final rift between Scargill and the party, which was in any case entering the terminal throes of its own internal divisions between Moscow-leaning hardliners and 'Eurocommunists'.

If he had not faced up to the real world during the strike, Scargill was totally unrepentant about it. His presidential address to the 1 July conference in 1985 was a model of self-congratulation. The strike had changed the course of British history. It had challenged the very heart

of the capitalist system. It had delivered the worst blow ever dealt to
the Thatcher government and created a crisis in international capital.
Traditional picket line militancy was not dead, and accurate historical
analysis would prove that beyond doubt. Orgreave had been a success.
The return to work without an agreement was a fundamental mistake,
and events had proved it to be so. The strike had brought forth
revolutionary changes within the union and within mining communities. Scargill repeated his guiding philosophy: 'We are involved in a
class war, and any attempt to deny that flies in the face of reality.
Confronted by our enemy's mobilisation, we are entitled, indeed
obliged, to call on our class for massive support.' He rejected any
'orgy of self-criticism', insisting: 'We should stand confident and
proud of what we have achieved, proclaiming the positive aspects of
the dispute, and the most important victory of all – the struggle
itself.' This argument was to be repeated ad infinitum until it became
an incantation, a spell, a strangely modified version of Marxism: 'The
means justifies the means.' It's the struggle that counts, not the winning. Two months later, Cortonwood colliery, the trigger for the
strike, closed without a murmur.

Nottinghamshire finally broke away on 7 July, prompting Scargill
to declare that secession 'raises the ghost of Spencerism, which in
the late 1920s led Notts miners into disastrous isolation'. The new
union could not join the TUC or affiliate to the Labour Party, but
it was quickly recognized by the Coal Board and thereafter placed
Scargill in the invidious position of having to sit down with the 'rebel'
union or refuse to negotiate. After losing a court action to exclude
the UDM, he chose splendid isolation, ensuring that NUM members
had to accept, belatedly, what their breakaway comrades had
negotiated.

Scargill's next battle was to commit a future Labour government
to reimburse the NUM for all its fines and financial losses during
the strike. The 1985 Blackpool Trades Union Congress overturned
the general council's recommendation and carried, by a slender margin, the mineworkers' demand. The vote irritated Neil Kinnock, who
had already blamed Scargill for the loss of the Brecon by-election in
July by only 559 votes, and there were moves to head off further
embarrassment at the party conference by negotiating a behind-the-
scenes pact. It was a forlorn hope. Scargill would no more compromise with Kinnock than with MacGregor. He carried the day at
Bournemouth, by 3.5 million votes to 2.9 million, a Pyrrhic victory

because it was not enough to force the Labour leader to include the commitment in his manifesto but quite sufficient to seal the final split with Kinnock.

He could no longer play politics with his executive, however. The breakdown of the old Left was never more in evidence than in October 1985, when Scotland and South Wales led the demand for him to 'bend the knee' to the High Court and purge his contempt so that the union could regain £8 million sequestrated during the strike. Scargill resisted the pressure as long as he could, and when the executive instructed him to apologize, he refused to do it in person. His own fine of £1,000 for contempt had already been paid by a mysterious unknown admirer. The TUC added its two-penn'orth to the pressure, and still he was unmoved. Not until 14 November did Scargill offer what Mr Justice Nicholls described as a 'perfunctory' apology, in writing, while sitting impassively in court listening to the story of how he had tried to evade the sequestration of NUM funds. The NUM was not out of the woods, however. Its funds remained in the hands of the receiver, Malcolm Arnold, on the instructions of another court. Not until 27 June 1986 did the Court of Appeal finally hand back to the NUM control over its funds, and then only because three new trustees 'whose integrity is not in question' had been appointed in place of Scargill, Heathfield and McGahey.

The court move came on the eve of the NUM conference in Tenby, South Wales, when McGahey emerged as the surprise instigator of a move to reconcile the union with the breakaway UDM. Scargill bitterly opposed the step, and it came to nothing. His presidential address, on the familiar theme that forty-two pits would be closed unless the union mounted a strike, was received with silence or only polite applause, even among Yorkshire delegates. His old rival Trevor Bell mourned: 'Mr Scargill is living in the past. No amount of rhetoric will rewrite the fact that we lost the strike.' But Scargill carried on like a hellfire preacher, and because he was still so much younger than the *ancien régime* who were in charge when he was first elected president, his position slowly began to revive as they reached retirement age. Moves by his old political rivals on the Left to make him a 'presidential pariah' failed. At the time of the Durham miners' gala, an official close to the 'McGahey–Kinnock axis' (an unlikely alliance) was quoted as saying: 'It is our belief that within a year he will either have lost all credibility or have resigned.'[11] Unfortunately for the plotters, the speculation was based on a false premise. Scargill is not a resigning man, and since he defines his own credibility, indeed redefines it to his own satisfaction as he goes along, he is not susceptible to being dethroned in the way his critics fondly imagined. Seven years later, he is still in office, while the fond originators of the failed coup are not.

In the aftermath of the strike, the tabloids found Scargill's personal life much more interesting than the ins and outs of labour movement politics. And with good reason. He furnished some splendid copy. In April 1986, he sued Peter Wright, chief constable of South Yorkshire Police, for 'exemplary damages' for alleged false imprisonment arising out of an incident outside his home at 2B Yews Lane, Worsbrough, nearly four years previously. The case came before a jury at the High Court in Manchester. Mike Mansfield, representing Scargill, said the early morning peace was shattered when four police cars containing seven officers converged on the spot. The scene could have indicated that a massive crime had been committed, but the police only wanted to question Scargill over an alleged speeding offence.

The jury heard that Scargill had been in London on the night before the incident in July 1982 for a radio interview with Carol Thatcher, daughter of his Conservative alter ego, the prime minister. He left London in a convoy, driving his Jaguar XJ6, with Jim Parker driving a Rover behind him. He could not have been driving at 110 to 120 m.p.h. on the M1, as later alleged, because both cars had 'governors' fitted to set the cruise control at seventy m.p.h. Five months later, Rotherham Magistrates Court had acquitted him of the speed charge.

On the night in question, as he parked outside his home and went to get suitcases out of the boot, a police car arrived and he was told to wait on the pavement for a motorway patrol car to arrive. He waited for more than thirty minutes, and police stopped him from going inside. Two other police Rover cars and a motorway patrol car finally appeared. His wife Anne, who had been watching the bizarre scene unfold from her bedroom window, came out into the street in her dressing gown and asked Scargill: 'What's wrong? Has there been a murder?' Scargill said: 'I felt like a criminal standing there in the middle of the road. The blue lights were flashing. It was like Blackpool illuminations. I told police it looked more like a scene from Starsky and Hutch. I said I was sorry, but could I go inside. She [Mrs Scargill] said: "Don't be silly, come on in." But the police officer replied: "He has got to stay here." I was under no illusion that I was not in a position to move at all. There is no doubt in my mind that if I had I would have been physically restrained.' Mr Mansfield told the jury that exemplary damages were awardable in 'circumstances surrounding unlawful acts which in your view are oppressive, arbitrary and unconstitutional, an abuse'. Scargill had been detained without authority for oppressive reasons.

Then the redoubtable George Carman, QC, perhaps Britain's leading counsel for this sort of case, to whom Scargill was to turn in later years, got to work on him. Carman, appearing for South Yorkshire Police, sought to get under Scargill's skin. He asked him to drop his television technique of avoiding giving direct answers to direct questions. 'You are a highly intelligent man and very used to being questioned. Just answer the questions being asked. You are not doing that. It may be something you have picked up from television. It would be better if you directed your mind to the questions being asked. I know it would be contrary to your nature. On television, they run out of time, but in court we have the time to wait for your answers and not let you steamroller your way through.'

Carman was particularly scathing about the statement of claim filed by Scargill's lawyers, which stated that he had 'suffered injury and damage'. What was the injury, Carman asked. The plaintiff said the circumstances of his detention on the pavement 'created injury in the sense that it was damaging to my reputation. It was published all over the British press ... I felt very deeply it was an infringement of my liberty.' His driver, Jim Parker, gave evidence about a 'fierce' policeman ordering the NUM president about, and Mrs Scargill also spoke of a 'very aggressive' policeman. A garage electrician, James Lamont, was produced to swear that the speed control device on the car could not have been working at the time Scargill claimed to have been using it when he was clocked on the M1. The car had been brought in to the garage where he worked about two days after the alleged speeding incident to get the unit working again. He was told if he did not get it working, the garage would lose the NUM business. Carman accused Scargill of having lied to the court over whether he had been pursued at excessive speed on the M1. His quarry retorted: 'That is not true, and I resent it.'

Carman's summing-up was a masterpiece. He described the plaintiff as 'a fading and flawed public figure' and his civil action as 'trivial and a fairy tale'. He told the jury: 'He seeks an award because he wants to have his stake in the pages of our contemporary history as a man who stood up as a champion of freedom and liberty. At the same time, he is seeking to expose the wicked behaviour of an oppressive police force. You may well take a deep breath indeed when you hear that claim because you may think to entrust Mr Scargill with the task of upholding your civil liberties might be regarded as dangerous as entrusting Satan with the task of abolishing sin.' The NUM leader was 'a self-admitted lawbreaker' who had been found in contempt of the High Court, and was therefore not perhaps the ideal candidate to crusade on behalf of his own civil liberties, much less others. He described the case as an 'extraordinary claim that may just deserve its place in the legal chronicle of our day. Rarely, if ever, has so much of other people's money been spent so freely and for so long over such a trivial claim.' Faced with such an onslaught, Scargill's counsel Mike Mansfield did his best, asking the jury if they could detect a note of hostility, a feeling of animosity, 'almost hatred', towards his client. 'Everything that could possibly be dredged up has been put before you. This is in danger of becoming a trial of Mr Scargill.'

If it was, the jury of six men and five women found against him after a three-and-a-half-hour retirement. Scargill was landed with costs of £100,000, though he was confident that none of this would fall on the union. He would donate the salary he had not been paid during the strike, and the rest would come from supporters. Perhaps the most curious thing about the case – apart from the unwiseness of bringing it at all – lay in the extraordinary delay. The 'unlawful imprisonment' had taken place nearly four years earlier. The strike had intervened. Why pursue the litigation, when there had been demonstrably no injury to his reputation save that self-inflicted by his conduct of the dispute?

The press had a field day with the court case, but there was an even bigger story building up. A small item in the *Evening Standard*'s 'Londoner's Diary' on 15 September 1986 headed 'Arthur on the move' told readers that, having persuaded the NCB to fork out for structural repairs to his bungalow in Worsbrough, Scargill had 'discreetly put the house on the market'. A small ad for 'Arthur's Bunker' had appeared in the local paper. It was described as an 'impressive and spacious' home with four bedrooms and two bathrooms, and viewing was by appointment only. The *Standard*'s mole said a large portrait of Che Guevara graced the entrance hall. The paper recorded that Scargill had bought the house for £3,500 twenty years previously, and had recently won a long battle to squeeze compensation from the NCB.

A paragraph in the following day's *Times* picked up the story, embellishing it with 'speculation that he is to buy a £125,000 house at Barnsley'. Curiouser and curiouser. In fact, the *Mail on Sunday* had reported in December 1985 that Scargill 'had twice tried to buy the £100,000 house now owned by his daughter's boyfriend'. Biology student David Roberts, aged twenty-three, denied that he had bought the oak-beamed property on the fringe of Worsbrough on behalf of Mr Scargill. He said he had bought the house with money from a trust left by his grandfather. He told the *Daily Mail* on 7 December 1985 that his future father-in-law was not involved in any way with the purchase of Treelands Cottage on Hound Hill. 'It's absolute rubbish to say that Arthur has bought this house. My grandfather owned a lot of property round here and had a bit of money. He left me quite a lot and that is the money I have used. Yes, it is a big house for a young couple. But it's lovely, isn't it? Contracts have been exchanged, but I don't know when I'm moving in because I've some studying to do yet.'

His grandfather may indeed have left him some money. But in other respects he was lying. The Lightman Inquiry report[12] discloses that Mr Roberts bought the house as a nominee for Scargill, on 16 September 1985. Completion took place on 1 October 1985. The source of the funding will be investigated later, but Scargill told Gavin Lightman, QC, he bought the house in this clandestine manner because 'he wished to conceal his identity as purchaser to avoid adverse publicity'.

And well he might. The secret purchase of one of the most desirable properties in his home village went through only six months after his members went back to work at the end of the most harrowing strike in post-war history. Hundreds, perhaps even thousands, lost their homes when they could no longer keep up their mortgage repayments. They did not have access to the kind of money that enabled Scargill to buy the house of his dreams. They did not even have the money to keep a roof over their head. Yet Scargill, the man who would not 'prostitute his principles' and sneered at those who did, could fork out £100,000 for a stone-built, three-bedroom house set in an acre of land. The estate agents rhapsodized about it, as they were entitled to do: 'This outstanding house is a monument of elegance and a home which combines the integrity of the past with

the virtues of present-day modernity.' The grounds include twin
monumental pools, a waterfall and a fountain. The property is
reached through wrought-iron pillars along a sweeping gravel drive.
It has beamed ceilings, oak floors, a Regency-style principal bedroom,
and a sunken bathroom. And Arthur has a sunken reputation.

The Scargill family is believed to have moved into the property
in the New Year of 1987, after workmen installed two 500-watt
searchlights at the front to deter intruders. On the front door, a new
brass knocker in the shape of a miner's safety lamp was installed.
Scargill has lived there in some comfort ever since. He did, however,
experience great difficulty in selling his bungalow in Yews Lane,
partly because he had made such a ballyhoo about mining subsidence
from nearby Barrow colliery. Eventually, it was sold privately – but
not before Scargill had tried another extraordinary trick. In late 1986,
soon after Lord (then Sir Robert) Haslam took over from Ian Mac-
Gregor as chairman of the NCB, the miners' leader asked for a
private, one-to-one meeting with him. Haslam was reluctant to
engage in such meetings, but he put aside his misgivings and agreed
to meet Scargill. He had a PA standing by just in case the NUM
president was about to make a Gormley-style secret initiative to break
the deadlock in the many problems facing the coal industry's industrial relations. It was the only time Scargill accepted a cup of tea
from the chairman. He did not have the problems of the industry on
his mind. Only his own problems. He told Haslam his house was on
the market and he was having difficulty selling it. Would the Coal
Board be interested? The asking price was £40,000 – rather less than
he had been asking in Barnsley. An astonished Haslam still said 'No'
and the tête-à-tête was terminated.

While all these fascinating events were going on in his private life,
it was politics as usual for the Squire of Treelands. In January 1987,
he was pressing Labour to enter the election with a commitment to
double the size of the coal industry by the year 2000. He appeared
on television to attack a Tory tormentor, Spencer Batiste, MP, who
claimed that leaked documents showed the NUM was £2 million in
debt. 'We are not going bust,' he declared. In South Wales, he suffered a rebuff as the NUM area leadership agreed to talks with the
NCB on possible six-day working at a planned £90 million super-pit
at Margam. But his candidate to succeed McGahey as vice-president,
Yorkshire area official Sammy Thompson, beat off the old Left's
challenger Eric Clarke. As the general election approached, his old

enemy Peter Walker emerged to play the Scargill card. He told a
Tory rally in South Yorkshire that Labour's first big campaign cheque
was for £400,000 from the NUM. Scargill was at the other side of
the Pennines, campaigning for Terry Fields, later disowned by
Labour for his Militant links. On the hustings in Liverpool, Scargill
demanded that a Kinnock government 'take into common ownership
the animals of Fleet Street' who had been prying into his private life.
When Mrs Thatcher won her record third term of office, he claimed
to have been 'gagged' during the election campaign. There had been
'undue pressure from the top of the party' to prevent him speaking
at rallies. He dismissed the idea that Labour had a 'brilliant' campaign. 'If it was brilliant, Labour would have been elected,' he said.
Sharing a platform with Neil Kinnock at the Yorkshire miners' gala,
he reiterated his belief in 'extra-parliamentary activity'.

Scargill's own future came under scrutiny at the NUM annual
conference. Delegates pushed through a rule change in July 1987
making him stand for re-election, which he had avoided hitherto by
not using his vote on the executive. New legislation would close that
loophole, but the miners decided to pre-empt that step. His stock
was rising. The Coal Board's vicious' new disciplinary code gave him
an opportunity to go back to the members in a pithead ballot. For
the first time since his own election, he won. The men voted by 77.5
per cent in favour of 'various forms of industrial action' after a dispute
over the disciplining of men at Frickley, the 'second to none' militant
pit near Doncaster. The result was hailed as Scargill's Second
Coming, but this assessment proved premature. A national overtime
ban was imposed, but it was operated in a half-hearted way and quietly
ditched some months later.

Scargill did not have a very good Congress that year, just retaining
the seat on the general council he had resumed in 1986 on McGahey's
retirement, but being kept down on the unglamorous committees
once again. His confrères insisted he was a 'new boy' and had to start
again at the bottom of the ladder. He also lost a key vote on nuclear
power – but he grabbed the headlines with the story of his derring-do
on the Blackpool seafront. With a billiard cue in his hand, picked up
in the pub where he had been drinking, management consultant
Geoffrey Hill, aged forty-six, approached Scargill in a telephone box
'to tell him he's done more damage to this country than anyone since
Hitler'. Scargill said: 'The man made some references to my political
attitudes and then he tried to hit me with a cue, so I flattened him.

I was very interested in judo for about ten years and I can look after myself. I was not hurt in any way, but he was.' The rash management consultant claimed that minder Jim Parker put his arm round his neck and pulled him back, and Scargill burst out of the phone box and tried to punch him. His glasses fell off, and in the scuffle he hurt his eye. At the time, Parker said nothing. Today, he supports Hill's version of events, adding for good measure that Scargill cowered in the phone box when Hill first opened the door.

If he came out of the phone box as Clark Kent rather than Superman, Scargill soon demonstrated he could still fly. On 12 November 1987, he caught the opposition on the hop by resigning the NUM presidency at a routine meeting of the executive called to discuss the flagging overtime ban. He immediately went into campaign gear, telling miners that if Mrs Thatcher and the Tories didn't want him, and nor did British Coal or Sir Robert Haslam, 'I can think of no better grounds for supporting me.' The ballot was called for January, five years after the previous poll, and he told the *Barnsley Chronicle*: 'I can expect support on the basis of integrity, commitment and unswerving loyalty.' Taken unprepared, the Right was in consternation. There was also outrage at 'legal advice' suddenly produced that any full-time official who wished to stand would first have to resign his post. But John Walsh, the North Yorkshire area agent, had no qualms about putting his job on the line. 'A large number of members are disillusioned with the leadership,' he argued.

Scargill knew that, and spared no effort to get re-elected. He appeared at more than thirty rallies, and was surprised to be nominated even by the old county enemy, Lancashire. There was one embarrassing interlude. He had been due to visit Australia for a conference of the International Mineworkers' Organization, of which he was also president. He called off the trip, but he had already prerecorded an interview with David Langsam, an Australian freelance journalist living in London, who sold it to *The Observer*. In the interview, he once again appeared to embrace Communism, recalling that he had learned his socialism from his father Harold, 'who was, and is, a Communist. Not the Eurocommunist variety, not the New Realist variety, but the real Communist who wants to see capitalism torn down and replaced by a system where people own and control the means of production, distribution and exchange. It's called, quite simply, Socialism. He convinced me at the time that it was right. I'm more passionately in support of that view now than I was then.'[13]

He took no chances on being re-elected. The Arthur Road Show was brought back into operation, making more than thirty appearances all over the country. The message was the same: no compromise, no collaboration. He offered a knout rather than an olive branch to the UDM, and rejected the idea of a flexible working week. But this was not a repeat of 1981. The Left was divided. His home county was divided, with two Yorkshiremen contending for the post. In South Elmsall, near Doncaster, when he spoke to Frickley supporters, in the streets outside the Pretoria working men's club were fly posters comparing the house he had when he became the national president and his new mansion. The unwritten message was that he had done rather well out of the job. The scandal of quite how he got the house was yet to break, however.

An infected right arm confined him briefly to hospital in the latter stages of the campaign, which went to a nail-biting finish. Scargill retained the presidency with fifty-four per cent of the poll, a slump from the seventy per cent he had achieved in 1981. He was predictably modest: 'My election victory in the present climate can only be described as a stunning win for the fundamental principles of trade unionism and represent a staggering defeat for "new realism".' Hardly 'stunning', but enough. He demanded a renewed attack on 'the common enemies', British Coal and the government. The immediate speculation was that he now had the job for life, but the Department of Employment indicated that labour laws took precedence over NUM rules, and he would have to stand again in 1993.

As the miners' numbers dwindled, Scargill lost his seat on the TUC general council. But he sustained his interest in pushing Tony Benn's political future, backing him personally for his bid for the Labour leadership in the summer of 1988. Benn had tried to get Scargill into Parliament with him, two years previously, when Roy Mason retired his Barnsley Central seat. Scargill had 'considered it seriously, but felt it wasn't right'. Benn flattered him that he could be 'highly significant' in rebuilding the party from the inside as an MP – particularly if he remained president of the NUM.[14] There would have been an outcry within the union had he tried to keep both jobs, but Scargill never had been attracted to the idea of being a back-bencher. He felt he had more power where he was, and there was precious little class war in the Commons. If 222 Euston Road was a den of metropolitan temptation, then what was the Palace of Westminster?

Nothing was too good for the workers, however. At the 1988 NUM conference, he unveiled a new charter demanding £20,000 a year, a four-day week, retirement at fifty and a permanent ban on systematic overtime. His ambitious plans, which most delegates felt to be completely out of touch with reality in the coalfields, received only dutiful applause, while his sentiments in support of two Welsh miners who killed a taxi driver during the strike stunned his audience. Scargill once again hijacked the headlines when he paid tribute to their 'spirit and courage', a view condemned by Neil Kinnock as 'disgusting' and by Norman Willis as 'insensitive and crass'. He went back to Sheffield to a pay dispute at union headquarters. Staff earning between £5,000 and £13,000 a year wanted 'parity' with their £39,000-a-year boss. The complaint was a familiar one: they felt 'at the mercy of a feudal lord who has total power'.

It was a thin year at the cutting edge of militancy. In December, Scargill's members voted fifty-one per cent 'No' in a ballot on industrial action to force British Coal to negotiate with the NUM at pits where the breakaway UDM had a majority. His authority was back on the erosion path, and one executive member, who (as usual) declined to be named, said: 'Nobody in authority who has a clue is talking to him. He is surrounded by hero-worshippers. Nobody says that the king is naked.' A delegate conference in the New Year of 1989 went on to approve what his critics called 'backward and undemocratic' rule changes that made it progressively harder for his position to be challenged. Candidates for senior office would have to secure nomination from areas representing twenty per cent of the union's 90,000 membership before getting on to the ballot paper. Only Yorkshire, Scargill's heartland, with more than a third of the total membership, qualified as a stand-alone coalfield under this rule. Had it been in operation during Scargill's most recent contest for the presidency, John Walsh, the man who took forty-six per cent of the vote and almost unseated him, would not even have been able to stand, because he had to go outside his own coalfield for a nomination. The Left's great drive for democracy had come to this.

Media interest in Scargill began to diminish. The fascination had been with what he could do on the great stage of British politics, and the story had now become whether he could sustain his own position as the undisputed leader of a middle-ranking union that had been forced to knuckle under. It wasn't just the media who tired of him. He even disappears from Tony Benn's memoirs, with only a single, cursory mention in the diaries from 24 January 1987 when he appeared along-

side the author on a platform outside Wapping) until the next great
public event in his life in March 1990. He wasn't muzzled. He just
wasn't reported any more. The box-office boy couldn't sell tickets, but
his desire to be in the headlines never diminished. It was just harder to
make it. He was up to the challenge. You just had to be more outrageous. Alas, nobody was listening any more. At the Yorkshire miners'
gala on 17 June 1989, he predicted that British Coal would cut the
industry from seventy-eight pits employing 76,000 men to fifty pits
employing 50,000 men. He was still right – though not right enough.
Less than four years later, there were fifty pits and fewer than 30,000
miners. Scargill continued to rant that 'there is only one way to save
the industry and that is by being prepared to take industrial action if
necessary'. The faithful applauded. But he was casting at straws. Some
of them were quite substantial. The idea was floated that he could
become treasurer of the Labour Party. It was firmly squashed by the
Transport and General Workers' Union, with whom the NUM had
begun merger talks. Then those negotiations, too, fell by the wayside.
The merger document suggested a new TGWU Energy Section in
which nuclear energy workers and opencast coal miners would have a
vote as well as NUM members. Scargill saw a chasm yawning, and his
executive declined to follow up the amalgamation proposals. He ended
the year in hospital in Sheffield, undergoing observation over the
Christmas period after complaining of chest pains. He knew the real
pain was yet to come.

CHAPTER IX

SCANDAL

THE STORM BROKE on 5 March 1990. Under a banner headline 'Scargill and the Libyan Money: The Facts', the *Daily Mirror* alleged that Arthur Scargill got £163,000 in strike support from Libya, and used a large chunk of it to pay off personal debts. While miners were losing their homes at the height of the bitter 1984–5 strike, the paper said, Scargill counted out £70,000 from 'a huge pile of cash strewn over an office table' and ordered it to be used to pay back his £25,000 mortgage to the NUM and the home loans of his two top officials, general secretary Peter Heathfield and chief executive Roger Windsor. Scargill had always denied accepting money from the terrorist-linked regime of Colonel Gaddafi, but the *Mirror* alleged that this was a BIG LIE. 'Our inquiries reveal that the president of the National Union of Mineworkers launched an incredible cloak and dagger operation to bring a secret hoard of Libyan money into Britain. The cash was intended to relieve the hardship of the embattled miners and their families. It was part of a torrent of money flowing into the NUM from all over the world – including secret funds, totalling £1 million, donated by Russia.'

Four inside pages were dominated by the story, and a series entitled 'The Scargill Affair' ran all week, with fresh allegations every day. On the same day that the first shocking 'revelations' were published, Central Television's investigative programme 'The Cook Report' screened a half-hour special entitled 'Where Did The Money Go?', an equally hard-hitting journalistic coup. Roger Cook, the fearless investigator, had persuaded Windsor and Jim Parker, Scargill's closest confidants, to appear on camera to talk about life with the president. They made the same allegations, and more besides.

Windsor, who had been videoed kissing the Libyan dictator in his tent in Tripoli in October 1984, told viewers he had received three packages each of £50,000 cash from Altaf Abbasi, a Pakistani who represented Libyan interests in Britain. He kept the money in old biscuit tins in his larder before taking it in a suitcase to the NUM offices in Sheffield. There, Scargill opened the suitcase and counted out four piles: £10,000 for the striking Nottinghamshire miners, £29,000 for his own bridging loan, £17,500 for Heathfield's home extension, and £25,000 for Scargill's own home in Yorkshire. He put the rest of the money back into the suitcase, and telephoned the union's accountant, Steve Hudson, to come down. He was asked to take away the bundles of money and give a receipt for each of the bundles to the persons concerned.

'The Cook Report' interviewed Dr Kim Howells, MP, who said that a delegation of Russian miners had told the South Wales area leaders that 'a large amount of money designated for the British miners' had left Moscow. They wondered what had happened to it. So did the Welsh miners. They had never heard of the donation. Windsor then told viewers that £1 million from the Russians had been received in an NUM bank account in Geneva.

These two allegations triggered the greatest personal and political crisis in Scargill's life, which still reverberates today. The full story has never been told. In so far as it is known, this is it. In July 1988, the NUM annual conference was held in Great Yarmouth, Norfolk, and attended by the Fleet Street 'mafia' of industrial reporters, including Terry Pattinson, industrial editor of the *Daily Mirror*. Pattinson, an occasionally abrasive Geordie of rather less than average height, an old-fashioned Labour loyalist and sometime leader of his office NUJ branch, chanced across Maurice Jones, editor of *The Miner*, a member of the Communist Party and Scargill stalwart for more than a decade. Jones was very disgruntled about life in 'Colditz', as staff called NUM headquarters. He was non-committal about rumours going round the conference that visiting Soviet miners were asking: 'What happened to our million pounds?' George Bolton, Scottish area executive member, knew 'categorically' that the cash had been sent, but had no proof. Scargill himself had been reported by *The Sunday Times* as telling a rally in Bedworth, Warwicks, that the Russians had donated half a million pounds. But nobody knew what had happened to it. 'Except Arthur,' volunteered Jones.

Then the trail went cold for a year. During that time, Parker's disillusionment with Scargill became total. Tiring of being a dogsbody to his hectoring boss, he took £15,000 voluntary redundancy in March 1989. At the NUM conference in July that year, Jones told

Pattinson that he too was about to quit. He and Parker had a document that would 'blow his mind'. The two met at St Pancras station the day after the conference closed. Jones told the *Mirror* man to disguise himself as a tourist, and dived on to the floor of his car when they left the station. They talked in a nearby pub, and Jones kept up the air of melodrama by insisting on facing the door. Clearly nervous, the *Miner* editor produced from his briefcase a photocopied Bank of Ireland monthly account statement dated April 1988 which had been sent to the International Miners' Organization, c/o Mr Arthur Scargill at NUM headquarters. The balance of the account was substantially more than a quarter of a million pounds. It seemed very curious that such a large sum of money was in a Dublin account, so long after the strike and the lifting of receivership of the NUM in June 1986. Pattinson showed the document to his editor, Richard Stott, who did not want an immediate story but gave the go-ahead for what became Operation Cyclops – the unmasking of Scargill. Embittered by his long years of virtual servitude, Parker spilled the beans to Pattinson about Scargill's alleged desire to get as much as £20 million out of the Russians, which he thought would match the £1 million given in 1926, after inflation.

Another critical piece of the jigsaw slotted in soon after. At the end of July, Roger Windsor, Scargill's right-hand man as chief executive, summoned Pattinson to Sheffield for an interview. He, too, had had enough of Scargill and was taking voluntary redundancy. He was moving to France, and he wanted to sell the story of his life and times at the court of King Arthur. The powers that be at the *Mirror* insisted on sending an investigative 'hard-man', Ulsterman Frank Thorne, to work with him. The two sat in Windsor's living room in Kenbourne Road, Sheffield, while the man who kissed Gaddafi opened his heart – at a price. He wanted £30,000. Negotiations were opened, and the tapes began to roll.

It was an extraordinary story. In September 1984, Scargill had picked up one of the many letters offering help that came into the NUM offices. 'This one needs following up,' he allegedly told Windsor. It came from Altaf Abbasi, a Pakistani shopkeeper in Doncaster. Windsor arranged a meeting at the home of a Pakistani friend in Sheffield. Abbasi told Windsor he had contacts at the highest levels in Libya, and financial assistance would be forthcoming to help the striking miners in their struggle against the Thatcher government. The conspiratorial atmosphere deepened when Abbasi – who still lives in Britain – suggested code names. He would be the Doctor, Scargill would be the Patient and the Libyan go-between in Tripoli would be the Consultant. Windsor arranged a meeting between Scargill and Abbasi a few weeks later in Blackpool, where the Labour Party conference was in session. According to Parker, there was a second meeting in Scargill's car on the seafront at Lytham St Annes. 'If my memory serves me right, he were asking for sort of two million quid in support of the strike,' he told 'The Cook Report'.

The upshot of those talks was a further meeting in Paris the following week with the Consultant, Salim Ibrahim, who was Gaddafi's bagman. They flew out from Manchester on 8 October, Scargill using the fictitious name of Smith. During talks in the offices of the French miners, Scargill volunteered Windsor to go out to Tripoli. Twelve days later, Windsor flew to Libya via Frankfurt. After kicking his heels for two days in a luxury hotel, he was summoned to the presence. He gave Gaddafi a detailed report on the strike, and told him that the NUM president 'had asked me to request sympathetic consideration for funds'.

Scargill had always denied that any such appeal had been made. When news of Windsor's visit hit the headlines during the strike, Scargill said: 'At no time have we received monies and at no time have we sought or been given any monies from the Libyan government.' This was echoed in a statement on 28 October 1984 by TUC general secretary Norman Willis, who said Scargill had given him a 'categorical assurance' that no financial support had been sought or received by, or would be accepted by, the NUM 'from the Libyan regime, which he, like myself, regards as an odious tyranny'. Then what possible purpose was there for such a mission? It strains imagination beyond the bounds of credulity to believe that Scargill would despatch his chief executive to Tripoli for the best part of a week at such a critical juncture – with a High Court-appointed sequestrator. taking control of the union's assets – simply to reiterate the familiar litany of hardship and accept the condolences of the Libyan 'trade unions'.

Because the video taken in Gaddafi's tent had been screened round the world even before he got home, Windsor was in deep trouble as soon as he got off the plane. But, he told the *Mirror*, 'Arthur was concerned not about the bad publicity but about how much money we had been promised and secondly that we should concoct a cover story to deal with the union's national executive.'[1]

When the heat was off, towards the end of November 1984, said Windsor, he was chauffeured by Parker in the presidential car to three separate drops, picking up cash to the tune of £163,000. This money was taken into the NUM offices on 3 December, he alleges, and divided up as the *Mirror* had detailed. 'Arthur looked on it as a clever thing to do. There was this money no one knew about, and it was protecting the union by protecting Scargill, Heathfield and me.'

This was the story he told to the *Mirror* duo, who were later joined on the story by another staff sleuth, Ted Oliver. They then turned their attention back to Jones and Parker, who were initially unwilling to divulge all they knew until Pattinson disclosed that Windsor had squealed, and had produced a briefcase full of photocopies of internal NUM documents. Their attitude changed to one of full co-operation. But Stott, the *Mirror* editor, still would not publish until he had further corroborative evidence. Thorne and Oliver, the 'hit men', were given the task of finding Altaf Abbasi – the Doctor. Pattinson enlisted Windsor's aid to find 'the fourth man', Steven Hudson, who had allegedly been present at the divvy-up of the cash. Windsor was unhappy about being used as an undercover reporter, but undertook to speak to Hudson, who was now working for CISWO, the coal industry social welfare organization, based in Barnsley. Its head, incidentally, was former NUM international secretary Vernon Jones, yet another refugee from Scargill's court. Windsor made a taped telephone call to Hudson, in which the former NUM accountant confirmed the basics of the story. Windsor then moved to the property he and his wife Angie had bought in the South of France. Stott took personal charge of the investigation, and told his publisher, Robert Maxwell. At a drinks function on the Trades Union Congress fringe the next month, Maxwell quizzed Pattinson about the probe and, intrigued by what he heard, told them to get it right. After all, if there was a libel action, he would have to foot the bill.

Thorne and Oliver tracked down Altaf Abbasi to a new address in Nottingham. They pretended to be *Mirror* journalists writing a book on the great strike, not a particularly convincing cover for desperate-looking men. Abbasi fled, thinking they were genuine hit men sent by Gaddafi. He took a lot of persuading – but no money – to talk. Abbasi is widely travelled on the political fringes, and he claimed to have been in contact with Scargill for more than a year before Windsor was sent out to Tripoli. He even fancied himself as an NUM-sponsored MP. Abbasi confirmed Windsor's version of events.

The *Mirror* team now had four solid, mutually corroborative accounts of the Scargill scandal. A fifth practically fell into their lap, in the unlikely shape of eighty-five-year-old John Platts-Mills, QC, globetrotter extraordinaire for left-wing causes. Pattinson spotted his name among the documents supplied by Windsor, and rang the barrister more in hope than expectation. But the old boy was only too happy to talk, not just once, but twice – and the second time he was taped. Platts-Mills admitted taking the miners' begging bowl to Moscow *and* Libya.

By now, the *Mirror*'s ferreting in dark corners had been noticed. Despite a blackout on Operation Cyclops, news of what was going on had filtered out as far as the producer of 'The Cook Report', Clive Entwistle, a former *Mirror* and *People* journalist of substantial repute. He suggested working together to tie the story up. Entwistle, working on a programme about the strike, heard everywhere that Pattinson had 'something big', and had guessed it was 'about Russia'. Rebuffed at first by the *Mirror*, Entwistle did his own digging. Through a Russian woman journalist distantly related to Gorbachov, he located Mikhail Srebny, the Russian miners' leader who sent the money to the NUM and now backed up Windsor's story. He told Pattinson of his discovery over a drink, and completed his dismay by saying they had got Abbasi – the Doctor – too. Reluctantly, the *Mirror* team agreed to a joint production on the story, with a synchronized launch.

However, time was passing. The story didn't run in September 1989, because Stott wasn't satisfied. Then they were into the party conference season, and the paper didn't want to spoil Labour's conference or present a political gift to the Tories. And then it was the run-up to Christmas, and there were other things on people's minds. Pattinson had virtually given up hope when two unexpected events sealed the fate of the story. Stott, who had temporized, was sacked by Maxwell in January 1990, and Roy Greenslade, assistant editor of *The Sunday Times* who took over the *Mirror* editorship, was keen to publish. And Steve Hudson, the elusive 'fourth man' in the drama, simply telephoned out of the blue and volunteered an interview. He went round to the *Mirror* office in Holborn and told Pattinson what he wanted to hear: that Windsor was 'telling the truth'.

It was just as well that Greenslade decided to publish. Scargill, who was deliberately being kept out of the picture to the very end so that the story could not be injuncted, had been tipped off about the investigation by Platts-Mills. Scargill launched a number of pre-emptive strikes. In October 1989, he brought out a special issue of *The Miner* – the first since Maurice Jones's departure – with a front page article headlined '*Mirror* Smears?' Aping Fleet Street style with an 'exclusive' box over Peter Heathfield's by-line, the splash asked: 'Has Robert Maxwell's "Daily Mirror" launched a special "smear" campaign against the NUM? And is its prime target Union President Arthur Scargill?'

Recent *Mirror* stories and its covert inquiries 'have led us to suspect that something rather sinister is going on,' the story continued. Since the union's annual conference in July, the *Mirror*'s industrial editor 'seems to have been thrown into searching for information to try and discredit Arthur Scargill'. Beneath the cross-heading 'Stolen Documents', *The Miner* reported that during the conference, several documents together with entire files 'were stolen from Mr Scargill's personal secretary's office. Included was a bank statement relating to the International Mineworkers' Organization, marked Private, and addressed to Arthur Scargill. This was not surprising, as he was president of the IMO, which had a membership of six million from mining unions in 43 countries, and he is a signatory to its bank accounts.'

A copy of the stolen bank statement had been handed to the *Mirror*, and Pattinson had begun a feverish hunt for information. But not one sentence had appeared in the *Mirror*. The *Mail on Sunday* had run the story, but it sank like a lead balloon. Lawyers acting for the IMO had demanded the document back, without success, both papers claiming they had destroyed their photocopies. Now Pattinson was off on the trail of something else 'in true James Bond [well, Basildon Bond] fashion' – another 'stolen' letter written by Scargill to John Platts-Mills, QC. 'There's no deep, dark mystery' about this, *The Miner* assured its readers. Platts-Mills had contacted the NUM offering to raise money internationally. Scargill had replied in January 1985, and again a month later, saying that the union needed help in raising money to maintain the NUM, pay legal costs and assist areas needing finance for picketing. He gave details of a bank account in Warsaw, belonging to the Miners' Trade Union International (forerunner of the IMO), where donations could be sent.

Letters like this had been sent all over the world, the article insisted (printing a copy of the one to Platts-Mills). So what was the *Mirror* up to? *The Miner* hazarded a guess that the *Mirror* was trying to sabotage a prospective merger between the NUM and the TGWU, concluding with a classic Scargill homily: 'It's time the trade union and labour movement took a stand against gutter journalism which seeks constantly to smear and vilify trade union leaders who stand by the principles on which they were elected.'

Plainly, Scargill was rattled. He also went to Sheffield Police to report the break-in at his office and to lay a complaint against Windsor concerning a company named Oakedge, of which he was secretary. Windsor and two other head office officials, industrial relations officer Mick Clapham (now MP for Penistone and Barnsley West) and David Feickert (the NUM's head of research until May 1993), had bought the firm 'off the shelf' for £85 as a shield against sequestration. The move had Scargill's backing and knowledge. But the company was never active apart from buying some office furniture. It was incorporated in November 1983, nearly four months before the strike started, and never filed reports and accounts. It was dissolved in May 1988 – more than a year before the alleged break-in. Sheffield fraud squad soon dismissed any suggestion of wrongdoing. Clapham dismissed the inquiry as 'a diversionary tactic'. Designed, it must be assumed, to discredit Windsor and divert attention from his impending disclosures. That Scargill should also wait three months before reporting the alleged break-in may also be of significance.

Scargill knew the big one was imminent. He had fobbed off Pattinson's questions faxed to his office about the IMO account statement, but he was aware that the *Mirror* team had 'fronted' Heathfield with allegations about the Libyan money. He also knew that Jim Parker had been consorting with the enemy. Heathfield had told the NUM executive on 1 March to expect 'press smears' to hit the newsstands the following Monday. From what little they told the executive (known to Scargill, evidently, as 'chicken feed times'), it is clear the two national officials knew enough to rehearse their defence. The minutes of the meeting record that the general secretary assured the committee that there was no truth in the allegations. They agreed to wait for publication.

Having synchronized their timing, the *Mirror* and Central TV went ahead. Rival tabloids had an inkling that something was coming, both from 'village' gossip in Fleet Street and from the knowledge that the scheduled 'Cook Report' programme had been pulled to provide a slot for the blockbuster. There is nothing the tabloids love better than to run a 'spoiler' against a rival's scoop, and this was no different. On 3 March, the *Sun* forecast that Scargill would come under heavy fire over Russian and Libyan money, but that was the nearest anyone else got.

A political furore greeted the publication of the *Mirror*'s 'exclusive' and the screening of 'The Cook Report'. Neil Kinnock called for a full inquiry. Tory back-benchers called for a Commons debate. Scargill called the story 'vicious lies'. But in the areas there was disquiet. In South Wales, George Rees said: 'Scargill has a million questions to answer.' Scottish leader George Bolton demanded that the president 'open all the books'. Scargill authorized a detailed statement, saying that he had neither a mortgage nor a loan, 'so no question of repayment could have been perceived'. Houses occupied by national officials were owned by the national union. Before the strike, the NUM had been in the process of buying the homes occupied by Scargill and Heathfield: in Scargill's case, from the president himself; in Heathfield's case, from the Derbyshire area of the NUM. The union had also spent some money on the properties. When court action was threatened which could have led to the seizure of the houses, it was decided to repay the NUM for the money spent. 'The money to do this came from a trust fund, and in the president's case, was repaid to that trust fund within four days from his own personal savings.' What trust fund, asked members of the executive. Scargill told BBC TV News: 'I had a £25,000 mortgage on my house and I paid that off in August 1984 from the Bradford and Bingley Building Society and the Co-op Bank with cheques.' He did not explain why, if he had money in the bank, he needed to use an NUM trust fund at all.

The *Mirror* taunted Scargill. If the paper was doing other than printing the facts, 'Mr Scargill has his remedy in the High Court.' Scargill conceded a special executive in Sheffield on 9 March to discuss the allegations, particularly the suggestion that £1 million of Soviet money intended to alleviate hardship could have ended up in an IMO account in Dublin, to which Scargill had access but of which the executive was ignorant. The mood building up was one of concern rather than a 'lynch-mob' mentality, but there was no stomach for an NUM-financed libel action.

Scargill should be left to swing in the wind, Scots miners decided. George Bolton, the area secretary, said: 'The NUM was never consulted, never involved and therefore has no responsibility. Our view is that the persons concerned should decide to sue or not to sue personally. The allegations are very grave indeed. And if they decide not to sue I would imagine that leaves a very great question mark.' Scargill, a notorious litigant, never did sue.

Further 'revelations' appeared in the *Mirror*. In a centre spread on Altaf Abbasi, the paper quoted him as saying that he had met Scargill for the first time in Blackpool, and that 'other meetings' followed. 'Scargill told me, "We need this money to feed our hungry." I recall that he said a child had died and they could not even afford to bury him.' Months after the strike, Abbasi alleged, there was a further meeting in Normandy at the holiday home of Alain Simon, an official of the MTUI and later general secretary of the IMO – and close trade union contact of the miners' president – with Windsor and. Heathfield.[2] At this meeting, the NUM was said to have asked for a further £2 million. Later, when 'the Doctor' learned of the *Mirror* investigation, he informed the Libyans, who sent 'investigators' to Europe.

Abbasi himself emerged as something of a mystery man, a 'peddler of revolutionary dreams'. He had been running a corner grocery store in Bennetthorpe, Doncaster, but was now a 'property developer' in Nottingham. He was styled as the European representative of Al Zulfikar – The Sword – a Libyan-backed terrorist group dedicated to the overthrow of General Zia's government in his home country of Pakistan. This forty-four-year-old father of five, his face badly pockmarked, stared grimly out of the centrefold.

Next day, the *Mirror* turned to less lurid but still damaging allegations. Ken Cameron, the charismatic left-wing leader of the Fire Brigade Union, related how he took £200,000 in a cardboard box to Scargill's flat in the Barbican with only Jim Parker to guard him. Parker himself claimed to have made numerous pick-ups of cash of up to £250,000 in the same way. The boxes had been Scargill's idea. 'He said he didn't want it to look obvious that we were picking up cash.' Parker's revelations had their comic side. He disclosed that Scargill's creative bouffant hairstyle, known among the staff as 'flying shredded wheat', was held in place by hair lacquer. 'He was so mean he would let me buy his cans of lacquer out of my pittance of a wage,' said his driver. Cans of 'extra-hold' Cossack spray rattled around the presidential limousine.

On the morning of the special NUM executive, the *Mirror* challenged the 'lies' alleged to have been told by Scargill as he battled

Arthur Scargill arrested at Orgreave coking plant in May 1984 during the great 'Strike for Jobs'

Below: Police give First Aid to the miners' leader following violent clashes between pickets and police outside Orgreave coking plant near Sheffield at the height of the strike, 16 June 1984

Above: The NUM 'Troika' at the 1984 TUC. *Left to right*: Peter Heathfield, General Secretary; Mick McGahey, the Communist Vice-President; and Scargill, for once refusing to comment. Over his left shoulder is Roger Windsor, the controversial Executive Officer, and behind him George Rees, the left-wing South Wales Miners' leader who broke with Scargill politically

Labour leader Neil Kinnock, privately deeply unhappy about the year-long miners' strike, on the only occasion he shared a platform with Scargill, Stoke-on-Trent, 30 November 1984

A break in peace talks, September 1984. *Left to right*: Scargill; Kevan Hunt, Industrial Relations Director of the Coal Board; and NCB Chairman Ian MacGregor

Biting his lip before asking the Labour movement to come to his aid: Scargill addressing the TUC at Brighton in September 1984 as his all-out strike began to crumble

John Walsh, Scargill's fiercest critic in his Yorkshire heartland. Walsh challenged him for the NUM Presidency in January 1988 and ran him close, taking 46 per cent of the votes. Had most of Nottinghamshire not quit the NUM, it is practically certain he would have ousted Scargill

Above: Scargill's mansion, Treelands, Worsbrough, near Barnsley, bought in 1985, shortly after the strike was over

Inset: The interior of Treelands

Yews Lane, Worsbrough, the Scargill family home for many years before the controversial move to Treelands

Right: Maurice Jones, the Yorkshire journalist who was Scargill's editor, first of the *Yorkshire Miner*, then of the *Miner*, the NUM national paper. He broke with Scargill in 1989 and, with the industrial editor of the *Daily Mirror* Terry Pattison (*far right*), began the 'detective journalism' that led to the controversial Lightman Inquiry

Left: Gavin Lightman QC who conducted the inquiry into allegations of Russian and Libyan financial donations to the Mine Workers' Union during the 1984 strike

Above: Arthur in his element, surrounded by the media, leaving his headquarters in Sheffield, March 1990

Roger Windsor, Executive Officer of the NUM appointed by Scargill, quit amid mutual recriminations in 1989 and made allegations about Libyan/Russian money that formed the basis of the *Daily Mirror* and Central TV's 'Cook Report' scandal

Jim Parker, Scargill's chauffeur and long-standing friend until they broke in 1989, supported Windsor's allegations

Altaf Abbasi, a Pakistani businessman who claimed to have been a money courier between Colonel Gadaffi and the NUM in 1989

Scargill seen with Jean McCrindle, a close associate who was a signatory to four of the secret accounts set up by Scargill to beat sequestration during the Great Strike of 1984–5

Inset: Ms Nell Myers, Scargill's press secretary from 1982

Scargill answers questions on the Lightman report at Bedworth, near Coventry, 2 August 1990

THE TRUTH

Above: Scargill and Norman Willis, General Secretary of the TUC, leaving Congress House on 14 October 1992, after crisis talks about Michael Heseltine's plans to close thirty-one collieries with the loss of 30,000 jobs

Taking a back seat: Scargill applauds his wife Anne as she gives a victor's salute after emerging from a four-day sit-in at the doomed Parkside Colliery on Merseyside, Easter 1993

to talk his way out of the crisis. Windsor was quoted as saying: 'Once Arthur has created a story, that becomes the truth and the truth then becomes a lie.' The paper then challenged miners' leaders to get to the truth by demanding the answers to two questions. Where did ALL the money come FROM? Where did ALL the money go TO? Roy Greenslade, the *Mirror*'s editor who sanctioned publication of the story, also moved quickly to stifle allegations that the week-long series of disclosures was an attempt by publisher Robert Maxwell to punish Scargill for damaging the Labour Party. 'There is no conspiracy or smear,' he told *The Sunday Times*.[3] 'It was a genuine piece of investigative journalism. I contributed to the miners' hardship fund and I have printed this more in sorrow than in anger.'

Greenslade added that Neil Kinnock was unaware of the allegations until two days before they were published. Presumably, he read about them in the *Sun*. A Kinnock aide denied that there had been collusion, volunteering: 'but Neil will not have lost any sleep ... the NUM strike was a major diversion and probably set back the Kinnock project to reform the Labour Party by a year or 18 months. It has made Neil unforgiving of Arthur Scargill.' Naturally, Tony Benn was more understanding. On the day the first allegations were published, he confided to his diary that he had spoken to Scargill, who could not go home because of the press siege of Treelands 'following vicious attacks' on him in the *Mirror*. Benn singled out an interview of Maxwell by Hugo Young in that day's *Guardian*, in which the publisher boasted of being a major factor in defeating the miners' strike and declared how much he admired Mrs Thatcher. 'He is a very powerful man,' concluded Benn. 'The news at midnight has been all about Arthur Scargill's categorical denial of all the charges. He is consulting his lawyers. If you have to choose between Maxwell and Scargill, there is no doubt who to believe. Arthur is a person of enormous integrity.'[4] Surprisingly, considering the way the story was to run in the media in the months that followed, Benn never mentions Scargill again in his published diaries for the rest of that tumultuous year.

The executive faced demands for an inquiry from a number of areas, and from Kevin Barron, an NUM-sponsored MP who had been Scargill's legman in Nottinghamshire during his bid for the presidency. Barron, who would become a key player in the drama, said the many thousands of miners who loyally went on strike and suffered for years after would want to know how all donations were used and with what authority. There should be a full investigation into all the accounts and how they were run. If any had not been published, this should be done immediately. Not even he expected the breathtaking array of secret fund-holding that finally emerged. The executive, who still had to enter the new NUM offices in Sheffield ignominiously through an underground car park because of a dispute between Scargill and the City Council over who should build steps to the front door, met for five hours.

A tightly worded press release then disclosed that the executive had unanimously accepted the recommendation of the national officials to appoint an independent inquiry into 'the allegations made by Central Television and the Mirror Group of Newspapers' against the national officials. The NEC agreed that the inquiry should consist of an eminent QC, whose terms of reference would be to investigate the allegations that the national officials had accepted money alleged to have come from Libya in 1984, and Soviet finances alleged to have come into the funds of the NUM, and the allegations that in December 1984 the officials used money alleged to have come from Libya to pay off their personal mortgages/loans. A five-man sub-committee composed of Jack Taylor (Yorkshire president, Scargill loyalist), George Rees (South Wales, Scargill critic), Gordon Butler (Derbyshire, becoming a critic), Idwal Morgan (cokeworkers, loyalist) and Henry Richardon (Nottinghamshire, loyalist) was set up. They were instructed to meet the Haldane Society of Lawyers to appoint a suitable QC. The society is, generally speaking, composed of left-wing lawyers.

It was already clear that he would have a massive task. Scargill blithely admitted to his executive that he had been running no fewer than fourteen secret bank accounts in order to evade sequestration. The coalfield barons listened open-mouthed as he explained in a voice filled with tension that the money was still there, three years after the lifting of sequestration. They were also told that home loans to Scargill, Heathfield and former chief executive Windsor had been paid from a 'trust fund' held in cash at NUM headquarters; money had indeed come from Russia, and nine bank accounts had been opened all over Europe by Scargill and his associates. The biggest account, the Miners' International Research, Education and Support Fund (or MIREDS), opened on 30 January while the TUC was wrestling to find a settlement in the dispute, was still current, and had in it £1.8 million. Other accounts were in Austria, Sheffield, Leeds and Dublin.

The announcement of an inquiry on Scargill's terms was greeted with derision by the tabloid press. The choice of Gavin Lightman, QC, a commercial law specialist, to head it was assumed to be further evidence of a 'whitewash' in the making, as he had acted for the NUM on a number of occasions, particularly during the cases of sequestration and receivership. The legal establishment, ever more cautious, insisted that the fifty-year-old barrister would do a thorough, independent job. He soon ran into difficulties. He decided that the inquiry ought to be in private, and that witnesses should not have to give evidence on oath. The *Mirror* and Central Television refused to co-operate. Their fears were misplaced. 'Fortunately,' Pattinson told the author, 'our boycott did not have tragic consequences.' Anyone who believed that Scargill had employed a tame pussycat in Lightman had made a serious error of judgement.'

As he interviewed witnesses, Lightman came to the view that his inquiry's terms of reference were too narrow. Ten weeks after he was appointed, he consulted the NUM's 'five wise men', and they agreed to add a further question to the Scargill litany. This was 'Has there been any misapplication of funds or assets of the NUM or any breach of duty by the national officials in connection with or arising out of the financial arrangements made by the NUM or the national officials during or in connection with the 1984–5 miners' strike?' From that point on, it was clear that Lightman was keen to hand down a moral judgement as well as technical findings. Lightman had also enlisted accountants Cork Gully to go through the bank accounts. And if he did not get the co-operation of *Mirror* and 'Cook Report' investigators, he could command answers from the NUM leaders involved.

Scargill tried to carry on his life as normal, though those close to him observed he was not his usual bouncy self. On Sunday 16 April, only a month after the Gaddafi–Soviet money scandal broke, he was involved in a serious road accident while driving his new Ford Granada Scorpio home alone from the office. He was knocked unconscious when an oncoming car skidded and crashed head-on into Scargill's car. A woman passer-by dragged the unconscious NUM president from behind the wheel, and ambulancemen gave him oxygen on the way to a Sheffield hospital. Police said both drivers were lucky to survive. Scargill suffered a black eye, cuts, bruises and whip lash injuries that forced him to wear a neck brace for a time. It was the second serious accident he had suffered. Five years previously, his Rover was written off when a car crashed into the rear while Scargill was parked in a lay-by reading a map.

As the time for Lightman to report neared, there was another little local difficulty. The NUM had been given grants of £300,000 by South Yorkshire Metropolitan Council to move to a new head-quarters, with a listed stone façade, right next to City Hall, on con-dition that the union set up a mining museum and library within five years. But what with one thing and another, seven years later not a book or a brass lamp was in sight. Rotherham Council, which took over the scheme, complained. A pit tub was hurriedly procured and artefacts hurriedly appeared on shelves. It was not entered for museum of the year.

The exhibit everyone was waiting for appeared on 3 July 1990 – a very fast turnaround for so complicated a task. A version of the find-ings flattering to Scargill had been leaked to the *Guardian* and the BBC that morning. It was said that he would be cleared of making any personal gain from monies donated during the strike. If only it were so simple. Lightman's report was given to the thirteen members of the executive present, plus Scargill and Heathfield, an hour before they met. They talked all day, and Scargill gave a briefing at eight p.m., which, according to those who attended, was more memorable for what it didn't say than for what it did. He told reporters he and Heathfield had been cleared, and went into a rapid, complicated spiel about loans that had been repaid at sixteen per cent interest rates. Only a handful of copies of the bulky, two-volume report were avail-able, and none of the journalists had had time to read it. And not all of them were there: in line with the continuing ban on Rupert Murdoch's papers, *The Times*, the *Sun* and *Today* were left out in the street. However, one sharp-eyed hack caught Lightman's strictures about 'breach of duty' and asked Scargill if he intended to resign. 'Certainly not,' rapped the president. 'Does anybody have any sen-sible questions to ask?'

The confidential minutes of that executive meeting make interest-ing reading. When the committee had read the report, Scargill and Heathfield handed out a written response to Lightman's criticism. After 'long and detailed discussion', the executive agreed:

'1. That the Lightman Inquiry has completely cleared the two National Officials of the allegation published in the *Daily Mirror* and broadcast on Central Television's Cook Report of using any monies received for or on behalf of the NUM or its members or for hardship purposes in order to repay personal mortgages or loans. The NEC fully accept the Lightman's findings that there has been no personal misappropriation of monies by the National Officials.

2. To accept the recommendations contained in the report, and ask the four-man team [Jack Taylor had already quit, having taken early retirement] to meet Mr Lightman and to take legal advice to determine if any monies in the MIREDS fund donated by the Soviet Miners' Union was or should belong to the NUM for the benefit of its members; to inquire if out of the £580,000 which had been placed by the MACF [Miners Action Committee Fund] into the MIREDS fund there should be any payment made to the NUM; to seek legal advice with a view to obtaining details of the Polish bank account, and to ascertain to whom the Mineworkers' Trust money belongs and the course of action which the NUM needs to take.

3. Mr Windsor's loan. To ask lawyers to write to Mr Windsor asking him to pay the £29,500 plus interest to the Miners' Solidarity Fund, bearing in mind he had indicated in the *Daily Mirror* and on the Cook Report he was willing to do so.'

Scargill might have believed what he told the press: 'I have done nothing wrong.' The press did not believe him. *The Times* headline was 'Scargill ran illegal accounts until last year.' *The Daily Telegraph* highlighted the loan for Treelands, its front-page headline reading: 'Breach of duty by Scargill over £100,000 loan.' The *Guardian* was a little kinder, offering: 'Scargill claims vindication over misuse of funds.' *Mirror* editor Roy Greenslade stood by his story: 'Once again I say to Arthur Scargill: "Sue Us." We are convinced that our story, which was properly researched over many months, was correct.'

Lightman did clear Scargill of paying off his mortgage with Libyan cash, but elsewhere he was damning. Scargill had said the Russians had not sent money to the miners. Lightman was 'quite satisfied' that money had been collected and sent by the Soviet miners for the benefit of the NUM, and Scargill's failure to make a full report was 'a remarkable breach of duty'. The Russian money ought to be returned to the NUM. Scargill had said repeatedly that he did not ask the Libyans for money. Lightman believed that Windsor 'probably did ask for financial assistance from the Libyan government'. He had given Gaddafi the secret Narodny bank account number in Warsaw, and so had Platts-Mills. It could not therefore be ruled out that Libya donated money to this account. Furthermore, he was satisfied that Windsor did bring at least £150,000 in cash into the

office at about the time he said he did. 'There is a real possibility
that the money came from Libya: but equally, there is a real possibility
that it came from elsewhere. The uncertain character of this conclusion is a reflection of the careless way the records of the unofficial
accounts were kept and monies dealt with by the national officials
during this period.'

Lightman found that Windsor's allegation that the cash he had
brought in was used to repay Scargill's mortgage was 'entirely untrue',
since the mortgage had been repaid in August. 'What was in fact
repaid was the sum of £6,860 expended on repairs.' The money for
these repairs, carried out at the union's expense in the middle of the
strike, was taken from a cash fund in the NUM offices known as the
'Miners' Action Committee Fund', which was in effect a big bag of
cash. Lightman agreed with Scargill that within a few days of using
the MACF fund to pay for the repairs, he repaid the sum of £6,861 in
cash 'into the brown paper parcel which was the MACF account'.
This was witnessed by his personal/press assistant Ms Nell Myers,
who signed a (falsely dated) receipt to that effect. Lightman was
satisfied that Scargill had sufficient cash available to make the repayment. The only question was: why go through such a rigmarole in
the first place. Scargill had the cash to repay the NUM for his house
repairs; why not give it straight to the union? He explained he didn't
have the cash available at the time, and told Heathfield he would pay
it back as soon as possible.

Turning to the purchase of Treelands, Lightman finally nailed the
lie that Scargill's son-in-law had bought the house for himself. The
NUM president freely admitted that he had wanted to buy the house
for some time. It came on the market in July 1985. The strike was
over, but Receiver Michael Arnold was still in charge of the union's
assets and Scargill was not being paid. He did not get his salary until
November 1986. Scargill 'took the view' that it would be impossible
to get a loan from any bank, and therefore turned to his old friend
Alain Simon, and asked him if his Miners' Trade Union International
could give him a loan. He needed a long-term mortgage and a bridging loan while he sold his bungalow in 2B Yews Lane.

Simon agreed, and £100,000 was paid in cash to Scargill on 12
August 1985. The money came from the MIREDS account in Dublin,
which came in turn from Russia, East Germany and Hungary, and
from MACF, the brown paper bag at union headquarters. This was
the first withdrawal of any kind from the MIREDS fund ('Miners'

International Research, Education and Support Fund', remember). Lightman decided that the MIREDS trust deed was a sham, that the trust was 'the ideal receptacle' for cash sloshing round head office in a bag and for Soviet and other international monies intended to be held for or given to the NUM. Indeed, more than half a million pounds had been put into it from the cash bag, and £1.4 million from the Eastern Bloc. So, from funds emanating in cash from Sheffield HQ or from what were then still Communist countries, officially for 'research, education and support', Scargill was able to borrow £100,000 at short notice to buy the house of his dreams, when all around the country his strike-shattered members were being put out on the street by the building societies.

He needed the money in a hurry, so the paperwork had to be done later. Simon kindly sent him a letter confirming the loan, and purporting to include the £100,000. The interest rate was fixed at two and a half per cent on the first £50,000 and twelve per cent on the second £50,000. Nice work, if you can get it. When his Miners' Trade Union International merged with the nascent International Mineworkers' Organization, of which Scargill was also president, Simon wrote to him saying that his debt was now to the IMO.

Completion of the sale of Treelands to Scargill took place on 1 October 1985, with David Roberts acting as nominee for his future father-in-law. Scargill did not need the whole £100,000 for the transaction. He used £34,000 out of his own savings, and £91,000 of the MIREDS account. Of that £34,000, £29,000 came from an account he had opened with the Jyske Bank in Denmark in the name of A. Pickering – the maiden name of his dead mother. He had put his personal funds abroad because he was afraid the sequestrators might take them. Steve Hudson, the NUM finance officer, had recommended the Jyske because it paid a very good rate of interest. The little boy from Worsbrough who hated capitalism and loved his mother so much had a funny way of showing it. In May 1987, he got a £50,000 mortgage from the Co-op, and paid back half his loan to the IMO. Treelands was transferred to him. In January 1989, after the sale of 2B Yews Lane, Scargill paid off the rest of his loan, plus some interest. Records of other interest payments to the IMO had been produced, and while there was doubt whether the payments had actually been made, Lightman was inclined to believe they had. 'That this doubt should exist is part of the price Mr Scargill must pay for borrowing money in cash from a trust fund and generally

conducting his affairs and the affairs of the NUM and the IMO in
the unbusinesslike manner in which they have been conducted,' said
Lightman reprovingly.

Heathfield was later able to get a similar home loan from the
MIREDS account, and Lightman said this arrangement disturbed
him considerably. First, the loans came from an account which was
either totally or substantially NUM money. Secondly, no notice was
ever given to and no consent sought from the NUM. Scargill's attitude was that it had nothing to do with the NUM. 'I do not agree.
It is to be borne in mind that Mr Scargill is full-time president of
the NUM as well as president of the IMO. It must be quite wrong
that he or Mr Heathfield should receive any benefit out of funds in
which the NUM were interested without the consent of the NUM
in any event.'

Lightman appeared to have difficulty in taking Scargill's explanations at face value. He found 'difficult to accept' the president's
assertion that he did not intend to mislead the executive about falsely
dated receipts for the home repairs loan. Turning to the disclosure
of accounts to KPMG Peat Marwick in late 1989 and early 1990,
Scargill said he wanted an audit to prevent any questions arising
thereafter. Hudson, the finance officer, said the myriad accounts were
revealed to him by Scargill because he was 'concerned about imminent revelations by Mr Windsor in the Press'. Lightman concludes:
'I cannot accept Mr Scargill's evidence on this question. I do not
believe that there would have been any disclosure or any report by
KPMG but for the falling out with Mr Windsor.'

Going back to his terms of reference, Lightman was satisfied that
'not merely did the NUM by Mr Scargill seek political help (in the
form in particular of cutting off oil supplies) but also financial help.'
A payment in the records attributed to the French CGT 'may have
been received from Libya', though he could reach no concluded view.
On the Russian connection, he found that at least £1 million, or
possibly $1 million, was raised by a levy on Soviet miners by their
union and sent to the MIREDS fund and was now owned by the
IMO. The NUM received little or no benefit from this fund 'and
most certainly not the benefit intended'. Using that money for the
IMO was a misapplication of funds.

On the home loans issue, Lightman found that no Libyan or Russian money was spent on home loans for either national official.
Scargill had already paid off his mortgage. But union money

amounting to £6,860.58 was spent on improvements to Scargill's bungalow and 'there was a degree of irregularity regarding authorisation for this payment'. But since this money had been repaid to the MACF – the office account-in-a-bag – 'I think no complaint can now be made.'

Answering the question he deliberately posed to himself on 1 June, Lightman said: 'In my view, as a matter of law, there have been a number of misapplications of funds and breaches of duty.' Since the beginning of sequestration, the union had in effect operated two sets of accounts: the official accounts properly administered and audited, and the unofficial accounts operated by the national officials – effectively, Scargill – with no supervision or control. 'The very existence of these separate funds, their collection and distribution, their retention and investment, and most of all their non-disclosure, involved breaches of duty by the national officials.'

Lightman distinguished two periods of time in which 'this state of affairs' continued: the receivership period, and the period since then. As a matter of law, raising secret funds during receivership was unlawful and a breach of duty. In the conditions of the dispute, the members may have gone along with it, but such acquiescence 'cannot in law constitute excuse'. After receivership, there was clearly a duty to make a clean breast of everything to the executive, which was entitled to know the full facts and the true financial condition of the union. 'A substantial price has been paid in loss of staff (and no doubt membership) morale, disturbed by the persistent evidence and rumours of secret accounts,' the inquiry disclosed.

Lightman found a 'quite unnecessary' delay in winding up the accounts. Receivership ended on 27 June 1986, yet the secret accounts were still going strong more than three years later – right up to the time disclosure in the press was imminent. 'The great problem is that Mr Scargill has acted throughout without the benefit of properly informed legal or accountancy advice. I regret that I am of the view that was in part because Mr Scargill was unwilling to accept the constraints which such advice would have placed upon him. Indeed when I put this view to Mr Scargill, he accepted that this was the case.'

It was wrong and a breach of duty to get their home loans from the MIREDS fund without the prior consent of the executive, and the loans should in any event have been reported. Both officials might have thought they were acting properly. 'However, I find it a matter of concern that in particular in the case of Mr Scargill, he did not recognise the impropriety of what seemed to me to have been so obviously wrong.'

The Soviet money, Lightman adds, was misapplied. The MIREDS trust held the Soviet money as trustee for the NUM 'and Mr Scargill has wrongfully allowed such monies to be treated as, and has wrongfully maintained that such monies are, in effect IMO monies'. If the money did not actually belong at that stage to the NUM, then Scargill was also wrong in assenting to the transfer of money raised for the NUM to the MIREDS trust. By allowing his role in the IMO to result in substantial benefits for that organization to be obtained at the expense of the NUM, Scargill had 'failed to recognise or implement his overriding duties' to the mineworkers' union he was supposed to lead.

This was the catalogue of wrongdoing that an unrepentant Scargill said 'in no way criticises' the national officials. Breathing ritual defiance, he declared: 'I will confess to one crime. I did everything in my power to beat sequestration and receivership. I think we did it and I think this is a matter of credit and should be a matter of congratulation not criticism that we were able to exist not merely in 1984–5 but in a very difficult period since.'

His executive's 'unanimous' statement concealed a huge row that day. Only three members supported him. He was mauled by his critics over the 'breach of duty' charges and the degree of deception involving so many clandestine accounts and the uses to which they were put. There were calls to quit the secretive IMO, Scargill's 'baby', and one executive member told *The Daily Telegraph*: 'Lightman is the most damning report I have ever read. It's a hundred times worse than I had imagined. You wouldn't run a darts club the way he ran the union.' Another said: 'If I'd been criticised like that I'd want to chuck myself out of the window.'

But Scargill is no quitter. His first hurdle was to get through the NUM annual conference the following week. Luckily, it was on 'home' ground, Red Hill, the headquarters of the Durham area of the union, once a bastion of the Right, but now fiercely loyal to the president. He also had to do something about Lightman's recommendation that the union should go after the funds dotted about Europe that might belong to the NUM. That would come later. Right now, he had to endure a torrent of media criticism. 'Unfit to lead the NUM' pronounced *The Independent*, a typical reaction. The *Mirror* was to the point: Lightman's report was the outcome of only hearing witnesses for the defence. 'Without even hearing from the "prosecution", Scargill is condemned,' the paper argued, calling Scargill once again to sue.

He put on a bullish front, insisting that the Soviet money – which he had once claimed never existed – was not missing but under his control in bank accounts in Dublin and Vienna. Yury Butchenko, a visiting Russian leader of a non-Communist miners' union in the Kuzbas, promptly asked for the money back, putting the true figure at between £3.6 and £10 million. He was disgusted that cash collected from Soviet pitmen had never reached the families for whom it was intended. Scargill was unimpressed. He won a ritual standing ovation from all but two of the delegations at Durham for saying that Lightman had vindicated him. He refused to apologize to anyone 'for the role I played in a period which has been tantamount to a state of war against everything we represent'. Everything he and Heathfield did 'was for the benefit of the union'. He was proud of having set up a system of accounts to confuse the sequestrators and camouflage funds to prevent them being seized by the state. The accounts had to be kept going until late 1989 or legal action by the receiver would have halted him repaying 'debt of honour' loans to friendly unions. The union's depleted squad of four wise men decided to talk to Lightman about getting back the money that belonged to the NUM. Scargill moved deftly. Nobody would be more delighted than he if the money was judged to be the NUM's.

Everybody got in on the act. The TUC general secretary Norman Willis wrote to Scargill asking whether he had been misled by the miners' leader in October 1984 when he was assured that the NUM had not sought or received funds from Libya. Scargill ducked and weaved. The TUC statement had been issued by Willis, not by him. In fact it was a joint statement. And in any event Windsor's claim about money from Libya came well after the TUC statement. This was disingenuousness at its best. MPs – Labour as well as Tory – clamoured for a police investigation, and Sir Geoffrey Howe, standing in for the prime minister, hoped that the 'appropriate authorities' would examine the evidence behind these 'gravely disquieting allegations'.

Scargill was already beginning to recover his poise at the close of the Durham conference. He was bolstered by comments in Moscow by Vladimir Louniov, the new president of the Soviet miners' union,

who said the Russians sent two million roubles' worth of food and
clothing, but no cash. This statement was distributed to delegates by
Ms Nell Myers, Scargill's faithful press secretary (known in the office
as 'Death Nell' for her habit of dressing in black). Louniov said the
Soviet miners would not have been able to send any hard currency.
Scargill seized on this as vindication of his argument that the Russians
had only sent money to the IMO for international purposes, not for
the striking British miners. At the Durham miners' gala after the
conference, the unthinkable happened: Scargill was booed by pitmen.
When his supporters took up the strike chant of 'Arthur Scargill,
Arthur Scargill, we'll support you ever more', his critics replied by
singing: 'We don't need you any more.' Some miners booed and gave
the thumbs-down sign.

His stock plummeted the next week, as the NUM executive voted
unanimously to sue Scargill and Heathfield as part of proceedings
for the recovery of £1.4 million in Russian money salted away. The
executive rejected Scargill's plea to sort out the issue by negotiation
or arbitration, and took Lightman's legal advice to go to law. Scargill
and Heathfield had to undergo the humiliation of being excluded
from their own executive meeting while the decision was taken.
Lawyers acting for the union appeared in private before Mr Justice
Mervyn Davies to secure injunctions preventing Scargill and
Heathfield disposing of their own assets. Bank accounts of the IMO
were frozen in Dublin and Vienna. Writs claiming breach of trust
were issued, alleging that the national officials had wrongly diverted
the Soviet money to MIREDS. Scargill raged. He described his
executive's decision as 'crackers' and fumed at the suggestion of resignation. 'What do you want me to do? Run a fish shop? You must be
joking . . . there has never been anything lame about me, mister,' he
snapped at reporters. The national officials had acted in good faith
and carried out the instructions of the donors.

But Louniov's support on this front was itself being undermined.
Mikhail Srebny, leader of the Soviet Miners' Union at the time of
the strike, had appeared on ITN News the night before to reiterate
that they *had* given money: £1 million. 'We wanted it to be used only
to give help to the miners, the striking miners,' he said. 'We did not
even think of it going for any other expenditure or outgoings.' Srebny
was shown a photograph of Treelands and was visibly shocked. When
told how Scargill had bought the property, he said: 'I am outraged to
the depths of my soul.' Scargill dismissed these words as 'a remarkable

change of mind'. But they ring true, truer than Scargill's windy rhetoric about international organization. Miners the world over understand each other, the privations they suffer – particularly when
engaged in struggle against an implacable employer. Soviet miners
were no different: indeed, better. They had a long record of co-
operation with the militant coalfields of Britain. They would have
put their hands in their pockets, and worked extra shifts, to send aid.

Besides, the IMO had not even been formed when the Russians
sent their cash out. It had been on the drawing board since 1982,
when Scargill became president of the NUM. He wanted to pull out
of the Western-orientated Miners' International Federation, based
in London and run by his old ex-Communist rival from Barnsley,
Peter Tait. In keeping with his socialist internationalist vision, not
to mention his desire to strut his stuff on the largest possible stage,
he wanted to forge a new global trade union body for miners in all
countries, East, West and Third World. In other hands, it would
have been a noble project. In his, it became (in the words of Kim
Howells, MP) 'a mickey mouse organisation, a kind of piggy bank
for Scargill and this unreconstructed Stalinist Alain Simon'. Simon
was an executive committee member of the French Communist trade
union centre CGT, who shared the original dream. He was also
secretary-general of the Miners' Trade Union International, part of
the Eastern-bloc World Federation of Trade Unions founded in 1949
when the Cold War split international trade unionism on political
lines.

But the talks dragged on, and the International Mineworkers'
Organization was not actually founded until September 1985, six
months after the strike ended and even longer after the despatch of
the Soviet cash. It was supposed to have six million members in
forty-three countries, but it only held a conference once every four
years and did not appear to do very much in between. Nobody knew,
because it published no reports of its activities, pleading the necessity
for secrecy in countries where miners laboured under repressive
regimes.

Simon refused to talk to Lightman, and in turn he was scathing
about the organization, pointing out that it has no financial records
or minutes of decisions. Its finances are 'practically impenetrable' and
Scargill could not get any information out of it even though he was
the president and with Simon had unrestricted and unaudited access
to funds in excess of £2 million. Lightman recommended that the

executive should give very serious thought to severing its connections with the IMO, which in five years had cost the NUM £105,200 in subscriptions, but which refused to co-operate with the inquiry and appeared to have no normal financial controls of audits. He also pointed out that for Scargill to continue as president of both the IMO and the NUM inevitably involved a conflict of interest, and the risk of a sacrifice of the interests of the NUM to the IMO – as had occurred. Three years later, he still has both jobs.

But on 20 July, all he had was a fistful of writs claiming damages for breach of trust and restraining him from disposing of funds in IMO bank accounts that his fellow union leaders insisted belonged to the NUM. Scargill thought it 'a little sad' to have writs served as he arrived for work, when a telephone call would have sufficed. In a scene worthy of the Pink Panther, Scargill decided to fly out to France the next day for secret talks with Simon. Wearing dark glasses and carrying a ticket in the name of Arthur Fenn (his secretary's name is Yvonne Fenn), he tried to board a Paris-bound flight at Leeds/Bradford airport. Somehow, the airline staff saw through his disguise, and made him go back and buy a ticket under his own name. He was travelling without his executive's knowledge or approval, but one member said: 'It was typical Arthur. He could easily have said he had to go because of the legal action, and no one would have questioned it. But instead he adopts this cloak and dagger stuff and looks stupid.'

Stupid or not, the initiative appeared to pay off. On 24 July, the NUM executive's four-man team liaising with Lightman flew to Paris to see Scargill, Heathfield and Simon in an attempt to sort out what the IMO general secretary was to call 'a lovers' quarrel'. As they did so, Whitehall confirmed that Employment Secretary Michael Howard was considering new legislation to block possible loopholes in the handling of trade union funds. And the Serious Fraud Squad was called in to investigate the Soviet money affair after a formal complaint was lodged by a 'former senior member' of the union, who was accompanied by Sergei Massalovitch, a Russian miners' official visiting the capital. Detective Chief Superintendent Tony McStravik of the Metropolitan and City Fraud Squad was put in charge of the inquiry. Scargill said plaintively: 'If it is not one allegation, it is another. It has been going on for three months. I am beginning to take the view that it is get Arthur Scargill time.'

Meanwhile, the negotiations at a hotel near Charles de Gaulle airport had gone well. Simon, who had the key to the IMO's financial web, had agreed to co-operate and open the books. He said: 'There is no more misunderstanding. All the obstacles are out of the way.' Well, not quite. On 26 July, the High Court granted a three-month moratorium on legal action to allow the NUM and the IMO to sort out repatriation of the Russian money. The NUM's four wise men then embarked on a tour of European capitals – Moscow, Paris and Budapest – to track down who had sent what to whom, and for what purpose. In the Soviet capital Mikhail Srebny repeated that £1 million had been sent for the striking mineworkers.

While the NUM leaders were scouring the continent, Scargill was doing what he knew best: getting the show on the road. John Sweeney, a spectator for *The Observer*, was duly impressed. 'Nostalgia is spread thick in the Arthur Scargill comeback road show. Sheffield City Hall seemed awash with sepia tints: the old war cries of the Great Miners' Strike rang out, apparently as ancient as the psalms, proving there is nothing so distant as the recent past.' Dennis Skinner warmed up the audience with 'good clean class poison'. Then Paul Foot, Socialist Workers' Party guru and *Daily Mirror* columnist, got the 800-strong audience into a lather about 'cheque book journalism of the meanest kind' – that of his own paper. Finally, at the end of the evening came Scargill's set-piece, 'a declamatory defence, rather than a forensic one'. His audience showed some unease as he ducked and weaved through the minutiae of his seventeen bank accounts, but warmed to his comic routine of a clash with Lightman. Mimicking his legal inquisitor's posh, Southern accent, Scargill played himself as the straight, blunt Yorkshireman who got the better of him. Lightman quizzes him about hiding the money from the sequestrators:

'How did you get the money?'
'In cash.'
'But it was £200,000!'
'Yes.'
'How did you receive it?'
'In a cardboard box.'
'Did you give him a receipt?'
'No.'
'Why not?'
'Because he never asked for one!'
'That money should have gone to the sequestrator.'
'Blow me down!'

It was classic Scargill theatre, and the audience loved it. Arthur's confidence seemed to flood back. The old vanity resurfaced. 'The City of London was thinking of offering Heathfield and me a job.' But Sweeney found an even more telling pay-off line: 'He finished on a note which was eerily familiar. Explaining why he wouldn't sue his detractors because of the biased legal system, he roared: "The only jury that matters is the working class", and then sat down to a standing ovation. Who else said that? Ceauşescu, just before they shot him.'

This knockabout music-hall turn was the nearest most miners got to the facts of Lightman, unless they bought the heavy papers which printed extracts, or the Penguin book which reprinted the report and appendices. Lightman urged that all delegates to the annual conference and all areas should have copies, and 'such newspapers as the national executive thinks appropriate'. Less than a handful of copies were made available to the media after the executive meeting, and few rank-and-file miners saw it. In Yorkshire, at least, there was not much appetite. At Frickley colliery, for instance, only a handful of men asked to see the copy in the NUM union 'box' at the pithead. Most miners either believed the press and television were lying, or were apathetic.

To accompany the road show, Scargill produced a twenty-four-page counterblast to Lightman, in which he said that Windsor went to Tripoli 'to explain the union's case and to seek political support to stop the supply of Libyan oil while British miners were on strike, but I was not seeking support from the Libyan government. I also made clear, however, that we would welcome financial assistance from trade unionists anywhere.' He claimed it would have been impossible to get his executive's permission for the loan to become Squire of Treelands 'because at the time the receiver was in charge of the NUM's assets'. Brushing aside Lightman's strictures on his clandestine accounts, he said throughout the entire period of sequestration and receivership all these accounts were operated on a 'need to know' basis. Press leaks from his own executive on 9 March after the *Mirror*/'Cook Report' allegations 'showed how correct we were in keeping these accounts confidential'. His first explanation was disingenuous: he knew, or should have known, that trade unions and government in Libya are one and the same thing. His second explanation similarly evades the point, and fails to address the farrago of lies told to avoid 'adverse publicity'. His third explanation is a majestic

piece of Scargill-speak: if he had told his executive of the accounts –
even three years after receivership ended – they might have told
somebody else. Precisely. The whole carefully contrived, cosy, cash-
lined labyrinth would have been opened to the public gaze. And down
it would have crashed.

While the road show was in the coalfields, Gaddafi gave an embarrassing interview to Marie Colvin, respected Middle East correspondent of *The Sunday Times*, in which he confirmed the basics of
Windsor's story. He told Colvin: 'Scargill's deputy came here. He
asked for humanitarian aid. He said that when miners' children died
they couldn't be buried because their parents had no money. I asked
the General Producers' Union of Libyan Workers to provide some
help for the miners. I do not know the details of the agreement, or
how much money was given.' There was talk of the Libyan government suing the NUM. Scargill, preparing for the TUC conference,
remained defiant: 'If Windsor got money from Libya, I've no knowledge of it.' Asked if he doubted Gaddafi's word, he shot back: 'Is he
a man you would want to associate with?' Perhaps not. Better send
the butler, Windsor.

He was back in the headlines at the annual Trades Union Congress
in Blackpool, clashing at the rostrum with general secretary Norman
Willis, who he had sneered at as 'a sumo wrestler' on his coalfield
tour. Willis pushed the new realist line, that a demand for complete
trade union immunities under the law and open-ended rights to take
secondary industrial action simply would not be accepted by the
voters. Scargill, supporting a move to abolish all 'anti-union' legislation, warned the movement its leaders were threatening to betray the
principles for which it had traditionally stood. In an unprecedented
interruption from the platform, Willis shouted: 'That's rubbish!'
Scargill smiled. He knows how to get under his opponent's skin. John
Lyons, leader of the power station managers' union, who heartily
detests the NUM president, was jeered when he told delegates: 'If
anyone here thinks Arthur Scargill is an electoral asset, he should
have his brains tested. The NUM has had a bellyful of his principles.'
Scargill lost the vote.

He was also kept out of his executive once again when the four-man
team made an interim report on the efforts to establish how much
the NUM was owed from the Russian money. Things were not going
his way. Srebny, the Soviet miners' union chief, described the IMO
account of events as 'fiction'. Anatoli Kapustin, deputy leader of the

All-Union Central Council of Trade Unions, Soviet equivalent of
the TUC, wrote to Simon expressing shock that Scargill had been
loaned £100,000 to buy Treelands, and demanding 'radical demo-
cratisation' of the IMO's activities. He also criticized its financial
arrangements as being under 'the uncontrolled and boundless disposal of one or two persons'. It wasn't Scargill's week. He was even
pilloried in full-page newspaper advertisements for a little-known
male anti-perspirant. Beneath a photograph of him in full flow was the
legend 'Mitchum, for when You're Really Sweating!' Leagas Delaney,
advertising agents for the deodorant, used him – without his consent –
because he was in the news. Neil Greatrex, president of the breakaway
UDM and a one-time Arthur fan, smirked: 'Appropriate, considering
the investigations taking place. It really does smell dodgy.'

Worse was to come. On 7 September, after a lengthy investigation,
the government-appointed Certification Officer Matthew Wake
brought criminal charges against Scargill and Heathfield at Sheffield
magistrates court. Scargill was charged with wilfully neglecting to
perform the union's duty to keep proper accounting records and
aiding and abetting Heathfield in wilfully failing to keep proper
accounting records. The third charge against him alleged that he
aided and abetted Heathfield in neglecting to maintain a satisfactory
system of accounting records. Similar charges were laid against
Heathfield, and three charges were also preferred against the NUM
for failing to send to the Certification Officer a 'true and fair balance
sheet'. All the charges were brought under section 12 of the 1974
Trades Union and Labour Relations Act – ironically, a law put on
the statute book by Michael Foot when, as Employment Secretary,
he repealed Edward Heath's hated 1971 Industrial Relations Act.
Each of the nine charges carried a maximum £400 fine. Scargill
promised to defend the action 'all the way'.

The impending prosecution appeared to hasten moves to reach an
out-of-court settlement of the Russian money issue. On 10 September, after five hours of hard bargaining – probably the most successful negotiation of Scargill's life – a compromise was reached
between the NUM team, composed of executive members of the
union, and the IMO team, composed of national officials of the NUM
and an international apparatchik. To avoid the issue going to the
High Court, the NUM team agreed to accept repatriation of
£742,000: rather less than the top figure of £2,033,000 that accountants Cork Gully thought the union was entitled to. Scargill was

credited with having come off the fence on the side of his union and against the IMO, which he also leads. This looks unlikely, given the draft text of the compromise in the hands of the author. Initially, the joint legal agreement said (clause two): 'The NUM, its Officers and National Executive Committee declare and acknowledge that the NUM has no further claim to or any interest in any funds or assets held by or under the control of the IMO otherwise as affiliated members of the IMO *and that those funds and/or assets are and at all times have been properly held by or on behalf of the IMO* [author's italics]; and the NUM, its officers and Executive Committee further undertake that they will not commence or attempt to cause, encourage or support financially or otherwise any legal proceedings anywhere in the world in which such a claim is made or any such interest is asserted.'

In other words, right until the signing of the deal, Scargill's IMO was trying to pretend that the Russian money did not really belong to the British miners at all. It had 'at all times . . . been properly held by or on behalf of the IMO'. The NUM team spotted the trap, and refused to sign until those weasel words were taken out. Had they remained, Scargill would have been able to say that he was right all along. The money was intended for the IMO for 'international purposes'. And his international body was simply being magnanimous in helping out the NUM in a tight corner. The ploy failed.

Back home in Sheffield, the miners' executive breathed a huge sigh of relief and voted unanimously to ratify the Paris accord. The Lightman Inquiry and subsequent court action had cost the union more than £350,000, and a full hearing of its High Court action against the two national officials and the IMO would have cost another £1 million. The case was dropped. Scargill still refused to accept that he had been wrong. The Paris accord also cleared the way for the Fraud Squad to call off their inquiry, which was getting nowhere. Detectives cited the passage of time, lack of evidence and problems of jurisdiction as reasons for bringing the investigation to a halt.

At the Labour Party conference which followed, Scargill was evidently showing signs of strain. He was admitted to a Blackpool hospital for checks for suspected pneumonia after collapsing at a guesthouse in the town. Ms Jo Richardson, the party chairman, prompted cheers and applause from delegates when she sent the conference's good wishes. He was well enough the next week to chair a special delegate conference on the Lightman Report at NUM headquarters, which by now was big enough to hold the dwindling band of coalfield representatives: 142 in all, appearing on behalf of 58,700 members – less than a third of the pre-strike figure. As customary for special conferences (on an old Gormley ruling), the press were excluded, and the miners were free to speak their mind. The official verbatim report makes clear that they did.

Des Dutfield, South Wales president, moved that Scargill and Heathfield stand down and offer themselves for re-election. He pointed out that even after receivership had ended, he and fellow members of the executive had been kept in the dark. 'These secret accounts should have been revealed, could have been revealed at an earlier date and would not have been if Windsor had not blown the whole story. We could find no justification for that secrecy to prevail once the receiver had left the union's business.' Such secrecy meant the union was being run as an autocracy, not a democracy, 'and that is why we feel so angered'. Lancashire and Derbyshire miners supported the call for new elections, and Scotland denounced Scargill's argument that the Russian money was meant for international purposes as 'pie in the sky . . . our membership don't believe that'. But the votes were stacked up against the dissidents. Yorkshire, the Midlands, Durham and Nottinghamshire were all decided in favour of Scargill before the proceedings began.

Scargill said he would be 'very brief', and went on being very brief for nearly 5,000 words. He excoriated Lightman for 'his absolute paranoiac desire to try and influence this union' to accept that money coming into the Miners' Action Committee Fund actually belonged to the NUM. 'They never were, and they never will be,' he insisted. Knowing he was already in the clear, he was able to say he never had any intention of reporting the secret accounts to the executive, because they were not NUM accounts. He apologized to nobody for the role he played in the 'miracle' of sustaining the union during the strike and afterwards. 'I have done nothing wrong,' he declared. 'Heathfield has done nothing wrong. Everything we have done between 1984 to date has been for the benefit of this organisation, of our union. I ask you to think back to the days when this took place, not to a cosy atmosphere in Lincoln's Inn in 1990, but to a period when we were involved in a class war against an enemy absolutely intent on destroying us . . . There is a concerted attempt to denigrate the tremendous achievements and sacrifice of men and women who went through that great dispute, men and women who wrote a new chapter in British history, who provided an inspiration not only in this country but throughout the world.'

As Lawrence Daly used to say to Gormley: 'Pull the lever Joe,' and the right-wing arms would go up, now the lever jerked up the Scargill-loyalist vote. Scargill's actions were endorsed. Membership of the IMO was approved. And, for good measure, the Durham miners got through a motion authorizing Scargill and the leadership to sue Lightman for publishing his report through Penguin Books without asking the permission of the NUM. That litigation still hangs over Lightman's head. By contrast, the Serious Fraud Office announced on 10 December 1990 that, after receiving the results of the Metropolitan Police investigation, 'we have advised them that the case does not fall within our statutory criteria'. Scargill also won his complaint to the Advertising Standards Association about the 'sweating' advertisement. The ASA criticized the advertisement as 'highly distasteful'.

But he fared less well at the hands of the men. A secret pithead ballot in mid-November on industrial action in support of a £50 a week pay claim resulted in a fifty-seven per cent 'No' vote. This was his fifth such defeat in a row, and prompted speculation that the union might disintegrate, with Scotland and South Wales going it alone and the central coalfields reconstituting themselves into what would effectively be a National Union of Yorkshire Miners. Scargill was obliged to go into the business of exporting his revolution – to Czechoslovakia, where strikes had effectively been outlawed under the Communist regime. He visited Prague twice to advise the new, free Czech mining union how to strike. 'The thinking of the Czech and British miners is absolutely the same,' said their leader Marian Mesiarik. 'There is a feeling that miners must strike for their rights if they are required to.' Employment Secretary Michael Howard advised them to think very hard before they negotiated a transfer to Scargill. 'Many of his own members no longer support him.'

The Lightman Inquiry came back to haunt both sides as the revisers got to work. In May 1991, a Channel 4 'Despatches' programme made by socialist film maker Ken Loach accused the *Daily Mirror* and 'The Cook Report' of a deliberate and uncorroborated smear campaign against Scargill. Roger Cook's foot-in-the-door journalism was dismissed as 'light entertainment', and 'Despatches' claimed that Windsor and Parker shared £130,000 for their role in the Gaddafi–Soviet money affair. Loach argued that the *Mirror* story and 'The

Cook Report' films were in line with the new face of the Labour Party. 'The last thing Kinnock wants to be faced with is a strong trade union movement.'

Scargill was certainly strengthened by the collapse on 19 June of the Certification Officer's prosecution for failing to keep proper records. The case before Stipendiary Magistrate Ian Crompton ran into trouble on the first day when the court ruled that all evidence submitted to the Lightman Inquiry was covered by privilege and could not be heard. The magistrate ruled that it would be 'manifestly and blatantly unfair' for the Certification Officer to use details of the NUM's finances given to Lightman during his investigation. The NUM leaders had been assured of confidentiality and had not been cautioned under the Police and Criminal Evidence Act. Nor would the magistrate allow Lightman to give evidence, on the grounds that that would breach the professional and legal privilege between a lawyer and his client. Defence lawyers submitted this left the prosecution with so little evidence that the charges should be dropped. Roger Ter Haar, appearing for the Certification Officer, sought a judicial review, but the magistrate refused to grant it and the case fell when the prosecution offered no further evidence.

Scargill was naturally delighted. 'All the charges have been dismissed. That fully vindicates our position,' he said. 'The prosecution should never have been brought in the first place, and I'm pleased to see that justice has been done in Sheffield.' Ms Gareth Peirce, solicitor for the national officials, accused the government of being politically inspired: 'There certainly is the strongest suggestion that this prosecution was brought for political motives, and I do not suggest that the Certification Officer was doing that himself. The prosecution happened in the context of attacks coming on the union from all directions last summer, so people can come to their own conclusions.'

Matthew Wake, the Certification Officer, was convinced that the prosecution was 'properly brought'. But he was sanguine: 'You win some and you lose some.' He considered an appeal for judicial review to the High Court, but dropped it after legal advice that it would be a waste of public money given the summary nature of the charges, and the time and cost involved. So the full story of the Doctor, the Patient and the Consultant never did emerge in court, the only place where all the evidence could have been dispassionately weighed and a binding verdict reached. That being the case, the controversy goes on. Windsor broods in his Gondeville manor, awaiting the opportunity to get into the witness box, while Scargill rests his case.

In August 1992, the Inland Revenue finally signed a legal agreement with the NUM accepting that secret accounts set up to avoid sequestration and receivership were valid trusts and not the property of the NUM. Mark Stephens, solicitor for the NUM, said the agreement established that there had been 'no impropriety' on the part of the national officials in the running of the fourteen secret accounts. So all's well that ends well. Except there is still the residual, nagging feeling that the Squire of Treelands is a great deal better at looking after number one than defending and advancing the terms and conditions of his members, which is, after all, what they pay him £60,000 a year for.

CHAPTER X

COMEBACK

O N 13 OCTOBER 1992, Michael Heseltine, president of the Board
of Trade, stood up in the House of Commons to announce
the virtual demise of the British coal industry. Of the fifty deep mines
still open, thirty-one would close by the end of the financial year,
and some within four days. Up to 30,000 miners and white-collar
workers would lose their jobs in the biggest redundancy operation
in the country's history, costing an estimated one billion pounds.
The knock-on effect in mining supply firms, the railways and services
trades would add a further 70,000 jobs to the holocaust so blithely
announced by Heseltine. There was uproar in Parliament and in the
country at large. Britons were still reeling from the impact of 'Black
Wednesday' only a month before, when the UK had to quit the
European Exchange Rate Mechanism and devalue the pound, and
the precipitate closure of more than half the nation's coal industry
in one fell swoop was more than they could take. 'Middle England'
rose up in revolt, in a spontaneous upswelling of emotional support
for the miners most poignantly expressed by Mrs Jean Nuttall of
Kings Langley, Herts: 'Why, on the evening following the news of
the closure of thirty-one coal mines, was I, a middle-class, somewhat
more than middle-aged housewife living in a nice house in leafy
suburbia, crying into the washing up?'

Scargill could scarcely believe his luck. The run-down was not
news to him. He had been telling anybody who would listen for
months what the government was about to do to the coal industry.
At the Labour Party conference in Blackpool two weeks previously,
he managed to wake up the delegates with an emergency motion
deploring pit closures. Brandishing his favourite weapon – the leaked
document – he disclosed that the Cabinet intended to shut thirty
collieries. The secret letter, dated 17 September, from Industry Minister Tim Sainsbury to Treasury Chief Secretary Michael Portillo

spoke of an announcement by British Coal in the second half of September. It also named the thirty collieries, and calculated the likely increase in unemployment. 'As you know, many communities are likely to be seriously hit by the closures,' confided Sainsbury. It was a begging letter, asking for £15 million 'windfall' money from the European Community to be directed to the hard-hit coalfields, a move for extra EC cash, and more money for government factory building. Sainsbury copied his letter to other relevant ministers, and added: 'This issue is manifestly extremely sensitive. I would be grateful if you would restrict copying of this letter to those who need to know.'

'I think miners need to know and I think the British people need to know,' the outraged miners' leader thundered to loud cheers from the conference hall. Nine years ago, he reminded delegates, he had warned that the government had a hit list of pits earmarked for closure. 'I was told I was telling lies. One hundred and forty pit closures and 140,000 redundancies later, I ask this question: who told the truth and who told the lies?' It was a classic Scargill stroke, followed by a swift piece of self-justification. He had seen the leader of the breakaway UDM on television saying how he felt betrayed by the government, whose policies would devastate mining communities. 'If those for whom he spoke had done the time-honoured thing and respected picket lines in 1984 we would not be in the situation we are in in 1992.' He offered no evidence for this self-serving assertion, but the words were well chosen. The working miners had not behaved with honour, had not 'respected' picket lines. It was the language of gentlemen of honour, a far cry from the sometimes brutal reality of flying pickets. He got his applause, but the party modernizers now firmly in the driving seat dismissed his intervention. Alistair Darling, MP, Labour's City spokesman, said: 'What you saw there was a nostalgic look back at the past.'

And, unaccountably, the coal story failed to pick up steam. Accurate speculation continued on the inside and business pages, but *The Observer* was the only paper to splash with it before the actual announcement. All that changed when Heseltine stood up at the despatch box. His well-advertised angst about the misery his closure programme would cause cut little ice. The *Daily Mirror*, Scargill's tormentor, pointed out that 'Prezza Hezza' was a rich man with an annual Cabinet salary three times the redundancy payments that would have to last sacked miners for the rest of their lives. 'What an unctuous creep he is. And what a hard-faced killer the Government is!' the *Mirror* roared.

Terry Pattinson, the paper's industrial editor, who had accused Scargill of taking money from Colonel Gaddafi, now gave him pride of place. The NUM president pledged a fight to the death to forestall the closures, and promised to recommend unspecified 'action' to a special delegate conference in Sheffield the next day. Asked if the action would be legal, he replied: 'It will be justified.' Somewhat belatedly, he was learning caution, but the old rhetoric was still there. 'The price of trusting the Tories and British Coal can be seen in the savage butchery announced today by the government with a total lack of compassion by a government and management devoid of anything but malice and vindictiveness. It is a determination to repay what they see as a defeat inflicted on them by the miners' union in 1974.'

He was ready for a strike, and Johnny Stones, veteran delegate from Frickley colliery, Yorkshire, announced his willingness to move a resolution for industrial action – the miners' 'last hurrah', he called it. Scargill was unimpressed by threats that miners taking action would lose a large chunk of their redundancy money, or by the huge stocks of coal inside the power stations, equivalent to a year's supply. 'Miners have a choice, either to lie down and let this happen or stand up and fight back,' he declared on the eve of the 15 October conference.

And then something happened. He listened to the voices of caution among the delegates, and took heed. As one coalfield representative put it, 'Arthur was listening and keeping his knee-jerk calls for a strike in check. We haven't seen it for a long while, but I call it leadership at last.' Buoyed up by the sudden surge in public support, delegates voted to stay their hand on industrial action. Looking unusually composed, his hands resting on the table instead of chopping the air, and speaking quietly to the camera, Scargill announced that the NUM was not looking for a confrontation with anybody, and would be going to see the TUC General Council in London that Saturday with a view to harnessing the wave of public and political indignation to save the threatened pits. 'We don't want a strike,' he insisted. 'All we want is to save the British coal industry and jobs.'

Was this a different Scargill to the loud-mouthed demagogue hell-bent on bringing down the wicked Tory government? Fellow union leaders who had not seen him on the general council and only knew him from his hardline appearances at the rostrum remarked that his finger-wagging demands for solidarity action had gone, to be replaced by a cool appraisal of the case for coal. He finished his presentation with the harrowing story of one of the industry's hapless 'gypsies', a miner who had moved house and pit six times in the past six years to stay in work. *The Financial Times* thought it detected more than just a change of style, wondering if Scargill was now 'quieter, less cocksure – as if his "martyrdom" has given him an inner assurance he used to lack'. The man himself dismissed such folly. 'You can say what you like, I know that I haven't changed. But the issues have been finally understood by the British people.'

He had evidently been 'got at' by members of his own executive and other sympathetic union leaders at a private meeting earlier in the week. The barons of the labour movement were not going to allow such a golden opportunity to put the government on the rack over the economy and jobs to slip through their fingers. The TUC moved quickly to organize a 'Jobs and Recovery Campaign' on the back of public unrest, taking the initiative out of Scargill's hands while allowing him to remain a front-bench propagandist in the battle to reverse government policy. The TUC set about organizing a national day of demonstration for 25 October, and supported Labour's moves in Parliament to win a moratorium on pit closures while the Select Committee on Trade and Industry investigated coal's future. Norman Willis undertook to lobby wavering Tory back-benchers, including Winston Churchill and Mrs Elizabeth Peacock, whose revolt looked likely to rob Heseltine of his Commons majority on the closure programme.

Middle England was on the march in the most unlikely places. Three thousand protesters paraded through Cheltenham with plac-ards demanding 'Sack Major, NOT 30,000 Miners' to a rally where Lord Neidpath told the cheering crowd that the prime minister would like to hear their opinions. To ringing cheers, he then read out the telephone number of 10 Downing Street. This time, even Woodrow Wyatt, right-wing columnist of the *News of the World*, refused to blame Scargill. Major was rattled, not by the prospect of respectable West Country folk berating him on the telephone, but by the increas-ing likelihood of a humiliating Commons defeat. With his majority reduced to only twenty-one in the April general election, it only required eleven Tory back-benchers to rebel to compel a U-turn. Eight MPs signalled their readiness to defy the Whips, and others promised to abstain. Amid front-page headlines like the *Daily Express*'s 'Can Major Survive?' the prime minister called an emergency Cabinet meeting on 19 October. Scargill, basking once again in the glow of public recognition, was also back in favour with the new Labour hierarchy. After discussing the coal crisis with MPs, he met Labour leader John Smith and the Shadow trade and industry secretary Robin Cook.

Major and Heseltine bought parliamentary peace with a freeze of the closures accompanied by a DTI investigation of possible new markets for coal, to report in the New Year. Six Tory dissidents marched into the Labour lobby, and five abstained, bringing the government's majority down to thirteen. Rebel Elizabeth Peacock, who angrily told her party: 'It's about people', was rewarded with dismissal from her post as parliamentary private secretary to the social security minister, Nicholas Scott.

It was a day to savour for Scargill in a different way. In the autumn sunshine, he led a column of more than 100,000 miners, their families and supporters through the West End to Hyde Park. It was the biggest outpouring of public wrath since the poll tax demonstrations, but it was peaceful. In Park Lane, Scargill was handed a bouquet of white chrysanthemums. Guests in the posh hotels of Kensington and Knightsbridge leaned out of their windows and cheered. Shoppers and tourists clapped, motorists tooted their horns. Newsmen said Scargill was mobbed like a film star, and when the march passed the five-star Royal Garden Hotel, a miner gesticulated to cheering guests: 'Look, they're rattling their jewellery for Arthur.' Scargill told the protesters what they wanted to hear: 'For the first time in years, working men and women have expressed their outrage and indignation at a government completely devoid of compassion and understanding.' To applause, he called Heseltine's measures 'a callous act that has aroused anger the length and breadth of the land'.

Heseltine, the leader writers noted glumly, had achieved the impossible. He had put 'our Arthur' back on his pedestal. Scargill savoured the front page of the *Daily Mirror*, which was almost entirely taken up with a picture of him accepting a bouquet, with smiling police officers and miners punching the air as a backdrop. The headline read: 'COR! Look what Major's done for old Arthur!' But the tabloids did not bother with Scargill's other main appearance of the day, at the Central Hall, Westminster, where the old warrior was on form. Speaking to activists at a ticket-only affair that only half filled the massive hall, he demanded that the campaign against closures should be stepped up, and insisted that not one pit should close. This was the real Scargill speaking. As he had made plain to *The Financial Times*, nothing had really changed. Four days later, as 200,000 people braved appalling rain to march again in the capital to back the miners, he was back in gear, demanding support until the policy was fully reversed, calling for mass demonstrations in every town and city to compel the government to withdraw, and exhuming the threat of industrial action should the Cabinet fail to back down under pressure from the public. It was a signal that his political recidivism, suppressed during the weeks of riding public anger over the closures, would eventually resurface.

For now, he was content to play the formal game of consultation and litigation. He flew to Strasbourg for talks with EC Energy Commissioner Antonio Cardoso de Cunha, winning support for an independent inquiry, and he got socialist Euro MPs on side. Meanwhile, British Coal was pursuing a 'closure by stealth' policy, keeping ten of the thirty-one pits abandoned by the government on a care and maintenance basis only, and sending home on basic pay the men who reported for work every day. The corporation also allowed miners to volunteer for redundancy, which they did – in a trickle at first, but then building up to more than 8,000 across the industry. At Grimethorpe, near Barnsley, home of the famous colliery band, coal production ceased on 30 October, and the men were bitter. Face worker Michael Haywood, aged twenty-five, burst out: 'It's hatred, right inside.' Scargill toured the country drumming up public support and battling against the odds to keep the miners' morale intact.

The campaign produced some astonishing cameos, but none more so than the dramatic reappearance of the senior police officer who arrested Scargill in the Battle of Orgreave to say: 'Arthur was right.' Chief Superintendent John Nesbit emerged from retirement to tell the *Daily Mirror*: 'Unfortunately, a lot of the forecasts made by Scargill during that time were spot-on. You have to concede what he said would happen to the coal industry has come to fruition.

'Major and the Tories have given him a platform again. He has public support – now I would like to see how he uses it. I do know this, Arthur must never go down the road towards violence again. He must not pitch miner against miner. He has a lot of loyal and trustworthy supporters and he must proceed in a moderate way.' Nesbit, who had been a boy miner like Scargill and a member of the

NUM, added: 'I believe Orgreave was a turning point in the strike. The wholesale violence turned public sympathy away from Arthur. I hope he has learned the lesson. I hope he fights this battle in a peaceful way, using public sympathy on behalf of the miners. And I hope he wins this time.'

This priceless confession appeared shortly before Scargill made another, unscheduled appearance before the TUC General Council to begin his long march back towards orthodox militancy. Union leaders agreed to hold their monthly meeting at the historic Mansion House in Doncaster in a show of solidarity with the mining communities. Scargill turned up and gave them a forty-minute oration on the state of the crisis. British Coal was 'blackmailing' miners to quit the industry, and the NUM would do 'anything and everything in our power' to halt plans to shut the ten collieries most at risk. He called on the general council to mount industrial action against the closure programme, but the TUC ruled out his demand. Outside, militant miners and ultra-Left demonstrators kept up a chant for 'General Strike Now!', but Norman Willis riposted: 'There is no way the TUC would put their head in a legal noose.' Scargill wanted secondary action to back the miners, knowing it was unlawful under the Tebbit legislation. His gradual shift back from 'no strike' towards a germinating conflict worried the ruling TUC moderates. They saw the pit closures as a political decision, giving them the first opportunity since 1979 to force a political U-turn on the government.

The Commons DTI Select Committee began taking evidence from interested parties, and British Coal came up with a compromise plan that would spare thirteen of the thirty-one pits and save 8,000 jobs. But the initiative was linked to drastic reforms of working practices, including repeal of the 1908 Coal Mines Regulation Act, which limits underground shifts to seven and a half hours. The men would work the same number of hours per year. But scrapping the act would allow twenty-four-hour coal production through three eight-hour shifts – which could actually be as long as ten hours including travelling time. The corporation cited American practice, which allowed mines to work round the clock seven days a week. Scargill was irate. He called a press conference in Sheffield to denounce British Coal's modification of its original closure plan as a 'cynical contempt' of British miners. 'Their package is an attempt to blackmail miners into accepting longer working hours and inferior working practices as a prelude to privatisation.' Where such practices operated in the USA, he claimed, accidents were five times greater than in British mines.

The initiative flopped, and on 9 December, declared National Recovery Day by the TUC, he recovered his confidence in the traditional remedy sufficiently to demand publicly that the labour movement bring out its millions on to the streets. The media had stopped writing about the campaign, he told a Congress House conference on coal. This was not strictly true, but true enough to be illustrative of his argument. Furthermore, the government was not listening. 'We have put the case and it has not been answered,' said Scargill. 'The TUC must decide where we go from here. It is not just mining jobs, it is rail, engineering jobs and other jobs too. We want the TUC to tell the government that unless there is a U-turn, we will call for a day of action with millions of people on the streets.'

Nor was Scargill too proud to invoke the Almighty. Despite his occasionally ambivalent remarks about Christianity in the past, a week later he joined a symbolic church service outside Grimethorpe colliery. Flanked by local clergy, he joined in the carol singing and read the lesson from Isaiah, chapter nine, beginning: 'The people walking in darkness have seen a great light; on those living in the land of the shadow of death a light has dawned.'

What he really wanted – all he seems ever to have wanted since becoming president – was to have a successful strike over jobs and pits. Baulked of this prize by the cautious TUC, he set about getting his way by a different route. On 17 December, he hijacked a press conference called by the Coalfield Communities Campaign at Westminster to announce his latest wheeze: a South African-style 'stayaway' day. The NUM would announce a set date when miners and their supporters would not go to work. This novel idea took the union's executive by surprise, and went through virtually on the nod. Only George Bolton, by now Scargill's fiercest critic within the leadership, opposed it. 'The anger and revulsion against pit closures have lit a torch from one end of the country to another,' said Scargill. 'We are not willing to accept the closure of the ten pits that have been identified by Michael Heseltine as being candidates for closure at the end of the 90-day consultation period.'

Scargill's first objective was to win the support of the railway workers, whose Rail, Maritime and Transport Union had conducted a brilliantly successful guerrilla campaign of one-day strikes in the long, hot summer of 1989. Jimmy Knapp, general secretary of the RMT, had been an admirer of the miners' leader, but the relationship had cooled somewhat after the great strike of 1984–5. In private, Knapp had taken to calling him a 'headbanger'. But the rail unions, the RMT and its traditional rival the footplatemen's union ASLEF, agreed to joint talks in the New Year on a possible 'stay-away'. Scargill had already pencilled 19 January 1993 in his diary as the date when British workers would emulate South African black workers.

He was on less firm ground, however, in seeking TUC support for the move. Scargill insisted that he was not seeking to defy the labour laws, though he had called for such defiance countless times. 'I have not mentioned industrial action. I have not mentioned a strike,' he pointed out. 'All I have mentioned is a stay-away campaign of action.' He knew full well that the greenest labour lawyer would swiftly strip away such a fig-leaf cover, but he gave notice that he would be asking the whole labour movement to back him. He would call on the TUC General Council 'to support that stay-away day of action and to call upon all affiliates to be fully involved'. Unless the government changed its pit closure policy, the action must go ahead 'because we are all involved'. Rallies and demonstrations, which are meat and drink to his campaigning style, were not enough.

The TUC would not back his adventurist new strategy, but support came from a different, unexpected quarter. On 21 December, the High Court ruled that the government had acted unlawfully in announcing its intention to close more than half the coal industry. Lord Justice Glidewell and Mr Justice Hidden found that the government and British Coal 'irrationally and unlawfully' ignored the right of mineworkers and their trade unions to be consulted. Furthermore, the judges quashed Heseltine's compromise policy of closing ten pits after a ninety-day consultation period and put the future of the remaining twenty-one threatened collieries to a review. Giving judgement on the NUM's appeal against the closures, the High Court found that the actions of ministers and British Coal put them in breach of the 1975 Employment Protection Act, which gives work people statutory rights of consultation on redundancies of more than ten people. They were possibly also in breach of European Community directives. Miners' rights were further enshrined in the industry's Modified Colliery Review Procedure operated from 1985, but unilaterally suspended by British Coal in October 1992 to accelerate pit closures. The High Court ruled that no colliery could be closed until the procedure had been exhausted.

The judgement, which took three hours to read out, came as a rude awakening for ministers and the corporation. Scargill left the Gothic court buildings in the Strand with a broad grin all over his face and told waiting newsmen: 'It is a good ruling, and demonstrates the correctness of bringing the case in the first place. The Coal Board and the government should never have announced the closure of 31 pits and the loss of 30,000 jobs.' On the face of it, the NUM had won. John Major now talked of having 'an open mind' on the industry, and Scargill demanded Heseltine's head on a platter. He also called for coal production to restart at the ten pits that were being run on a care and maintenance basis. In the mining communities, the High Court decision was hailed as the best Christmas present the miners could have wished for. The *Yorkshire Post* opined that, politically, 'the disaster is total'. The government had damaged its credibility as a fair-minded employer, resurrected doubts about electricity privatization and united the rival mining unions in defence of common interests. 'And it has put Arthur Scargill back on his favourite pedestal as a champion of the oppressed.'[1]

But the euphoria was short-lived. The worldly-wise pointed out that British Coal had always got its way on closures eventually, and in the meantime men reduced to basic rates at idle pits were voting with their feet in their thousands. Mark Stephens, the NUM's solicitor, said it was 'disgraceful' that men were still being sent home from the ten pits most at risk. 'It follows as night follows day that coaling should resume, and these men should be put back to work.' Failure to resume production could put Heseltine in contempt, he added. But the pits stayed idle, and by Christmas more than 5,000 men had taken voluntary redundancy. Moreover, the TUC General Council thankfully seized on the judgement to reject the NUM's proposal for a 'stay-away' day of action, arguing that it was now 'inappropriate'. Scargill was unfazed. The protest would go ahead, if British Coal did not resume production *and* development work at the ten pits.

With such a public argy-bargy going on, Scargill might have been forgiven for thinking that his private concerns would no longer interest the media. He could not have been more wrong. On Christmas Eve, *The Independent* ran an inside page lead headlined: 'Scargill heads for legal clash on union presidency.'[2] The story, by Labour Editor Barrie Clement, recounted how his second five-year term of office would expire at the end of January, and employment legislation required him to stand for re-election. But the NUM executive had yet to set in motion the election process, which could take up to ten weeks to complete. Perhaps tongue in cheek, the story continued: 'His detractors within the union are unable to understand his reluctance to trigger the election, given his new-found popularity both inside and outside the union. No one on the NUM executive has broached the issue and Mr Scargill has remained inscrutable on the issue.'

He had not been available for comment, so the paper freely offered its own, speculating that Scargill might be seeking to evade the labour laws. One escape route could be the union's rule that officials over fifty-five need not seek re-election, and NUM rules should take precedence over 'Thatcher's laws'. It was also significant that he had assumed a new post of joint president/general secretary since the retirement of Heathfield the previous summer. This step might make the law inoperable. Yet another 'ploy' under consideration was a merger of the Yorkshire, Nottinghamshire and North-East areas into a new, truly national – i.e. non-federal – union, on whose executive he could sit. However, it was pointed out that, since 1989, even non-voting members of union executives have to submit themselves to periodic election by secret postal ballot.

What was Arthur playing at? The procedures for executive elections had been set in motion. But he kept mum about his own position. Nobody inside the leadership dared raise the issue. Nobody outside the union felt brave enough to invoke the commissioner for trade union affairs, a government-appointed busybody charged with looking after the rights and interests of individual trade union members. The government had been told but, having quite enough on its plate with the coal crisis, wisely kept out of the controversy.

Scargill's stay-away day idea did not find universal approval, Ken Capstick, vice-president of the Yorkshire miners, thought it would get a cool response from the rest of the trade union movement. 'Arthur should let it fizzle away – it could all be forgotten in a couple of days,' he said.[3] Scargill's newfound friends on the Tory backbenches were even less impressed. 'Muscle-flexing of this kind is disastrous,' said Mrs Elizabeth Peacock, MP for Batley and Spen. 'A one-day strike is the worst possible thing the union could do. It would lose a lot of popular support.'

Scargill was unpersuaded. Though the original 19 January date slipped quietly out of the calendar, he stepped up his demands for mass action and for the first time reverted to his theme of the great strike: getting rid of the Conservative government by people power.

Speaking in Keighley, West Yorkshire, at his fifty-seventh rally of the campaign on 11 January, he congratulated the TUC for what it had done, but added: 'This is not enough. If, at the end of the day, this government is not prepared to listen to logic, then I urge the TUC and the entire Labour and socialist movement to call the same type of day of action that we have seen throughout Eastern Europe. As we go into this New Year, it can herald not only the reversal of the pit closure programme but it may also mean that we must have a mass day of action with millions taking to the streets of Britain. In the process we can begin the campaign to get rid of a government which has lost the confidence of the British people and replace it with one that will give to our people a sense of dignity and hope.'

His twin obsessions, being 'right' and changing society through the mass mobilization of the citizenry, are nowhere more evident than in the Keighley speech, which did not receive very wide publication. By now, his regular daytime, evening and weekend appearances had lost their newsworthiness. Very often it was the same material pepped up with a few music hall turns. Reporters would listen rather than take notes, joking among themselves that Scargill had the world's cheapest deep-mined clichés. It is difficult to see how he could have varied his central theme of the wrongness of pit closures. But as the days and weeks passed, and the long-awaited Heseltine White Paper on coal failed to appear, the commingling of the NUM's industrial objectives and his own messianic agenda became more and more pronounced.

The Keighley speech is a case in point. His own arguments are now baldly presented as 'logic'. They are irrefutable. He is right, and everybody else is wrong. Ergo, he is morally empowered to demand that millions of people must take to the street in a campaign to rid the country of a Conservative administration that has been in office less than nine months. He does not say how the government will fall, or what will take its place, or what kind of society will ensue from such revolutionary change. He is offering slogans rather than coherent political thinking. And, at heart, the slogans are about himself as much as they are about the crisis of the coal industry. They spring from an ironclad conviction that he has a uniquely clear political understanding of the situation, and that therefore he alone knows the way ahead and the masses have a duty to follow. There is something of the 'leading and guiding role' of his Communist Party days here. But there is even more of the invincible sense of being right and the fixity of purpose that have made Arthur Scargill such an inadequate yet dangerously appealing leader. His tragic flaw is his immoderate self-belief. He believes so much in himself that he can overpower the critical faculties of an audience, of his followers, of those who desperately want it all to be true anyway, and of his members, whose keenly developed sense of loyalty to their union makes them an easy prey for a leader of his manipulative genius.

Despite protests that he was not looking for a strike only twelve weeks earlier, Scargill's entire energies were now engaged in promoting one. He met the rail unions on 5 January, and though RMT and ASLEF leaders were in two minds about the wisdom of concerted industrial action, British Rail's refusal to give a guarantee of no compulsory redundancies in the run-up to privatization of the system gave them grounds for mounting their own dispute in parallel with the miners. A new date for the first 'day of action', – 18 February – was discarded because the rail unions said they did not have enough time to win a 'Yes' vote in the secret ballot required by law. The pit ballot date was fixed for 5 March. The rail vote was also to begin that day, but continue for a fortnight. The hard-Left's battle plan was leaked by Dave Douglass, Communist activist at Hatfield colliery in South Yorkshire, in the *Daily Worker*: 'Ballots will seek support for a rolling set of one-day strikes, and the real potential of embracing the concept of generalised strike action' that had been pushed by the Left since the start of the campaign 'appears now to be a reality'.[4]

The publication of the Commons Trade and Industry Select Committe's report on 29 January was greeted with near-contempt by Scargill. The committee, chaired by Sheffield Labour MP Dick Caborn, had done a magnificent job both in proposing new markets for coal and in squaring the political circle of persuading a Tory-dominated body to offer a Conservative industry secretary to pump subsidies into a state-owned enterprise unionized by their hated adversary Arthur Scargill. The MPs urged Heseltine to give British Coal a five-year subsidy until 1998, and to take a number of other measures such as cutting back opencast coalmining, ending the import of French electricity and banning the burning of the oil-based fuel Orimulsion. Such a package would yield an extra market of sixteen million tonnes of coal in the electricity generating industry, and three million tonnes among other customers. The cost would be £500 million – half the price tag of the original redundancy programme.

Scargill was unimpressed by this 'fudge'. The report did not demand the saving of all thirty-one pits, and was therefore 'unacceptable'. He criticized the role played in the exercise by Labour MPs, including his own former head of industrial relations at NUM headquarters, Mick Clapham, who had entered the Commons at the last general election. Labour leaders were privately furious. Caborn had achieved a near-miracle in winning a unanimous vote for the report, even if he did have to water down some of the thirty-nine recommendations to the government, and deserved better than Scargill's sneers that the report was 'an abysmal failure' that was completely contrary to NUM, TUC and Labour Party policy. Scargill was also 'implacably opposed' to any reform of working hours legislation. He preferred a blueprint put forward by Mrs Peacock because she wanted bigger subsidies. The MP for Batley and Spen was in no position to deliver her proposals, which carried virtually no political weight, but Scargill found her contribution 'infinitely better' than the Select Committee's rescue plan. His contempt was no doubt of some comfort to Heseltine, who was not inclined to change his initial judgement on the future of the industry and only did so because of the huge public outcry. After Scargill's comprehensive rubbishing of the report, he was under less pressure to implement its findings. Mostly, he ignored them. British Coal followed suit.

Heseltine allowed the timetable for his White Paper to drift on beyond the end of January, when it was originally promised, into February and then March, teasing out Scargill's true intentions and wearing down the Tory back-bench rebels, whose votes he needed to secure his coal strategy and his own political neck. Westminster's dissident Conservative Coal Group agreed to go for the full Select Committee report. The group's chief spokesman, Winston Churchill, warned that if Heseltine came to the House with proposals to save significantly fewer than twenty of the threatened pits he would be 'taking a significant risk' with the government's majority. But his coalition, always an unstable group, began to fall apart as the day of reckoning neared. Judicious leaks from the Heseltine camp suggested that no more than twelve to fourteen pits would be saved by his review. Soundings taken among back-benchers, as an NUM delegate conference voted to ballot on strike action, indicated that this would be enough to carry the day.

The NUM strike vote gave Scargill his first victory at the ballot box since being re-elected in 1988, and only his second win in ten years. Miners voted sixty to forty in favour of industrial action, in a poll that showed marked regional variations, an unusually low turnout and a chilling decline in members – even since the mid-October closure announcement. Overall, 12,913 pitmen voted for a strike, with 8,465 against. Turnout was estimated at about sixty per cent, indicating that the true membership of the NUM was down to 30,000. Derbyshire, Scotland and North Wales voted against the strike. Yorkshire, South Wales, the Midlands, Nottinghamshire (with few NUM members) and the North-East were in favour, but the latter, now regarded as the 'barometer' coalfield, by only 50.1 per cent. Scargill was quietly satisfied, telling a rally in Newcastle-under-Lyme, Staffs: 'We shall now campaign with all the power at our elbow for all the jobs threatened in our industry.' He would also call on the rest of the trade union movement to join in the day of action, already secretly set for Friday, 2 April. British Coal's reaction was predictable. Industrial action would be reckless, and would lose miners the credibility they had re-won over the last seven years by increased productivity, and would reduce the benefits of those who may have to face redundancy, warned Kevan Hunt, director of industrial relations.

More critically, the strike vote dismayed and angered the very Tory back-benchers on whose already equivocal support the NUM depended for a political lifeline. Winston Churchill did not mince his words: 'It would be a very major own goal if he were to repeat the tactics that he tried with such disastrous results in the Eighties. There is a lot of sympathy for the miners. There is zero sympathy for Scargill's tactics.'⁵ Dick Caborn, MP, was more understanding, arguing that the vote was more a 'cry for help' than a re-run of the militant years. Norman Willis, general secretary of the TUC, was also emollient: 'This vote is directly due to Mr Heseltine and British Coal, who have been stumbling between bludgeoning and blundering. Between them, they have produced a vote of anger and frustration that millions of people will readily understand.'

They might have been a little more understanding had Scargill not succeeded in his two-pronged strike strategy. The railway workers voted to join the 2 April walkout, threatening commuter and long-distance travellers in the week before Easter. Scargill, whose alliances can be as temporary as they are unlikely, had by now fallen out with Mrs Peacock. She thought his strike was the worst possible thing the miners could do. It would not help to save jobs; quite the reverse.

He was unrepentant, denying that industrial action would lose valuable public support. That support had been 'extremely good', but after six months the miners had reached the stage where they had to take further action because the government was not listening to their logical arguments. He did not think it unreasonable to ask his members to stop work for one day to prevent the government and British Coal stopping them from working ever again.

It was a choice sound-bite, but it glossed over the reality. A one-day walkout is really a token protest. Against the backdrop of a year's supply of coal stocked on the ground, it was only a pinprick. But he knew that the 2 April stoppage was only to be the precursor of something much bigger: certainly, more 'rolling stoppages' and a general call to all trade unions to join in. The 'concept of generalized strike action' was foreshadowed by Dave Douglass a month before. At that time he had cautioned that the wording of the strike ballot paper would be crucial 'since an all-embracing question may frighten the faint-hearted into believing they are being tricked into all-out industrial action. At this stage, we must win support for the rolling days of action.'[6] He was being frank (if a little cynical) with the comrades, but there are uneasy echoes of the slide into all-out confrontation of almost exactly nine years previously. Except that, this time, Scargill had held a ballot.

Heseltine blamed the power generators for the delay in producing his White Paper. They were reluctant to sign binding agreements to buy British coal over the next three years. Then, with a flourish, Scargill produced another leaked document, this time showing that the privatized energy companies did not want to be landed with the huge costs of stocking British coal that they did not want to buy anyway because it was dearer than imported coal. Heseltine celebrated his sixtieth birthday at his stately pile, Thenford House, near Banbury, Oxon, in more muted style than his fiftieth, when there were fireworks, a disco and 150 guests. He had a lot to be low-key about, facing the certainty of political oblivion if he repeated the parliamentary fiasco of the previous autumn. He was quietly confident. The Whips had sewn up a deal with the Ulster Unionists giving Northern Ireland an undersea gas pipeline in return for their crucial votes. The 'City Comment' in *The Daily Telegraph* breezily speculated that Scargill and the impending strike would turn out to be Heseltine's 'best hope' of selling his policy to the Commons. Meanwhile, the government discreetly extended from 31 March to the end of

1993 the deadline for miners to go out on redundancy terms worth up to £37,000. More than 8,000 men had already given up the struggle and quit.

By the time Heseltine produced his White Paper, two months later, on 25 March, the steady onslaught of events and the notoriously short attention span of the media had contrived to dissipate the public outrage that had greeted his original announcement. He offered very little to his critics. The much-vaunted review did not guarantee a single extra ton of coal, only subsidies of up to £500 million to help British Coal seek out new markets in the short time available before the industry was privatized. Of the thirty-one pits earmarked for closure, eighteen would either shut or go into mothballs, while thirteen were given a short-term reprieve of up to two years while production costs were brought down to internationally competitive levels. In addition, a further £200 million regional aid was promised, with new enterprise zones in Nottinghamshire and Yorkshire. It was enough for most of the potential rebels. Heseltine's Commons fixer, Keith Hampson, MP for Leeds North-West, said the government had been more generous with subsidies than the Trade and Industry Select Committee (of which he is a member) had recommended. But he took a side-swipe at the old adversary: 'Arthur Scargill will fight the one thing that will give the remaining pits a chance: changes in working practices, more flexible shifts and longer hours cutting coal.'

The next day's papers all agreed that 'Hezza' had rescued his own future, if not that of the coal industry. It was a measure of the marginalization of the NUM that Scargill's future was not even mentioned. Indeed, on this day of days, where was he? Where were the fire and brimstone quotes? Why was the great British public served up another helping of Ken Capstick complaining that the White Paper was an absolute disgrace that had not saved a single pit? On the day the future of his members' industry was announced to a crowded Commons, Scargill was not even in the country. He was in New York, appearing before an obscure United Nations subcommittee in his capacity as president of the IMO. His mission, said supporters, was to win funds for education and training for IMO unions.

The initial relief on the Tory back-benches gave way to apprehension when closer examination of the White Paper revealed its flaws. The electricity generators were not obliged to buy one extra cobble of coal. It was only an 'enabling' package, and if the power industry did not pick up the opportunity, the miners were back where they started. Nervousness increased when British Coal signed contracts with the generators for forty million tonnes of coal in 1993 4, falling to only thirty million tonnes a year for the four years thereafter. This left the industry with the insurmountable task of finding markets for those extra ten million tonnes on top of the 12.8 million tonnes produced at the twelve collieries 'reprieved' by Heseltine. Rising productivity, the year's stock of coal inside power station gates and the contribution of the new 'super-pit' (ordered by Nigel Lawson) coming on stream all multiplied the problems facing Scargill. A doleful British Coal spokesman said: 'It's going to be a severe challenge. One scenario may be that we have to close down more capacity.' So the pits were not saved after all.

An irritated Heseltine described British Coal's claim as 'worst case speculation'. He blamed the closures on the NUM, saying the union had delayed change for so long that the market had been filled by fuels more competitive than British coal. It was 'tragic' that their huge productivity gains had come too late. He pointed out that in February, the shortest month of the year, the industry produced no less than five million tonnes of coal – with the ten provisionally closed pits standing idle and with more than 8,000 men having left the industry. Heseltine had made up his mind to go for privatization at breakneck pace, even if that meant selling the mines at knockdown prices – less than the value of the plant and equipment. 'We want to drive privatization as fast as possible,' he said. Subsidies offered in the White Paper to make the coal competitive with imports would then pass to the private operators. Heseltine's deputy Tim Eggar, who suffers from a permanent smirk, argued that miners, being 'skilled, strong and highly disciplined workers of high repute', would find it easier than most jobless people to find work. 'We reckon that 84 per cent of those who have taken voluntary redundancy are in other work within 18 months,' he claimed.

Ministerial assurances were, as usual, not worth the paper they were not written on. But the Whips had done their work and, as the critical vote neared, Heseltine could relax. With a thousand miners demonstrating outside the House, he threw in a few extra concessions: three enterprise zones in the worst-hit areas of Easington, County Durham, the Dearne Valley, South Yorkshire, and Mansfield, Nottinghamshire. Social Services Secretary Peter Lilley also announced

that bronchitis and emphysema for miners with more than twenty
years service underground would now attract disablement benefit.
This was a long-overdue ruling. Bringing it to the House then made
it look shabby and cynical. But it worked. Despite refusing to give
any guarantees about the future market for coal, the government won
a majority of twenty-two for the White Paper. Only four die-hard
Tory rebels voted against: Elizabeth Peacock (Batley and Spen),
Richard Alexander (Newark), William Cash (Stafford) and Nicholas
Winterton (Macclesfield). Winston Churchill (Davyhulme), Steven
Day (Cheadle), Patrick Cormack (Staffordshire South) abstained. The
Conservative Coal Group had demonstrated it was more Conserva-
tive than coal.

Scargill felt vindicated once again. The Select Committee had
failed. The dissident Tories had melted like snow in summer, as he
predicted. He had the labour movement on side: Norman Willis
called the White Paper 'an early start to a slow poisoning of the
industry'. Women Against Pit Closures activist Betty Heathfield (now
estranged from Peter Heathfield) called for 'massive direct action' to
save the industry. Scargill returned to his baseline demand for all
thirty-one pits to be saved. 'The NUM is not concerned with trade-
offs or secret agreements.' He demanded that 'every worker in
Britain' should be out on Friday that week in support of the miners.
He sought to draw in the TUC and the Labour Party, arguing: 'Don't
make the mistakes of 1984. Act now in defence not only of miners
and rail workers, but the health, local government and social services.'
Simon Hughes, Liberal Democrat MP for Bermondsey, on the platform with Scargill was sufficiently carried away to support the NUM
president. The TUC and Labour leaders stayed mum, oblivious to
Scargill's insistence that 'only the mass action of the British people'
would defeat the closure plan.

On 2 April, all the NUM pits were stopped, but the strike was not
a hundred per cent. At Easington colliery in County Durham, seventy
per cent of the midnight shift went in, followed by forty per cent of
the six a.m. shift. The traditionally moderate Manton pit, part of the
Yorkshire NUM area but situated in Worksop, Nottinghamshire,
worked during the morning. However, these were the exception
rather than the rule. Only thirteen of British Coal's pits – all bulwarks
of the rival UDM, which belatedly began its own strike ballot – were
at work. In Yorkshire, pit deputies joined the walkout. Corporation
management described the strike as 'a pointless exercise'. Scargill

stayed on his home patch, leading a march through Barnsley. He declared the day of action a huge success and called on 'every union in Britain' to support the next one. There had to be a next one, of course: the Scargill mind-set demanded that. He insisted that the one-day strike had 'attained the objectives that we set' – to focus attention on the disgraceful behaviour of the government in closing down coal mines. If that was truly the objective, it was eclipsed by the one-day rail strike that accompanied it. Almost all media attention was focused on the railways, where only one passenger train ran and one goods train – embarrassingly, a coal merry-go-round service in Yorkshire. The objective of the next strike would be to protect jobs 'and help restore democracy in this country'. He declaimed: 'I want people to understand that what we are saying now is a message of hope and inspiration for the future.'

British Coal retaliated swiftly by ending the NUM's check-off system from 10 April at all the pits that struck. This was a serious financial blow for the union. Under check-off, union dues are automatically deducted from a miner's pay packet and sent direct to the area. Check-off saves considerable administrative expense, but, more importantly, it sustains trade union membership at a high level. Men who want to quit the union have to make a positive decision to opt out, and communicate that in writing to management. Without check-off, the NUM branches had to go back to the cumbersome collection of subscriptions manually and individually. Even with the loss of the de facto closed shop during the great strike, membership of the NUM had remained extremely high – in excess of ninety per cent. This latest punitive action was designed to drive down membership. The loss of check-off, NUM officials feared, would reduce membership to less than eighty per cent of manpower, creating a pool of non-union labour at every colliery.

Scargill argued that the first national coal strike for eight years had been a success, insisting: 'This is not the end of the campaign, it's the beginning.' It was, in fact, the beginning of the end. A few days later, members of the rival UDM voted by 3,673 to 2,943 against taking industrial action, and the first steps towards closures took place. The UDM agreed to the shutdown of two mines, Silverhill and Cotgrave, on condition that men redundant there could take the place of miners wanting to quit at other pits in Nottinghamshire. This move cleared the way for British Coal to increase the pressure elsewhere. After an offer of enhanced redundancy terms, coal production stopped at Easington and Westoe collieries in Durham, at Maltby and Rossington in Yorkshire, and at Clipstone and Bevercotes in Nottinghamshire. By the end of April, sixteen of the thirty-one pits originally slated for closure had ceased to produce, and were at varying stages of shutdown.

Meanwhile, Anne Scargill stole the headlines from her husband. On 9 April, using her maiden name of Harper, she evaded security checks and, along with three other members of Women Against Pit Closures, joined a party of teachers on an underground visit to Parkside colliery, Newton-le-Willows, Lancashire's last remaining pit. The mine had been on a 'care and maintenance' basis since ceasing production six months previously, and why British Coal allowed such a visit at such a time remains a mystery. However, Mrs Scargill inveigled her way down, and then refused to come back up again. She and her fellow protesters 'sat in' 2,000 feet below the surface for four nights throughout the Easter weekend, eating sandwiches and water supplied by management and passing the time by playing I-spy, singing songs and playing cards. Managers prevented them from speaking to men carrying out maintenance work.

The four protesters conveniently re-emerged for the TV cameras on Bank Holiday Monday afternoon as Arthur Scargill was making a speech. Anne Scargill was kissed and hugged by Arthur, and told the waiting rally: 'Get the kettle on. We haven't had a hot drink for days.' She said the managers had not allowed them to sleep, kicking their feet when they lay down to rest. It was a propaganda coup for the NUM, but short-lived, and it brought down the wrath of the pit management on the union branch. Some women activists claimed they had not been consulted on the 'sit in', and local NUM members were openly sceptical of Scargill's insistence that he knew nothing of the women's action until he heard it on the news.

However, the action did have its intended effect of raising the profile of the pit closure dispute in the media. Scargill insisted that the government was leaning on the newspapers to make them ignore the conflict. This could well have been true, though it was rather more likely that the tabloids' notoriously short attention span had long been exhausted. The Parkside interlude did bring Anne Scargill to public notice more than any previous action. The Press Association put out a profile of her – the first that anyone could remember of a trade union leader's wife.

She had already unburdened herself in a sympathetic interview in *The Independent on Sunday* on 21 February 1993. Writer Geraldine Bedell found her 'an unlikely activist: not in the least aggressive, motherly rather than chippy'. She had missed an earlier interview after being detained for attempting to chain herself to the railings of Michael Heseltine's DTI offices in Victoria Street. Anne Scargill used her husband's slogans: 'One hundred thousand people could lose their jobs if these pits go. Yet we mine the cheapest deep-mined coal in the world. We're not dots on a computer screen.'

But she was at her most interesting when talking about their private life. 'I'm not saying we haven't had our ups and downs. He doesn't quarrel, Arthur, he's one of those frustrating people who just ignores you when you get angry with him. We argue about silly things, like when he promises to meet me and then something turns up and he doesn't come home for a day and a half.' She defends Arthur: 'He's a very shy man. He works incredibly hard, and he really passionately cares about people. But he doesn't tell lies, and people don't always want to hear.' Anne Scargill even exculpates her husband from any blame for the outcome of the 1984 strike: 'He had an executive committee. It wasn't just him.'

On one thing they agreed: the renewed flush of public esteem would be transitory. 'I say to him: "Enjoy your popularity, love, cause it'll not last."' Scargill admitted to Hunter Davies two months later: 'A friend asked me if I wasn't worried my new popularity would disappear with the 24-hour strikes. If it's a choice between popularity and principle, I'll choose principle any time.' Being liked would not last. 'I give it three months.'

In truth, his popularity was already on the wane, not just among the general public but among his own men. When the second one-day strike took place on 16 April, British Coal reported 'an increasing number' of miners turning up for work. Coal was produced at twenty of the forty operational pits during the morning shift, twice as many as during the first strike on 2 April. More significantly, voting for a new national executive showed a shift against Scargill that threatened to rob him of his eight–six in-built majority. Scargill loyalists in the North-East and the white-collar section COSA were defeated by more independent candidates, indicating a rightward shift among the membership. His hold in Yorkshire remained solid, but his insistence on pursuing industrial action had clearly taken its toll. Scargill was unmoved: 'The combined effects of the coal and rail twenty-four-hour strikes are inflicting incalculable losses on the government, but minimum damage to the public and trade union members,' he claimed.

Scargill was whistling in the wind. Events, the bane of all politicians, were moving against him. First, the vital link with the railwaymen snapped. After long talks with British Rail on a compromise wording about job security, RMT leaders put a new formula to a ballot of their members. They narrowly voted against having any further strikes, isolating the miners once again. Discreetly, the idea of more stoppages in the pits, leading up to an all-out confrontation, was dropped. Without the railwaymen fighting alongside them, it was unlikely that the miners would heed a third strike call.

Then, on 26 May, the High Court reversed its earlier posture and ruled that British Coal had now 'consulted genuinely' about the first ten pits scheduled for closure, and could now go ahead with the shutdown. Brian Sedgemore, Labour MP for Hackney South and Shoreditch, said the judges must be 'off their trolley'.

Robbed of the strike weapon, and left in the lurch by the courts, Scargill was unable to halt the tide of closures, which by late June began to overwhelm even the twelve pits supposedly 'reprieved' by Heseltine's White Paper. The electricity generators showed no interest in buying more British coal – even at subsidized prices. By the early summer of 1994, 33 collieries had been closed – more than originally threatened. Of these, half a dozen were disposed of under licence to private operators, and reopened with drastically reduced workforces. Almost 40,000 men had lost their jobs, and the NUM was in the grip of a financial crisis. Scargill sought to survive by merging his union with the Yorkshire Area of the NUM (which was still a union in its own right, and solvent). Yorkshire miners indicated their support for him by voting 88.5 per cent in favour of this stratagem. But the NUM was now down to about 8,000 paying members.

Seemingly unfazed by the carnage of his industry, Scargill turned his fire on the prospect of denationalization. Addressing the Yorkshire Miners' Gala in Wakefield on 19 June, he said privatization had to be opposed with the same vigour as was used to oppose pit closures. 'And to anyone daft enough to buy pits, we say that if they change our terms and conditions and they reduce safety standards, then we will close all the pits.' But by now, his threats warranted only a couple of paragraphs in the press.

CHAPTER XI

REAPPRAISAL

ARTHUR SCARGILL CARRIES around in his pocket a postcard-sized memento mori of the coal industry. He takes it out with a flourish for the edification of the few journalists who penetrate the formidable defences to reach his bunker. Headed 'A. Scargill's predictions', it reads: 'In 1984, I predicted the closure of 70 pits and this prediction proved accurate. In 1985/6 I predicted the closure of a further 50 pits down to 70 and this proved accurate. In 1987 (on the basis of K. Moses' presentation) I predicted a reduction of a further 20 pits to 50 by 1992/3 and this proved accurate. In 1991 I predicted that there would be a reduction to 30 pits if no action was taken against the Tory government and Coal Board policies.'

Should the reporter's shorthand not be up to the job, Scargill will happily fax a life-sized copy of the postcard of predictions to his office. This is his self-justification: that he was right, and history will judge him so. It is also the reason most often given by his supporters for their adulation. Even those who cannot go along with his manifest sense of destiny concede that he foresaw the accelerated run-down of the British coal industry.

His was by no means a voice in the wilderness. Many other industry experts and industrial journalists were saying much the same thing at much the same time, based in part at least on the same secret documents coming out of the giant colander that was Hobart House. And there was a powerful degree of self-fulfilment in his prophecies. By presenting a totally uncompromising front to successive Energy Secretaries and to the management of the industry, he hastened the very process he so vehemently condemned. Once freed of the constraints of state ownership, the electricity generators were always going to move as quickly as public policy would allow to rid themselves of dependence on British Coal and the constant sabre-rattling of Arthur Scargill.

The more baleful his threats from the presidential rostrum, the quicker the 'dash for gas' became, and the faster the development of comprehensive new facilities for bulk coal imports. This was a clear, if unstated, line of thinking in government. Cecil Parkinson, the Cabinet minister who privatized the electricity supply industry, later confessed: 'Mr Scargill and the National Union of Mineworkers made his predictions a self-fulfilling prophecy. He proved in 1985 that no government could allow itself to be at the mercy of an industry and a trade union which would use its economic power for political purposes. He underlined, in a way which made the contraction of the industry inevitable, his belief that it was his duty to bring down a Conservative government whatever the views of the electorate.'[1] Scargill's critics on the Left concur, arguing that the collapse of the NUM under his leadership helped to speed up the closure programme.

But there is a deeper significance to Arthur's postcard. He actually *needs* the threat, real or imagined, of pit closures. His whole outlook is built on conflict, from which he will emerge as both the winner and the great wise leader. 'He thought he was the new Messiah,' observed Emlyn Williams, his canny rival on the Left who grew disillusioned with Scargill.

Jimmy Reid, his one-time political mentor in the YCL, thinks that Scargill sees himself as an apostolic successor to A. J. Cook: 'I'm convinced that he thought he was the reincarnation of A. J. Cook. It was almost metaphysical. It was a kind of emotion. It didn't define itself in any ideology. He was Cook Mark Two, but this time it would be a different result. He was very much led by the perception of the great role he was going to play. He thinks of himself as a pivotal figure who makes things happen.'[2]

Many elements fuse into this self-deluding sense of destiny that, ultimately, is his tragic flaw. There is the little boy, shunned and bullied at school, anxious to please teacher and show his classmates 'what for'. There is the secondary school pupil, fired by the passionate prose of Jack London, who wants in his naive way to make the world a better place. There is the young worker, desperate to show his Marxist teachers he is as good as – if not better than – they are. There is the principled pit militant, determined to be a leader of men, struggling against the dead hand of the repressive, worldly mafiosi of Woolley colliery. There is the champion of the burgeoning hard-Left of the Yorkshire coalfield, grabbing airtime to ventilate his members' grievances. There is the opinionated delegate anxious to shine in front of his elders and betters in the area council of the NUM. There is the ambitious lay official scheming to rid the county of its effete and gullible leaders. There is the hero of Saltley, battling to reverse history and snatch the presidential crown from the corrupt forces of moderation. There is the victorious successor to the wheeler-dealer Joe Gormley who takes on 'the American butcher' and Margaret Thatcher's hated Tory government. Always fighting, fighting, fighting. There is always somebody else to fight. Once one dragon is slain, another rises from the dust. The warrior cannot rest. He must buckle on his sword and sally forth. And so it goes on.

This is not really a class war. It is a personal war. Scargill is taking on the world to show how 'right' he is. And for that to be shown, there has to be an approving audience. For the boy at Worsbrough primary, it was the teacher to whom he hurried, urging: 'Please Miss, I've finished. What do I do now?' For the man pitting himself against Capital, it has to be the deep roar from miners' throats at the mass rallies that feeds him spiritual refreshment. His aides have noticed how, during the great strike, he would appear in the coalfields looking exhausted and depressed. 'But when he had an audience, he would change.' Beaming, he would confide to his driver Jim Parker that he'd been 'firing on eight cylinders. I'd got them! I had them in the palm of my hand. I could do anything with them.' Unwholesome, maybe, but true. Diffident at close quarters, he comes alive in front of a sea of undifferentiated faces.

Those who have been close to him complain that implicit in his boasts of being able to raise and drop an audience virtually at will lies a condescending view of the miners: they are cannon fodder in the struggle. Perhaps it ought not to be taken to extremes, but there is something in this criticism. Scargill has always been on the lookout for his next move, his next audience, and there is a hard, self-regarding edge to his ambition. Politics is a hard business, and he exhibited early the necessary personal skills.

Scargill always wants to be taken seriously as a political figure. He emphasizes this dimension of his life in interviews time and again. He has been a member of the Labour Party for thirty years, but he has shown little personal interest in orthodox political advancement. He told Sue Lawley that he was 'actually tempted in my younger days when I was fifteen, sixteen, seventeen, to try for a full-blooded career which would involve standing for the local council, which I did. And eventually standing for Parliament.' In fact, he was twenty-two when he stood unsuccessfully as Communist Party candidate for Worsbrough Urban District Council.

He has boasted many times of the 'safe' parliamentary seats he has been offered. Sometimes the figure is four, sometimes six, sometimes more. He always insists he has never been tempted to take these 'certain offers'. Nor has he ever revealed where they are, or who 'offered' them to him. No party activist has gone on record disclosing the identity of any such constituency. There is only Scargill's word that any such offer was ever made. On the other hand, these proposals, and his lofty rejection of them in the interests of working for the NUM, have become part of the comprehensive myth of his life.

Only one piece of objective evidence on this score is traceable, and this is equivocal. Tony Benn confided to his diary on 1 November 1986 that he had gone to Sheffield to try to persuade Scargill to put his name forward for the safe seat of Barnsley Central. Scargill was tempted. Benn wrote, 'He said he had considered it seriously but he felt it wasn't right.' Benn suggested that he remain president of the NUM while becoming an MP – an extraordinary proposition which would have caused uproar in the union – but even this beguiling prospect could not clinch the issue. Arthur 'was not keen'. The seat eventually went to Eric Illsley, an administrative officer of the York-shire area of the Union in Barnsley, who remains an NUM-sponsored MP. So he could have had that seat, had he wanted it.

Scargill insisted that 'in real terms, power is in the trade union and labour movement'. The position of an MP 'is not really comparable. If you're a back-bench MP in Parliament and you look at the record, they can't get very much done. That's not to criticise them because they do as well as they can in the circumstances that present themselves to them.' He was less charitable to Labour MPs in January 1993 when they signed the Commons Trade and Industry Select Committee report advocating measures to increase the coal market. He was scathing about them for refusing to demand that all thirty-one threatened pits stay open at whatever cost.

Unless you are a Cabinet minister, he has argued, 'then you're not really in a position where you're going to be able to achieve anything and if you look at the average span when a person is in the Cabinet, it's very limited indeed, with a few notable exceptions. But if you ask somebody, for example, who is the MP for so-and-so constituency, they'd have very great difficulty in telling you. On the other hand, if you ask them who's the president of the NUM or who's the general secretary of the Transport and General Workers' Union, I've no doubt they'd tell you instantly.' That may be true, though it would certainly be less true now than when he said it five years ago. But as a test of political value, it shows poverty of understanding.

Perhaps more revealing is the fact that he never allowed his name to go forward to any of the constituencies where he was allegedly welcome. There are reasons other than the ones he cites. To become an MP, he would have had to go through the tiresome mill of selection conferences, approval by Walworth Road party chiefs, and an election campaign in which his candidature would have come under immense media scrutiny. He would have had to go through the ritual of promising to represent all his constituents, not just the ones who agreed with him. Given his record as compensation agent, he would probably have made a good constituency member, in terms of sorting out people's problems.

But once in Parliament, he would have had to accept the Labour Whip, the collective discipline of his party. He would have had to accept the hierarchy of the PLP and the responsibility of serving on obscure parliamentary committees. To speak inside the House, where he would simply have been one of hundreds of back-benchers, he would have to attract the Speaker's eye. Outside Parliament, he would have had to pay at least lip service to party policy. Worst of all, he would have had to live in London much of the week, and spend most of his waking hours in the Palace of Westminster, rubbing shoulders with 'the class enemy' in the corridors of power, eating and drinking in the tea rooms with men and women for whom he nursed a not very secret contempt.

All that would have been anathema. The indignity of having to go through the democratic process to get elected would have been tedious, not to mention the frightening risk that he might actually lose. The goad of having to accept party discipline would have been unendurable. The enforced resumption of relations with the great whore, London, would have been unthinkable. When he left the capital in April 1983, Scargill breathed a huge sigh of relief. 'London is a place where you can be very easily sucked into the system, and I have no intention of allowing that to happen,' he said. Westminster is the very heart of that 'system', and he couldn't cope with the idea of being part of it. He offers political mistrust of the Establishment as his explanation. That was surely present, as was the provincial insecurity and lack of self-confidence that compelled him to go back to the small pond where he knew he could be a big fish. When he moved the NUM to Sheffield, it gave him an enormous psychological advantage. Instead of all coming together in the capital as more or less equals, the other members of the executive came to the court of King Arthur if not as subjects, then as courtiers.

Scargill also had, or affected to have, the genuine revolutionary's mistrust of parliamentary democracy. In 1981, he told Dave Priscott, Leeds district secretary of the Communist Party, that anyone who believed that socialism could be achieved simply by electing a number of MPs was deluding himself. 'We will win parliamentary power, we will win real political power, we will win working-class power to the extent that we organize people in this country to fight for, and sustain, the alternative socialist system that we want to see. Parliaments do not necessarily reflect the views of ordinary people, and if you have a Parliament that is not being pushed by a working-class movement demanding change, expecting and requiring change, then you will not get that change.'

A decade later, a disillusioned Priscott observed to the author: 'A little Marxism is a dangerous thing. He acquired crude Marxism rather than creative Marxism, and he has tried to live his life on a very small stock of intellectual capital.'

This analysis gets to the heart of the matter. Ian MacGregor, the political rhinoceros who loathed him, talked often of 'Scargillism' and 'Scargillites', as though he led a party or a tendency that had beliefs and adherents. But is there such a thing as Scargillism: a connected body of social and political thought which, if translated into reality, would bring about a different society? Has he given birth to a philosophy, a political creed, that will outlive him, and fire future generations with the zeal that has marked every stage of his own stormy career?

In one sense, the jury is still out because Scargill has been clever – or naive – enough to express his views about the future with such romantic imprecision that he cannot easily be called to account. On 'Desert Island Discs', he insisted he was 'not a dreamer, but a realist' and then went on to talk in the most starry-eyed manner about the inevitability of socialism. 'The one thing I would never do is to be daft enough to commit myself to say it will occur on such and such a day or at such and such a time. I know from experience, not only here but in many parts of the world, that circumstances can alter quite dramatically and change things literally overnight. So all I would say is that the inevitability of socialism is there for all to see, because we can't carry on with a system where we do produce too much food and we put it into great big warehouses to rot at the same time as we see people die of starvation in the Third World. And if for no other reason than that and for wanting to bring about a world without nuclear weapons, a world of peace, I think that Britain and its people will eventually turn towards a socialist alternative.'

Such sentiments would not be out of place on the letters page of a children's newspaper, and could not seriously be described as a political philosophy. In his one extended discussion, in *New Left Review* in 1975, of how a socialist society would come about, and what it would look like, he was equally simplistic. The British ruling class had created the crisis of capital, he argued, and they must pay to solve it. 'And if they're not prepared to pay, *then we take over*, as we should do anyway, all the means of production, distribution and exchange. Then we'll have a look to see what we can do to resolve all the problems in Britain. That's how I look at it – very simple.'³

He thought the revolution could come about in one of two ways. Either the Left would win the leadership of the unions, and then win the Labour Party through commitment to conference policies to 'the positions which are necessary to change society'. Or a strike situation similar to 1972 or 1974 could come about where 'another Saltley' could occur. 'If we get another Saltley then the whole picture changes from one where you can have a peaceful road to one where you do not have such a peaceful road.'

Whichever route was taken, the outcome must be the same: the immediate implementation of Clause Four. 'It's no good compromising. History is littered with abortive attempts to reform capitalism. You cannot reform this system out of existence. What we need is a complete and utter change of society. What we must create is a new socialist society.' He believed that such change could happen 'very swiftly'. Vague 'developments' taking place then – in 1975 – 'could make the day when we have a socialist state in Western Europe much nearer than people think'.⁴

Later, in August 1979, Scargill tailored his exposition to a different audience, but some of the earlier elements reappeared. He told BBC TV's 'Person to Person' programme that 'a lot of things that none of us can envisage at the moment are likely to come suddenly to the fore'. With the constant star of Saltley before him, he said: 'It may be that there will be an industrial confrontation that turns into a political confrontation. It may be that the world of European events, such as the election of a socialist government somewhere in Europe with a real socialist policy, will have a decisive influence upon the British electorate. It may be a combination of all these things, but, whatever it is, I'm convinced that in the not too distant future – and by that I mean ten, twenty years – Britain will start to move towards a new type of society.'5 His ten years are long gone, and his twenty have not long to go, but neither the confrontation at home nor the socialist advances abroad have materialized. Indeed, both Britain and Europe have travelled a long way in the opposite direction.

In 1981, he was still looking for a Left takeover of the trade union and labour movement which would 'inevitably' commit the Parliamentary Labour Party to bringing about political change – 'but only if it's backed by mass mobilization of ordinary working people desirous of change. If we do that then we've got the basis for a real revolutionary change in British politics that I want to see: the basis for the kind of system of society that the socialist pioneers in our movement dreamed about and fought for all their lives.'6 Scargill made these remarks in an interview for *Marxism Today*, then the theoretical organ of the Communist Party. His words were taped, but he asked for a text of the interview and liberally rewrote what he had said before allowing it to be published – another sign of the intense desire to have the last say, and to control.

If there is a common strand in his political discourse, it is the notion that the masses have to be mobilized, preferably on the streets as at Saltley or in industrial action, as a necessary preliminary to radical change in society. This view places him squarely in the tradition of syndicalism, the achievement of social and political change through mass action, chiefly strikes. Syndicalism had a brief flowering at the turn of the century in the USA and some continental countries. But it never took root in Britain, not least because the trade unions here formed the Labour Party as the voice of the masses in the political process.

In so far as Scargill can be pinned down philosophically, argues Jimmy Reid, he is a syndicalist, though 'there isn't a great deal of evidence of a thought-out position. He said he could have been a Labour MP, but who wanted to be an MP? He had more authority as Yorkshire leader of the NUM. There was always this implication that militant trade unionism on its own almost could become the dynamo of changing society. Syndicalism has been tried in other countries and abandoned because it doesn't work. That is not to say that trade unions don't have a political role. But Arthur was saying more than that.' He also conceived of a bigger role for himself in this process. On the YCL National Committee, he 'seemed to imply that he was pivotal to some big, latent development among the Left and the miners. He had a rather exaggerated perception of what was likely to be the political development in his area.'

Exaggerated or not, he did try to put his theory into practice. His great strike of 1984-5 was the industrial confrontation designed to turn into a political confrontation. By his own lights, it has been Scargill's greatest achievement. In his presidential address to the NUM's annual conference on 1 July 1985, he said the strike had changed the course of British history. The miners had challenged the very heart of the capitalist system, and had delivered the worst blow ever to the Thatcher government. Miners should stand proud of what they had achieved: 'the most important victory of all – the struggle itself'. The NUM's contribution to history and humanity was a triumph: 'Let our great strike be the beginning of the fight not only to save jobs and pits, but to strengthen our union, and help create the conditions for electing a Labour government pledged to fulfil the aims and principles upon which the NUM was founded.'

His rousing peroration, with its incantation of the classic Marxist phrases about 'creating the conditions' for socialism, brought him a standing ovation from the delegates. But there were fewer of them than the year before, and their numbers went into steep decline thereafter. For all his rhetoric, the strike was a failure. If anything, it accelerated pit closures because the NUM, weakened by a year-long struggle and by the breakaway of Nottinghamshire miners to form their own union, was unable to offer serious resistance to the savage run-down of the industry.

Scargill will never change his own assessment of the strike. It was worth it, because the miners showed they could do it. 'The victory is the struggle, the struggle is the victory' is his justification. There is precious little evidence to support his contention that the great strike was an inspiration for workers at home and abroad. Strike figures in the UK dived even more sharply than the NUM membership after 1985, and in 1992 were running at their lowest level since records began.

Scargill's personal vindication of the strike finds few backers. Hugh Scanlon, left-wing president of the engineering workers and the scourge of the Heath government, now a peer, argued: 'If ever defeat was snatched from the jaws of victory, it was the miners' strike. I think they could have got a settlement with honour. I think when you say either we're going to bring the government down, or you say not one man must be declared redundant, when you put those demands, then I think you are heading for defeat. Whereas there could be no doubt that there were many, many influential people within the Tory government and within the Coal Board who were perfectly willing to give a satisfactory settlement.'[7]

Bill Jordan, Scanlon's right-wing successor, is even more scathing: 'In retrospect, I think everyone regards the miners' strike as a disaster. It was a disaster for the mining union, it was a disaster for the movement. It was a fight that was led from a position of seeming impregnability. I think most people will realize that certainly there are very few things that can counter the strength of a determined and powerful union. There is probably only one strength that can equal that and that is the might of government.' Sid Weighell, former leader of the railwaymen, shares this view, and lays the blame at Scargill's door: 'A once powerful union, the most powerful in Britain, has got no teeth left at all, due entirely to the leadership of one man. Old Joe Gormley wouldn't have done that to his union in a thousand years.'

There are dissenting voices of support. Jim Mortimer, who has been a trade union official, head of the conciliation service ACAS and general secretary of the Labour Party, believes: 'if I had been a miner, I would have done as they did'. He points to the tremendous upsurge in enthusiasm among rank-and-file members of the Labour Party prompted by the strike, and laments that this enthusiasm was not reflected in Labour's parliamentary leadership. The parameters of the strike were set for the NUM, as they most often are in disputes. 'In the circumstances, they were right to stand and fight. The result could have been different, but that was not the fault of the miners.'

Mortimer discerns among the Yorkshire miners a determination to defend their interests 'really second to none'. Their political traditions may have been different to those of Scotland and South Wales, but their industrial militancy was unquestionable. 'Arthur Scargill embodies all the fighting spirit and militancy and solidarity of the mining tradition. His contribution has been a positive one. He expressed and personified the readiness of the miners to fight for their jobs and their communities.' He also sees parallels with 1926, when despite the great defeat of the general strike, the heroic struggle of the miners influenced a generation of young, active trade unionists.

There is something of value here, if not on the scale that Scargill would wish it to be. He does embody the fighting spirit of the miners and other sections of the working class. In the words of Ken Gill, former leader of the white-collar union MSF and probably the most successful Communist trade union leader of his generation, Scargill 'is a rebel, really'. He personifies the spirit of 'agin': rebellion against the company bosses, against the union bureaucrats, against the carefully crafted labour legislation passed since 1979 to crush the combative spirit of working people. This is a very healthy, very British – indeed, very Yorkshire – quality that can make the difference between life being bearable and unbearable. In Scargill, being 'agin' comes naturally. He is aware of the fact, and consciously models himself on other great rebels of history. His idols are A. J. Cook, Fidel Castro, Nelson Mandela and Tony Benn, and he sees himself as part of a historical continuum stretching back through the labour movement pioneers to the early radicals and socialists, even to medieval figures like Wat Tyler.

In his second presidential address in July 1983, he argued that 'faced with possible parliamentary destruction of all that is good and compassionate in our society', the only course open to the working class would be extra-parliamentary action. 'As for us, miners will have to take direct action if we are to save our industry, our self-respect and dignity. That action will, however, only be effective if it is infused with the ideals, the hopes and aspirations upon which our movement was founded. We have inherited the dreams of Wat Tyler, the Chartists, of Keir Hardie and the suffragettes, of our own early leaders such as A. J. Cook.'

Scargill married this quality of rebelliousness to his own sense of destiny, to produce a personal, almost religious crusade. It was a seductive, evangelical gospel delivered as if he were a revivalist preacher, and it attracted worshippers rather than just supporters. 'To carry out those dreams we must fight for a social framework in which all people can live and grow, work, learn and create. I ask this conference to raise its eyes and look to a new horizon,' he cried. 'Be prepared to stand and fight for our industry, and alongside our fellow workers in other industries. Let us begin to practise those passionate beliefs our movement preaches. If we dedicate ourselves to this end, we shall not only save our industry – we will pave the way towards a caring and truly democratic socialist system of society.'

His style here owes more to Wesley than to Marx, and more to his deeply religious mother than to his Communist father. Scargill has equivocated about his religious background. In 1979, he said: 'I'm a Christian, and I've also got faith not only in my belief as a socialist but a tremendous belief in human beings, and I know we can produce a society where man will cease simply to go to work and have a little leisure, but will release his latent talent and ability and begin to produce in the cultural sense all the things that he is capable of – music, poetry, writing, sculpture, whole works of art that, at the moment, are literally lying dormant simply because we as a society are not able to tap it.'

Three years after this glimpse of mystical Utopianism, he was in rather more irreverent mood when John Mortimer asked him if he was religious. 'I certainly think Jesus Christ existed. And I remember this when they say I have unpopular views. When Christ was about to be crucified, he couldn't even find a seconder, let alone anyone to vote for him.' An anonymous writer of 1988 pointed out that many of the miners' leaders were products of the Sunday schools. John Normansall, the giant of the nineteenth century, A. J. Cook, and Joe Hall, the great Yorkshire leader, were all educated at Sunday school when they were children. 'In later life, at public meetings, they sounded like evangelists. I know Arthur Scargill is not a religious man, but he adopted the oratory style and delivery of the old-fashioned firebrand preacher, if not the philosophy.' Quite so, though, as so often with Scargill, it is difficult to prise the man out of the myth.

Critics and friends alike find the frenetic pace of his activity bewildering at times. He is a natural fidget. Nothing he comes into contact with is ever quite right. Everything has to be reshaped to his satisfaction, by him. This is as true of big institutions as of small matters, such as who opens the post. So he naturally latched on to the hard-Left reformers of the Labour Party in the seventies, with the result that the NUM is now virtually without influence in the party. He opposed the outlawing of the Militant Tendency and the expulsions that followed. He persisted with unilateral nuclear disarmament long after it had gone out of fashion. He was fire and brimstone against the European Community, 'an unmitigated disaster for Britain'. He saw the pressure group Trade Unions for Labour Victory, set up in the summer of 1978 (and now retitled Trade Unions for Labour), as a sinister right-wing Trojan horse, and sought to undermine it. He fought the conference platform tirelessly, helping in numerous well-publicized defeats including the 1985 demand for a total amnesty for miners sacked during the great strike. He consistently criticized Neil Kinnock – who happily traded insults with him.

For the NUM, his behaviour was a total somersault from the post-war years, right up to the mid-seventies, when the miners could be relied upon to marshal the block vote in favour of the Labour leadership. Yet Scargill knew that, traditionally, the miners were solidly in the centre of the party. He even claimed, quite wrongly, that 'the miners' union were responsible for the creation of the Labour Party and have been in the vanguard in sustaining it throughout its life'.[8] In fact, the miners flirted for decades with the Liberal Party, because they came to politics early – long before Labour was formed – and only the Liberals could offer the parliamentary support they needed for legislative reforms. The miners were among the last big unions to affiliate to the Labour Party, and did not do so until 1909.

Scargill inherited the policy of 'no truck with TULV' from Gormley, who had quit the body (which had thirty-seven members representing ninety per cent of affiliated trade unionists) in 1980. The generally accepted view was that Gormley was 'too busy watching Scargill and the NUM Left over his shoulder'[9] to take part in TULV work. The miners first blocked, and then boycotted, the setting up of a Yorkshire TULV. These were extraordinary actions, when set against the historic support of the NUM for mainstream Labour politics, and Scargill's own high political profile. He allied himself with the Left on the party executive against the Callaghan government. When that fell after the so-called Winter of Discontent, he first supported Michael Foot and then urged Tony Benn to supplant him. His hard-Left instincts led the NUM up a political cul-de-sac, and it has stuck there.

Scargill's work on the international front has been obscured by excessive secrecy. Shortly after becoming president, he argued for an end to the Cold War divisions within the trade union movement. Miners in the West and some Third World countries belonged to the Miners' International Federation, based in London and with Peter Tait, the quondam Yorkshire Communist, as its secretary-general. Miners in the Eastern Bloc belonged to the Prague-based, Communist-dominated World Federation of Trade Unions. Scargill wanted to bring the two warring organizations together into a single international body, 'thus enabling us to provide the basis for government throughout the world to produce policies that will lead to nuclear disarmament and a lasting world peace'.

His characteristically modest proposal produced a meeting in Paris in April 1983, sponsored by Scargill and the Communist French trade union centre, CGT. This was the embryo of the International Miners' Organization, of which Scargill immediately became president. The initiative provoked uproar in the MIF, prompting Britain's expulsion from the organization, which would brook no fraternizing with the Communists. Apart from playing a deeply controversial role in the Lightman affair, the IMO has done very little to achieve the exotic objectives set for it by Scargill a decade ago. It holds periodic conferences, the most recent in Algeria in May 1993, but reports of its activities are very scanty. Most British miners have probably never heard of it, yet it costs the NUM many thousands of pounds a year in affiliation fees.

Scargill has a greater impact in South Africa, where he is accorded more of a hero's welcome than in his own country. He has been a genuine and committed opponent of apartheid since his teenage days in the YCL, and played a key, unselfconscious role in helping black South Africans to form their own union, also named the National Union of Mineworkers. He encouraged its charismatic young leader Cyril Ramaphosa – now secretary-general of the African National Congress and heir-apparent of Nelson Mandela – bringing him to Britain for NUM conferences and introducing him to British supporters. Mandela has paid public tribute to Scargill, saying he was 'my working-class hero all those years in jail'. In turn, Scargill feels more able to relax in South Africa. Some of the grim public stance he so often adopts at home fades, says Ken Gill, to be replaced by 'a very warm, open approach'. 'They absolutely love him there. I was at mass meetings in Cape Town in 1992 when he spoke, and they cheered him to the echo. He more than anyone helped organize the South African NUM.'

In the end, any *tour d'horizon* of Scargill's life and achievements ends up returning to the great strike. That year was his philosophy put into practice. Faced with hard questions about his tactics, he ducks and weaves. Harried by the relentless questions of Darcus

Howe on Channel 4's 'The Devil's Advocate' in March 1993, he first took refuge in the argument that other unions such as the steelworkers and engineering workers had also been decimated. But none have lost the same proportion – nearly ninety per cent – as the NUM. Challenged about taking on the government when the power stations had a year's supply of coal in stock, he insisted he did not choose when to fight, only whether to fight. Miners could either lie down and see pits closed and their union destroyed. Or they could fight back, 'and I believe that history will judge that they were right to fight back'.

It is true that he did not begin the strike, though he had amply prepared for it and had exhibited an almost obsessive desire for such a conflict for many years. But he does carry the largest personal responsibility for prolonging the strike. His was the most powerful voice on the executive for keeping it going. He could have signalled a shift in policy that would have enabled the NUM leadership to accept a historic compromise. He would have allowed the union to walk away from the battlefield with a vestigial unity, and live to fight another day. Most, if not all, other union leaders would have seized on the draft settlement available in July, or the NACODS formula on the table in late October, and presented it to the members as a famous victory – even if it was not, and could not have been.

The July formula envisaged that only pits that were capable of being 'beneficially' worked could be kept open. MacGregor argued that this meant 'beneficial to the community. Beneficial to the community of those who work in the industry. Beneficial to the mining communities, beneficial to the community of people who live in Britain.' These are ambiguous words, which MacGregor would have used to close pits. But long before he arrived on the scene, miners' leaders had already sold the pass on economic closures. The surrender was spelled out ten years before, in Labour's Plan for Coal, drawn up in the shadow of the 1974 strike victory, which laid down that uneconomic pits would go to the wall. All the parties agreed that the industry would keep down production costs so as to preserve coal's competitive margin. And 'with the transformed outlook for coal, providing that costs remain competitive overall ... the need to close pits on economic grounds should be much reduced. But inevitably some pits will have to close as their useful economic reserves of coal are depleted.' Thus did paragraph 29 of the Tripartite Plan for Coal, signed by government, NCB and NUM, make a nonsense of the impossible demands of Scargill. His hero Tony Benn, while Energy Secretary, had confirmed the situation as late as 4 December 1978 when he told the Commons: 'I have never found the NUM in any way unreasonable where closures are necessary because of exhaustion or because pits are out of line in economic terms.'

A settlement in July or October 1984 would have minimized the great hardship among the miners and their families. Scargill should have settled. By prolonging the strike he prolonged their agony. It is no use saying that he was simply carrying out their wishes. Even if that were true, and it was only true for a dwindling number, it is a cop-out. Understandably, workers in such depths of struggle have the greatest difficulty in accepting defeat, and acknowledging that their sacrifices have been to no avail. It is the duty and responsibility of their leaders to take on themselves the obloquy of failure. By so doing, they ameliorate the crushing sense of loss.

Scargill could have done that, but he chose not to. He chose to live in an increasingly unreal world of victory just around the corner. Given his inability to use his casting vote, either for continuing the strike or calling it off on that fateful Sunday in March 1985, the question has to be asked: is he a genuine leader at all? Or is the whole thing a myth sustained by blustering hype and slogans of 'no surrender'? Only in the context of the ultra-loyal mining communities could such a figure survive, because only there are the normal objective criteria of leadership set aside for 'one of us'.

Of course, a deal of the kind on offer would have allowed the NCB to close pits, but that had already been conceded in the Plan for Coal. At least the National Union of Mineworkers would have been national in fact as well as in name. An agreement in 1984 would almost certainly have halted the formation of the breakaway Union of Democratic Mineworkers in Nottinghamshire. In turn, this would have kept in place the bargaining procedures that have operated in the industry since nationalization. Instead, on Scargill's insistence, the NUM has refused to negotiate at the same table as the UDM and he has not negotiated a pay rise for his members since the strike ended. NUM members annually endure the humiliation of having the 'scab union' pay rise imposed on them.

Scargill blames everybody but himself – and the miners – for the outcome of the strike. He told his Channel 4 interrogator: 'The only problem was that the British labour and trade union movement, to its cost, didn't give us the support that we deserved and to which we were entitled.' Yet for months he refused to allow the TUC to get near 'his' strike, for fear that its direction would be wrested from his control. They would probably get it wrong, as they had in 1926. He knew that he could never persuade other trade union leaders to get on his political roller coaster. Their dilemma was often expressed in private as 'How do we prevent the miners from going down to defeat, while at the same time denying Arthur a victory?' Not being paid-up class warriors, they did not have the luxury of saying: 'I am not in the business of compromise.' That was very much the business they were in. It kept them in business, and Scargill knew it before he finally submitted to asking the TUC for support. They were, nonetheless, a useful scapegoat for the failure of his own strategy.

Finally, it came down to this personal thing: he could not give way, on anything, to anybody. Not even to his closest party comrades. He threw on the floor of his office a peace formula proposed by Bert Ramelson, his Communist mentor, because it smacked of accommodation with the enemy. He was right, and everybody else was wrong. He still insists he was right. Asking for Edith Piaf's 'Je ne regrette rien' in 1988, he told Sue Lawley that he would not have done anything differently. 'I don't accept that in the end we lost. I think if you look at the strike itself and take it into context, I think you'll see that it led to an inspiration as far as the labour and trade union movement was concerned. And it's often been said in history that people have lost things. It was said that the suffragettes lost, but you know that the suffragettes didn't lose. It was said that the Tolpuddle Martyrs lost, but when we look back we know that the trade union movement in this country and in other parts of the world flourished because of their sacrifice. And I think we shall see not only the triumph of working people in establishing the right to work but we shall see the establishment of socialism – because of, not in spite of, the miners' strike.'

He insisted he had never quietly, privately, briefly cracked during the dispute 'and the reason's a simple one. I believed passionately in what I was doing and I knew that the cause was absolutely right. And when I'm sitting on that desert island I'll be able to sit back under that palm tree looking over that beautiful stretch of sand and say to myself that what I did was right and above all I never sold out the men.' Scargill can enjoy this stupendous moral self-indulgence because he determines what is a sell-out and what is not. The industry has crashed around his ears, but it is not his fault because he predicted it, and if only others had done as he proposed, it would not have happened. His union is practically in ruins, but he cannot be blamed because he never compromised on the absolutist platform on which he ran for office. Socialism has not arrived on time, but it would have if the mass picketing of Orgreave had gone on for long enough. By such effortless, brilliant chop-logic he maintains his chirpy superiority. Delivered from a platform, it gets audiences to their feet. In cold print, it is possible to see it for what it is: an intellectual sham.

Scargill's career is not yet over. But his great years are unquestionably behind him, and some kind of balance sheet can be drawn up. The figures are not very flattering. Scargill inherited a union of 220,000 members working in almost two hundred collieries. Today, the once mighty NUM is not very much more than a tenth of that size, and there are only twenty collieries with an assured future. Like the Irish political parties still divided between the different sides of Eire's Civil War seventy years ago, the miners are split into two unions divided by loyalties forged during the great strike. Because Scargill cannot accept a reunification of the two warring factions, except on his own impossible terms, the colliers are sundered and the break plays into the hands of the management and Conservative ministers. Because he will not sit down and negotiate with the breakaway UDM, his members have to accept whatever the smaller, non-militant union gets. Suggestions of a re-merger with the UDM, possibly in a new alignment with the much-reduced pit deputies' union NACODS, have been cold-shouldered by Scargill.

His most faithful fellow member of the troika during the strike, Mick McGahey, has only once broken his silence to give a coded judgement on Scargill. In December 1990, McGahey told the *Scottish Miner*: 'The National Union of Mineworkers has lost its credibility and has been isolated in the trade union and labour movement.' He made an impassioned plea for reunification with the miners of Nottinghamshire, and argued that the NUM should sit down with the UDM to negotiate on pay.

Without naming Scargill, but plainly referring to him, McGahey added: 'No one should stand loftily on their own particular principle. The interest of the miner, his wife and family is what matters. I find it difficult to comprehend why my union is not negotiating when overtime is rising, when bonus payments have become a major part of wages and when questions of safety are involved. We cannot stand outside the negotiating chamber. We must be in there arguing our case.' McGahey had retired from the NUM vice-presidency in 1988. He found the continuing rift with Nottinghamshire particularly distressing. 'The miners must be reunited. Nottinghamshire miners are solid miners and they are miners above everything else. It is not good enough to say that there will always be room for the Notts miners but not for the UDM leaders, when the Notts miners have democratically elected their leaders.' Of course if the Nottinghamshire miners had been reunited with the NUM after the strike, but before January 1988, Scargill would almost certainly not have been re-elected in the presidential ballot of that year.

As McGahey also observed, the outlook on the broader political front was deeply depressing, and it remains so. The NUM is no longer represented on the TUC General Council. Dismissive of the labour movement's ruling body when he had an automatic right to a seat, Scargill now finds it impossible to secure election to it, and no other nominee is put forward to win back the miners' lost authority. Likewise the Labour Party. Ignominiously pushed off the party's national executive, the mineworkers are relegated to the sidelines. The power of the trade union block vote, on which Scargill pinned so many revolutionary hopes, is dramatically on the wane and appears certain to disappear altogether in a year or two. Even if it remains in truncated form, at the party conference and in the constituency parties, the NUM has lost power and influence through falling numbers and through being on the wrong side in the battle over ideological and organizational reform.

The NUM could not even hold on to its sponsorship of Hemsworth, a Yorkshire mining constituency where it was said they weighed Labour votes rather than counted them. In the 1991 by-election, Yorkshire area vice-president Ken Capstick was vetoed as Labour's choice by the party hierarchy largely because he was seen as too close to Scargill, and therefore 'the wrong type of candidate' – even for a safe seat that retains strong mining links. Despite official denials, the retributive hand of Kinnock was seen behind Walworth Road's determination not to let 'Scargill's man' into the Commons. The group of NUM-sponsored MPs, bolstered somewhat at the last election, is also divided between ultra-loyalists like Denis Skinner, the 'beast of Bolsover', and Jimmy Hood, one-time branch secretary at Ollerton and now member for Clydesdale, and those who believe the Commons Select Committee on Trade and Industry did a good job last winter in its ground-breaking report on pit closures.

Of course, not all the decline in the NUM's fortunes can be laid at the door of one man. Not even Arthur Scargill. The anti-myth that has grown up around him, in neat counterpoint to the myth he has spun around himself, makes him the culprit for every defeat, every reverse. But it is not quite so. By their actions and inaction, the miners have shown their willingness to tolerate his leadership, even if they do not always wish to follow it. By their all but supine acquiescence, his critics on the NUM national executive have given him a virtual free run. Even the older hands shake their heads and confess to having been 'mesmerized' by his overpowering personality. His reign may be wayward and adventurist, but it is undisputed.

Short of being unhorsed by a legal challenge, he will stay in the job until he is sixty-five in January 2003. He is proud of his ox-like constitution, and even in this aspect feels compelled to compare his lot with that of his great hero. Naturally, he comes off better. At the height of the Lightman affair, he told Seamus Milne of *The Guardian*: 'There are parallels with A. J. Cook, but there are also differences. In his day, it was very amateurish. Cook was battered, not only psychologically from the desertion of colleagues and friends, but also physically. Apart from one or two hiccups, I have a very strong constitution and an amazing power of recuperation.'

His reputation certainly made a comeback in the aftermath of Heseltine's bungled pit closure announcements. How history will judge him, it is too early to tell. Certainly, he invites judgement. He sees himself as the Margaret Thatcher of his class, quipping 'like me' when a television interviewer described her as 'not a halfway person'. When challenged that he lost the battle with the Iron Lady, he retorts: 'She's gone. I'm here.' He sees himself as a symbol of the struggle against 'the Tory juggernaut' whose name and example will endure.

Jimmy Reid finds closer parallels with Mrs Thatcher than with A. J. Cook. 'She has closed her mind to the possibility of being wrong. He never admitted to having any doubts at all. He has that frightening certitude, so has she. Although they were both apparently poles apart, politically, philosophically and ideologically, they are both dogmatists. The difference is that she had the whole state machine at her disposal.' In a devastating critique that confirmed the total political break with his former YCL comrade, published shortly before the end of the great strike, Reid argued: 'I reject the notion that Scargill is leading some crusade against Thatcherite Toryism. Beneath the rhetoric, Scargillism and Thatcherism are political allies. I would put it this way: the political spectrum is not linear but circular. In my experience the extreme Left always ends up rubbing shoulders with the extreme Right. They are philosophically blood brothers.'[10]

Thatcher and Scargill are both conviction politicians (though he has more convictions than her, usually for obstructing the police). He sees himself as the obverse of the same coin. She became queen of the Establishment. He wants to be thought of as the guerrilla leader, bringing his men out of the hills like Fidel Castro to change society at a stroke. 'I would rather be a member of a resistance movement than collaborate,' he told an interviewer in late 1992. 'The trouble with collaborating is that fifty years on, when the archives are discovered, people get found out.'

It is a mistake to seek to understand Scargill solely in political terms, even if that is the way he would wish to be assessed. His comrades on the Left of the mineworkers' union listened when he insisted that collective policy and decision-making was more important than personalities. For the most part, they believed him. That is how Scargill sees himself, in public at least. But there are other, just as powerful, forces at work: his clamoring for attention, his relentless drive, his hypnotic self-belief, his total conviction that he is right. In the words of one Welsh NUM leader who attended the Left caucus meetings during the Yorkshireman's rise to power: 'We didn't realize that Arthur's ego was even bigger than the office he was taking on.' By the time they did realize, it was too late. Scargill's law insisted that once he had been elected on his revolutionary platform, there was no going back. The miners must be 'politicized'. They had to follow their ayatollah. The boy from Worsbrough was convinced he was leading his people to a better world. And his exaggerated belief in his destiny made him believe his own rhetoric. That is his tragedy, and the tragedy of the National Union of Mineworkers.

By all the formal criteria of success, he has failed. But something of Scargill will live on. Just as A. J. Cook is remembered as the sea-green incorruptible leader of men – even if this image does not strictly accord with the facts – Scargill will be remembered as the man who said 'no' to the entrenched forces of capitalism and state authority. His refusal to tack, to make himself and the NUM acceptable to the political middle ground, helped substantially to keep alive a vital spirit of defiance in the British people. Workers in struggle, anywhere, over whatever issue, knew where to look for a beacon of support. Long after his manifest failure as a syndicalist revolutionary is forgotten, he will be honoured for that. He may be fatally flawed, but he has assured himself of a niche in history.

Notes and References

CHAPTER II
1. Joan Bakewell, *Illustrated London News*, July 1978, p. 36.
2. Anthony Bailey, *Observer Magazine*, 17 June 1979.
3. Bakewell, op. cit.
4. Ibid.
5. Ibid.
6. Interview with the author, 29 December 1992.
7. Michael Crick, *Scargill and the Miners*, Penguin, 1984, p. 26.
8. Quoted in *The Observer*, 3 February 1974.
9. Interview with the author, 29 December 1992.
10. Bailey, op. cit.
11. Crick, op. cit., p. 27.
12. Bakewell, op. cit.
13. Interview with the author, 29 December 1992.
14. Bakewell, op. cit.
15. Len Doherty, *Sheffield Star*, 28 February 1972.
16. John Mortimer, *The Sunday Times*, 10 January 1982.
17. Doherty, op. cit.
18. Mortimer, op. cit.
19. Roger Cross, *Yorkshire Post*, 29 January 1974.
20. *Daily Mail*, 10 December 1974, quoted in Crick, op. cit.
21. *New Left Review*, July/August 1975.
22. David Dimbleby, 'Person to Person', *The Listener*, 9 August 1979.
23. Telephone interview with the author, 18 December 1992.
24. Ibid.
25. Interview with the author, 4 January 1993.
26. *Daily Mail*, 9 December 1977.
27. Crick, op. cit., p. 30.
28. Interview with Jimmy Reid, Glasgow, 7 February 1993.
29. Interview with Bert Ramelson, London, 2 December 1992.
30. Frank Watters, *Being Frank*, Monkspring Publications, p. 14.
31. Ibid., p. 14.
32. Crick, op. cit., p. 18.
33. Watters, op. cit., p. 15.
34. Bakewell, op. cit.
35. Dimbleby, op. cit.
36. Ibid.

37. *New Left Review*, 92, July/August 1975.
38. Ibid.
39. Ibid.
40. Watters, p. 35.
41. *Newsday*, quoted by Crick, op. cit., p. 33.
42. *New Left Review*, op. cit.
43. Bakewell, op. cit.
44. Mortimer, op. cit.

CHAPTER III
1. Mortimer, op. cit.
2. Will Paynter, *My Generation*, Allen and Unwin, 1972, pp. 33–34.
3. Ibid., p. 155.
4. Bakewell, op. cit.
5. Ibid.
6. *Yorkshire Evening Post*, 7 June 1973.
7. *Daily Mail*, 9 December 1977, quoted Crick, op. cit., p. 32.
8. *Scargill the Stalinist*, Nicholas Hagger, Oaktree Books, 1984, p. 81.
9. *Daily Mirror*, 25 November 1980, quoted Crick.
10. Watters, op. cit., p. 31.
11. Dimbleby, op. cit., p. 166.
12. *Sheffield Independent*, 30 March 1861.
13. Andrew Taylor, *The Politics of the Yorkshire Miners*, Croom Helm, 1984, p. 25.
14. Interview with the author, 30 December 1992.
15. Ibid.
16. Taylor, op. cit., p. 30.

17. 'Desert Island Discs'.
18. *Daily Mirror*, November 1980, quoted Crick, op. cit.
19. Bakewell, op. cit.
20. Interview with the author, Castleford, 20 January 1993.
21. 'Desert Island Discs'.
22. Interview with the author, 20 January 1993.
23. *The Times*, 28 November 1977, quoted by Crick, op. cit.
24. Interview with the author, Wakefield, 4 January 1993.
25. Crick, op. cit., p. 33.
26. Bailey, op. cit.
27. Dimbleby, op. cit.
28. Mortimer, op. cit.
29. Interview with the author, 3 December 1992.
30. Watters, quoted Crick, p. 35.
31. *New Left Review*, July/August 1975, p. 6.
32. *The Sunday Times*, 17 November 1974.
33. Interview with the author, Grimethorpe, 1 March 1993.
34. Interview with the author, 3 March 1993.
35. Ibid.
36. *New Left Review*, op. cit., p. 6.
37. Ibid., p. 8.

CHAPTER IV
1. Taylor, op. cit., p. 54.
2. CMND 2798, quoted by Taylor, op. cit., p. 55.

3. TUC General Council report to Congress, quoted by Taylor, op. cit., p. 55.
4. Interview with the author, 1 March 1993.
5. Ibid.
6. V. L. Allen, *The Militancy of British Miners*, The Moor Press, 1981, p. 139.
7. Interview with the author, 30 December 1992.
8. Allen, op. cit., p. 140.
9. Ibid., p. 135.
10. Interview with the author, 3 March 1993.
11. Taylor, op. cit., p. 69.
12. Robens, *Ten Year Stint*, Cassell, 1972, p. 22.
13. *New Left Review*, 92, p. 9.
14. Robens, op. cit., p. 24.
15. Ibid., p. 24.
16. *New Left Review*, op. cit., p. 11.
17. Taylor, op. cit., p. 100.
18. Ibid., p. 205.
19. Tape of interview with Hywel Francis, 1980.
20. *The Times*, 7 January 1991.
21. Taylor, op. cit., p. 206.
22. Crick, op. cit., 51.
23. *New Left Review*, op. cit., p. 11.
24. Ibid., p. 12.
25. Interview with the author, 1 March 1993.
26. Ibid.
27. Watters, op. cit., p. 21.
28. *New Left Review*, 92, p. 13.
29. Ibid., p. 18.
30. Ibid., p. 19.
31. Watters, op. cit., p. 63.
32. Watters, op. cit., p. 224.
33. 'The Saltley Incident', A Report by F. L. Ffoulkes, British Gas Corporation, March 1985.
34. Taylor, op. cit.

CHAPTER V
1. *Sheffield Star*, 28 February 1972.
2. Ibid.
3. Interview with the author, 4 January 1993.
4. Allen, op. cit., p. 224.
5. Interview, 30 December 1992.
6. Interview, 29 December 1992.
7. Interview, ? December 1992.
8. Allen, op. cit., p. 226.
9. Ibid., p. 226.
10. Ibid., p. 229.
11. *Yorkshire Evening Post*, 7 June 1973.
12. *New Left Review*, 92, p. 21.
13. Ibid.
14. Ibid.
15. Joe Gormley, *Battered Cherub*, Hamish Hamilton, 1982, p. 139.
16. *New Left Review*, 92, p. 21.
17. *The Times*, 4 January 1974.
18. *The Times*, 30 January 1974.
19. *New Left Review*, 92, p. 22.
20. Taylor, op. cit., p. 224.
21. Tony Benn, *Against The Tide*, Hutchinson, p. 101.
22. Gormley, op. cit., p. 144.
23. Allen, op. cit., p. 258.

24. *Yorkshire Evening Post*, 7 June 1973.

25. *Observer Magazine*, 17 June 1979.

26. Interview with the author, 8 February 1993.

27. Interview with the author, 4 January 1993.

28. Interview with the author, 30 December 1992.

29. Crick, op. cit., p. 67.

30. Recollection of author, present at lunch.

31. Tony Benn, op. cit., p. 222.

32. Gormley, op. cit., p. 149.

33. *New Left Review*, 92, p. 24.

34. *The Times*, 8 November 1974.

35. Reprinted in Jonathan Winterton and Ruth Winterton, *Coal, Crisis and Conflict*, Manchester University Press, 1989, p. 11.

36. Interview with the author, 24 January 1993.

37. Allen, op. cit., p. 290.

38. Bakewell, op. cit.

39. Interview with the author, 30 December 1992.

40. Jack Dromey and Graham Taylor, *Grunwick: The Workers' Story*, Lawrence and Wishart, 1978, p. 124.

41. Arthur Scargill, *Miners in the Eighties*, pub: NUM Yorkshire Area, 1 September 1981.

42. Gormley, op. cit., p. 207.

CHAPTER VI

1. *The Observer*, 6 December 1981.

2. Interview with the author, 15 December 1992.

3. Interview with the author, 24 January 1993.

4. Gormley, op. cit., p. 208.

5. *The Times*, 10 December 1981.

6. Interview with the author, 5 January 1993.

7. *The Times*, 14 January 1982.

8. Gormley, op. cit., p. 211.

9. *The Times*, 12 March 1982.

10. Ibid.

11. Interview with the author, 19 January 1993.

12. *The Times*, 17 June 1982.

13. *Morning Telegraph*, 4 January 1983.

14. *The Times*, 9 July 1982.

15. *The Times*, 23 August 1982.

16. *The Times*, 16 April 1983.

17. Tony Benn, op. cit., p. 400.

18. Ibid., p. 523.

19. Tony Benn, *Conflict of Interest*, Hutchinson, 1990, p. 413.

20. Ibid., p. 56.

21. Tony Benn, *The End of an Era*, Hutchinson, 1992, p. 87.

22. *The Times*, 10 April 1981.

23. Benn, op. cit., p. 154.

24. Ibid., p. 158.

25. Ibid., p. 226.

26. Ibid., p. 248.

27. *The Times*, 6 May 1983.

28. Taylor, op. cit., p. 291.

29. Presidential Address,

NUM conference, Perth, 4 July 1983.

30. *The Times*, 7 July 1983.

31. Interview with the author, 21 January 1993.

32. *The Times*, 25 August 1983.

33. Nicholas Ridley, *My Style of Government*, Hutchinson, 1991, p. 67.

34. Ibid., p. 67.

35. Ibid., p. 70.

36. Peter Walker, *Staying Power: An Autobiography*, Bloomsbury, 1991, p. 166.

37. Ibid., p. 167.

38. Ibid., p. 169.

39. Nigel Lawson, *The View From No 11*, Bantam Press, 1992, p. 142.

40. Ibid., p. 143.

41. Ibid., p. 146.

42. Ibid., p. 146.

43. Ibid., p. 147.

44. Ibid., p. 148.

45. Ibid., p. 149.

46. Ibid., p. 154.

47. Ibid., p. 157.

48. Ian MacGregor, *The Enemies Within*, Collins, 1986, p. 115.

49. Ibid., p. 18.

50. Ibid., p. 34.

51. Ibid., p. 72.

52. Ibid., p. 116.

53. *The Times*, 9 September 1983.

54. Kim Howells, interview with the author, 15 December 1992.

55. Terry Thomas, interview with the author, 24 January 1993.

56. Ibid.

CHAPTER VII

1. Interview with the author, 21 December 1992.

2. Geoffrey Goodman, *The Miners' Strike*, Pluto Press, 1985, p. 67.

3. Martin Adeney and John Lloyd, *The Miners' Strike*, Routledge & Kegan Paul, 1988, p. 86.

4. Ibid., p. 69.

5. Interview with the author, 21 December 1992.

6. Goodman, op. cit., p. 71.

7. Ibid., p. 70.

8. Interview with the author, 21 December 1992.

9. Adeney and Lloyd, op. cit., p. 82.

10. *The Times*, 11 March 1983.

11. Ian MacGregor, op. cit., p. 146.

12. Ibid., p. 147.

13. Adeney and Lloyd, op. cit., p. 83.

14. Ibid., p. 84.

15. *The Lightman Report*, Penguin, 1990, p. 15.

16. Adeney and Lloyd, op. cit., p. 84.

17. CINCC minutes, pp. 3–6.

18. Roy Ottey, *The Strike*, Sidgwick and Jackson, 1985, pp. 60–1.

19. Ibid., p. 68.

20. Ibid., p. 69.

21. Ibid., p. 70.

22. Ibid., p. 72.

23. Ibid., p. 73.

24. Tony Benn, *The End of An Era*, p. 324.

25. Ibid., p. 346.

26. Interview with the author, 21 December 1992.

27. Tony Benn, op. cit., p. 349.

28. Ibid., p. 348.

29. *The Times*, 24 May 1984.

30. P. Wright, *Policing the Coal Dispute*, p. 8.

31. *The Times*, 30 May 1984.

32. Interview with the author, 5 January 1993.

33. Wright, op. cit., p. 10.

34. Ibid., p. 12.

35. Geoffrey Goodman, *The Miners' Strike*, Pluto Press, 1985, p. 107.

36. Tony Benn, op. cit., p. 345.

37. Wright, op. cit.

38. Interview with the author, 7 January 1993.

39. Ian MacGregor, op. cit., p. 205.

40. Interview with the author, 11 January 1993.

41. Interview with the author, 5 January 1993.

42. MacGregor, op. cit., p. 245.

43. *The Times*, 12 June 1984.

44. Tony Benn, op. cit., p. 365.

45. Ibid., p. 366.

46. MacGregor, op. cit., p. 252.

CHAPTER VIII

1. Tony Benn, op. cit., pp. 368–9.

2. Interview with the author, 7 January 1993.

3. MacGregor, op. cit., p. 288.

4. Ibid., p. 282.

5. Interview with the author, 8 February 1993.

6. Interview with the author, 21 December 1992.

7. Interview with the author, 24 January 1993.

8. Interview with the author, 15 December 1992.

9. Interview with the author, 25 January 1993.

10. Interview with the author, 11 January 1993.

11. *The Observer*, 13 July 1987.

12. *Lightman Inquiry Report*, Penguin, 1985, p. 91.

13. *The Observer*, 22 November 1987.

14. Tony Benn, op. cit., p. 479.

CHAPTER IX

1. *Daily Mirror*, 5 March 1990.

2. *Daily Mirror*, 7 March 1990.

3. *The Sunday Times*, 11 March 1990.

4. Tony Benn, op. cit., p. 588.

CHAPTER X

1. *Yorkshire Post*, 22 December 1992.

2. *The Independent*, 24 December 1992.

3. *Yorkshire on Sunday*, 27 December 1992.

4. *Daily Worker*, 30 January 1993.

5. *The Observer*, 7 March 1993.

6. *Daily Worker*, 30 January 1993.

CHAPTER XI
1. Cecil Parkinson, *Right at the Centre*, Weidenfeld & Nicolson, 1992, p. 281.
2. Interview with the author, 7 February 1993.
3. *New Left Review*, July 1975, p. 25.
4. Ibid., pp. 31–3.

5. *The Listener*, 9 August 1979.
6. *Marxism Today*, April 1981.
7. 'Brothers', BBC Radio 4, February 1992.
8. Presidential address, Yorkshire area, March 1981.
9. *The Contentious Alliance*, Lewis Minkin, Edinburgh University Press, 1992, p. 492.
10. *The Listener*, 17 January 1985, p. 93.

Index

Hollywood vs. America
Popular Culture and the War on Traditional Values

Michael Medved

This book has struck a raw nerve. Film stars, commentators and politicians joined the fierce debate fuelled by Michael Medved's trenchant critique of the film industry – the most provocative study of the moral implications of popular culture ever written. His condemnation of sex, violence, bad language, and the seemingly consistent attack on traditional values, has given rise to feverish discussions on both sides of the Atlantic. Jane Fonda has accused Hollywood of immortality. Sir Anthony Hopkins may not now recreate the monstrous role of Hannibal Lecter.

Why do so many films attack religion, glorify violence and undermine the family? What is the cost of big-screen brutality? Have we become impervious to the increasingly grotesque violence erupting from our cinema screens and high-street video shops?

Greeted both with cheers of support and howls of enraged dissent, *Hollywood vs. America* confronts head on one of the most significant issues of our time.

'Real dynamite . . . The author says his book will make him the most hated man in Hollywood. On the other hand, it might save an industry that seems bent on self-destruction.' *Daily Mail*

ISBN 0 00 638235 5

This is Orson Welles

Orson Welles and Peter Bogdanovich

This is the book that Welles ultimately considered his auto-biography, but it's a memoir like no other. At once accessible, entertaining and revealing, Welles and Bogdanovich's collaboration is an unforgettable collection of penetrating, fascinating and often hilarious conversations undertaken over many years, on both sides of the Atlantic. With *This is Orson Welles* the master illusionist and self-confessed 'faker', in his own words, 'puts the record straight'.

'The Art of Bogdanovich's interrogation conceals itself in the ease of good friends talking, yet it elicits from Welles answers which show us his position and his character under the arc-light thrown upon them by his brilliant tongue . . . Such humorous charm is captivating'　　　　　　　　　　Philip Glazebrook, *Spectator*

'This is a book you must beg, borrow or steal . . . Welles pulls no punches: reading it is like being a privileged guest at his table, savouring that inimitable voice, as the pearls drop in abundance'
　　　　　　　　　　Bryan Forbes, *Mail on Sunday*

'Fascinating. A treasure-trove of insights'　　　　　　　John Lahr

'Welles at his roaring best'　　　　*New York Times Book Review*

ISBN 0 00 638232 0

The New Emperors

Mao and Deng: A Dual Biography

Harrison E. Salisbury

'A fascinating story . . . enlivened by personal anecdotes and packed with splendid reports of the two "New Emperors" that will make addictive reading not only for diplomats, scholars and their colleagues, but also for businessmen and tourists.'

Clare Hollingworth, *Daily Telegraph*

Harrison Salisbury's knowledge of China and its leaders – based on twenty years of study and first-hand research – has produced an epic narrative history of the new Communist dynasty. As he surveys the convulsive events that shaped modern China – the Nationalist–Communist civil war, the Communist takeover, the mass famine following the Great Leap Forward, the Cultural Revolution – Salisbury focuses on Mao and Deng and their complex relationship.

How Deng won Mao's favour by building Mao's secret Third Line, a gigantic industrial redoubt whose crippling cost was in inverse proportion to its ultimate strategic value, and rose to power; how he was ousted and persecuted by Mao during the Cultural Revolution; how he was recalled by Mao and then toppled by Mao's wife; and how General Ye Jianying plotted to overthrow the Gang of Four and install Deng as the 'new emperor' – all are sketched in dramatic detail.

'A stunningly detailed account of two enigmatic figures'

Financial Times

ISBN 0 586 21864 5

The Honourable Company

A History of the English East India Company

John Keay

'The first accessible narrative history of the English East India Company which has appeared for some time . . . Keay recounts his story with the sweep of a James Michener, but one anchored in the meticulous scholarship of historians . . . Commercial successes and failures, battles and politics from Table Bay to Tokyo Bay are treated with verve and clarity.'

Christopher Bayly, *The Observer*

Over two centuries, the East India Company grew from a loose association of Elizabethan tradesmen into 'the Grandest Society of Merchants in the Universe' – a huge commercial enterprise which controlled half the world's trade and also administered an embryonic empire. A tenth of the British exchequer's total revenue derived from customs receipts on the Company's UK imports; its armed forces exceeded those of most sovereign states. Without it there would have been no British India and no British Empire.

ISBN 0 00 638072 7

☐	A LOOK AROUND THE CORNER Margery Jolley	0-00-638333-5	£4.99
☐	IDOL WORSHIP Ed. Chris Robets	0-00-638266-5	£5.99
☐	LOVE LIES Deborah McKinlay	0-00-255529-8	£7.99
☐	HOW NOT TO RAISE A PERFECT CHILD Libby Purves	0-00-637598-7	£6.99

All these books are available from your local bookseller or can be ordered direct from the publishers.

To order direct just tick the titles you want and fill in the form below:

Name: _____

Address: _____

_____

Postcode: _____

Send to: HarperCollins Mail Order, Dept 8, HarperCollins*Publishers*, Westerhill Road, Bishopbriggs, Glasgow G64 2QT.

Please enclose a cheque or postal order or your authority to debit your Visa/Access account –

Credit card no: _____

Expiry date: _____

Signature: _____

– to the value of the cover price plus:

UK & BFPO: Add £1.00 for the first and 25p for each additional book ordered.

Overseas orders including Eire, please add £2.95 service charge.

Books will be sent by surface mail but quotes for airmail despatches will be given on request.

24 HOUR TELEPHONE ORDERING SERVICE FOR
ACCESS/VISA CARDHOLDERS –
TEL: GLASGOW 041-772 2281 or LONDON 081-307 4052